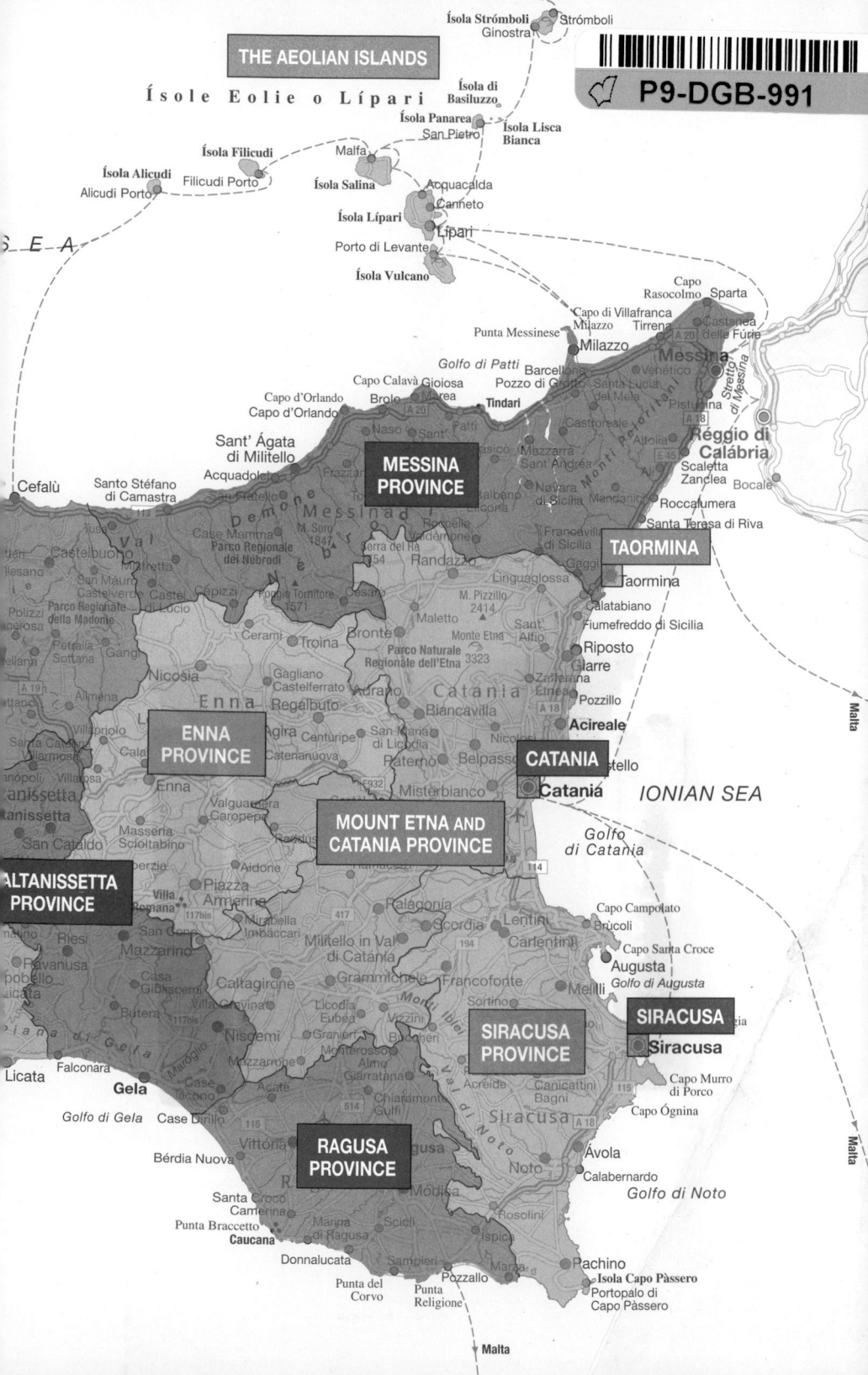

INSIGHT ⊙ GUIDES

SICILY

◉ Walking Eye App

YOUR FREE DESTINATION CONTENT AND EBOOK AVAILABLE THROUGH THE WALKING EYE APP

Your guide now includes a free eBook and destination content for your chosen destination, all for the same great price as before. Simply download the Walking Eye App from the App Store or Google Play to access your free eBook and destination content.

HOW THE WALKING EYE APP WORKS

Through the Walking Eye App, you can purchase a range of eBooks and destination content. However, when you buy this book, you can download the corresponding eBook and destination content for free. Just see below in the grey panels where to find your free content and then scan the QR code at the bottom of this page.

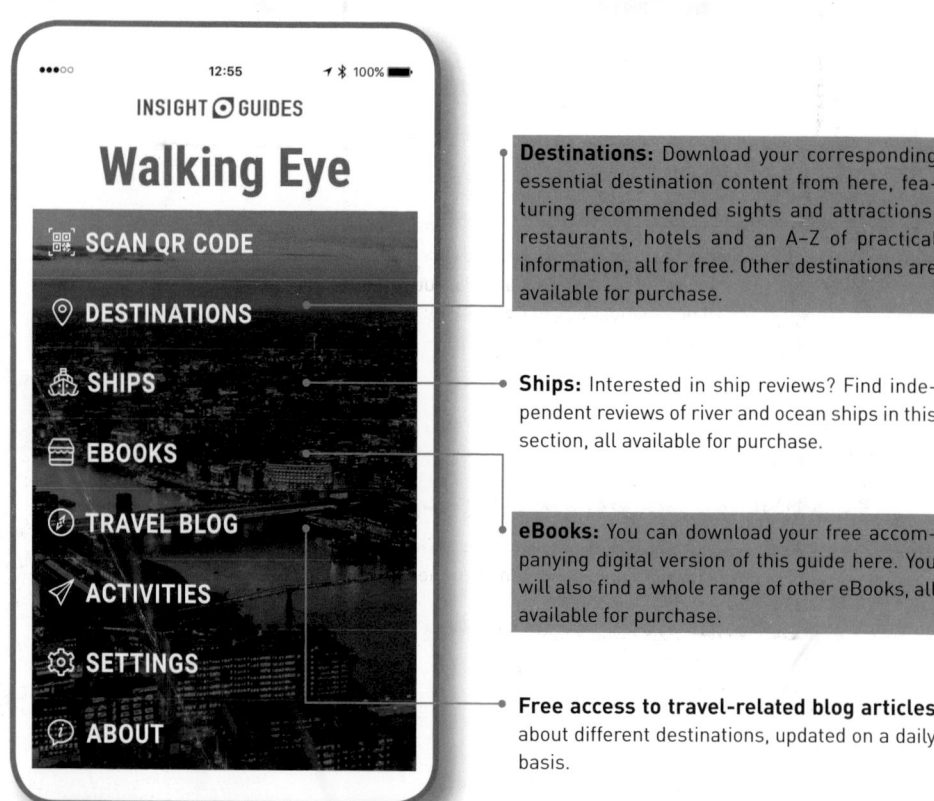

Destinations: Download your corresponding essential destination content from here, featuring recommended sights and attractions, restaurants, hotels and an A–Z of practical information, all for free. Other destinations are available for purchase.

Ships: Interested in ship reviews? Find independent reviews of river and ocean ships in this section, all available for purchase.

eBooks: You can download your free accompanying digital version of this guide here. You will also find a whole range of other eBooks, all available for purchase.

Free access to travel-related blog articles about different destinations, updated on a daily basis.

HOW THE DESTINATION CONTENT WORKS

Each destination includes a short introduction, an A–Z of practical information and recommended points of interest, split into 4 different categories:

• Highlights
• Accommodation
• Eating out
• What to do

You can view the location of every point of interest and save it by adding it to your Favourites. In the 'Around Me' section you can view all the points of interest within 5km.

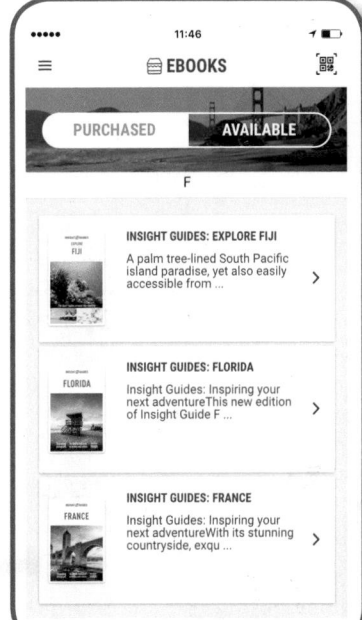

HOW THE EBOOKS WORK

The eBooks are provided in EPUB file format. Please note that you will need an eBook reader installed on your device to open the file. Many devices come with this as standard, but you may still need to install one manually from Google Play.

The eBook content is identical to the content in the printed guide.

HOW TO DOWNLOAD THE WALKING EYE APP

1. Download the Walking Eye App from the App Store or Google Play.
2. Open the app and select the scanning function from the main menu.
3. Scan the QR code on this page – you will then be asked a security question to verify ownership of the book.
4. Once this has been verified, you will see your eBook and destination content in the purchased ebook and destination sections, where you will be able to download them.

Other destination apps and eBooks are available for purchase separately or are free with the purchase of the Insight Guide book.

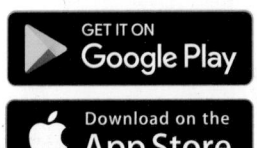

CONTENTS

Travel tips

TRANSPORT

A – Z

LANGUAGE

FURTHER READING

Maps

LEGEND

  Insight on

  Photo story

THE BEST OF SICILY: TOP ATTRACTIONS

△ **Mount Etna**. Europe's largest active volcano can be reached by cable car, with a hike to the craters up the basalt-encrusted slopes or a trail-bashing jeep ride up to the ragged summits; you can even ski on Mount Etna. See page 213.

△ **The Riserva dello Zíngaro**. Set on the rugged coastline between Scopello and San Vito Lo Capo, this is Sicily's most successful nature reserve, with walks, beaches, birdlife and cosy guesthouses nearby. See pages 53 and 105.

▷ **Sicilian Baroque in the Val di Noto**. This Unesco World Heritage site in southeastern Sicily embraces a cluster of cities where the Baroque architecture is often matched by the rugged scenery beyond. See page 191.

◁ **The Valley of the Temples**. Agrigento's Greek temples are as fine as any ancient ruins remaining in Greece. February's almond blossom festival is a lovely time to visit. See page 126.

◁ **Palermo's Arab-Norman heart**. From the Moorish, red-domed churches to the royal palace and the Cappella Palatina to the pleasure dome of La Zisa, these exotic monuments evoke *The Arabian Nights*. See pages 70, 81 and 98.

△ **Sicilian castles**. Sweep away the cobwebs by visiting great medieval castles, including those in Sperlinga, Cáccamo, Catania, Enna, Erice and Siracusa, generally built by the Normans or the Swabians. See page 99.

◁ **Granitas**. Flavoured with fruit, almonds or coffee, these Sicilian sorbets are often eaten for breakfast, with sweet brioche. The best haunts include the Bam Bar in Taormina and Caffè Sicilia in Noto. See pages 226 and 192.

◁ **Wine tasting in an estate**. Whether a grand estate such as Florio in Marsala or the organic Sirignano Wine Resort near Alcamo, this is a great experience, possibly including lunch or even a cookery course. See page 49 .

▽ **Island-hopping around the Aeolian Islands**. Vulcano boasts a smouldering volcano, as does Strómboli; Salina is sleepy and family-friendly; Panarea is chic; remote Alicudi is the land that time forgot. See page 245.

▽ **Villa Romana mosaics**. This superb villa in Piazza Armerina boasts some of the most extensive and beautiful Roman mosaics ever known, even if ongoing restoration means parts may be closed. See page 159.

THE BEST OF SICILY: EDITOR'S CHOICE

BEST SICILIAN EXPERIENCES

Train around the volcano. Dramatic sightseeing on the Circumetnea Railway, which circles the base of Etna on a three-hour trip from Catania to Riposto, with several stops on the way. See page 213.

The Alcántara Gorge adventure. Gola dell'Alcántara, near Taormina, is a wild gorge carved by the river. You can simply walk the gorge path or hire waders or wetsuits – the water is freezing. Buses from Taormina and Catania. Avoid Sundays. See page 215.

Hiking and eating in the Madonie mountains. Follow limestone paths through meadows and woodlands of cork and holm to medieval villages and Slow Food feasts. See page 94.

To the islands by sea. Ferries and hydrofoils sail from Palermo, Cefalù and Milazzo to islands off the Tyrrhenian coast – **Vulcano, Lípari** and **Salina** are closest. Sail to the **Egadi Islands** from Trápani. (Travel agents can organise trips from Catania, Messina and Taormina.) See page 254.

The *passeggiata*. The classic early evening stroll, with ices or *aperitivi*; an especially engaging experience in Alcamo, Cefalù, Noto, Ortigia, Ragusa Ibla, Scicli, Taormina, Trápani and, in summer, Mondello and the beach resorts.

Passeggiata at twilight on Piazza Aprile in Taormina.

TOP TOWNS

Cefalù. Charming medieval seaside resort and gentle introduction to Sicily, with its great cathedral and leisurely pace of life. See page 92.

Erice. The island's moodiest medieval town is lovely in any season, even swathed in winter mists. See page 103.

Noto. Sicily's most stunning Baroque city is a luminous stage set which lures you in to play a part. See page 191.

Palermo. Both a glorious assault on the senses and the glittering summation of Arab-Norman Sicily. See page 67.

Ragusa (Ibla). Steeped in atmosphere, yet arguably the island's most civilised and hospitable centre. See page 164.

Siracusa (Ortigia). Sicily's most lyrical city, especially in sleepy Ortigia, an island apart. See page 179.

Taormina.Chic hotels and cosmopolitan confidence make the resort a seductive retreat from Sicilian intensity. See page 225.

View over Ragusa Ibla in the south of the island.

THE FINEST CHURCHES

Cappella Palatina, Palermo. The Palatine Chapel boasts Byzantine and Arab-Norman mosaics. See page 71.
Oratorio di San Lorenzo, Palermo. Near Piazza Marina,

Madonna and Child statue in Monreale Cathedral near Palermo.

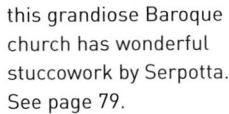

this grandiose Baroque church has wonderful stuccowork by Serpotta. See page 79.
Duomo, Monreale. Monreale Cathedral is a glittering tapestry of mosaics matched by stunning mosaics in the cloisters – all of which helped it become a Unesco World Heritage site in 2015. See page 87.
Duomo, Cefalù. The mystical Arab-Norman cathedral is now a Unesco World Heritage site, alongside Monreale. See page 93.
Duomo, Siracusa. A Sicilian hybrid: a Greek Temple of Athena converted into an early Christian church, but later remodelled in exuberant Baroque style. See page 186.

Greek temple at Selinunte.

TOP TEMPLES

Sicily has more ancient Greek temples than Greece. The best are:
Agrigento. Ancient Akragas, the most hedonistic city in Greek Sicily, is the island's most celebrated ancient site. Set in the Valley of the Temples, it is the world's largest temple. See page 126.
Segesta, Trápani province. The majestic Doric temple stands in solemn isolation facing Monte Barbaro. See page 106.
Selinunte, Trápani province. A glorious setting for a ruined city founded around 650 BC but ravaged by the Carthaginians. See page 111.
Mozia, Trápani province. Not a temple but the site of a Carthaginian city on an island in the Stagnone lagoon. See page 108.

BEST BEACHES

San Vito Lo Capo. Near Erice, is acclaimed for its wild scenery and peacefulness. See page 105.
Mondello, Cefalù and Isola Bella. Over-popular they may be but a perfect introduction to the Sicilian beach scene. See pages 83, 92 and 230.
Vendìcari. South of Siracusa, Vendìcari boasts unspoilt beaches

in a nature reserve, with even wilder beaches near **Capo Pàssero**. See page 195.
The islands. Lovely, diverse, often volcanic, the beaches on Ustica, the Egadi and the Aeolian Islands are in demand. See pages 96, 115 and 245.
Ragusa Province. This area has some of Sicily's best beaches. See page 177.

Golden sandy beach in Ragusa Province.

BEST STREET FOOD

Sfinciuni. Slightly spicy Sicilian pizza with anchovies, oregano and breadcrumbs.
Arancini. Deep-fried rice balls filled with meat or vegetables and bought from market or street stalls.
Pane e panelle. Deep-fried chickpea fritters served in a warm sesame bun.
Pani ca' meusa. Veal spleen sandwich, a Palermitan special for those with strong stomachs.
Seafood snacks. From *calamari fritti* to seafood nibbles such as clams, oysters, sardines or even boiled octopus.

THE SWEETEST DESSERTS

Cannoli. Crunchy, rich, ricotta-filled sweet pastries studded with candied fruit and chocolate.
Cassata. Made from sweetened ricotta, candied fruit, almond paste and sponge cake.
Gelati. Sicilians claim to having invented ice cream and make some of the best.
Granita. Sorbet made with fresh fruit or coffee and often served with a brioche.
Frutta alla Martorana. Invented by nuns, with marzipan moulded into convincing recreations of fresh fruit.

Caltagirone vase.

Seafood stew, just one of many culinary highlights.

ONLY IN SICILY

Sicilian Baroque. Palaces and churches created in a sumptuously theatrical style, characterised by fantasy and ornamentation. Noto might be the best-preserved Baroque town, but neighbouring Scicli, Ragusa and Módica are also superb, rebuilt after the 1693 earthquake. Catania and Acireale are also Baroque gems, as are the Serpotta oratories in Palermo.
Puppet theatre. Puppet shows are a Sicilian tradition. Their stories are based on the adventures of the brave knights of Charlemagne (Carlo Magno), with the moral: the importance of honour and chivalry. The best in Palermo is Mimmo Cuticchio. See page 200.
Classical drama. Theatres at classical sites often return to their original function, with Greek drama from May to July. Watch the Classics at Siracusa, Segesta, Taormina, Catania and Morgantina. See page 181.
Easter festivals. Nothing is as it seems in Sicily as the festivals are often a fusion of Christian and pagan rites, such as Prizzi's Dance of the Devils, depicting the battle between Good and Evil. See page 142.
Caltagirone pottery. Famous for its ceramics since ancient times, Caltagirone majolica is unmistakable, painted in blue, green and yellow. The other two important ceramics centres on the island are Sciacca and Santa Stefano di Camastra (just outside Cefalù). See page 201.

THE BOLDEST LANDSCAPES

Riserva dello Zíngaro. Sicily's model nature reserve boasts stunning beaches with a mountainous backdrop. See page 53.

Mount Etna's volcanic park. Includes the vast gullies of the Valley del Bove on the southeastern flank, created by the collapse of an ancient caldera. See page 213.

Le Saline. Tràpani's saltpans, with windmills and piles of "white gold" are an arresting sight best seen between May and September. See page 108.

Parco delle Madonie. Set in the sun-baked mountains south of Cefalù, with villages built on vertiginous slopes. See page 94.

Lo Stagnone. North of Marsala, Sicily's largest lagoon is a mysterious place, home to Punic Mozia. See page 108.

Rock canyons. The best are **Pantálica** (see page 197), **Ispica**, **Alcántara** and in the **Monti Iblei**, near Ragusa. See pages 197, 175, 215 and 169.

The sun-baked mountains of Parco delle Madonie in the northwest of the island.

THE BEST OF PALERMO

Palazzo dei Normanni. Houses the Sicilian Parliament and the Royal Apartments. Don't miss the **Cappella Palatina** with Byzantine and Arab-Norman mosaics.

Markets. Great for atmosphere, and for the freshest food for picnics. **Ballarò** is the liveliest, surpassing the more established **Vucciria** and the **Capo**, which is good for clothes.

Churches. The **Norman cathedral** contains royal tombs and a small museum. **San Giovanni degli Eremiti**, with its cloistered oriental garden, is yet another Arab-Norman church worth visiting besides the dreamlike **La Martorana**. The **Convento dei Cappuccini** is a gruesome catacombs containing 8,000 mummified Palermitans.

Museums and Opera. The **Museo Archeologico Regionale** is one of the richest archaeological collections in Italy. The 15th-century **Palazzo Abatellis** is home to the Galleria Regionale della Sicilia, with medieval sculptures as well as Renaissance paintings by Antonello da Messina. The **Teatro Massimo** is a vast but elegant neoclassical and Art Nouveau opera house that was the setting for a compelling massacre in The Godfather series.

Gardens. The **Orto Botánico**, one of Europe's leading botanical gardens, now also marks the start of a delightful seafront stroll that runs to the Foro Italico and the revamped port. **Parco della Favorita** is a lovely park laid out by the Bourbons. See page 67.

Teatro Massimo, Palermo.

Seller at the fish market in Catania.

A bakery in Mazara del Vallo, Trápani.

Santo Stéfano di Camastra
ceramics.

A VOLCANIC HERITAGE

Sicily's complex history has produced an island with a unique character – proud, introspective, enigmatic and irreverent.

The rocky coastline at Cefalù.

Sicily may be Italian, but the islanders are Latin only by adoption. They may look back at Magna Graecia or Moorish Sicily but tend to be bored by their exotic past. Mostly, they sleepwalk their way through history, as if it were a bad play in a long-forgotten language. Floating not far beneath the surface is a kaleidoscope of swirling foreignness against a backdrop of Sicilian fatalism.

This is the legacy of a land whose heyday was over 700 years ago. It is most visible in the diversity of architectural styles, brought together under one roof in a remarkable mongrel, Siracusa Cathedral.

The Greeks' lessons in democracy fell on stony ground: the Sicilians responded with a race of full-blooded tyrants. The Mafia showed equal disdain for democratic niceties: their shadowy state within a state became more effective than the pale, public model. Poor Sicilians knuckled under or emigrated, often flourishing on foreign soil. Until recently, most landed, educated Sicilians declined public office, pre-ferring private gain to public good. As the Prince says in Lampedusa's *The Leopard*: "I cannot lift a finger in politics. It would only get bitten."

Painted cart in Palermo.

This is the deadly product served by Sicilian history. As the writer Leonardo Sciascia says: "History has been a wicked stepmother to us Sicilians." Yet it is this heritage of doom, drama and excess that draws visi-tors to an island marooned between Europe and Africa.

Recently, a renaissance of sorts has been under way, including a refusal to support the Mafia in many quarters. Sicily has also revamped its image, with restored historic centres, reopened museums and re-energised cit-ies. Superb wine estates, seductive farmstays, stylish villa holidays, Sicil-ian cookery courses and guided nature trails are also part of the dazzling new landscape.

Goethe, too, found Sicily intoxicating, from the classical temples and Etna's eruptions to the volcanic Sicilians themselves. "To have seen Italy without seeing Sicily", he wrote, "is not to have seen Italy at all – for Sicily is the key to everything."

THE SICILIANS

Brooding, fatalistic and passionately pessimistic – or celebratory, sensitive and overwhelmingly hospitable? The Sicilians are a mass of apparent contradictions.

Sicilians have a reputation for being brooding, suspicious and unfathomable. Closer contact reveals stoicism, conservatism and deep sensibility. This contradictory character does not match the sunny Mediterranean stereotype of *dolce far niente*, but outsiders may nonetheless encounter overwhelming hospitality, boundless curiosity and smothering friendship on the slimmest of pretexts.

Campaigning Sicilian journalist Giuseppe Fava once said of his beloved island: "The inability to structure society is the Sicilian tragedy."

In 1814 the British Governor of Sicily was perplexed that "Sicilians expect everything to be done for them; they have always been so accustomed to obedience." His Sicilian minister argued for absolutism: "Too much liberty is for the Sicilians what would be a pistol or stiletto in the hands of a boy or a madman." Critics claim that Sicilians remain sluggish citizens, subsidy junkies with little sense of self-help. Sicilians reply that power and prestige lie elsewhere. History has taught them to have no faith in institutions.

THE MEANING OF FAMILY

In the face of this, the traditional responses are emigration, resignation, complicity or withdrawal into a private world. Though emigration has been the choice of millions, most Sicilians choose to stay but avoid confrontation with the shadow-state of patronage and the Mafia. They prefer to live intensely, but

Local character in Mazara del Vallo.

in private. As a result, their world is circumscribed by the family, the bedrock of island life.

Palermo is emblematic of the retreat from the world and also of an ambivalence about class. It goes against the grain of Sicilian sentimentality to admit that the middle classes have fled the historic centre in droves to settle in safe leafy villages or in the suburbs. Optimists point to a gradual return of the middle classes to the *centro storico*, with one square held up as a shining example, a socially mixed island which could be the city's salvation. But elsewhere, gentrification looks a long way off. Arab and African immigrants occupy derelict buildings by the port while hovels lurk in the shadow of splendid mansions. The Sicilian upper classes lead such a separate lifestyle that a social vacuum is inevitable. In rural Sicily, the divide is further consolidated by education, Mafia affiliation and isolation.

Yet within a cocoon of personal loyalty to friends and family, individuals cultivate their patch. In a traditionally oppressed culture, one's word is one's bond; lives have depended on *parole d'onore*, so promises must be kept. But in the eyes of a pessimistic or powerless individual, betrayal can happen only too easily, sparked off by a casual rebuff. Any rejection of hospitality is seen as a betrayal. As a Palermitan lawyer says: "For us, hospitality is a joy and a duty with obligations on both sides. A refusal is not just rude but fuels our *complessi di tradimento* [betrayal complex]."

PRINCELY HOSPITALITY

The joy, of course, comes when the fortress doors are opened and through that chink appears a prince, welcoming you to a courtly scene straight out of Lampedusa's *The Leopard*, that Sicilian masterpiece of decline and fall. Sicily nurtures the seductive illusion that you are a treasured guest rather than a common tourist. But it may not be an illusion: Sicilian hospitality is legendary, as suffocatingly sweet as the local *cassata* sponge cake.

Appearances matter in Sicily: the word azzizzare (to beautify) comes from the Arabic; orfanità is Spanish-Palermitan dialect for looking good; spagnolismo (Hispanicism) means seeming better than you are.

Particularly in Palermo and Ragusa, many leading families have decided to open their ancestral homes – and even their hearts – to the general public. Conte Federico, who welcomes guests to his Palermitan palace, embodies this spirit. The unaffected count, who can trace his lineage back to the great Emperor Frederick II of Sicily, enchants guests with an evening of feasting and fantasy in princely proportions, including opera sung by his soprano wife. Before cocktails by candlelight in the Arab-Norman tower, fortunate guests can stroll through the staterooms and admire the suits of armour in the knights' hall. Dinner is based on exotic recipes dating from when Sicily was under Arab-Norman rule, and the centre of civilised Europe (www.contefederico.com).

Elsewhere, life has moved on, and the princess herself may be turning down your bedsheets (even princesses need to keep a roof over their heads). But the generous Sicilian

High spirits at the fish market in Catania.

spirit remains the same. And this is true of the welcome in the simplest farmstay in the Madonie mountains. Whether a sumptuous palace with a Baroque ballroom or a boutique wine resort near Alcamo, these are genuine homes, and the pleasures are deeply domestic.

Not that hospitality is ever a simple commercial transaction in Sicily. The truest hospitality comes to foreigners whose slightest friendly gesture is rewarded with fresh pastries, a bunch of just-picked grapes, the keys to a long-closed church, or an insistence on a tour of an obscure archaeological site. Possibly all at once. It is delightful, even when the offers bear no relation to what you wanted.

FOREIGN FUSION

The story of private virtues and public vices is linked to Sicily's hybrid past. As the writer Gesualdo Bufalino says: "The Greeks shaped our sensitivity to light and harmony. The Muslims brought us a fragrance of oriental gardens, of legendary *Thousand and One Nights*; but they also sowed in us a fanatical exaltation and an inclination to deceit and voluptuousness. The Spanish gave us hyperbole and haughtiness, the magnificence of words and rites, the magnanimity of our code of

Friendly smile in Catania.

honour, but also a strong taste of ashes and death." Even today, the Arab west is overladen with inscrutability, Spanish manners and ceremony, while the Greek east is more democratic, with closer links to the Italian mainland. Sicily's miscegenation lives on in the language. *Cristiani* (Christians) is a generic word for people, just as *turchi* (Turks) refers to heathens.

Sicily's Baroque architecture is another hybrid – Spanish, Roman and Sicilian fusion, reflected in the islanders' Baroque temperament. As writer Stefano Malatesta says: "Everything's Baroque, excessive and eccentric: look at the lavish, multicoloured food, the decadent nobles, the elaborate courtesy, the contorted human relationships, the fine 18th-century minds, tinged by arrogance and aimlessness."

In Ragusa's Duomo, celebrity chef Ciccio Sultano concurs: "my cooking is voluptuously Baroque because I am Baroque: I never remove anything from my recipes but just pile on more."

A PASSION FOR THE PRESENT

Despite their Baroque spirit and the burden of the past, Sicilians have a passion for the present. Thanks to a heightened sense of history, the islanders attach supreme importance to time. They see themselves as volatile forces of nature, as violent as Etna, but imbued with a sense of the sacred. Spirituality is expressed in spontaneous church services led by lay women. In festivals, classical polytheism merges with Christianity. But the everyday intimacy of the relationship with God implies a chatty equality and an acceptance of Him in any guise.

Sicilian proverbs reflect a dog-eat-dog society: "whoever makes himself a sheep will be eaten by a wolf" and "to the docile dog, the wolf seems ferocious."

Lampedusa's *The Leopard* is illuminating in unravelling this state of being Sicilian: "Sicilians never wish to improve for the simple reason that they believe themselves perfect. Their vanity is stronger than their misery. Every invasion by outsiders upsets their illusion of achieved perfection, and risks disturbing their self-satisfied waiting for nothing at all."

Still, this melancholic immutability is enlivened by a zest for life best felt in Palermo's bustling Ballarò market, the haunt of artisans and students, housewives and bootleggers. Ballarò is raucous and exotic, with spicy scents and sounds that transport you back to Moorish times. As local actress Teresa Mannino admits, "In Sicily everything screams – the people, the seagulls, even the sea itself."

THE NEW SICILY

Change is in the air and is cause for cautious celebration, from the resurgent southeast to urban regeneration and rural renewal across the island.

Against the odds, Sicilian renewal is under way, even if it would be foolhardy to speak of a Sicilian renaissance: the island is too flawed and fatalistic for that. Still, the Sicilians have a talent for turning the painful past into something of beauty, with the *coppola storta* ("twisted cap") a testament to this talent. The cap, the traditional symbol of a lowlife *mafioso*, is now a cult design object, seen as reclaiming a "true" Sicilian identity. Similarly, land expropriated from the Mafia has been reborn as wine estates for the common good. And once feared symbols such as Palermo's palace of the Inquisition have been turned into telling museums. It's symbolic but also part of the redemption of Sicily.

Known as "an island within an island", the Val di Noto is currently the most dynamic part of Sicily. The locals attribute its unspoilt countryside, entrepreneurial spirit and escape from the tentacles of the Mafia to good fortune. When the Spanish kings ruled Sicily, the west was divided into vast estates run by absentee barons while the southeast was handed over to the local gentry who cherished their small estates. Partly as a result, in Noto, Módica, Ragusa, Scicli and Siracusa, the Unesco-listed Baroque gems in the Val di Noto, regeneration has taken root, with the cities looking increasingly splendid.

The long restoration of the fabulous Unesco-listed Villa Romana proved challenging but it was finally completed at the end of 2012. Neighbouring Aidone has a fine new museum, showcasing Sicilian-Greek treasures "recuperated" from the Getty collection in Malibu. Elsewhere, the island abounds in Unesco World Heritage sites, with Palermo's Arab-Norman treasures and Monreale and Cefalù's churches the most recent additions (2015). On the west coast, Trápani has revamped its historic centre and coastal promenade, while Mazaro del Vallo deserves praise for its Dancing Satyr Museum and vibrant Kasbah. Just along the coast is Marsala's magnificent Punic Ship Museum and Trápani's restored saltpans.

In the top resort of Taormina, both the Grand Timeo and San Domenico are standard bearers for

Moto taxi tour in Noto.

Sicilian luxury. The moody former monastery of San Domenico has acquired its second Michelin star, while the revamped Grand Timeo enjoys Taormina's finest views, with Mount Etna, a Unesco natural heritage site since 2013, snow-capped or spouting molten lava. In Siracusa, Scicli, Ragusa and Palermo chic boutique hotels vie with palatial B&Bs.

In the countryside, a glut of gorgeous *agriturismi* (farmstays) and wine resorts now offer a lovely alternative to villa-living, especially when run by an effusive owner. For a very reasonable price, you can find a Slow Food farmstay overlooking a timeless scene of dry-stone walls and ancient olive groves. Not so much "new Sicily" as "old Sicily" reclaimed.

Taormina and Mount Etna,
drawing by Adolphe Rouargue.

DECISIVE DATES

20000–10000 BC
Old Stone Age settlers live in caves on Monte Pellegrino and the Egadi Islands.

2000–1000 BC
Bronze Age Sicilians trade with Mycenaean Greeks.

*c.***1250 BC**
The Siculi (Sicels), Sicani (Sicans) and Elymni (Elymians) settle.

*c.***860 BC**
Carthaginians (Phoenicians from North Africa) establish trading sites at Panormus (modern Palermo), Solus (Solunto) and Motya (Mozia).

Greek ruins at Selinunte.

*c.***734–700 BC**
Naxos, the first Greek colony in Sicily, is founded, followed by colonies at Siracusa, Megara Hyblaea, Gela, Selinus (modern Selinunte) and Akragas (Agrigento).

5th century BC
Height of Greek civilisation in Sicily. Siracusa rivals Athens in power and prestige.

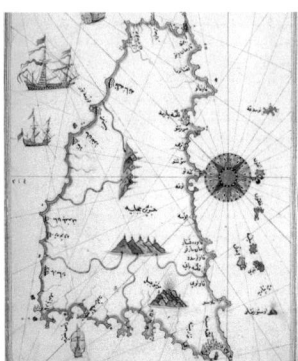

Portolan chart of Sicily.

480 BC
Gela, Akragas and Siracusa defeat the Carthaginians at the battle of Himera.

409–407 BC
Carthage sacks Selinus, Himera, Akragas and Gela. Plague forces Carthaginians to withdraw.

264–241 BC
First Punic War. Sicily is the battleground as Romans wage war on Carthaginians.

ROME AND BYZANTIUM
212 BC
Siracusa falls to the Romans; the island is ruled by Rome.

2nd century AD
Spread of Christianity in Sicily.

395
Sicily is part of the Western Roman Empire.

535
The Byzantines conquer Sicily, which is now under Emperor Justinian.

652
First major Arab raid on Sicily.

ARABS AND NORMANS
831–78
Palermo falls to the Saracens (Arabs). Arabs capture Messina, Modica, Ragusa and Enna. Siracusa is taken by storm and destroyed.

965
Sicily under Arab control. Palermo second in size only to Constantinople.

1061
The Normans land in Sicily: they struggle against the Arabs.

1072
Norman Count Roger de Hauteville takes Palermo "for Christendom".

1091
Noto, the last major Muslim stronghold, falls to the all-conquering Normans.

1130
Count Roger's son, Roger II, becomes king of Sicily.

1198–1250
Emperor Frederick II rules Sicily.

1266
Charles of Anjou is crowned king of Sicily.

1282
The Sicilian Vespers. Popular Sicilian uprising against the French.

SPANISH RULE
1302
The Aragonese begin 200-year domination.

1442
Alfonso V, king of Aragon, reunites Naples and Sicily and takes the title king of the Two Sicilies.

1502
The Spanish crown controls Sicily.

1513
The Spanish Inquisition arrives in Sicily.

1669
Etna erupts, destroying Catania.

1693
Massive earthquake strikes the east.

1713
Treaty of Utrecht. Victor Amadeus II of Piedmont-Savoy made king of Sicily.

1720
Austrian viceroys rule Sicily.

1734–1860
Spanish Bourbons rule Sicily through viceroys.

1759
Kingdom of Naples and Sicily passes to Ferdinand IV.

1806–15
British occupation of Sicily.

1816
The kingdom of the Two Sicilies is created under the Bourbons.

REVOLUTION AND UNIFICATION

1848–9
Sicilian Revolution.

1860
Garibaldi forces the Bourbons off Sicily.

Ferdinand I, king of the Two Sicilies, in 1816.

1861
Sicily joins kingdom of Italy.

1908
Messina destroyed by an earthquake.

1915
Italy joins the Allies in World War I.

1943
Sicily is invaded by Allies in World War II.

MODERN SICILY

1951–75
One million Sicilians emigrate, especially to the US.

1968
Disastrous earthquake in the Belice Valley.

1986
The Mafia maxi-trials indict hundreds.

1992
Mafia assassinate two judges. Mount Etna erupts.

1995
Giulio Andreotti, seven times prime minister of Italy, is brought to Palermo to face charges of collaborating with the Mafia.

2002
Etna erupts. Days later, Strómboli also erupts.

2006
Mafia boss Bernardo Provenzano is caught after 43 years in hiding.

2011
Etna erupts repeatedly. Berlusconi forced out.

2013
Comiso airport opens for low-cost flights.

2015
Palermo-born Sergio Mattarella is the first Sicilian to become Italy's president. The provinces of Agrigento, Caltanissetta, Enna, Ragusa, Siracusa and Trápani become part of the Free Municipal Consortia while the provinces of Catania, Messina and Palermo become Metropolitan Cities.

2017
Nello Musumeci of the Diventerà Bellissima party is elected president of Sicily.

2018
Palermo is the Italian Capital of Culture.

Mount Etna erupting in 2002 as seen from the air.

THE SHAPING OF SICILY

The island's warring tribes were subdued by the Romans, whose seven centuries of dominance were followed by a succession of foreign powers, including the Greeks, Germans, French, Spanish and Habsburgs. Although it became part of Italy in 1861, Sicily is in many ways un-Italian.

Sicilian history is a cavalcade of invasion by ancient tribes. The Sicani, Siculi, and Elymni were the first. Then came the Carthaginians and Greeks, the Romans, Arabs, mercenaries and slaves, Vandals, Goths, Saracens, Normans and Spaniards. Most remained for long periods, adding rich layers to Sicily's extraordinary fusion of genes and culture.

The islanders were not great shapers of their own destiny but the powers of their subversiveness and survival were substantial. When invaded and occupied, they proved themselves to be a ball and chain around the neck of each conqueror.

In response to invasion, the Sicilians were sullen, slothful and uncooperative – a millstone dragging its rulers into futile conflict while leaving the Sicilians themselves free to live in their own luxurious private theatre.

Fifth-century BC sculpture unearthed in Agrigento.

THE KEY TO POWER

In days when the known world was limited to the lands lining the Mediterranean, the boundaries were Phoenicia (today's Lebanon) and the Straits of Gibraltar. Carthage was only 160km (100 miles) away, in Tunisia. Sicily was not only in the centre, but it divided "the world" into two. Ancient superpowers could dominate one side or the other but in order to control both, they had to possess Sicily.

Although not a large island, Sicily was big enough for enemies like the Phoenicians and Greeks to occupy separate parts yet never quite big enough to be a power in its own right, even though Siracusa (Syracuse) was once considered

the greatest city in Europe. The island was always at the mercy of larger forces swirling around its shores and dragged into almost every major Mediterranean war. However, three indigenous groups with separate cultures and languages were established: the Elymni (Elymians) in the northwest, the Sicani (Sicans) in the west and the Siculi (Sicels) in the east.

When the Phoenicians arrived, they occupied northwestern Sicily and welcomed the resident Sicani as neighbours. They fortified their settlements like Solunto and Panormus (Palermo) only when their livelihood was threatened by Greek expansion. On the island of Motya (modern Mozia), their base for attacking the Greeks, there were sensationalist aspects of their culture, such as sacred prostitution and human sacrifice. Numerous jars of charred babies imply that Motya was a grim place. The balance of power swung from Siculi to Sicani and back again. But since Sicily is named after the Siculi race, it is clear that they ultimately triumphed, in name at least.

The Sicilian Greek colonies were ruled by "tyrants", a term that originally meant men who seized power instead of inheriting it – an early form of today's dictators.

Perseus slays Medusa, from Temple C at Selinunte.

○ THE NAME SICILY

The Siculi, who gave their name to Sicily, came from Liguria in the 13th century BC. According to Thucydides, they "defeated the Sicani in battle, drove them to the south and west of the island, and renamed it Sicily instead of Sicania." These seafarers and farmers were gradually Hellenised by Greek settlers on the east coast. However, in settlements like Siracusa, the Siculi were reduced to serfdom. They were seldom granted Greek citizenship, though a few were elevated from the status of barbarians, to persons qualified to marry Greeks – the ultimate accolade. Sicily abounds with Siculi settlements, with the best one at Ispica.

ENTER THE GREEKS

When Sicily formed part of Magna Graecia (Greater Greece) it had a population of more than 3 million – greater than Athens and Sparta combined. The islanders spoke Greek and practised Greek art. Agriculture flourished, and the island became the granary of the Mediterranean.

But none of this was evident when the Greek migrants first arrived. Nor were they aware that there were Phoenician settlements on the western shore. The first colony on the east coast was Naxos (734 BC). Then came Zankle (Messina), Leontinoi (Lentini) and Katane (Catania). In the south, with settlers from Rhodes and Crete, were Gela, Akragas (Agrigento), Selinunte and Heraclea Minoa. Syrakusai (Siracusa), the greatest colony, was founded by Corinthian Greeks.

Sicily's first taste of the battles ahead occurred in 480 BC, when the Carthaginian commander Hamilcar invaded Sicily with 300,000 mercenaries aboard 200 galleys and 3,000 transport ships. He besieged Himera (Términi Imerese) by land and sea, prompting the tyrant Theron to appeal for help from Gelon, the tyrant of Siracusa. Gelon responded with 50,000 men and 5,000 cavalry and 150,000 Carthaginians were slain in the ensuing battle.

ATHENS INTERVENES

Sicilian cities were always ready to fight and, when Selinunte and Segesta quarrelled, Selinunte asked Siracusa for help, so Segesta approached Athens. After Segesta offered to cover the costs of military aid, Athens fell for Segesta's creditworthiness and did battle on its behalf (see box).

The battle for control of Siracusa's great harbour took place in 413 BC, with Greeks fighting Greeks. The Athenians were humiliated. Their generals were executed and the 7,000 captured troops were lowered 30 metres (100ft) into stone quarries, into a hell which was stifling hot by day and freezing at night. After 10 weeks, those who survived were sold as slaves.

Naturally, the Sicilian Greeks went back to fighting among themselves, thus triggering a second Carthaginian invasion. Hannibal, the eldest son of Hamilcar, had a score to settle with the city where Hamilcar died. In 409 BC he arrived with a powerful force and razed Selinunte to the ground. Then, at Himera, he sought personal vengeance with a massacre: 3,000 male survivors were taken to where Hamilcar had died, tortured and offered as sacrifices to the memory of the dead general.

A year later, Hannibal attacked Akragas. But, while digging trenches, the Carthaginians had exposed corpses and a plague swept through the camp, killing Hannibal. The city eventually fell after an eight-month siege.

After blaming Siracusan generals for the defeat, in 405 BC a spirited demagogue, one Dionysius, came to power and ruled efficiently for 38 years, to be followed by Timoleon (345–336 BC), who restored a democracy of sorts. The next ruler was Agathocles (315–289 BC), who returned to the bellicose old days, seizing remaining Carthaginian land. Finally Hieron II (265–215 BC) brought a measure of stability, forging a treaty between Siracusa and Carthage. Then he changed the course of history by making an alliance with the newly expanding Mediterranean superpower: Rome.

ROME AND BYZANTIUM

In 264 BC the Punic Wars triggered momentous changes in Sicily. Sandwiched between the rival powers of Rome and Carthage, it was a battleground. Popular images of the Punic Wars are dominated by Hannibal's crossing the Apennines with elephants to attack Rome, but the first rounds were fought in Sicily, bringing the island firmly within the Roman Empire.

Rome's takeover was methodical. First, Akragas (Agrigento) fell in 261 BC and 25,000 of its inhabitants were sold into slavery. Then Panormus (Palermo) and Selinunte and, ultimately, after a two-year siege, Siracusa. The island became Rome's first province (as opposed to being incorporated in the Republic) because it was deemed too Hellenised, too Greek in its culture. So Greek language and traditions prevailed. The next 50 years saw revolts by slaves which were brutally curbed.

In common with the rest of the Empire, the Sicilians became recognised Roman citizens in AD 212 – the island was now an extension of Italy. It acquired a reputation as a Roman resort, beloved by the likes of Caligula. A tantalising glimpse of Sicily as the playground of rich Romans can be seen in the Villa Romana at Casale (see page 159).

Mosaics show a phantasmagoria of bathing, dancing, fishing, hunting, wine-pressing, music and drama – a vision of earthly paradise a wealthy, contented pagan would see while relaxing on holiday.

VANDALS AND GOTHS

Then Sicily exploded under the onslaught of the unmitigated louts of Western history – the Vandals. Having been expelled from Germany, they planned to use Sicily as a springboard back to Europe. But Sicily, like Rome and the rest of Italy,

Greek vase depicting Hephaestus and Dionysius raising a cup, 5th century BC.

fell to yet another Germanic race, the Goths. As Italy grew too chaotic to remain the seat of the empire, the emperor decamped to Constantinople, or Byzantium, as the Eastern Empire was named. In time, his Byzantine general Belisarius was ordered to invade Sicily to reclaim Greek heritage; the Sicilians sighed with relief. But joy was premature. Emperor Constans II proceeded to seize property, tax extortionately and sell debtors into slavery. It was a slave who redressed the balance in AD 668. While Constans was being soaped in his bath, the slave picked up the soap box and brought it down on the emperor's head.

Visitors to Byzantine Sicily noted the women's love of ornament. Their jewels were a testament to the skills of Byzantine goldsmiths and a worldly counterpoint to shimmering church mosaics. Byzantine art is well served here even today, with cupolas emblazoned with austere Greek bishops and inscrutable saints. Classical naturalism ceded to Eastern stylisation and realism was replaced by decorative patterns and abstraction.

The Arab domination enhanced Byzantine art and architecture. The emirs employed Byzantine craftsmen so earlier decorative patterns and stylisation suffused Islamic art. A thousand years of Greek-infused values could not be so easily erased.

ARABS AND NORMANS

During the Byzantine period, Sicily was the target of frequent piratical raids by Syrians, Egyp-

A portrait of Hercules, detail from the Labours of Hercules mosaic at the Villa Romana del Casale.

tians and Moors from North Africa. As early as AD 652, Saracens from Kairouan (Tunisia) made incursions into the island. Then, in 827, came the fully fledged Arab invasion.

A fleet of 100 ships was despatched, with 10,000 troops, mainly Arabs, Berbers and Spanish Muslims. The Arabs slowly gained a foothold and, in 878, Siracusa, Sicily's first city for 1,500 years, fell. It now took second place to Palermo, as Christianity did to Islam, and Greek to Arabic. Palermo Cathedral was converted into a mosque and resounded to Muslim prayers for nearly 250 years. There was an influx of Arab settlers known as Saracens, a term that encompassed Arabs, Berbers and Spanish Moors.

As virtually an independent emirate, Sicily played a privileged role as a bridge between Africa and Europe. Trade flourished and taxation was low. The tolerant regime allowed subjects to abide by their own laws. Despite freedom of worship, Christians freely converted to Islam: there were soon hundreds of mosques in Palermo. As well as Arabs from Spain, Syria and Egypt, there were Berbers, Black Africans, Jews, Persians, Greeks, Lombards and Slavs. Western Sicily prospered.

Sicilian conservatism made for a smooth transition from Byzantine to Islamic architecture. Although many churches were converted into mosques, the Arabs happily encased Byzantine art and symbolism in Islamic ornamentation. Christian and Islamic symbolism were conveniently fused.

Already a presence in Italy, the Normans were dismissed as "wolves" by the Arabs, who singled out their ferocity, barbarism and native cunning. Nonetheless, the "wolves" were invited to invade western Sicily by the emirs of Catania and Siracusa, as they were disgruntled by the concentration

⊘ SEGESTA'S CUNNING RUSE

The Athenians were tricked into funding Segesta's war with Selinunte in 413 BC. Segesta misrepresented its wealth with a show of splendour at the temple of Aphrodite on Mount Eryx (Erice). The Athenian ambassadors enjoyed sumptuous banquets, eating off gold and silver plates. So awed were they that they had no hesitation in recommending ships be put at the disposal of Segesta. What the Athenians didn't know was that the temple treasures were fakes. The gold and silver plate was borrowed from the Siculi. But the fraud was never exposed and the 250 ships that sailed from Piraeus with 25,000 men was the largest ever Greek armada.

of power there. The Norman Hautevilles, Christian freebooters, needed no encouragement.

THE NORMAN CONQUEST

In 1068, Count Roger and his elder brother, Robert Guiscard, a fortune-hunting Norman knight, defeated the Arabs at Misilmeri, then during the siege of Palermo in 1072. Robert urged his men on to seize the city, which was "hateful to God and subject to devils".

The great Palermo mosque was quickly reconsecrated to Christ. Robert magnani-

Count Roger died in 1101, leaving Sicily governed by his widow until the coronation of his son, Roger II, in 1130. Revelling in glory, this Roger spent lavishly on palaces, mosques, gardens and education. As the richest king in Christendom, he indulged his love of Arab art and culture. He also patronised astronomers and astrologers, Koranic scholars and Sicilian poets. This charismatic king was well versed in three languages. His cosmopolitan court was home to French *jongleurs* and balladeers who followed the itinerant Norman knights.

The Saracens at the assault of Messina, from Jean Skylitzes' Byzantine Chronicles.

mously shared the Sicilian spoils with Count Roger (also known as Conte Ruggero and King Roger I). He was an autocratic ruler, buttressed by the Byzantine concept of divine rule but, under Arab influence, was transformed from a foolhardy crusader and rough diamond into a cultured figure.

Arab influence did not wane with the Norman conquest. The Normans recognised Saracen superiority in culture and commerce, so welcomed Muslim courtiers and merchants. Most Arabs retained their castles, palaces and lands as well as their social prestige. Arab craftsmanship was prized in the conversion of mosques to cathedrals while their administrative skills, erudition and poetry were appreciated at court.

⊘ ARAB ENLIGHTENMENT

On their arrival the Arabs instigated land reforms and encouraged the spread of smallholdings. They created the fountains, baths, reservoirs and storage towers still visible today, including in La Ziza in Palermo. Sulphur, lead, silver, antimony and alum were refined. They cultivated citrus fruits and introduced sugar cane, cotton, mulberries, palms, melons, pistachio nuts, papyrus and flax. Ice from Mount Etna was used to make sorbets and sherbets, while sea salt was dried at Trápani. They introduced coral and tuna fishing. Nor did the Islamic faith deter these sophisticated Arabs from planting *zubbibbu* grapes for wine.

> *In between empire-building, Frederick I of Sicily founded a school of Sicilian poetry, wrote a book on falconry and studied science, pondering such questions as the workings of Mount Etna and the precise location of hell.*

As in Arab times, this liberalism decreed that "Latins, Greeks, Jews and Saracens be judged according to their own laws". Norman French,

The Normans vanquishing the Saracens, sculpted on the cathedral of Mazara del Vallo.

Greek, Arabic and Latin were all spoken. Even so, cultural and economic pressures led the Arabs gradually to retreat inland, away from the coastal cities.

Only the Normans were granted fiefdoms, and the rise of the baronial class was the most dubious Norman legacy. But these rugged kings also bequeathed an efficient administration and a relatively liberal regime. In its day, this melting pot of racial talent made for Christendom's most culturally creative society.

FROM BAD TO GOOD

Roger was succeeded by William I, posthumously nicknamed "the Bad" because he

aroused jealousies by being "more a Mohammedan than a Christian in belief, in character and in manners". He lived like an Arab emir in a palace that contained a bodyguard of black slaves and a harem under eunuch management. His lifestyle was a matter of taste, not faith, because he had no qualms about raiding the Muslims in North Africa on behalf of the Pope.

His son, William the Good, was only 14 when crowned in 1166, and his reign was guided by Walter of the Mill, the English Archbishop of Palermo and architect of Palermo Cathedral. The English connection was strengthened when William II married Joanna, King Richard the Lionheart's sister. Richard raided Messina while on his way to the Crusades but presented Tancred, William's successor, with Excalibur, King Arthur's sword, a fitting tribute to the end of a legendary line of warrior kings.

EMPERORS, KINGS AND VICEROYS

The death of William the Good in 1189 without an heir sent the succession reeling back to the House of Hohenstaufen (the Swabians) which produced the Prussian kings and Holy Roman Emperors. Apart from a few interludes, Norman and Spanish blood would reign over Sicily until 1860.

After Roger's line petered out, Henry VI, the Holy Roman Emperor, moved in. Next was his son, Frederick I of Sicily, who was, confusingly, crowned Emperor Frederick II. Born in Palermo of a Norman mother, he never considered himself Sicilian yet was known as a "baptised Sultan", thanks to his predilection for a *seraglio* and Saracen pages. Despite the Arabian lifestyle, however, Muslims were discriminated against and rural settlements gave way to baronial estates – and complex fortifications running from Messina to Siracusa.

Successors such as Charles of Anjou called themselves king of Sicily, using the title as an adornment as they pursued greater ambitions abroad. Backed by the pope, Charles plundered the island and taxed so punitively that rebellion hung in the air. Charles moved his capital from Palermo to Naples.

The Easter rebellion in 1282, the most significant uprising in Sicily's history, was both a patriotic insurrection and a revolt against feudalism. But far from freeing Sicilians from a foreign yoke, it led to the War of the Vespers. It all began when the Easter Monday procession in Palermo was joined by French soldiers from Charles's garrison. The festive mood turned to silence as Sicilian men were searched by the French troops for concealed weapons. As the bell called the faithful to Vespers, the French captain ordered his men to search the women too. "He himself laid hands upon the fairest, and pretending to look for a knife upon her, he thrust his hand out to her bosom." She fainted in the arms of her husband, who let out the ringing cry: "*Moranu i franchiski*" (Death to the French), and the French officer was struck down dead at the feet of the woman he had insulted.

an annual tax to Naples and recognised the dominance of the pope. This was submission under the guise of independence. Under the rule of a series of viceroys, the island was little more than a source of revenue for Spain, and was drained to fund the Reconquista and wars against the Turks.

A PAWN IN THE GAME

After Charles II died in 1700, Sicily could do little but sit back and watch as the Wars of the Spanish Succession made Sicily little more than a bargaining chip tossed between contending European

Medieval-style decorative plaque depicting Constance of Hauteville, Count Roger and Frederick II at the Alessi manufacture in Caltagirone.

The incident led to a riot which, with the encouragement of the local aristocracy, became an all-out revolt. The uprising spread from Palermo throughout Sicily, and in the massacre that followed no Frenchman was safe. The nobles of Palermo invited Peter II of Aragon to intervene on their behalf, and the Spaniard readily agreed, taking the title king of Sicily while promising to respect the freedom of Sicilians. Charles withdrew and French influence on the island ended.

Friction between the Spaniards in Sicily and the Normans in Naples frequently erupted into open warfare until 1372, when Naples agreed to Sicilian self-rule provided that the Sicilian ruler paid

powers. The Treaty of Utrecht of 1713 awarded the island to the northern Italian House of Savoy.

Victor Amadeus, Duke of Piedmont-Savoy and the new king, arrived in an English ship, Britain having decided that Sicily should be given to a weak Italian power rather than the stronger Austrian Habsburgs who still retained Naples. The Sicilian nobility hoped the new king would restore the glitter of the Spanish court and were nonplussed when he appeared in clothes made of undyed wool.

The king's survey of the economy underlined how far Sicily had degenerated. Why were there so many unemployed people in Palermo when agriculture was crying out for labour? Agriculture had dwindled so seriously that cereals had to be imported. Tax collection was put out to commercial tender, and the highest bidder unleashed a private army of thugs to recoup the cost.

In 1718 the Spanish invaded to recover their former land. The Sicilians, smarting under the Italian king's austerity measures, welcomed the 20,000 troops. Sicilian grandees brought their Spanish finery out of mothballs. The war climaxed at Francavilla, the biggest battle on Sicilian soil since Roman times. The victorious Habsburg emperor became king of Sicily.

His rule was short. Another Spanish fleet arrived in 1734 and, in a bloodless coup, took Sicily back. Sicily was yet again joined to Naples, under Charles of Bourbon, the Spanish infante. Then, when he succeeded to the Spanish throne in 1759, he handed it over to his son Ferdinand, whose reign lasted 66 years.

After Nelson's defeat of the French fleet in 1798, Ferdinand felt emboldened to attack French forces in Italy, but was forced to flee to Palermo under Nelson's protection. The king rewarded Nelson with the dukedom of Bronte, an estate near Mount

Garibaldi's troops taking Messina in July 1860.

⊘ THE SPANISH INQUISITION

After 1487 the Inquisition was powerful in Sicily. (Palermo boasts the newly restored Palazzo Chiaramonte, a severe palace that became the seat of the Inquisition with, carved on the prison walls, *pane, pazienza e tempo*, an appeal for bread, patience and time. Outside, heretics were burned.) The Spanish spy system used a grim police force to expel all Jews. Intellectual and cultural life suffocated. The system enforced the nobles' loyalty to the Spanish crown. But, tied to feudalism, the peasants reverted to banditry. Now popularly perceived as honourable, brigandry was the breeding ground for the birth of the Mafia.

Etna. Britain retained an interest in Sicily, if only to prevent Napoleon from moving in. In 1806, Ferdinand IV invited Britain to take over Sicily's defence – which made Sicily richer than it had been for centuries. British subsidies encouraged mining and reduced unemployment. While Ferdinand went on hunting trips, the real governor was William Bentinck, the British commander.

Britain could never decide what to do with Sicily. In the event, an Austrian reconquest of Naples meant that Britain withdrew and in 1816, the kingdom of the Two Sicilies was created. The kingdoms of Naples and Palermo were unified and Ferdinand became their king. Immediately he abolished the Sicilian flag and took to his court in Naples. Four years later, during the

St Rosalia celebrations, Palermo rose against him, a rebellion only put down after the arrival of 10,000 Austrian troops.

Palermo again provided the flashpoint for a revolt in 1848. In the aftermath, the king offered a liberal constitution, but this was rejected in favour of an independent Sicily. The Bourbon flag was replaced by the Tricolour.

GARIBALDI INTERVENES

That was the backdrop to another revolt in Palermo in 1860, which spurred Giuseppe Gari-

Turin. To many Sicilians, this fate sounded more like annexation than union.

UNDER THE ITALIAN FLAG

Union with Italy under King Vittorio Emanuele II brought little but poverty, abortive uprisings and mass emigration. The new parliamentary system ushered in democracy of a sort, but as only 1 percent of the island's population was eligible to vote, few could see much improvement. Economically, the island's fortunes went from poor to poorer. There were abortive uprisings which

Messina after the earthquake in 1908.

baldi to choose Sicily as the starting point for his unification of Italy. On 11 May he arrived at Marsala with 1,000 men to liberate the island from Bourbon rule in the name of the Piedmont House of Savoy.

Garibaldi's skill at guerrilla warfare and the growing support from the Sicilian peasantry ensured the victory over 15,000 Bourbon troops at Calatafimi. Within days, Garibaldi occupied Palermo and proclaimed himself dictator of the island, ruling on behalf of Vittorio Emanuele of Piedmont.

In a plebiscite, Sicilians voted almost unanimously for unification of Italy. This meant the end of Garibaldi's brief dictatorship and the assumption of power by Count Camillo Cavour in

By the end of the 19th century, emigration seemed the only escape from poverty. Many villages lost their menfolk to America, Argentina and Brazil. In a single year, Sicily lost 20 percent of its population.

were savagely repressed. In the last decades of the 19th century, the only escape from poverty seemed to be emigration.

The 20th century began ominously with the 1908 Messina earthquake which killed up to 84,000 people and destroyed thousands of homes. Then the conquest of Libya in 1912 was followed by World War I, taking a toll on the Sicilian economy. In 1934, swept along by Benito Mussolini's rhetoric in Rome, a plebiscite showed that only 116 Sicilians out of 4 million rejected Fascism.

Il Duce's master-plan was to industrialise the influential north and use Sicily as the provider of raw materials. He also planned to bring the Mafia to heel. Initially the Mafia were all for Mussolini; not so when he despatched Cesare Mori, an expert in uprisings, to eradicate the scourge. Various Dons were rounded

Benito Mussolini, who won Sicily to his cause.

⊘ THE MAFIA MEETS THE ALLIES

The Mafia played an unexpectedly important role in the Allied conquest of Sicily, and Vito Genovese, wanted for murder and other crimes by police in the United States, turned up as a liaison officer attached to a US army unit. Unwittingly, the Allies helped restore the Mafia's authority in Sicily and so erased Mussolini's only solid achievement: his bringing of the country's criminal families under control. In the absence of the previous Fascist administrators, the army invited a likely-looking candidate, Don Calógero Vizzini, to take on the job without looking into his background. He had been locked up by Mussolini as one of the most undesirable *mafiosi*.

up, while the carrying of firearms was forbidden. Mussolini announced that the Mafia had been eliminated, the murder rate, he said, had dropped from 10 a day to only three a week. The net result was to drive the criminal families deeper underground.

Then, as the tide turned in World War II, the Allies chose Sicily as the landing stage for the war against Hitler in Europe. The coast was defenceless, air cover minimal and, even had there been good roads, most of the artillery was still horse-drawn. The US 7th Army under General Patton landed at Gela in July 1943 while British and Canadian forces tackled the east coast. The German and Italian forces scrambled across the Straits of Messina. Once more, Sicily came under foreign control.

AFTER THE WAR

In 1946, Italy's new government granted Sicily autonomy in areas such as agriculture, mining and industry. In elections it would be a contest between Christian Democrats on the one hand and Socialists and Communists on the other.

The balance of power lay in the hands of prominent *mafioso* Don Calógero Vizzini. For the Mafia, the issue was merely one of choosing political partners that would facilitate the allocation of building licences, import permits and state contracts. Don Vizzini made his choice: the Christian Democrats doubled their number of seats and were comfortably installed as the majority party for the next 40 years. Subsequent demands for government action against the Mafia fell on curiously deaf ears.

As for the faltering economy, Gulf Oil struck lucky near Ragusa in 1953 and later near Gela. Suddenly the island was key to Italy's oil industry and by 1966 one of several refineries was handling 8 million tons of crude a year. The petroleum industry attracted its chemical derivatives; gas was discovered, and Sicily at last commanded the power to make industrialisation practicable.

Relative prosperity started to filter through to the island, with the per capita income quadrupling compared with the 1950s. And the tourism industry ground into gear, as did the wine industry. Life had begun to get sweeter. Or possibly only bitter-sweet, which is a more Sicilian concept, born of centuries of distilled disappointment.

SICILY TODAY

Sicilian society has been shaken out of its torpor. But it is an ambivalent awakening, reflecting Lampedusa's famous line: "Everything must change so that everything can stay the same".

Today, that oft-quoted line from Lampedusa's *The Leopard* could be paraphrased as: "Some things have changed, but some things remain the same." What hasn't changed is that Sicily seems to veer between stasis and crisis, currently concerning refugees. Even before the revolutions in North Africa, Sicily was struggling to cope with the influx of refugees, first Albanians, then Tunisians and Libyans. As the "back door to Europe", Sicily's coastline has been assailed by boatloads of Tunisians, with over 20,000 washed up on the shores of Lampedusa after Tunisia's president was overthrown in 2011. Waters surrounding the small island saw another tragedy when a boat full of migrants sunk in 2013 leaving at least 360 people dead. Two years later another 900 people drowned off the Lampedusa coast resulting in a major migrant crisis, and a EU plan to stop and destroy migrants' boats departing from war-torn Libya. The migrant crisis was the subject of a 2016 Italian documentary, *Fire at Sea*, directed by Gianfranco Rosi; shot on Lampedusa, it was nominated in the Best Documentary Feature category at the 2017 Oscars and won the Golden Bear at the 2016 Berlin Festival.

What hasn't changed is that jobs are scarce, and looking out for oneself, and one's clan, is a matter of survival. Underemployed and undercapitalised, many people piece together a livelihood from a variety of jobs. The eternal Sicilian dilemma is whether to stay in the beloved homeland, and suffer economically, or to seek success abroad. Sicily's challenge is to convince its young that they have a future. But what *has* changed is the Sicilian mindset, bringing stirrings of civic responsibility and the awakening of legions of "ordinary heroes". Sicilian heroes tend to be dead, ideally martyred like St Agata, while state-sanctioned heroes like the murdered anti-Mafia Judge Falcone are honoured too late. Any hero trying to change the system is

scorned with the ultimate insult: *"Idu nu du è"* (he's a nobody). Yet Sicily is full of unsung heroes. The grassroots association Addiopizzo fights against the payment of the *"pizzo"*, protection money widely paid to the Mafia. Founded in 2004, it burst onto the scene with the slogan, "A people who pay the *pizzo* are a people without dignity" plastered all over Palermo. Since then, over 800 businesses have signed up.

Using an Addiopizzo map, anyone can patronise shops, bars, restaurants and B&Bs that are standing up to the Mafia. There was another step forward when Confindustria, the national business association, announced that it would expel members caught paying the *"pizzo"*.

Father and daughter in Palermo.

Civic-minded Sicilians also support Libera Terra shops and cooperatives, which sell pasta, oil, cheese and wine produced from confiscated Mafia lands. In 2013, the police seized Mafia assets worth €1.3 bn and arrested Don Vito Nicastri, a boss from Tràpani, known as "The King of Wind Energy." In January–February 2018 alone, no less than 89 people with ties to mafia crimes were arrested in Palermo, Catania, Enna and other towns.

These small but significant steps still mark the start of a grassroots movement in favour of civil society. But as a respected Palermo publisher said: "We Sicilians have always been subjects, never citizens. The awakening of a civic consciousness is new: give us time to learn how to become citizens." Sicily is still due its renaissance.

📷 BUILDING FOR POSTERITY

The ancient Greeks, who held sway in Sicily, left the island with an unrivalled heritage of noble public buildings and domestic architecture.

Of the three great ancient civilisations that held sway in Sicily, the Greeks left the most enduring architectural legacy. The Carthaginians' buildings and artefacts were largely destroyed by Greeks – an exception being the remains at Mozia, including fine pebble mosaics. And little remains of Roman temples and public buildings – ironically because of Rome's more sophisticated building technology.

Where the Greeks built with solid stone, the Romans used cement within brick casings and faced buildings with a veneer of high-quality stone or marble. Once this was plundered by later generations, the cement and brick soon crumbled. The most enduring Roman remains include indestructible amphitheatres built into hillsides (e.g. Siracusa) and lavish additions to Greek buildings (e.g. the theatre at Taormina).

The Greeks built most of their public buildings in the Doric style, with simple, austere lines and a perfect harmony of proportion. The earliest large-scale temple (575 BC) can be found at Siracusa. Its imposing design was reproduced, with variations, over two centuries at Himera, Segesta, Akrakas (Agrigento) and elsewhere, but most splendidly at Selinunte, where at least nine majestic temples were built in the period from 580 to 480 BC.

Segesta's Greek theatre (3rd century BC). The tiers of seats face west, towards the Bay of Castellammare.

The theatre at Taormina was built by Greeks for drama, but later enlarged by the Romans, who used it for circus games

Statue of a young man in a tunic, dating from the 5th century BC, at the Whitaker Museum in Mozia, which was a flourishing Phoenician colony.

Greek pottery on display in Aidone's museum.

Remains to be Seen

Sicily's archaeological museums showcase civilisations ranging from the Phoenicians to the Greeks and Romans. Palermo's Museo Archeologico contains Carthaginian and Egyptian treasures, Roman sarcophagi and sculptures, notably a huge Emperor Claudius enthroned like Zeus, as well as magnificent friezes from Selinunte (see page 75).

Siracusa's museum houses a hugely diverse collection, featuring sensual statues, gruesome theatrical masks, huge burial urns and poignant sarcophagi (see page 184).

Agrigento's equivalent includes intriguing Bronze Age finds, beautifully painted Attic vases, Hellenistic statuary, and Roman tombs and mosaics. The highlight is a huge *telamon* from the Temple of Zeus (see page 128).

Newer museums with stunning exhibits include: Aidone ("the stolen Aphrodite"; see page 162); Marsala (the Punic ship; see page 109); and Mazara del Vallo (the Dancing Satyr; see page 111).

Doric temple, ruins of the ancient Greek city of Egesta, ow known as Segesta.

he Temple of Olympian Zeus at Agrigento once had 38 of ese colossal telamones (giants) set on its outer wall ting as supporting columns.

The Temple of Concord is one of the best-preserved Greek temples anywhere. It was built around 430 BC.

THE MAFIA

With its tradition of private justice and its code of silence, the Mafia has long seemed impervious to justice – but increasing public indignation means that the tide may be turning.

"If we can eliminate Cosa Nostra then the country can grow: a Sicily without the Mafia will be a Sicily that can start to develop again," declared prosecutor Ignazio De Francisci. Speaking after the arrest of Gaetano Riina, head of the Corleone Mafia in 2011, the prosecutor could allow himself a glimmer of optimism. Gaetano had taken over from his notorious brother, Godfather Toto Riina, who was arrested in 1993 after 23 years on the run. Despite an entrenched Mafia culture in Corleone, the prosecutor put his faith in the people: "It's not the same town it was five or 10 years ago – civil society has taken enormous steps forward."

> *The Mafia earns over €130 billion a year – around 10 percent of GDP – illicit income acquired from arms-dealing, drug-trafficking, prostitution, protection rackets and the embezzlement of European Union funds.*

Lucky Luciano, who forged links between the Sicilian and American mafias.

The revulsion of Sicilians to the 1992 murders of Mafia-fighting judges Giovanni Falcone and Paolo Borsellino has weakened the Mafia's grip on public opinion, its greatest weapon, and dented the age-old code of loyalty (*omertà*). A rise in civic responsibility, tougher laws and greater police determination have driven Sicily's *mafiosi* underground. But the cause is far from won.

MURKY BEGINNINGS

The origins of what is arguably Italy's biggest blight and its second-largest company can be traced to medieval times and a mysterious religious sect, the Beati Paoli, whose hooded members lurked, armed with pikes and swords, in underground passages beneath the streets of Palermo. The modern Mafia took shape in the early 19th century, in the form of brotherhoods, formed to protect Sicilians from corruption, foreign oppression and feudal malpractice. Criminal interests quickly seeped in, and before long the brotherhoods were feeding on the misery from which they pretended to defend their members.

Between 1872 and World War I, poverty forced 500,000 Sicilians to emigrate, mostly to the Americas. There, many joined brotherhoods based on those back home, and the foundations of Cosa Nostra were laid.

In 1925, Mussolini, appalled at the Mafia's new importance as a surrogate state, sent his prefect Cesare Mori to Sicily, and two years later victory was proclaimed for Mori's heavy-handed tactics. But Mori was also a threat to powerful agrarian *mafiosi*. Soon Sicily's landed interests struck a deal with the Fascists, and Mori left the island. In return, the agrarian *mafiosi* saw to it that Sicily's supposedly more criminal urban Mafia were almost wiped out. But the criminals won a reprieve in 1943, when they were given the job of clearing the way for the Allied invasion. Fearing that war between the US and Italy would damage their interests, Italian-American mobsters such as Lucky Luciano had struck a deal with US authorities in 1940. In return for their help, they were to be left alone. Local *mafiosi*, armed with weapons taken from captured Italian troops, were installed by the Allies as mayors of key Sicilian towns.

After the war, organised criminals began supporting Sicily's pro-separatist movement, backed by agrarian interests. Together with the authorities, the Mafia joined in the suppression of banditry, which had made inroads into its territory during the Fascist blitz.

GANGLAND MASSACRES

In 1957 the American and Sicilian mafias met in Palermo's Grand Hotel Et Des Palmes for a summit, called to create the *Cupola* or Commission, and to establish the Sicilians' heroin franchise. The result was a criminal organisation with a clear pyramid structure.

The island's *mammasantissima* also had the satisfaction of securing the import and distribution of all heroin in the United States. It was known as the Pizza Connection since pizza parlours were a cover for money-laundering. Sicily emerged as a strategic centre for drugs, arms and international crime, confirming the shift of the Mafia's economic centre of gravity from the country to the city.

In the early 1980s a Mafia war left Palermo's streets strewn with blood and the Corleone-based clan undisputed victors. In response to charges of government complicity, a crackdown on the Mafia was launched. Thousands of suspects were rounded up and an anti-Mafia pool of magistrates, which included Giovanni Falcone and Paolo Borsellino, was assembled. One "maxi-trial" resulted in 18 life sentences.

MURDERING THE MAGISTRATES

In spite of their success, the anti-Mafia pool of magistrates was mysteriously disbanded in 1988. Falcone moved to Rome as Director

---

It is unrealistic for the state to eradicate the Mafia without tackling the social conditions that fuel it, ranging from poverty to high youth unemployment and stagnant economic growth.

The aftermath of the bombing of Magistrate Giovanni Falcone's car.

of Penal Affairs and lobbied for a force with powers similar to the American FBI. In May 1992, he was on the point of being nominated *super-procuratore*, its head, when the Mafia took their revenge. As he drove with his wife, Judge Francesca Morvillo, along the *auto-strada* from the airport to Palermo, their car passed over a remote-controlled mine. The two judges and their three-man escort were killed instantly, their cars reduced to twisted burning metal, and a huge crater blown in the motorway. Today, the Falcone memorial is one of the first sights to greet visitors driving from Palermo airport, itself renamed in honour of the heroic magistrates.

Two months later, fellow-magistrate Paolo Borsellino, Falcone's boyhood friend and obvious successor, became another "illustrious corpse". He had just arrived at his mother's home when an 80kg (175lb) bomb in his car was detonated, also killing his five bodyguards.

The terror continued in 1993 with bombs in Milan and Rome that killed bystanders and devastated churches; an explosion at Florence's Uffizi gallery destroyed minor masterpieces. But the Mafia had miscalculated. The assassinations of the two Palermo judges and the attempt to destroy the nation's cultural treasures only served to tighten the resolve of the Italians and their government against the Mafia.

END OF THE UNTOUCHABLES

In 1995 Giulio Andreotti, seven times prime minister and one of Italy's most respected elder statesmen, was accused of being a protector and friend of the Mafia in return for votes. Although he was acquitted, the message was clear to *mafiosi* and politicans alike: henceforth no one could be considered "untouchable". Even media tycoon Silvio Berlusconi, until 2011 the Italian prime minister, faces persistent charges of Mafia collusion, which he stoutly denies.

In response to changing circumstances, the Mafia has gone to ground, not murdering but money-laundering, or focusing on arms-dealing, extortion and property speculation. As the old Mafia guard languishes in jail, a more sophisticated organisation, based on "old Mafia values", has filled the power vacuum. The new-generation gangster is likely to be as ruthless on the stock exchange floor as on the streets of Palermo. No one could pretend that Cosa Nostra has disappeared. It is simply mutating, a Sicilian leopard – only with slightly less distinctive spots.

PUBLIC REVULSION

But in society, there has been a shift in public attitudes towards silent acquiescence. Ever the cynic, Falcone called himself "simply a servant of the state *in terra infidelium*" (the land of disbelievers). But finally the believers are in the majority. Where once *mafioso* activity was seen as revolt against the state, justified by centuries of foreign oppression, today the population is less tolerant, particularly the young. The confiscation of Mafia property continues apace, and there is a genuine grassroots movement calling for change. The revelations of political complicity at the highest level have destroyed any fanciful notion that the Mafia somehow represented the private citizen against the forces of authority.

While there is no doubt that Sicily still harbours some dangerous criminals, they can no longer rely on support, or even consent, from most Sicilians. The *mafiosi* haven't gone away, but they are no longer untouchable.

Children take part in an anti-Mafia demonstration.

⊘ THE BEDSHEET PROTEST

In Sicily the murder of the magistrates in 1992 sparked a popular backlash against the Mafia's excesses. On the evening of Falcone's assassination, three Palermo sisters and their daughters hung bedsheets with anti-Mafia slogans from the balconies of their apartments. Soon other Palermitans joined in. The bedsheet protest caught on until it seemed that most of Palermo was making a personal stand against the Mafia. As anti-Mafia mayor Leoluca Orlando said later, "On certain days, you could look up at an apartment building and see where the Mafia Don lived – it was the apartment without a sheet hanging from the window."

SICILY IN THE MOVIES

Sicily is a gift to film directors – both intensely visual and an island of extremes, it is a place of passion, where life and death embrace.

Hollywood's infatuation with the glamour of gangster-land is legendary, especially in the assured hands of Francis Ford Coppola. In movies, the Mafia capital, Corleone, lends its jagged rocks and sullen populace to *The Godfather* trilogy, while the mountains around Montelepre, once the home of Salvatore Giuliano, Sicily's Robin Hood, echo to the sound of banditry.

The island's first international success was Visconti's *La Terra Trema* (*The Earth Shook*, 1947) based on Giovanni Verga's *I Malavoglia*, a tale of poverty and destiny in a fishing community. Naturally, the cast were real fishermen with impenetrable Sicilian accents. Then came *Stromboli: Terra di Dio* (1950), a chronicle of torrid passion between a Lithuanian refugee and a fisherman, an affair as doomed as the brooding melodrama of the movie.

Later, while Francesco Rosi's *Salvatore Giuliano* (1961) told the tragic tale of Sicily's greatest folk hero with the grandeur of a Greek myth, Visconti's glorious 1963 epic, *The Leopard*, exuded impeccable lushness, faded grandeur and decadence.

By 1984 the Italian mood was changing. Set in rural Sicily, the Taviani brothers' *Kaos* was a chaotic universe of legends and lost loves, of mother love and ties with the land. Then *Cinema Paradiso* (1988) brought a nostalgic slice of history following the arrival of the Talkies in small-town Sicily seen through the eyes of a young projectionist, and six years later, *Il Postino (The Postman)*, shot on the island of Salina, told a 1950s tale of a fisherman's son who delivers mail to exiled Chilean poet Pablo Neruda. Over time, he develops an appreciation of poetry (which helps him win the heart of the local beauty) and of Communism (which finally gets him killed).

THE MAFIA THEME

But the most recurring popular theme in the Sicilian film canon is the Mafia. Leonardo Sciascia's anti-Mafia fiction inspired many Italian directors with strong plots and moral dilemmas, starting in 1968 with *Il Giorno della Civeta* (Day of the Owl).

But true commercial successes, heretically, were American: Coppola's *The Godfather* trilogy, inspired by Mario Puzo's novel concerning Mafia wars in the 1950s, allowed Marlon Brando to play the Godfather with relish. The three movies' atmosphere made for operatic intensity; indeed *Part III* (1990) climaxed at

Nuovomondo (2006), a film about a family's emigration from Sicily to New York City at the beginning of the 20th century.

Palermo's Teatro Massimo during Mascagni's foreboding opera, *Cavalleria Rusticana*. A more realistic view of the mafia was recently portrayed in the acclaimed Gomorra television series based on a book by Roberto Saviano.

German director Margarethe von Trotta's *Il Lungo Silenzio (The Long Silence)* dealt with anti-Mafia magistrates and won applause from Mafia widows, while *Nuovomondo* (New World) by Emanuele Crialese (2006) focused on the eternal Sicilian dilemma: whether to stay or leave. His latest, *Terraferma* (2011), portrays Sicily as the "Promised Land" for desperate North African immigrants washed up on Linosa.

FOOD AND WINE

Sicily's exotic past, volcanic soil and teeming seas combine to produce a powerful, opulent cuisine, now matched by increasingly impressive wines.

One of Sicily's best-kept secrets is its cuisine. Only a few Sicilian dishes, like the sweet-and-sour aubergine side dish known as *caponata* or the ricotta-filled *cannoli*, have crossed the Straits of Messina to find fame and fortune abroad.

The Greek colonists who arrived in the 8th century BC were astonished at the fertility of Sicily's volcanic soil, and Siracusa soon became the gastronomic capital of the classical world. By the 5th century BC the city had produced the first cookbook written in the West, Mithaecus' *Lost Art of Cooking*, and the first school for chefs.

On the coast, the sea sets the agenda – it may be a classic insalata di mare (seafood with oil, lemon and herbs), pesce spada affumicato (smoked swordfish) or a dish of thumbnail-sized fried cuttlefish.

Fish is a favourite.

THE ARAB LEGACY

The Arabs brought innovative agricultural and culinary techniques and introduced crops that enriched Sicilian cooking; citrus, rice and aubergines became staples. They also made Sicilian cuisine sweet and spicy. Cane sugar was introduced, as was the Middle Eastern taste for sumptuous sweets – still a classic Sicilian trademark.

By the end of the Saracen occupation, the mould of Sicilian cooking had been set. The Normans employed Arab chefs and, until the Renaissance, Sicily exported pasta, sugar, confectionery and citrus to northern Italy. But while the Spanish brought chocolate and tomatoes from the New World and French chefs were

⊘ STREET FOOD AND MARKETS

Sicily has a long tradition of delicious snacks, especially in Palermo and Catania: chickpea fritters (*panelle*), potato croquettes (*crocche di patate*) and fried rice balls filled with meat and peas (*arancini*) provide a movable feast. The food markets serve up gastro-porn at its most deadly: writhing octopus, slithery eels and swordfish glisten on ice blocks; beyond are barrels of olives and lemons, bunches of basil and mint, sacks of oriental spices and trays of almond-encrusted pastries. In Palermo, Antica Focacceria provides a taster of street food, as do stalls in Ballarò market.

fashionable in the 19th century, Sicilian cuisine reflected class lines.

The poor survived on bread and wild greens; the aristocracy lived on lavish "baronial cuisine". It was left to the emerging *borghesia* to create contemporary Sicilian cooking: extravagant festive dishes, and simpler daily fare, always dedicated to exalting the extraordinary flavours of the produce.

THE SICILIAN MENU

Restaurant starters: As *antipasti*, the classic dishes are *sarde a beccafico*, sardines rolled in

ricotta melt into a magical blend. Pasta can also be paired with *fritella*, a spring sauté of new peas, fava beans and tiny artichokes, or simpler combinations garnished with sautéed courgettes.

Couscous: In the Trápani area, where the Arab influence is strongest, a local version of *couscous*, steamed in a fish broth, supplants pasta. This is best tasted during the vibrant September Couscous Festival at San Vito lo Capo.

Fish and meat: The mountain pastures of the Madonie and Nebrodi produce exceptional lamb and pork. Beef is best stuffed and braised in

Seafood couscous.

Market produce.

breadcrumbs, with a pine-nut and currant filling, baked with bay leaves, or *involtini di melanzane*, stuffed aubergines in tomato sauce. In the mountain towns of the Madonie and Nebrodi, rustic *antipasti* include salami, cow's-milk cheeses (*caciotta* and *caciocavallo*), sheep's-milk cheeses (such as *tuma*) and wild mushrooms *sott'olio*. Sicily's finest cheese is arguably a mature Ragusano DOP, from the Monti Iblei hills near Ragusa.

Pasta: Most Sicilians feel pasta to be the proper first course. Under Arab rule, Sicily was the first place to produce dried pasta on a commercial scale. Today's best-loved dish is *pasta con le melanzane*, known in eastern Sicily as *pasta alla Norma* (after Bellini's operatic heroine). Here, tomatoes, basil, fried aubergines and a sprinkling of salted

tomato sauce or skewered and grilled (*involtini alla siciliana*). But fish and seafood predominate in Sicily, whether as a main course (*pesce spada alla griglia*, grilled swordfish, or *tonno alla marinara*, tuna with olives, capers and tomatoes) or as a starter. Western Sicily's exotic *pasta con sarde* was invented in the 9th century by Arab army cooks who used whatever was at hand: sardines, saffron, pine nuts, dried currants and sprigs of wild fennel. In the east, a potent sauce of anchovies and breadcrumbs is still popular (*anclova e muddica*). In another dish, grated smoked tuna roe mixed with olive oil and parsley is poured over spaghetti.

Vegetables: *Melanzane alla parmigiana* (aubergine baked with parmesan), a Sicilian invention, reigns supreme. Equally fine is *peperonata* (sweet roasted peppers), or orange and fennel salad, a legacy of the Arabs, or artichokes fried, stuffed, roasted on coals, or braised with oil, parsley and garlic. Or bright-green cauliflower cooked with anchovies, cheese, olives and red wine. The interior boasts a survivor from classical times: *maccu*, a purée made from dried fava or broad beans flavoured with oil and wild fennel seeds.

Sweets: Choice becomes hardest towards the end of a meal. Sicilians have had a passion for sweet pastries since Arab times, and for ice cream since the 18th century (see box).

Colourful cassata.

⊘ THE MARSALA MERCHANTS

Marsala, produced around the town for which it is named, was created by 18th-century English merchants as an alternative to port. By 1773, John Woodhouse, originally a soap merchant, had found a way of both improving the taste of the wine and making it last longer. The fortified wine soon found favour with Nelson's fleet, with sailors at sea rewarded with a glass at sunset. Merchant Benjamin Ingham opened a rival winery in 1806, followed by Vincenzo Florio in 1833. Marsala, made by strengthening a base wine with grape brandy and ageing the result, rivals top sherries, Madeiras and ports.

> *From Marsala and Malvasia dessert wines to Bordeaux-style Mount Etna wines, from floral white to full-bodied red Nero d'Avola and cherry-coloured Cerasuolo di Vittoria – reputable estates include Gulfi, Hauner and Marchesi di Gregorio.*

SURPRISING WINES

"Sicilian wines encompass the spirit of 20 civilisations" claims wine buff Bruno Pastera. Certainly, Sicilian wines have a great pedigree, dating back to Phoenician and Greek times, but traditionally underperformed. With their prodigious amounts of sugar, they were despatched north for blending, to bump up the strength of better-known wines. More recently, there has been a full-scale return to producing serious drinking wines using native grape varieties.

Best known is Marsala, in the west of Sicily, still mistakenly synonymous with sickly-sweet liqueurs, but the best (known as *Vergine* or *Riserva*) are excellent, dry, smooth sherry-like wines.

Marsala might be Sicily's most famous wine but the island abounds in award-winning wines. Veronica Bonelli, former sommelier at Sicily's finest hotel, the Grand Timeo in Taormina, sums up the wine scene: "The west is better known, especially Nero d'Avola near Ragusa, and important wine-growing areas around Alcamo and Menfi, but there are also exciting wines coming from Mount Etna and the volcanic islands, such as the powerful but balanced wines made by the Hauner estate on Vulcano and Salina."

Even if modern Sicilian winemaking depends on merit alone, some of the best original estates were founded by the local nobility. The emblematic Regaleali estate, south of Palermo, is owned by the Conte Tasca d'Almerita, but has expanded to include estates on Mount Etna, as well as on the island of Mozia, near Marsala, and on the island of Salina. Given this range, the estate produces Rosso del Conte, a structured Nero d'Avola; Nozze d'Oro, a blend of native Inzolia and Sauvignon; dessert wines on Salina; and Etna wines based on the indigenous Nerello Mascalese varietal.

New-wave Etna wine-growers, such as the Passopisciaro estate in scenic Castiglione della Sicilia, use Nerello Mascalese to make award-winning Bordeaux-style reds. Instead, Catarratto and Inzolia are two native grape varieties that make superior whites, including dry, delicately floral wines around Alcamo. As for dessert wines, on the island of Pantelleria they favour Moscato, called Zibibbo, trained as low bushes against the incessant winds. The island of Salina has a similar tradition but with Malvasia rather than Moscato vines; the Carlo Hauner estate is recommended.

WINE RESORTS

These are wine estates where you can usually stay, dine, or do a cookery or wine-tasting course. Just outside Alcamo, the Sirignano Wine Resort is a delightful organic estate run by the Marchese de Gregori. Guests stay in converted farm workers' cottages on the estate, and sample the marquess's superb wines over meals cooked by an outstanding chef.

Other fine wine resorts include La Foresteria dell'Azienda Planeta, near Menfi, and Capofaro Malvasia on Salina, owned by the aristocratic Tasca d'Almerita family, who were one of the first to offer wine and cookery courses on their estates.

Ricotta-filled cannoli.

At the bar.

⊘ SWEET DREAMS ARE MADE OF THIS

The most famous dish of Arab descent is *cassata siciliana*, the spectacular, exceedingly sweet *gâteau* filled with ricotta cream and decorated with almond paste and candied fruit. "As beautiful as *cassata*" is high praise in Palermo. Instead, Sicilian artisanal ice cream comes in a bewildering array of flavours, from pistachio to pine nut, marzipan to ricotta.

Then there are Sicilian pastries. From the chewy *mustazzoli* biscuits or the nut-and-fig-flavoured *buccellato* to the opulent Arab tradition of *cannoli*. For centuries, the chief pastry cooks were nuns: Palermo alone had more than a score of convents, each famous for a particular sweet. A few convents still sell their pastries, including an atmospheric one in Mazara. Instead, in Erice, the tradition is carried on by women who learned their trade in convent orphanages.

On All Souls' Day, Sicilian children awake to find sugar dolls and baskets of fruit at the foot of their beds, left there by "the souls of their forefathers". The fruit is made of marzipan, known as *pasta reale* or *martorana*, one of Sicily's most delightful culinary traditions. Nowadays, *martorana* is available all year round, and designed to resemble fruit, though visitors with more salacious tastes may be transported by other versions, the nuns' sweet triumphs: virgins' breasts (*minni di vergini*) or chancellors' buttocks (*fedde del cancelliere*).

WILD PLACES

From mountains to volcanoes, nature reserves to marine parks, specks of islands to slithers of beaches, Sicily's wild places are slowly winning over adventurous travellers.

At Francavilla, we hike up the hill to the ruined Norman castle, from where there is a fabulous view across the Arab citrus orchards and the Greek citadel of Castiglione to the stately, smoking, snow-capped bulk of Mount Etna." Nigel, a guide with Ramblers Worldwide, enthuses over how a simple hike in Sicily embraces several civilisations and scenery that stays with you for ever.

Sicily has increasing appeal for active visitors, whether you're looking for a speedy helicopter ride over Mount Etna or a Slow Travel walking holiday in the Madonie mountains. From salt-pans to steaming fumeroles, the island offers bewildering choice. The diversity of landscape is unmatched by other Mediterranean islands and, what's more, you can combine several experiences on the same day. At a stretch you could even ski Etna in the morning and sun yourself on the beach in the afternoon. More typically, you may be wading through a volcanic river gorge in the morning and wading through Greek

Sicilian wall lizard (Podarcis waglerianus) on the Aeolian island of Panarea.

⊘ ANIMALS OF THE ISLAND

Though some creatures such as the wolf have vanished, the crested porcupine is still resident, as are the red fox, hare, wild cat, pine marten, weasel and edible dormouse. Among the island's eight species of bat are the mouse-eared bat and the rare Kuhl's pipistrelle and Savi's pipistrelle. Reptiles include the green lizard, black snake, dark green snake, grass snake and viper, and nocturnal geckos attracted by any outside light. The shy land tortoise is around, but hard to spot with its camouflage. In fresh water you may see the European pond turtle. Amphibians include the common toad, edible frog, tree frog and painted frog.

mythology in the afternoon, enthralled by the wild setting of Selinunte. What also sets Sicily apart is that a "nature trip" is often a voyage back into Sicilian history as well as geography.

DIPPING INTO LAGOONS, ISLANDS AND MARINE RESERVES

South of Trápani, the moody **Stagnone lagoon** embraces the Phoenician island of Mózia, stretching to the ancient salt marshes of the **Saline di Trápani**. These mysterious shallow lagoons are now protected so the tradition of salt extraction will survive, along with the solitary windmills.

The three **Egadi Islands**, only 30 minutes by hydrofoil from Trápani, are ringed by caves, creeks and miniature beaches. The clarity of the water and variety of marine life make swimming, sailing and diving a joy. Footpaths lead to secluded areas, but be prepared for rocky scrambles.

Closer to Palermo, **Ustica** is a well-established reserve and centre for marine studies. The rugged coastline is riddled with caverns and coves, partly accessible along coastal paths. On Ustica you can also explore the underwater sea world of sponges, corals and fish, or follow a sub-aqua archaeological trail in search of Roman wrecks or amphorae. Sub-aqua and marine biology courses are on the rise, helped by the accessibility of Ustica via hydrofoil and ferry services from Palermo.

For adventure-lovers, the **Aeolian Islands** are the most dramatic in Sicily, shaped by volcanic eruption and wind erosion. Strómboli, in particular, is a byword for pyrotechnics. The Aeolians also represent a paradise for ecologists, with geophysicists intrigued by seismic phenomena and molten lava brews. Nor can visitors fail to be impressed by the pervasive sulphurous smells and subaqueous burblings, phenomena matched by weirdly lovely lavic rock formations.

People walking on the rim of Vulcano's crater.

⊘ THE WILD AND WINDY AEOLIANS

The Aeolian Islands form a dazzling archipelago of seven volcanic islands, and represent one of Sicily's most compelling wild attractions. Named after Aeolus, the god of the winds, these elemental islands still exude an otherworldly air. The mustard-tinted radioactive waters and shores are buffeted by the choppiest seas in the Tyrrhenian. The senses are bombarded by a kaleidoscope of colours, from black swirling sand dunes to the rusty red seams of iron and aluminium sulphates. Elsewhere, the sprinklings of white pumice stone contrast with glittering black volcanic rock, while deep-green capers throw bronze-coloured beaches into relief.

For drama, it is difficult to compete with the volcanic activity on Strómboli's seething crater. Other natural wonders include hot springs on Lípari and Panarea, with fumeroles, holes emitting volcanic gases, bubbling underwater on Vulcano and Strómboli. Apart from pyrotechnics, the archipelago also promises sapphire-coloured seas and a dramatic coastline.

On Vulcano, the Gran Cratere marks the start of a fairly arduous ascent of the eerie main crater. An hour's walk across black sands leads to the moonscape of the volcanic crust and a startling sense of the acrid vaporous emissions. Climbing up the crater is a rite of passage for many visitors.

EXPLORING PARKS AND NATURE RESERVES

Sicily is also blessed with an array of protected places that attract both serious hikers and Sunday cyclists. The **Riserva dello Zíngaro** is the showcase Sicilian nature reserve (see box).

East of Palermo, the **Parco delle Madonie** flaunt the most beguiling peaks, often dubbed "the Sicilian Alps." Wooded, mountainous slopes are topped by medieval hamlets and, in winter, the odd ski resort. **Parco dei Nebrodi**, east of the Madonie, is Sicily's largest designated park, covering the mountainous region from Santo Stefano di Camastra to the foot of Etna. Swathed in ancient beech and oak forests, the Nebrodi are a popular place for horse-riding.

The **Vendicari** salt marshes south of Siracusa appeal to both beach-lovers and birdwatchers. Autumn or winter sees waders and ducks sharing the sheltered waters with flamingos, storks and egrets. Full immersion in nature often means full immersion in ancient history.

West of Siracusa lie protected gorges lined with prehistoric necropolis. The **Necrópoli di Pantálica**

Beach in the Riserva dello Zíngaro.

⊘ BIRDS WORTH SPOTTING

More than 150 species of birds, both migratory and nesting, have been logged on the island. The predators include the golden eagle and the peregrine falcon, but they are not the only birds of prey sustained by the island's small mammals and lizards: you may see Bonelli's eagles, red kites, marsh harriers, European sparrowhawks and owls. Besides the blackbirds, crows, robins, skylarks and thrushes, you may spot the hoopoe, red-billed chough, nuthatch, coal tit, Sicilian long-tailed tit, redstart, blackcap, greenfinch, quail and cirl bunting. On summer evenings swifts, swallows and martins join the bats swooping round the terraces.

and Valle dell'Anapo accommodate extraordinary Bronze Age cave dwellings and walks along the Anapo River Valley, alongside dramatic gorges and canyons.

The **Parco dell'Etna**, enveloping Etna's dramatic mountain and crater, can be explored on an afternoon jaunt or on organised treks, including the five-day Grande Traversata Etnea. On the lower slopes, lush citrus groves and bananas give way to pine groves and, finally, to volcanic terrain where only hardy flowers like the Etna violet can survive the extremes of temperature.

WILD FAMILY FUN

When temples pall and tempers fray, nothing beats a trip up **Mount Etna** to astound fractious children. Although Sicily does have theme parks, such as **Etnaland**, nothing compares with the real thing. Etnaland, with its suspended cableway and water park, delivers only a token nod to the elemental surroundings. Instead, **Etnavventura**, set on the southern flanks of Mount Etna, offers more contact with nature. Best of all, it's an adventure park conveniently close to the cable car at Rifugio Sapienza, so can be seamlessly combined with an educational (ish) ascent of Etna (see page 213).

Leave the car at **Rifugio Sapienza** and then chug up the cable car, some 2,500 metres (8,200ft) above sea level, marvelling at the mounds of lava. A jeep transfer then winds its way to the summit, crunching through a barren lunar landscape. If the crunch of clinker is too tame for teenagers, then opt for a guided Etna hike or helicopter tour.

Also in eastern Sicily, close to Etna, is the **Golea dell'Alcántara**, another unmissable experience for youngsters at ease with rushing water. Carved into rock-hard basalt, this 20-metre (66ft) -deep lava-stone gorge is the creation of one of Mount Etna's ancient eruptions. Teenagers will enjoy wading in the freezing waters, but the tougher canyoning experience (in a hired wetsuit) is only suitable for those over 16.

On the Palermo side of Sicily, in the Madonie mountains, the **Parco Avventura Madonie** is the island's best adventure playground. On offer are rope-ladder-walking, tree-climbing, cable slides, mountain-biking, hiking and horse-riding through the woods. The park provides a similar experience to Etnavventura, plus you can pre-book a picnic lunch.

Nor do the archaeological sites need to be a challenge if approached in the right way. **Selinunte** is probably the most child-friendly classical site.

Follow your guide's advice in choosing the right Etna trail as, depending on volcanic activity, Etna can be a damp squib smelling of rotten eggs or prove the most dramatic memory of your stay.

Flamingos on the saltpans at Nubia.

ⵔ RISERVA DELLO ZÍNGARO – SICILY'S MODEL NATURE RESERVE

The Riserva dello Zíngaro (tel: 0924 35108, www.riservaz-ingaro.it) is a Sicilian success story. Commonly known as Lo Zíngaro, it is both a glorious nature reserve sloping down to the sea and an emblem of Sicilian pride. In 1980, in response to plans to carve a main road through this pristine coast, a massive outcry from environmentalists mobilised public opinion and legislation was swiftly passed, securing the future of parks and reserves in Sicily.

Sandwiched between the mountains and the sea, the reserve boasts a Caribbean-style beach, secret coves and rocky headlands – complemented by artfully distressed stone cottages and ancient tuna fisheries. The Tonnara di

Scopello, where tuna was processed until 1984, is one of the most evocative sights in Sicily. The fishery and bay are framed by majestic stack rocks and a medieval watchtower. Well-marked walking trails include one running from the scenic fishing hamlet of Scopello to Tonarella, an easy 6km (4-mile) hike. En route, walkers are torn between the drama of the promontory plunging into the sea and the scent of wild fennel, which often finds its way into *pasta con le sarde*, pasta with sardines. With a cosy atmosphere and an array of rustic apartments, Scopello and San Vito lo Capo make homely bases. Raptors love it here too: the reserve is home to peregrine falcons, golden eagles, kites and Bonelli's eagles.

Greek temple at Selinunte.

View of the Aeolian Islands
from Vulcano.

Teatro Massimo, Palermo.

Driving through Ragusa Ibla.

INTRODUCTION

A detailed guide to Sicily and its islands, with principal sites clearly cross-referenced by number to the maps.

Catania's fish market.

Sicilian scenery is dramatic, sometimes harsh but seldom graceless. Today this granary of ancient Rome contains citrus groves, pastureland and vineyards as well as endless vistas of wheatfields. Away from the coast, an intriguing volcanic hinterland unfolds with wild mountains, gorges and sweeps of rich ochre-coloured earth. Between Catania and Messina, Mount Etna's smoking plumes hover above the ski slopes, citrus farms, vineyards and nonchalant villages that climb the volcano's skirts.

To most visitors, sophisticated yet elemental Taormina is the acceptable face of Sicily, a place of undiluted pleasure where culture shock is absent. On the northern coast is Cefalù, Taormina's rival resort, and a cocooning retreat after the intense capital, Palermo. Outside these cosmopolitan pockets, the adventure begins. The souks and inlaid street patterns of Mazara del Vallo would not be out of place in Morocco. The perfect medieval town of Erice is a shrine to pagan goddesses. The island of Mozia reveals its Phoenician port and sacrificial burial grounds. Built to intimidate the gods, the Greek temples of Agrigento, Segesta and Selinunte are a divine reflection of Magna Graecia. The Romans responded to the Greeks with the vivid mosaics of Piazza Armerina as an imprint of a sophisticated culture.

Mosaic in Monreale Cathedral.

Then, in Palermo, Cefalù and Monreale are cathedrals and churches that testify to Byzantine craftsmanship, Arab imagery and Norman scale. Elsewhere, Moorish palaces, Swabian castles and domed churches offer reinterpretations of this inspired Sicilian hybrid. To top it all, Baroque explodes in the architectural fireworks of Noto, Siracusa, Scicli and Ragusa, seductive cities in the newly revitalised southeast.

Sicily is to be explored and, while the island's rich architectural heritage beckons, the beaches, volcanic islands, wine routes and wild places are equally compelling. But the sun-baked island would be diminished without Sicilian hospitality, whether in a simple farmstay or in a family-owned palazzo run by princely hosts. The welcome can be as sweetly enveloping as *cassata*, the island's legendary dessert.

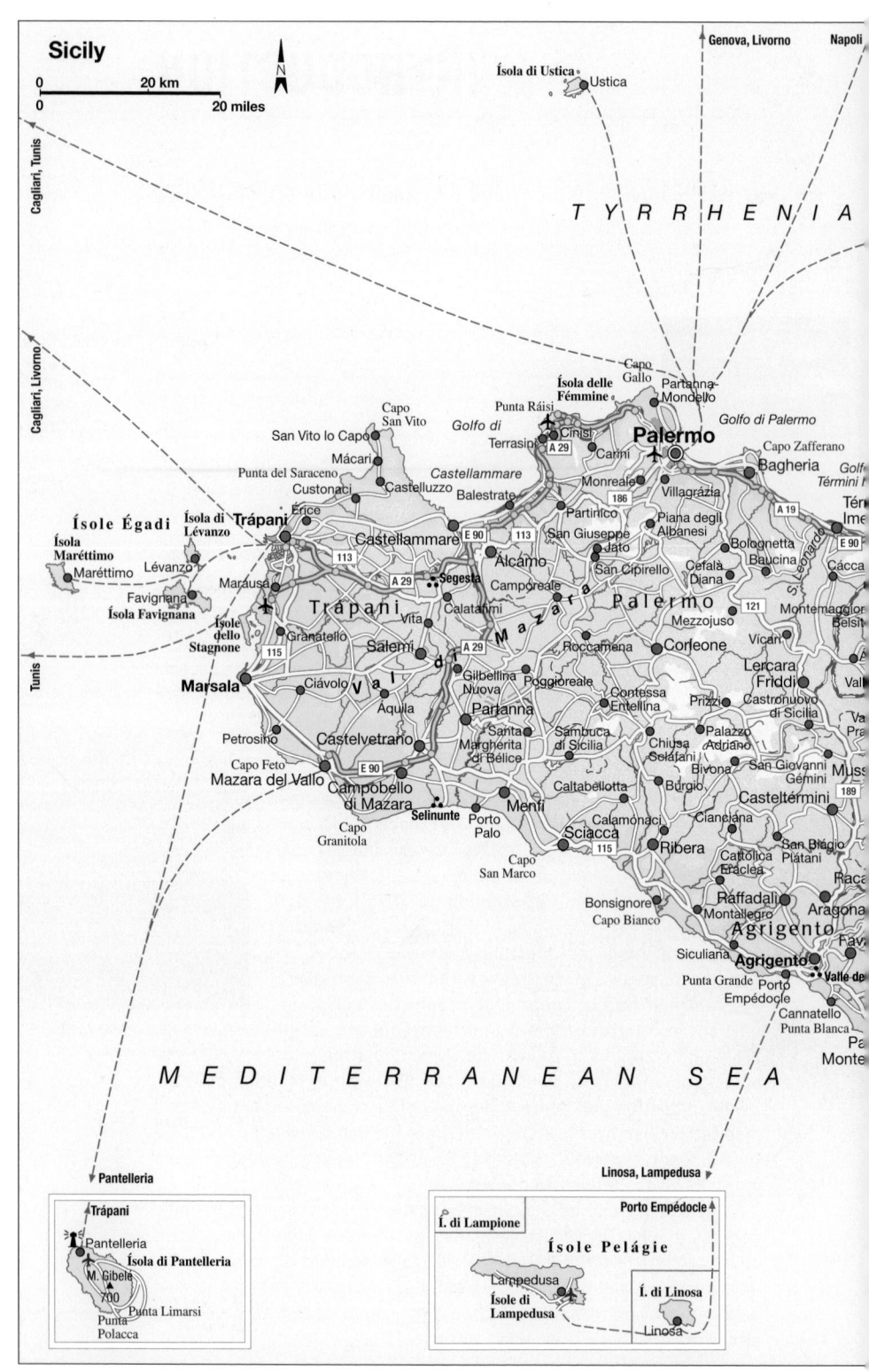

Sicily

0   20 km

0   20 miles

N

Cagliari, Tunis

Cagliari, Livorno

Tunis

Genova, Livorno   Napoli

Ísola di Ustica   Ustica

T Y R R H E N I A

Capo Gallo

Ísola delle Fémmine   Partanna-Mondello

Golfo di Palermo

Punta Ráisi

Capo San Vito

Golfo di

San Vito lo Capo

Terrasini   Cinisi

A 29

Carini

Palermo

Capo Zafferano

Bagheria

Golfo Términi I

Tér Ime

Mácari

Castellammare

Monreale

Villagrázia

Punta del Saraceno

186

A 19

Custonaci   Castelluzzo   Balestrate

Partinico

Piana degli Albanesi

Ísole Égadi   Ísola di Lévanzo   **Trápani**   Érice

E 90   113

San Giuseppe Jato

Bolognetta

E 90

Ísola Maréttimo

Castellammare

113

Álcamo

San Cipirello

Cáccia

Maréttimo   Lévanzo

Marausa

113

Segesta

Camporeale

Cefalà Diana

Baucina

Ísola Favignana

Trápani

Vita

Calatafimi

121

Montemaggior

Favignana

A 29

M a z a r a

Palermo

Belsì

Ísole dello Stagnone

Granatello

Salemi

d i

Roccamena

Corleone

Mezzojuso

Vícari

115

V a l

Gilbellina Nuova

Poggioreale

Lercara Friddi

Val

Marsala

Ciávolo

Contessa Entellina

Prizzi

Castronuovo di Sicilia

Pra

Petrosino

Áquila

Partanna

Palazzo Adriano

Santa Margherita di Bélice

Sámbuca di Sicilia

Chiusa Sclàfani

San Giovanni Gémini

Muss

Castelvetrano

Bivona

189

Capo Feto

E 90

Búrgio

Casteltérmini

Mazara del Vallo

Campobello di Mazara

Caltabellotta

Cianciana

Selinunte   Porto Palo

Menfi

Calamónaci

San Blagio

Capo Granitola

Sciacca

Ribera

Cattólica Plátani

Raca

Capo San Marco

115

Cattólica Eraclea

Bonsignore

Montallegro

Raffadali

Aragona

Capo Bianco

Agrigento

Siculiana

Fav

Punta Grande   Porto Empédocle

Agrigento   Valle de

Cannatello

Punta Blanca

Pa Monte

M E D I T E R R A N E A N   S E A

Pantelleria

Linosa, Lampedusa

Trápani

Pantelleria

Ísola di Pantelleria

M. Gibelè

700

Punta Limarsi

Punta Polacca

Porto Empédocle

Í. di Lampione

Ísole Pelágie

Lampedusa

Ísole di Lampedusa

Í. di Linosa

Linosa

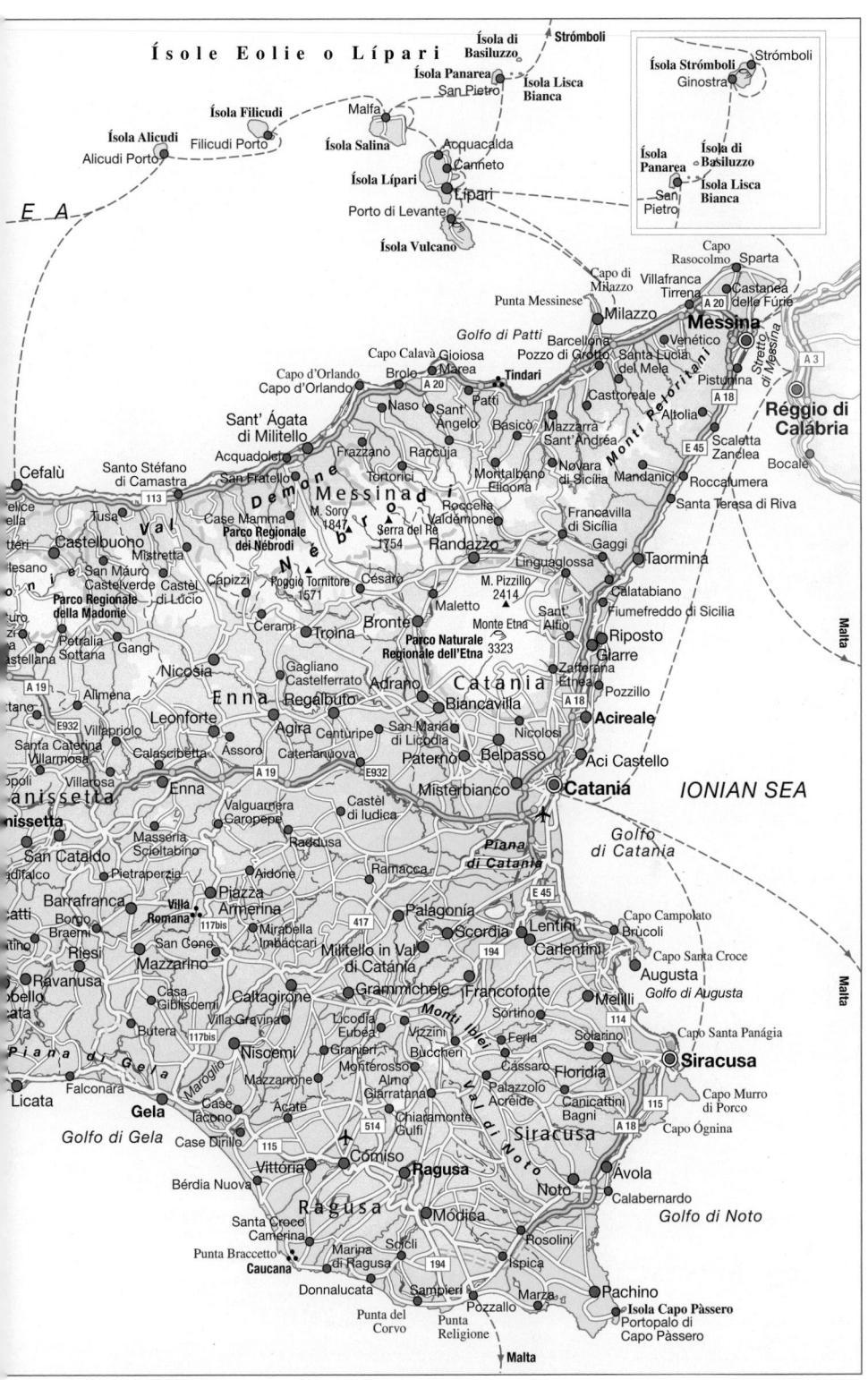

Ísole Eolie o Lípari

Ísola di Basiluzzo
Strómboli
Ísola Panarea
Isola Lisca Bianca
San Pietro
Malfa
Acquacalda
Ísola Filicudi
Ísola Salina
Canneto
Filicudi Porto
Ísola Alicudi
Ísola Lípari
San
Lípari
Alicudi Porto
Porto di Levante
EA
Ísola Vulcano

Ísola Strómboli   Strómboli
Ginostra
Ísola   Ísola di
Panarea   Basiluzzo
San   Ísola Lisca
Pietro   Bianca

Capo
Rasocolmo   Sparta
Capo di   Villafranca   Castanea
Milazzo   Punta Messinese   Tirrena   delle Fúrie
Messina
Milazzo   Venético
Golfo di Patti   Barcellona   Santa Lúcia   Pistunina
Capo Calavà Gioiosa   Pozzo di Grotto   del Mela
Brolo   Marea   Patti   Castoreale   Altofla   Scaletta
Capo d'Orlando   Tindari   Mazzarrà   Zanclea   Bocale
Capo d'Orlando   Naso   Sant'   Basicò   Sant'Andréa   Santa Teresa di Riva
Sant' Ágata   Ángelo   Montalbano   Nóvara   Mandanici
di Militello   Frazzanò   Raccuja   Elicona   di Sicilia   Roccalumera
Acquadolci   Tortorici   Roccella   Francavilla
Santo Stéfano   San Fratello   Valdèmone   di Sicilia
Cefalù   di Camastra   Messinad   M. Soro   Serra del Re   Gaggi
113   Case Mamma   1847   1754   Randazzo   Linguaglossa   Taormina
Tusa   Val   Parco Regionale   Césaro   M. Pizzillo   Calatabiano
Castelbuono   dei Nébrodi   2414   Sant'   Fiumefreddo di Sicilia
Mistretta   Poggio Tornitore   Maletto   Alfio   Riposto
Parco Regionale   San Máuro   1571   Monte Etna   Giarre
della Madonie   Castelverde Castel   Cerami   Bronte   Zafferana   Pozzillo
Petralia   di Lúcio   Troina   Parco Naturale   3323   Etnea   Acireale
Sottana   Gangi   Cápizzi   Regionale dell'Etna
Nicosia   Gagliano   Adrano   Catania   Aci Castello
A 19   Castelferrato   Biancavilla   Nicolosi
Alimena   Enna   Regalbuto   San Maria   Belpasso
Leonforte   Centúripe   di Licodia   Paternò   Catania
Agira   Assoro   Catenanuova
Calascibetta   A 19   Misterbianco   IONIAN SEA
Enna   Valguarnera   Castèl   Golfo
Caropepe   di ludica   di Catania
Masseria   Piana
Scioltabino   Raddusa   di Catania
San Cataldo   Pietraperzia   Aidone   Ramacca
Piazza   Palagonia   E 45   Capo Campolato
Barrafranca   Villa   Armerina   Brúcoli
Romana   Mirabella   417   Scordia   Lentini
Riesi   San Cono   Imbáccari   194   Carlentini   Capo Santa Croce
Ravanusa   Mazzarino   Militello in Val   Augusta
Casa   di Catánia   Francofonte   Melilli   Golfo di Augusta
Gibliscemi   Caltagirone   Grammichele   114
Butera   Villa Gravina   Licodia   Sortino   Solarino   Capo Santa Panágia
Niscemi   Eubéa   Vizzini   Ferla
Piana di Gela   Granieri   Buccheri   Cássaro   Floridia   Siracusa
Falconára   Montèrosso   Palazzolo   Canicattini   Capo Murro
Licata   Mazzarrone   Almo   Acréide   Bagni   di Porco
Gela   Case   Acate   Giarratana   115   Capo Ógnina
Iácono   Chiaramonte   Siracusa
Case Dirillo   514   Gulfi   A 18
Golfo di Gela   115   Cómiso   Ávola
Vittória   Ragusa   Noto
Bérdia Nuova   Calabernardo
Ragusa   Módica   Golfo di Noto
Santa Croce   Rosolini
Camerina   Marina   Scicli
Punta Bracchetto   di Ragusa   194   Íspica
Caucana   Marza   Pachino
Donnalucata   Sampieri   Ísola Capo Pàssero
Punta del   Pòzzallo   Portopalo di
Corvo   Punta   Capo Pàssero
Religione   Malta

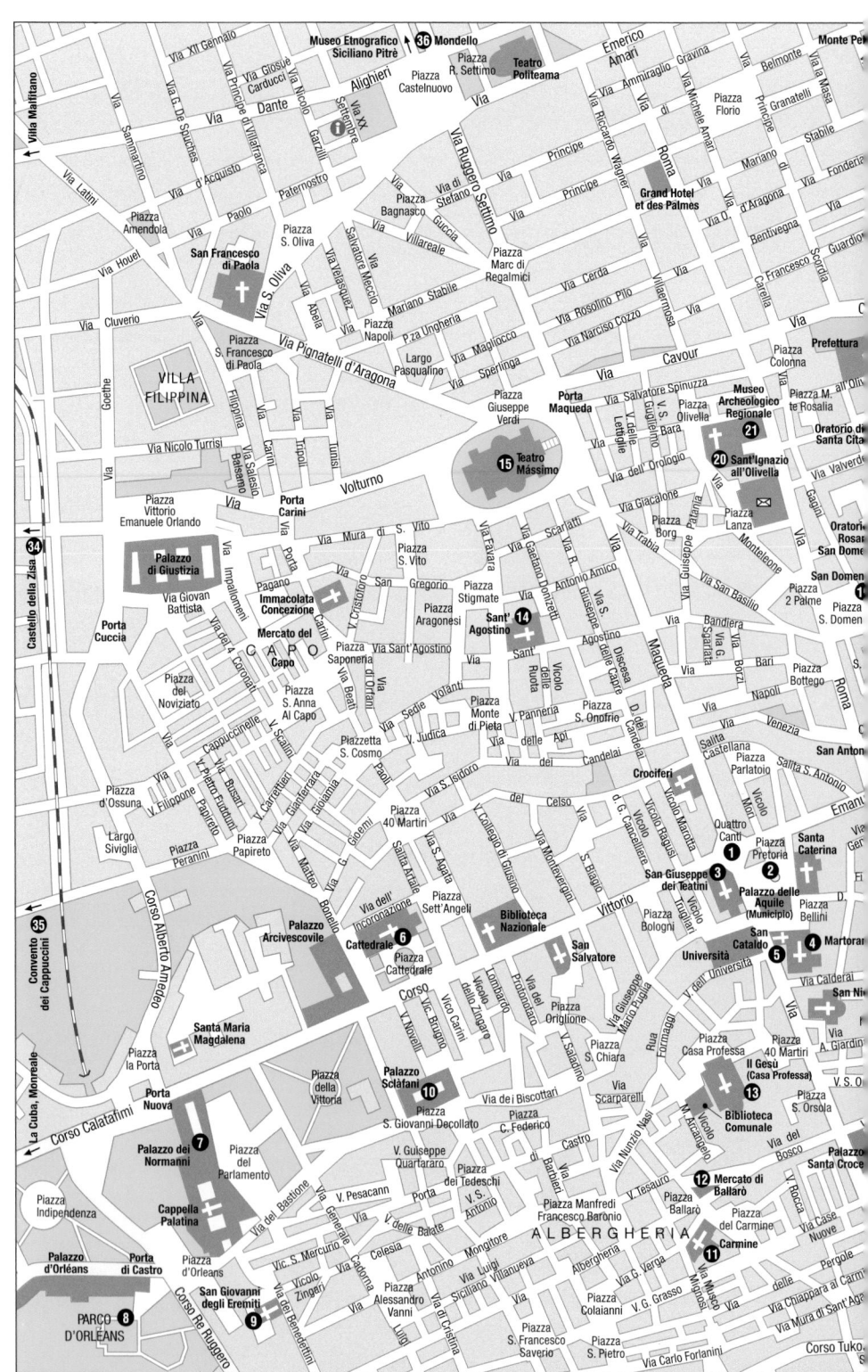

Palermo

0 — 200 m
0 — 200 yds

N

Molo Sud

Golfo di

Palermo

Castellammare

Piazza Cap.
di Porto

Porta
Felice

La Cala

Cala

Via del Mare

Via
atuano

Via
Piazza
ittime

Crispi

io
ovesi

Castello

Via
ianciolo

Tavola
Piazza
onderia

CIRIA
Via

Piazza
arzana

Cassari

Via
Galileo Ferraris

Via Filippo Patti

Via Gaspare Bivona

S. Sebastiano

Via

Via
F. Matera

Santa Maria
della Catena
19

Porta
Carbone

Piazza
Castello

Piazza
S. Spirito

Museo Internazionale
delle Marionette
32

Palazzo
Butera
31

VILLA

A

MARE

Via Emanuele

Vittorio

Corso
Via Bottai

Piazzetta
Dogana

Piazza
Marina
26

V. Niscemi

V. del Franisci

Via Butera

Foro Italico (Umberto I)

Mura delle Cattive

Salita Mura
di Cattive

Oratorio di
San Lorenzo
29

San Francesco
d'Assisi
28

Antica
Focacceria
. Francesco

ssa
io

Cibetta

30
alleria
d'Arte
oderna
(GAM)

dei Vespri

Santa Maria
dei Miracoli

Palazzo
Chiaramonte
25

Palazzo
Lanza
Tomasi

La Pietà

Porta
Dei Greci

Via dell'Intendenza

V. IV Aprile
Pi all'alloro

Via Scopari

Aloro

Via

Galleria Regionale
(Palazzo Abatellis)
24

Palazzo
Mirto
27

V. Merlo

Resuttana

V. Lungarini

Piazza
S. Francesco
d'Assisi

A. Paternostro

Via di Blasi

V. Sciarra

Cefalà

La Gancia

Piazza
Spasimo

Savona

Santa Teresa
Piazza
della Kalsa

Via S. Teresa

Teatro
Politeama
Garibaldi

Piazza
Rivoluzione

V. S.
Carlo

Via Schiavuzzo

C. all'Alloro

Vicolo

Francesco Riso

V. del Sole

Piazza
S. Eumo

della Vittoria

Spasimo

Piazza
Ventimiglia

Vicolo
del Pallone

Cervelo

Lincoln

Divisi

Via Garibaldi

Palazzo
Ajutamicristo
23

V. Filippo
Garibaldi

La
Magione
22

Piazza
Magione

Via
dello

Via
C. Pardi

LA KALSA

Lo Spasimo

Porta
Reale

Abramo

Foro Italico (Umberto I)

Monte
anta

Via
Gorizia

Via Garibaldi

Magione

Via
della Pace

Via G. Filangieri

Lincoln

Porta
Castro Filippo

VILLA

GIULIA

Via

Via
Milano

Corso

Porta
Garibaldi

Abramo

V. M. Cipolla

Via A. di Rudini

Lincoln

V. M. Cipolla

Via Antonio Ugo

ORTO

33

BOTÁNICO

Piazza
Tonnarazza

Via Ponte di Mare

Via Trio a Segno

Piazza
Giulio Cesare

Via V.
Manzoni

Via del
Rosario Gregorio

Palmieri

Mille

Via Paci

Architrafi

Stazione
Centrale

San Giovanni dei Lebbrosi

SANT'ERASMO

Bagheria

PALERMO

Love it or loathe it, Palermo pulls a punch, with the ongoing restoration of the city centre hailed a success – so let an array of Arab-Norman architecture and exotic street food dazzle your senses.

Palermo is both an essay in chaos and a jewel-box of a city: no map does justice to the city's confusion. Sicily's capital is a synthesis of bombsites and beauty, with sumptuous Arab-Norman and Baroque splendour interspersed with an intriguing Moorish muddle. Indeed, Palermo is not merely a crucible of Mediterranean culture but of world culture, given its history of conquest by Phoenicians, Romans, Byzantine Greeks, Arabs, Normans and Spaniards. As a result, the Spanish grid system is subverted by Moorish blind alleys, while domed churches may resemble mosques. Even the Palazzo dei Normanni, the royal palace, is built on Punic walls, but looks Moorish, Byzantine and Baroque by turns.

As a complex city culture that knows many masters, Palermo is, by nature, secretive yet seductive. Many masters, past and present, have been corrupt or neglectful. The cosmopolitan city was devastated during the Allied invasion of Italy when, in 1943, Allied bombs shattered the port and historic centre. Afterwards, the Mafia, in league with corrupt politicians, stepped in, accepting funds from Rome and, later, the European Union, for the rebuilding of the *centro storico,* only to siphon off the money for their own pleasures.

Il Gesù, also known as Casa Professa, Sicily's first Jesuit church.

Public attitudes only changed with the Mafia murders of magistrates Giovanni Falcone and Paolo Borsellino in 1992 (see page 42). Palermitans experienced a wave of revulsion, and citizens were no longer willing to be silently dominated by the Mafia. After a period of political stagnation, a feeling of hope now permeates the air as the Sicilian authorities combat corruption with some success. A citizen-led anti-Mafia movement and new civic pride seems to have taken root, despite a compromised city administration.

Main attractions

Chiesa della Martorana
Cattedrale (Cathedral)
Palazzo dei Normanni
San Giovanni degli Eremiti
Ballarò market
Oratorio del Rosario di San Domenico
Museo Archeologico Regionale
Palazzo Abatellis
Orto Botánico
Castello della Zisa

Map on page 64

THE HISTORIC CENTRE

Statues adorning Piazza Pretoria.

Palermo is divided into four sections by the **Quattro Canti ❶**, the crossroads at Piazza Vigliena, where "four corners of the city" are formed by two great arteries, **Via Maqueda** and **Corso Vittorio Emanuele**, the main street, built over a Phoenician road. The corners, embellished with Baroque stonework and fountains, are hard to appreciate amid the roar of traffic and the clatter of horses' hooves.

Northwest of Corso Emanuele is the **Capo** quarter and southwest the **Albergheria**. Northeast of Via Roma is the **Vucciria** and southeast lies the **Kalsa**. Each quarter reveals a picturesque clutter of mansions, markets and forbidding Baroque churches with luminous interiors.

Just along from Quattro Canti is **Piazza Pretoria ❷**, dominated by the Fontana Pretoria. This Baroque square was once disparagingly nicknamed **Piazza della Vergogna** (the Square of Shame) because of its abundance of flagrantly nude statues that make up the 16th-century Tuscan fountain.

Porta Nuova.

More than 30 near-naked nymphs, tritons, gods and youths surround its vast circular basin. Allegedly, the local nuns chopped off the noses of many of the naked men (but stopped short of castration). The statues are now restored and ornamental railings have been added to prevent further mishaps.

Adjoining the square is the **Palazzo delle Aquile**, the remodelled town hall, with eagles decorating the exterior. The towering presence here, however, is **San Giuseppe dei Teatini ❸** (Mon–Sat 9.30am–noon, 5.30pm–8pm, Sun 8.30am–1.15pm, 6–8pm; free), whose opulent interior exudes a Baroque spirit, beginning with the majolica-encrusted cupola. During the 17th and 18th centuries the church was theatrically decorated with multicoloured marble and with eight massive columns in grey marble to support the dome, which is emblazoned with a fresco of the *Triumph of Sant'Andrea Avellino* (1724) by Borremans.

On neighbouring Piazza Bellini the campanile of **Chiesa della Martorana ❹** (Mon–Sat 9.30am–1pm

⊘ GETTING AROUND

The historic centre, where you'll be spending nearly all your time, is best tackled on foot – driving is stressful and parking a problem. The hop-on-hop-off sightseeing buses are a useful way of getting your bearings and handy when tiredness sets in. Taxis are best telephoned, or found at taxi ranks or outside big hotels (check the meter is switched on). A horse-drawn carriage *(carrozza)* may be tempting but both you (and the blinkered horses) may be exposed to heavy traffic, summer heat and pollution.

City Sightseeing Palermo: "hop-on-hop-off" tours in red, open-top double-decker buses (24-hour ticket €20, lines A, B plus Monreale €25) with night tours in summer too, and bus links to Monreale. For information on routes and tariffs, visit www.city-sightseeing.it/it/palermo.

Cars: parking in Palermo can be a challenge (you can park only along streets with the blue lines) and even if there is space, it won't come cheap (rates start from €1 per hour). Part of the city centre is a Limited Traffic Zone (ZTL) with access only for drivers with a permit. You can check the location of car parks in Palermo by visiting www.car-parking.eu.

Taxis: tel: 091 513 311 or tel: 091 225 455.

Carriages: Pick up a horse-drawn carriage from outside the Teatro Massimo (from €50).

Transport network: information on city buses and parking, www.amat.pa.it.

and 3.30pm–5.30pm, Sun 9–10.30am) stands tall alongside the three small red domes of San Cataldo. La Martorana was established in 1143 by George of Antioch, an admiral whose successes brought such fortune to Norman Sicily that Roger II honoured him with the title emir. (The church was originally called Santa Maria dell'Ammiraglio, or St Mary of the Admiral, in his honour.) Greek Byzantine craftsmen made the splendid mosaics. In the cupola is *Christ Pantocrator Blessing from the Throne*; elsewhere, with angels and apostles, are scenes from the Ascension, the Annunciation, the Birth of Christ and Roger II crowned king by Christ. It is one of the most beautiful Norman churches in Sicily, but may have been even finer had not the nuns from the nearby convent demolished and altered much of it. Their Order, founded by Eloisa Martorana, was given the church in 1233, but Mussolini returned it to the Greek Orthodox community in 1935 as their cathedral.

The triple-domed church of **San Cataldo** ❺ (daily 9.30am–12.30pm and 3–6pm) is one of the last sacred buildings built in the Arab-Norman style. If the interior appears plain, it is probably only because of comparison to its gilded neighbour, La Martorana. Subdued light reveals the three domes supported by squinches and piers; the Fatimid capitals are so delicate they appear to float. The mosaic floor and lattice windows are original; in the crypt are sections of Palermo's ancient Roman walls.

To the west of Piazza Pretoria, at Corso Vittorio Emanuele 365, is the **Museo d'Arte Contemporanea RISO** (www.poloartecontemporanea.it; Tue, Wed, Sun 10am–7.30pm, Thu–Sat 10am–11.30pm). Housed in the beautifully renovated neoclassical Palazzo Belmonte Riso, the museum comprises works by Sicilian, Italian and international contemporary artists who worked on the island.

THE CATTEDRALE

West from Quattro Canti, Corso Vittorio Emanuele leads away from the port towards the cathedral, separating the Albergheria and Capo quarters. This

Piazza Pretoria.

main thoroughfare was once known as Via Cassaro Vecchio, vecchio being old and *cassaro* derived from *qasr*, Arabic for castle.

The **Cattedrale ❻** (www.cattedrale.palermo.it; Mon–Sat 9am–5.30pm, Sun 9am–1pm, 4–7pm; the roof by night summer 8.30pm–midnight) is a Sicilian hybrid: mentally erase the incongruous dome and focus on the desert-coloured stone, sculpted doorway and Moorish decoration, and the geometric Arab-Norman apses behind the cathedral. It was begun in 1185 on the site of a basilica that replaced a mosque in the 9th century. The cathedral was the work of an Englishman, Walter of the Mill, who went on to become Archbishop of Palermo in 1168. The mosaic over the portal came from the original Byzantine church while, on the left-hand column, an inscription from the Koran came from the original mosque.

The Baroque interior is a cool shell, a wan setting for six **royal Norman tombs** that include that of Roger II, the first king of Sicily (d. 1197) and Frederick II (d. 1250), emperor of Germany and king

The exquisite Cappella Palatina.

of Sicily. Borne by crouching lions, the sarcophagi are made of rare pink porphyry and sculpted by Arab masters, the only craftsmen who knew the technique in Norman times. In the nave are statues of saints by Antonello Gagini. The treasury contains royal mantles and the crown of Constance of Aragon (d. 1222), bedecked with jewels. Constance was 24 when she married Emperor Frederick II, age 14. In the crypt are 23 tombs, many of them Roman.

THE PALAZZO DEI NORMANNI

Beyond the cathedral on the Corso is **Piazza della Vittoria**, with a garden sheltered by palm trees and a triumphal gate, the **Porta Nuova**, erected in 1535 to celebrate Charles V's victory in Tunisia. Also here is the Unesco-listed **Palazzo dei Normanni ❼**, the eclectic royal palace and centre of power since Roger II converted the original 9th-century Arab towered castle into his residence, an Arab-Norman palace. It houses the city's greatest site, the superb **Cappella Palatina** (Palatine Chapel).

⊙ CRUCIBLE OF CULTURE

Palermo is a bewildering jumble of periods and styles. A Phoenician colony existed here from the 8th century BC, perched on the water's edge and sheltered by mountains, but it was only after Palermo fell to the Arabs in AD 831 (having been under Roman rule since 254 BC) that it came into its own. By the 9th century the city flourished as a great centre of scholarship and art, the home of Jewish and Lombard merchants, Greek craftsmen, Turkish and Syrian artisans, Persian artists and African slaves. It had the most multiracial population in Europe. Under Arab rule, there were 300 mosques, and the city was ringed by pleasure palaces like La Zisa and hunting lodges like La Cuba. Around 1050, with a population of 350,000, Palermo was one of the largest towns in Europe, second only to Córdoba – Islamic Spain's capital. By 1091 Norman rule coincided with Palermo's own golden age, one of expansion, enlightenment, prosperity and cultural riches, incorporating Greek, Roman and Arab traditions.

Under the Spanish rule that followed, the Moorish city was remodelled along grand Baroque arteries. Yet behind the grand Quattro Canti crossroads that divide the city into four *quartieri* (districts), the old Moorish maze continues to swirl with crooked alleys, lively markets and cosmopolitan chatter.

Now the seat of the Sicilian Parliament, this cube-shaped palazzo has walled gardens overgrown with orchids, papyrus, banyan trees, *ficus beniamine*, as well as dwarf palms, whose leaves are reputed to take 50 years to grow, and African kapoks, said to be a favourite with monkeys in their natural habitat because they store water in their barrel-like trunks. As the main building was turned into the home of the **Sicilian Regional Assembly** in 1947, its visiting hours are limited (www.federicosecondo.org; Mon–Sat 8.15am–5.40pm, Sun 8.15am–1pm, the royal apartments closed Tue–Thu).

CAPPELLA PALATINA

Leading off a lovely loggia is the superb **Cappella Palatina** (Mon–Sat 8.15am–5.40pm, Sun 8.15am–1pm), the royal chapel built for Roger II between 1130 and 1140. He ensured each of the religions in his kingdom – Muslim, Catholic and Greek Orthodox – was represented within the chapel. The interior displays glittering mosaics on the dome and apse, recalling the life of Roger II as well as Christian themes. These include sumptuous Biblical scenes incorporating the Annunciation, the Raising of Lazarus, the Building of the Ark, the Nativity and the Destruction of Sodom. The inlaid floors, marble walls, columns and candle holders and a 3-metre (10ft) tall paschal candlestick, richly decorated with animals carved in white marble, were made by Romans, while Arab craftsmen created the exquisitely carved and painted wooden ceiling; it portrays Christian paradise (as seen through Muslim eyes) with naked maidens surrounded by Normans prudishly clothed and crowned with haloes. The *muqarna* ceiling is remarkable, made by master-craftsmen from Syria, Iraq and Libya. Where else can you see Persian octagonal stars meet Islamic stalactites with palm trees and peacocks while men play chess, hunt and drink among entwined dancers and female musicians? Unique in a Christian church, it is a composition of ineffable oriental splendour.

On the top floor of the palace are the **Royal Apartments**, mostly decorated in

The Palazzo dei Normanni, dating back to the 9th century, is home to the Sicilian Parliament.

Palermo's Cattedrale.

The multicoloured dome of San Giovanni degli Eremiti.

Bourbon style, reflecting the tastes of the Spanish viceroys. The **Sala da Ballo** has a fine view to the sea. However, the loveliest rooms are Arab-Norman, especially the **Sala di Re Ruggero** (1140) with its splendid mosaics of hunting scenes. More recently revealed sections include the **Mura Puniche**, the Punic walls and postern – the oldest part of the palace – and the **Chiesa Inferiore**, mistakenly called the crypt as it lies below the Cappella Palatina, but actually the Lower Church, used for ceremonies and burials in Arab-Norman times.

Through Porta Nuova is Piazza Indipendenza, Palazzo d'Orléans and the **Parco d'Orléans** ❽ (Mon–Fri 9am–1pm, 3–6pm, Sat–Sun 9am–1pm; ornithological garden 9am–1pm only), lush gardens belonging to the Palazzo, the official residence of the Sicilian president. Mothers play here with children, men play cards and office-workers eat ice creams sandwiched in buns, a Palermitan speciality.

THE ALBERGHERIA QUARTER

Teatro Massimo.

South of Corso Emanuele, the Albergheria Quarter was once the home of Norman court officials and rich merchants from Pisa and Amalfi. Although many dilapidated houses are home to illegal immigrants, a sense of community prevails over scenes of urban decay.

The romantic **San Giovanni degli Eremiti** ❾ (Mon–Sat 9am–7pm, Sun 9am–1.30pm), with its distinctive five red cupolas, lies just south of the royal palace on Via dei Benedettini, at the western edge of the Albergheria Quarter. It illustrates the Arab influence favoured when its construction was begun by Roger II in 1132, a year after he had been elected king. Built over a Benedictine monastery founded in 581, this Moorish spot reveals Arab squinches, filigree windows and elegant Norman cloisters overgrown with jasmine, citrus, mimosa and pomegranate. Its restoration and new route stress hitherto neglected aspects, from the well and concealed cistern to the secret underground river.

Arab architectural motifs haunt **Palazzo Sclafani** ❿, a fortified medieval palazzo north of San Giovanni, built in 1330 by one of the most powerful feudal families.

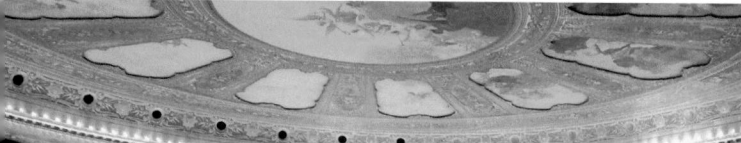

Further east, on Piazza del Carmine, is the fabulously domed church of **Carmine Maggiore** ⑪ (daily 8.45–10.45am) with fine paintings and majolica. This is the heart of **Ballarò market** ⑫, a noisy haunt of artisans and students, housewives and bootleggers. Currently Palermo's liveliest daily market, it is raucous, authentic and sprawling, with the hurly-burly of the exotic food stalls clashing with the second-hand clothes stalls.

Sicily's first Jesuit church, **Il Gesù** ⑬ (Mon–Fri 9.30am–1.30pm, Sat 9.30am–4pm), is on Piazza Casa Professa. Also known as Casa Professa for its learned Jesuit origins, its interior is beautifully decorated with colourful marble, sculptures, tritons and cherubs. It has been restored after being damaged in World War II.

THE CAPO QUARTER

The battered *Capo quartiere* lies north of the cathedral. Since its origins as the slave traders' quarter, the Capo has been isolated, historically the poorest area of the city. It is a maze of alleys,

but the centrepiece, masked by market stalls, is the church of **Sant'Agostino** ⑭ (Mon–Sat 7am–noon, 4pm–6pm, Sun 7.30am–noon), the sober remains of a medieval monastery, adorned with crests of the powerful Chiaramonte and Sclafani dynasties. Their crests and some lava mosaics decorate a delicate late 13th-century portal surmounted by a 14th-century rose window. Inside are gilded stuccoes by Giacomo Serpotta (c.1711), matched by charming 16th-century cloisters and a small garden.

Ballarò market.

This warren of streets conceals restored churches such as the **Immacolata Concezione** (Mon–Sat 9am–1pm) on Via Porta Carini, but others lie derelict. Some have been put to new uses like San Marco, which is now a care home. These streets are the setting for the **Capo market**, an inexpensive source of food, clothes and household goods.

Within walking distance of the market, northwards on Via Maqueda, historic Capo gives way to 19th- and 20th-century Palermo with the **Teatro Massimo** ⑮, the city's vast opera

Cloisters of San Giovanni.

On the lovely piazza beside the Teatro Massimo are two kiosks designed by Battista Basile's son Ernesto; they are in the Art Nouveau style that he used for much of his work in Palermo.

Getting married in Sant'Ignazio all'Olivella.

house, dominating Piazza Verdi (www. teatromassimo.it; tours daily 9.30am–6pm, unless there's a rehearsal; for opera tel: 091 605 3580). The well-restored building, first opened in 1897, was designed by Palermo's illustrious Giovanni Battista Basile in eclectic rather than neoclassical style. The portico, graced by Corinthian columns, is of Greek inspiration, while the cylindrical shapes of the building and the cupola owe more to Roman ideal. Inside, the grandiose main staircase is Baroque while the decor, rich in floral motifs, is decidedly Art Nouveau.

THE VUCCIRIA QUARTER

The name of this quarter is a corruption of the French *boucherie*, thanks to the quantity of meat traditionally on sale in the **Vucciria market** (Mon–Sat until 2pm) The stalls straggle along alleys from Via Roma to **San Domenico** ⓰ (Tue–Fri 8am–1.30pm, Sat–Sun 8.30am–1.30pm, 5–7pm), a Baroque church with an impressive facade that has its foundations in the 1300s but was altered around 1636 by the Domenican Order. In the

18th century, the Spanish viceroys tried to impose order on Palermo's most chaotic market but failed dismally. Little has changed and the names of the surrounding streets echo the old local trades: silversmiths, ironmongers, pasta makers, shoemakers. The colourful stalls display capers and pine nuts, spices and sun-dried tomatoes, endless varieties of meat and sausages and bootleg tapes, and are particularly charming as night falls and the red awnings are illuminated. However, the success of Ballarò market means that the Vucciria market truly bustles only on Saturdays.

If the Vucciria palls, leave the market and consider a drink in the faded *belle époque* grandeur of the **Grand Hotel et des Palmes** at 398 Via Roma. Wagner reputedly completed *Parsifal* in a gilded salon here in 1882, while the wartime Mafia boss, Lucky Luciano, later held court in the dining room.

Behind the church of San Domenico, on Via Bambinai, a doll makers' street that has stayed close to its roots by selling Christmas crib figures as well as votive offerings, is a Baroque jewel, the **Oratorio del Rosario di San Domenico** ⓱ (winter Mon–Sat 9am–2pm, summer until 6pm). It is a theatrical chapel created by the master in stuccowork, Giacomo Serpotta (see page 85), with putti playing cellos amidst seashells, eagles and allegorical exotica. The altarpiece, the *Madonna of the Rosary*, is the work of Van Dyck (c.1624) and considered one of the finest in Sicily and Italy.

Just around the corner, on Via Valverde, lies another celebrated oratory, **Oratorio di Santa Cita** ⓲ (winter Mon–Sat 9am–2pm, summer until 6pm), reached through lush gardens. The oratories were places where nobles gathered, centres for charitable works as well as for displays of personal status and wealth. In Santa Cita, Serpotta's ravishing stuccowork depicts the *Intercession of the Virgin in the Battle of Lepanto* with all of the boats exquisitely differentiated.

LA CALA

Beyond the chapel is **La Cala**, the scruffy portside edged by Via Cala. Fishing boats bob against a backdrop of bombed palazzi whose cellars house immigrant families. However, regeneration is gradually seeping into this semi-derelict quarter with the restoration of churches, like **San Giorgio dei Genovesi** (winter Mon–Sat 9am–2pm, summer until 6pm; free), which is now an exhibition centre. The transformation of La Cala and the old port area is the city's biggest project in coming years, including the **Castello a Mare**, the archaeological zone on the far side of the bay. This area suffered most from bomb damage in World War II, and the city was moved further from the sea by an accumulation of falling masonry, which is gradually being removed. The striking site, which includes crumbling Arab bastions, is now used for concerts and events.

Sandwiched between the port and Piazza Marina is **Santa Maria della Catena** ⑲ (daily 10am–6pm), a well-restored 15th-century church with an early Renaissance portico at the top of a flight of stairs. The church was named after the medieval chain (catena) that sealed the harbour in times of war. Inside, a 16th-century baldacchino covers a charming 14th-century fresco of The Madonna and Child.

PIAZZA OLIVELLA

From the port, if you retrace your steps to Via Roma and turn into Via Bara, you come to **Piazza Olivella**, part of a charming artisans' quarter of puppet-makers, pastry shops and inns. The grand Baroque church of **Sant'Ignazio Martire all'Olivella** ⑳ (Mon–Tue, Thu, Sat 7–10am, 5–8pm, Wed 7–8am, 5–8pm, Sun 9am–1pm) begun in 1598 but with a 17th-century facade, has some fine pictures.

Adjoining the Olivella church is the recently revamped **Museo Archeologico Regionale 'Antonio Salinas'** ㉑ (www.regione.sicilia.it/beniculturali/salinas;

Tue–Sat 9.30am–6.30pm, Sun until 2pm). This is the essence of classical Sicily encased in a late Renaissance monastery, with artefacts that illustrate the region's glorious historical roots, from prehistoric times to the Roman era. There are inscrutable Egyptian priestly figures found near Mozia, and anthropomorphic sarcophagi stare out of Semitic faces and square bodies. In a large cloister is a tangle of lush vegetation and a lily pond.

The museum's most important treasures are in the eastern wing entirely devoted to **Selinunte**, including carved stone reliefs (the metopes) that were set above the columns at Selinunte in about 470 BC (see page 111). The friezes depict deities, such as Athena protecting Perseus as he tussles with Medusa; Hercules slaying dwarves or battling a Cretan bull; Zeus marrying a frosty Hera on Mount Ida; Actaeon turning into a stag. Other highlights are the terracotta votive offerings from Selinunte; as well as the celebrated bronze ram that once stood over the gate of Castello Maniace in Siracusa.

Tango dancing is popular on summer evenings in the city.

Detail of Intercession of the Virgin in the Battle of Lepanto.

Interior of La Magione.

The Museo Archeologico also displays an Etruscan collection with sculptures and painted terracotta works from the 6th to 5th centuries BC uncovered in Chiusi (Tuscany). Superb Greek vases of the same period depict the *Myth of Tripolemus* and the *Battle of Athena against the Giants*. There are also casts of engravings from Addaura on nearby Monte Pellegrino and a Roman mosaic showing Orpheus enchanting wild beasts.

LA KALSA QUARTER

In Arab times the Kalsa Quarter was where the emir lived in splendour, and in the Middle Ages it became the chosen district for the homes of wealthy merchants. The word *kalsa* comes from the Arabic *khalisa*, meaning "pure" or "chosen".

Little of this purity shows today. La Kalsa may be picturesque, but it is impoverished, having been badly damaged during World War II as it fringes the harbour. When Mother Teresa's mission settled close to bomb-struck Piazza Magione, wealthy Palermitans were horrified to be lectured by an Albanian nun, even one incarnating sainthood. Her message was that since Palermo was as poor as the Third World, charity should begin at home. The message, however, seems to have struck a chord since the area is being slowly regenerated with a cheery materialism heralded by new bars, especially close to the delightfully gentrified **Piazza Marina**.

This seemingly abandoned corner of Palermo houses a wonderful Norman church as well as the late Mother Teresa's nuns and the church of **Santa Teresa alla Kalsa** (Fri–Wed 8–11am, 4.30–6pm, Thu 4.30–6pm).

On neighbouring Piazza Magione, Moorish filigree windows and blind arcading announce the ancestry of **La Magione ㉒** (Mon–Sat 9am–7pm, Sun winter 9am–1pm, summer 9am–7pm). This imposing Cistercian church was founded in 1151 but was then presented to the Imperial Teutonic Order by Henry VI in 1197. Norman architecture predominates, with a gracious interior complemented by a 14th-century altar and painted Crucifix. The delicate cloisters contain a 15th-century fresco of

☉ PRINCELY PASTIMES

As a Spanish vassal, Sicily indulged in conspicuous consumption on grandiose city palaces. The foreign viceroys sold feudal privileges and titles to fill their coffers and inflate the numbers of the aristocracy. Under the Neapolitan Bourbons, Palermo's population doubled and the city boasted more palaces than in the entire British Empire. Yet Palermo is oddly democratic, with all classes living hugger-mugger in the historic centre. Many palazzi have remained temples to Sicilian secrecy, but others have opened their ornate portals to prying eyes, and their ballrooms to privileged parties. Beyond the Baroque courtyards are Gothic loggias and Moorish watchtowers, restored private chapels and Rococo staterooms.

You can now stay in several castle-like palaces in Palermo, including with Conte Federico (www.contefederico.com), or in a boutique hotel such as Palazzo Brunaccini (www.palazzobrunaccini.it), which is superbly located in the heart of the historic city centre. Other palatial homes can be visited, including Palazzo Alliata di Pietragliata (Via Bandiera 14, tel: 039 347 526 4276; www.palazzoalliata.it) or the last home of Tomasi di Lampedusa, Palazzo Lanza Tomasi, in Via Butera 28 (groups only, tel: 039 333 316 5432, www.butera28.it). Apart from beguiling "private" visits, the patrician owners may offer recitals and classical concerts, cookery courses and tastings on ancestral wine estates.

the Crucifixion. Around the church is a charming garden of palm trees.

On Piazza Magione is a memorial to the magistrate Giovanni Falcone, assassinated by the Mafia in 1992 and, to one side of the piazza, is **Teatro Politeama Garibaldi** (1861), a small theatre seemingly saved from ruin, now the seat of the Orchestra Sinfonica Siciliana (www.orchestrasinfonicasiciliana.it). Just east of Piazza Magione, in the honeycomb heart of the Kalsa, is **Lo Spasimo** (Tue–Sun 9.30am–6.30pm). This evocative entertainment complex is set in a former 16th-century monastery. Jazz concerts are held in the cloisters and the roofless church which, given a sultry, starry night and swaying palms, creates a romantic, Moorish atmosphere.

Via Magione leads into Via Garibaldi with, among the palazzi, **Palazzo Ajutamicristo** ㉓, (http://palazzoajutamicristo.it), a Catalan-Gothic mansion built in 1490 containing a loggia and porticoed courtyard. It was along Via Garibaldi, and what is now Corso dei Mille, that Giuseppe Garibaldi made his triumphant advance into Palermo on 27 May 1860.

THE REGIONAL ART GALLERY

Just east, Via Alloro, the city's patrician centre in the Middle Ages and the principal street in the Kalsa, leads to **Palazzo Abatellis** (1488), a grand Catalan-Gothic mansion that is home to the **Galleria Regionale** ㉔ (Thu–Fri 9am–6pm, Sat–Sun 9am–1pm). This regional gallery houses Sicily's most endearing art collection, with the treasures complemented by the charming setting.

Set off a Renaissance courtyard and loggia, over two floors, the collection offers a journey back through Sicilian art, showcasing paintings and sculpture from the 15th and 16th centuries. The highlights include a serene bust of *Eleanor of Aragon* by Francesco Laurana, engaging Gagini sculptures by a Sicilian master and a haunting *Annunciation* (1476) by Antonello da Messina, Sicily's greatest painter of the 1400s.

The undoubted masterpiece is the powerful 15th-century *Triumph of Death*, with a skeleton archer as the grim reaper of Death riding on a spectral horse, cutting a swathe through wealthy bishops, nobles and fair maidens. Here, Death shoots only at those who do not want to die because they are enjoying life to the full; he ignores the poor and disabled, who pray for divine intervention and a release from their earthbound troubles. The subject is macabre but strangely compelling.

Next to the gallery is the austere **La Gancia**, the 15th-century church of **Santa Maria degli Angeli** (Mon–Sat 9.30am–1.30pm). On display are works by Antonello Gagini, Pietro Novelli and Giacomo Serpotta.

PALAZZO CHIARAMONTE

A short walk away is **Palazzo Chiaramonte** ㉕ (Tue–Sat 9am–1pm and 2.30–6.30pm, Sun 10am–2pm), a baronial palace built by the Chiaramonte dynasty in 1307. It became the palace of the Spanish viceroys and then the seat of the Inquisition from 1605 to

La Kalsa.

The cloisters of Palazzo Ajutamicristo.

Triumph of Death fresco at Palazzo Abatellis.

1782. Carved on the grim prison walls inside is a poignant plea for *pane, pazienza e tempo* (bread, patience and time). Heretics and dissenters were burned to death outside, but so too were artists and intellectuals, damned as subversives. Commonly known as Lo Steri, the building was restored for the Chancellor of Palermo University but is also a fascinating museum.

A formidable inner courtyard leads to the Inquisition prisons, which are covered in pleas and etchings. Off the first-floor loggia is the Sala Magna (Great Hall), where the Spanish viceroys met, and which is adorned with a superb medieval coffered ceiling.

Other highlights include the Chiesa di Sant'Antonio Abate, a Gothic gem once linked to the palace by an overhead passageway and, incongruously, *Vucceria*, Guttuso's languid depiction of Palermo's best-known market.

PIAZZA MARINA

Alongside Palazzo Chiaramonte is **Piazza Marina ㉖**, originally a muddy inlet that silted up and was reclaimed in Saracen times. Since then the square has witnessed the shame and glory of city history. It was used by the Aragonese for weddings and jousts and, because it was close to the prisons, for public executions too. In the centre is Giardino Garibaldi. As it is the only gentrified square in the old quarter, the locals are self-consciously proud of its shady park and well-tended banyan trees. The square holds a bric-a-brac market on Saturday afternoons and Sunday mornings. Across the square is the charming Renaissance church of **Santa Maria dei Miracoli** (Mon–Fri 9am–5pm, Sat 9am–1.30pm).

Close by, on Via Merlo, is **Palazzo Mirto ㉗**, an unprepossessing palazzo with a delightful interior. This Palermitan palace may be the embodiment of the "voluptuous torpor" described in *The Leopard*, but is far from unique. In 1982 the palace and its contents were donated to the state by the descendants of the Princes of Lanza Filangri, whose ancestors have lived in the palazzo since the 17th century.

Now a museum (Tue–Sat 9am–6pm, Sun 9am–1pm), the *palazzo* provides an insight into how a grand family lived and lays bare the eclectic tastes of the Palermitan aristocracy in the 18th century. Below *trompe l'œil* ceilings are Louis XVI chairs, rustic panelling, heroic tapestries, crib figures and, of course, a personal altar. A chinoiserie salon has lacquered oriental cabinets, porcelain and pagoda-style seats.

ST FRANCES AND ST LAWRENCE

A little further along Via Merlo, across from Palazzo Mirto, is **San Francesco d'Assisi ㉘** (Mon–Sat 7–11.30am, 4–6pm, Sun 7am–1pm, 4–6.30pm), one of Palermo's loveliest Gothic churches, its austerity softened by a beautiful portal and delicate rose window. It was damaged during World War II but well restored. The nave (1255–77) is edged

with 14th-century chapels and eight statues by Serpotta (1723).

Nearby, on Via Immacolatella, is the **Oratorio di San Lorenzo** ㉙ (daily 10am–6pm). The interior is a whimsical yet overwrought extravaganza of stucco by Giacomo Serpotta. The masterpiece is based on the lives of Saints Francis and Lawrence, with every surface awash with cheeky cherubs and lavish allegories. One of Caravaggio's last paintings, a *Nativity*, hung over the altar but was stolen in 1969.

Opposite the church of San Francesco, at 58 Via Paternostro, is **Antica Focacceria di San Lorenzo**, a legendary inn with battered bow windows matched by marble slabs and a gleaming brass stove. This period piece has a reputation for rustic snacks like *panini di panelle* (fried chickpea squares) and, an acquired taste, *pani cu' la meusa* (tripe served in a bun). The owner was also the first Palermitan restaurateur to challenge the notion of paying the *pizzo*, extortion money, and won, helping to lend support for the anti-Mafia Addiopizzo movement.

MODERN ART MUSEUM

From here, walk to neighbouring Via Sant'Anna and the **GAM** ㉚ (Galleria d'Arte Moderna, www.gampalermo. it; Tue–Sun 9.30am–6.30pm). Set in a lovely Catalan mansion and former convent, this stylish museum covers such movements as neoclassicism and Romanticism, especially through Sicilian art. The museum has the added attraction of a good restaurant.

THE REVITALISED SEAFRONT

Until very recently, Palermo turned its back on the sea and the stark waterfront was lined with shoddy stalls. But now a 2km (1.25-mile) trail known as the **Passeggiata a Mare**, the promenade along Foro Italico, has brought the locals back to the seafront. Palermitans either stroll along, admiring the headlands and one another, or lounge on funky, marble-clad beds dotted along the shore.

Much of this area was reduced to rubble by Allied bombing during the war, including **Palazzo Butera** ㉛, eulogised by Goethe. Once Sicily's grandest palace, it is now often used

Antonio di Francesco's 14th-century Madonna with Child at Palazzo Abatellis.

Banyan tree in Piazza Marina.

⊙ Tip

"A people who pay the *pizzo* (protection money) are a people without dignity" runs the slogan. Support a good cause by taking home local organic produce (such as wine, chickpeas, sun-dried tomatoes) by shopping at the Bottega dei Sapori (http://bottegaliberaterra.it) on Piazza Castelnuovo 13, Palermo. It's part of Libera Terra, an anti-Mafia association which farms land confiscated from the Mafia (see page 39).

Grim display in the Convento dei Cappuccini.

for receptions or as a film set (tel: 091 611 0162). As part of the ongoing regeneration of the waterfront, the council has restored the terraced **Mura delle Cattive** below Palazzo Butera. Decorated with statues, this was nicknamed "Wall of the Nasty Women" in honour of the sour-faced widows and spinsters who once glowered at lovers strolling by. In the 18th century, this was the place for illicit evening assignations on the pretence that the terrace had fine views over the seafront to Monte Pellegrino and that the heat here was less oppressive.

The marina below was Palermo's grand seafront in the heady days of the *belle époque* and was both a public parade and chance for louche encounters. Now known as **Foro Italico**, this area fell into decline until the creation of the promenade. The waterfront walk now features landscaped gardens popular with joggers and sunbathers, and stretches all the way to Villa Giulia and the Orto Botánico, the botanical gardens.

Off Via Butera, in Piazzetta Niscemi, is the Puppet Museum, **Museo Internazionale delle Marionette** ㉜ (www.museodellemarionette.it; Tue–Sat 10am–6pm, Sun–Mon 10am–2pm), with a collection of around 3,000 puppets from Palermo, Catania and Naples, as well as from Africa and the Far East. Puppet shows are staged there throughout the year, as are children's puppet-making activities.

Instead, off Foro Italico, close to the elegant **Porta Reale** (1786), is **Villa Giulia** (8am–sunset; free) with an attractive garden and the **Orto Botánico** ㉝ (www.ortobotanico.unipa.it; daily summer 9am–8pm, until 6pm in winter). These delightful botanical gardens are dotted with pavilions, sphinxes and a lily pond and enlivened by bamboo and bougainvillea, banyans and magnolias, pineapples and petticoat palms.

Further south, in a former railway depot at Via Messina Marine 27, is the Ecomuseum Mare Memoria Viva (www.marememoriaviva.it; Tue–Sun 10am–6.30pm), which is all about the sea and its relation with the city. Another branch of this museum, in the Royal Arsenal at Via dell'Arsenale 142

⊙ TERRASINI

Further along the coast, away from Mondello on the A29, are two more resorts. Isole delle Femmine is best avoided. It may face an island of the same name, but is surrounded by an industrial zone and the sea is often polluted. Terrasini, however, overlooks the Golfo di Castellammare and is a former fishing village with sandy beaches and clean sea. The 19th-century Palazzo D'Aumale (www.poloartecontemporanea.it/museo_dAumale; Tue–Sun 9am–7pm) hosts three sections of the civic museum: the Antiquarium with ancient finds from the sea, the Museo del Carreto with a folklore collection that includes traditional Sicilian painted carts, and the Museo di Storia Naturale, the natural history museum.

(Mon–Fri 9am–1pm), is dedicated to the history of the port and the shipyard.

THE WESTERN SUBURBS

Beyond the Capo Quarter, off Via Guglielmo Buono, is **Piazza Zisa** and one of the most impressive examples of Arab-Norman secular architecture in Sicily. It is purely Islamic in its inspiration. In Norman times palaces encircled the city "like gold coins around the neck of a bosomy girl", – the vivid description by the Arab poet Ibn Jubayr. The poet's words evoke the pleasure dome of **Castello della Zisa** ❸, now home to the Museo d'Arte Islamica di Palermo (Mon–Sat 9am–7pm, Sun 9am–1.30pm; take buses 101 or 106 there).

Begun in 1160 by William I, and known as La Zisa (from the Arabic for magnificent), this was to be a place of joy and splendour. An Arabic inscription by its entrance conjures up earthly paradise within. The palace later became a fortress and grand residence before returning to its Moorish roots. Now restored, with the Moorish gardens reinstated, La Zisa is magnificent once more.

An Arab arch leads to a palace built on the site of a Roman villa so that it could exploit an existing aqueduct. Devoted to water, the Arabs installed a system of canals, feeding water from the aqueduct into a charming fountain in a vaulted vestibule which, in turn, fed a pond outside. In fact, La Zisa's most charming spot is the vestibule, adorned by honeycomb vaults, the fountain and a glorious mosaic of peacocks and huntsmen. On the top floor, the hall was originally an atrium with the side rooms thought to have formed the harem.

Just north of the Castello, the former industrial area of **Il Cantieri Culturali della Zisa** now houses the Goethe-Institut, the Gramsci Institute, a cinematographic school and several studios.

South of La Zisa, screened by walls, is **La Cuba** (Mon–Sat 9am–7pm), the final piece of the Moorish jigsaw. Once domed, this disappointing pavilion lies along Corso Calatafimi, but in Arab times was set in a lake within the luxuriant grounds of La Zisa. In *The Decameron* Boccaccio set a story of illicit love in this "sumptuous villa" which is

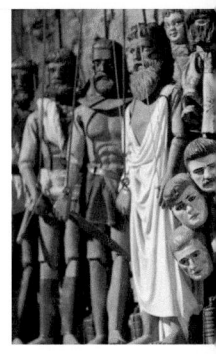

A display at the Puppet Museum, where puppet shows are put on throughout the year.

Relaxing on the Foro Italico.

⊙ LEOPARD CHANGING ITS SPOTS?

Although endlessly fascinating, Palermo is also gritty, chaotic and fatalistic about the future, so hardly provides the perfect blueprint for urban regeneration. Yet after a long slumber, the city is being revitalised, albeit on a small scale. The celebrated Serpotta oratories have been restored, along with other significant churches and museums, including Palazzo Abatellis, one of the island's major art collections. Churches and museums are being revamped and the archaeological museum has recently reopened following restoration and reconstruction. Exotic monuments such as the Palazzina Cinese folly and the Moorish palace of La Zisa have also been restored. Palermo's seafront, for so long neglected, has finally been given back to its citizens, with a proper promenade and gardens. Elsewhere, increased pedestrianisation would bring some peace to the historic centre, but so far there have only been tentative small-scale experiments, as in Via Principe di Belmonte, a popular spot for cocktails. Cautious experiments in hectic areas such as Via Roma have not been expanded. In a city which gave birth to *The Leopard*, a hymn to nostalgia and decadence, it would be foolish to expect a leopard to change its spots, but the leopard is certainly flexing its muscles.

now, although partly restored, a ruin marooned in an army barracks.

The **Convento dei Cappuccini** ㉟ (www. catacombepalermo.it; daily 9am–1pm, 3–6pm, Oct–Mar closed on Sun afternoons), the Capuchin friars' convent with its grim catacombs, lies on Via Cappuccini midway between La Cuba and La Zisa. In macabre Sicilian style, corpses of the clergy, nobles, lawyers and the bourgeoisie were mummified here from the 16th century to 1881. In these galleries embalmers have stored over 8,000 dearly departed souls. Many are hung on walls, dressed and grimacing at visitors.

NORTH AND CONCA D'ORO

Travelling northward towards the chic resort of Mondello, you come to the city outskirts and the legendary "golden shell", the **Conca d'Oro** plain, carved between coast and mountains. This should be carpeted with marigolds and citrus groves, but land speculation and corruption have ensured that Palermo's countryside is mostly encased in concrete, with environmental laws circumnavigated by unscrupulous builders.

Villa Igiea (http://villa-igiea.com), Palermo's de luxe seaside hotel on the east coast, is a survivor, a fine example of the city's Art Nouveau era. Ernesto Basile, son of the architect of the Teatro Massimo, designed it for the entrepreneurial Florio family who chose this terraced setting overlooking the sea. The Art Nouveau dining room is a harmonious composition of elegant cabinets, functional furnishings and ethereal frescoes.

On the northern outskirts, the road leads to Palermo's park, the former hunting grounds of the **Parco della Favorita** (daily) at the foot of Mount Pellegrino; this was purchased by the exiled Bourbon king Ferdinand in 1799 to make his exile from Naples more bearable. His domineering consort, Maria Carolina, conceived of the **Palazzina Cinese** (Tue–Sat 9am–7pm) as a Petit Trianon to rival the creation of her sister, Marie Antoinette. This restored oriental folly combines Chinese decorative motifs with Gothic and Egyptian flourishes.

Next door is **Villa Niscemi** (Sun 9am–1pm, Mon–Sat from 9am by arrangement; tel: 091 740 4822), whose fate seems assured as an entertainment centre. The villa was used as Giuseppe di Lampedusa's model for Tancredi's home in *The Leopard*. Owned by a noble family who came to Sicily with the Normans, the villa blends elegance with rustic charm.

Di Lampedusa's own ancestral home, **Villa Lampedusa** (www.villalampedusa.it), built in 1770 but bought by the Principe around 1845 and now a luxury hotel, is also nearby and well signposted. (For information on more Lampedusa sites, see "On the trail of *The Leopard*", page 135.)

Also here is the **Museo Etnografico Siciliano Pitrè** (closed for renovation and reconstruction), which houses an ethnographic collection that illustrates Sicilian life, customs and folklore. There are costumes, painted carts, musical instruments and carriages, including a model of the 18th-century carriage designed to transport a statue of Santa Rosalia.

Mondello at night.

From the coast, a scenic road climbs Monte Pellegrino, the city's holy mountain, passing citrus groves and shrubland. In the sandstone slopes, the **Grotto di Adduara caves** (closed) have revealed prehistoric drawings carved into the walls. It is a beautiful location, crowded at weekends with cars and picnickers. From the terraced slopes, sweeping views span the bay of the Conca d'Oro.

On the mountainside the **Santuario Santa Rosalia** (www.santuariosantarosalia. it; 7.30am–12.30pm and 2–6.30pm) is a shrine to Palermo's revered patron saint. According to legend, Rosalia renounced the world on the death of her father, becoming a religious recluse in this hermitage, where she died in 1166. In 1624, while Palermo was in the throes of a deadly plague, Rosalia appeared to a visitor on the mountain asking him to search for her remains in the cave and give her a Christian burial. Her grave found, she was disinterred and her relics carried in procession into Palermo where the plague miraculously ceased. Such was the spread of religious devotion to her that within a year a chapel with its cavern sanctuary was established in her honour, a place of pilgrimage. Mountain views and souvenir stalls are the additional rewards for trailing up to this sanctuary.

MONDELLO

Set in the lee of Monte Pellegrino is the fashionable resort of **Mondello** ㊱, easily reached from Palermo by bus from Viale della Libertà. The resort, pioneered by the Bourbons, began as a tuna-fishing village but was turned into a garden suburb in the 1890s and reached its heyday in the interwar years. Even if the ArtNouveau villas are now engulfed by ribbon development, Mondello has a certain charm. It remains a popular meeting place for Palermitans who come to the lido to swim, socialise and dine on fresh fish.

The centre of attraction is the striking Art Nouveau pier. Other attractions are slight but seductive, from summer sea breezes to a ruined medieval watchtower, as well as cool beach clubs and the chic Alle Terrazze restaurant (www.alleterrazze.it) on the pier: Palermo at its most docile.

Orto Botánico.

📷 A FLOWERING OF FLAMBOYANCE

The earthquake of 1693 wiped the architectural slate clean in many Sicilian cities and gave free rein to the new, ornate tastes of the ruling class.

The Baroque of the 18th century was a golden age for Sicilian architecture, a tantalising game of silhouettes and perspectives, an opportunity for wild ornamentation, with sculpted cornices, fanciful balconies and flowing staircases.

Roberto Ando, the Palermitan film director, believes Baroque as "a paradigm of Sicily – tortuous, eccentric, secretive, the endless search for a form".

In Palermo, *spagnolismo*, the love of ostentation, found its natural soulmate in Baroque taste. Urban planning led to grandiose squares and fancy streets. Convents, churches and oratories sprang up in the historic centre, and city palazzi competed for attention. Balconies and cornices were adorned with angels, nymphs, gargoyles and grimacing monsters.

The capital's church of San Giuseppe dei Teatini exudes a Baroque spirit, as does the stucco-encrusted Immacolata and the well-restored Casa Professa. As for palaces, Palermo boasts Palazzo Mirto, both a Baroque world and a showcase to the Sicilian nobility.

In Bagheria, villas acquired opulent staircases and marble-encrusted ballrooms. The distinguished Baroque cities of Ragusa and Módica indulged in spatial experiment, theatrical vistas flanked by flights of steps. In Noto, Baroque meant spaciousness, symmetry and loftiness. It is a stage set of a city, sculpted in golden stone, exuding a sense of *joie de vivre*.

Statue of San Marziano on the Duomo, Siracusa; he was the first bishop of the city.

The ceiling of Il Gesù, Sicily's first Jesuit church, is decorated in flamboyant Baroque style.

Marble carving of a cherub in the church of Santa Chiara, Noto.

A smiling example of Serpotta's work.

The Plaster Master

Giacomo Serpotta, born in Palermo in 1656, was a genius in stucco, who elevated Sicilian plasterwork from a craft to an art. His most breathtaking creations can be seen today in several of Palermo's well-restored oratories.

In the Vucceria market area, itself a manifestation of the restless Baroque spirit, Serpotta's lavish Oratorio del Rosario di San Domenico combines frothy statues of the Virtues with a joyful abundance of capering cherubs. The neighbouring Oratorio di Santa Cita is another masterwork. A host of exuberant angels and cherubs clamber over walls and window frames; allegorical statues seem to float in space, while an intricate stucco panel depicting a sea battle in relief employs metal wire for the ships' rigging. Closer to Piazza Marina, Serpotta's Oratorio di San Lorenzo has a fragile beauty bordering on the overblown, every creamy surface festooned with allegorical stucco figures.

Plan your independent (or guided) Serpotta tour online, through the association that manages the Serpotta masterpieces (www.ilgeniodipalermo.com, tel: 091 332 779, oratories open mornings only).

The dazzling concave-convex exterior of San Giovanni in Scicli is matched by an equally impressive interior. The whole town of Scicli, in Ragusa province, is a Baroque gem.

...tail from the Fountain of Orion in Messina, sculpted by ...ovanni Angelo Montorsoli in 1547.

Cloisters of the stunning 12th-century cathedral at Monreale.

PALERMO PROVINCE

Leave the bustling capital to explore Monreale's glittering Arab-Norman cathedral, the remote Madonie mountains, the brooding heartland that was home to the Mafia, and the island of Ustica.

Outside **Palermo** ❶ is a province of extreme light and shade, of exuberant festivals and shimmering cathedrals. This was once the Mafia heartland, with gulleys and mountain lairs nurtured by the mythology of banditry and poverty. Now, as the small towns begin to flourish again, the spiritual isolation that made this a wild province is evaporating.

MONREALE

These remote rural pockets feel far away from the Moorish voluptuousness and sophistication of **Monreale** ❷, 8km (5 miles) from the capital. In the words of a Sicilian proverb: "He who goes to Palermo without seeing Monreale leaves a donkey and comes back an ass."

Certainly, its sumptuous cathedral is the apogee of Arab-Norman art and a Unesco World Heritage site since 2015. The **Duomo di Monreale** (www.monrealeduomo.it; Apr–Oct Mon– Sat 8.30am–12.30pm, 2.30–4.45pm, Sun 8am–9.15am, 2.30–4.45pm, Nov–Mar Mon–Sat 8.30am–12.30pm, 2.30–4.30pm, Sun 8am–9.30am, 2.30– 4.30pm) and Benedictine monastery were built by William II, c.1183, on a hill overlooking the Conca d'Oro. Flanked by square bell towers, the cathedral dedicated to the Assumption is not instantly awe-inspiring, yet its details are exquisite. An arched 18th-century Romanesque portal frames a greenish bronze door decorated with Biblical scenes by Bonanno da Pisa (1185). The portal displays sculpted bands of garlands, figures and beasts alternating with multicoloured mosaics. To the left, a Gagini porch shelters another bronze door, by Barisano da Trani (1179), inspired by the delicacy of Byzantine inlaid ivory. The apses are Sicily's most opulent: interlacing limestone and lava arches, sculpted as delicately as wood.

Main attractions

Monreale (Duomo)
Piana degli Albanesi
Corleone
Solunto
Villa Palagonia (Bagheria)
Castello di Cáccamo
Cefalù
Parco Regionale delle Madonie (Madonie Mountains)
Castelbuono
Ustica

Map on page 88

The exquisite interior of the Unesco-listed cathedral.

Column detail in Monreale.

Monreale drew craftsmen from Persia, Africa, Asia, Greece, Venice, Pisa and Provence. The glistening gold interior fuses Arab purity of volume with Byzantine majesty. The shimmering (restored) mosaics are unequalled anywhere.

In the apse the *Christ Pantocrator*, about 6 metres (20ft) tall, is an authoritarian God presiding over the Madonna, angels and saints. Look for Thomas à Becket, who entered sainthood after Henry II of England had him murdered. (Henry was William's father-in-law.) Above the royal throne is a mosaic of *Christ Crowning William the Good*, a tribute to the king whose world embraced concubines, eunuchs and black slaves. Other delights include Cosmati paving, Roman capitals incorporating busts of Ceres and Proserpine, and a gilded ceiling whose rafters resemble the spines of beautifully bound books.

The garden cloisters (daily 9am–6.30pm) express William's love of Islamic art and are the most sumptuous 12th-century cloisters in the world. Every second pair of white marble columns has a vivid zigzag mosaic pattern spiralling up the shaft. Many sculptures echo the mosaics but add a personal note, including the name of a mason, or musicians playing Sicilian instruments. The *Allegory of the Seasons*, an enchanting marble composition, depicts tree-planting and pig-killing. In one corner, a loggia creates a chiaroscuro effect with a glorious, slightly phallic fountain. Shaped like a palm tree trunk, the shaft is crowned by lions' heads.

After raucous Palermo, Monreale exudes provincial calm, and while the town is probably an anticlimax after seeing the cathedral's mosaics, a stroll offers a chance to savour the pedestrianised centre, with its crumbling Baroque churches and shops selling ceramics or fine ices. The **Chiesa del Monte** has stuccowork by Serpotta while the church of **Madonna delle Croci**, set higher on the hill, offers a last lingering view from the cathedral to the coast.

BANDIT COUNTRY

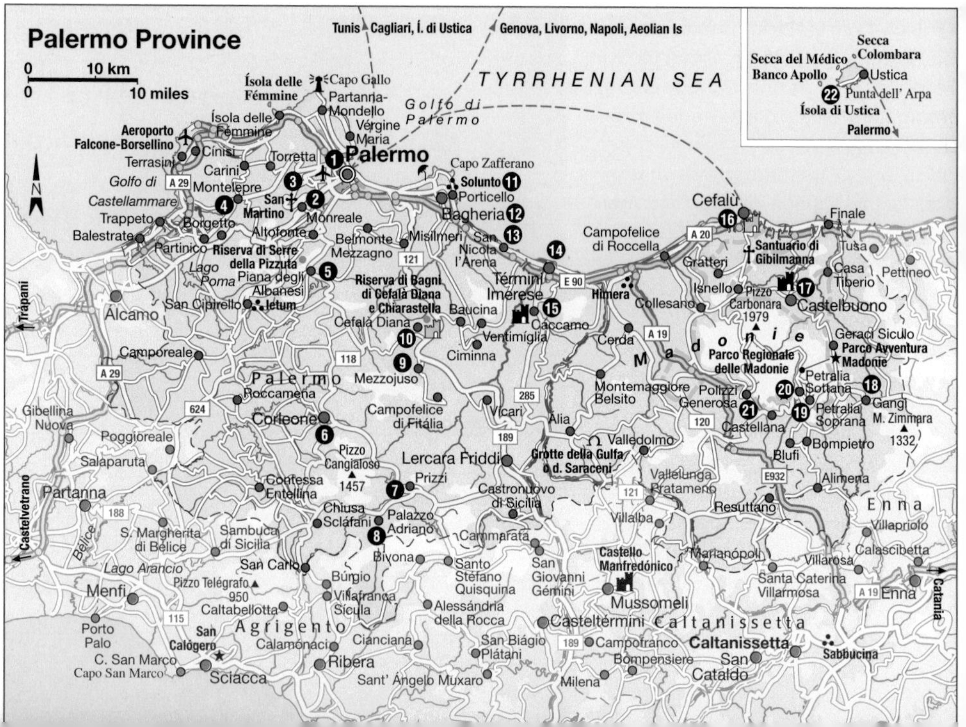

In the lushly mountainous landscape towards **Boccadifalco** is the hill resort of **San Martino delle Scale** with the Benedictine **Abbazia di San Martino** ❸ (www.abbaziadisanmartino.it; Mon–Sat 6.45am–12.30pm, 4–6pm, Sun 7.30am–1pm, 4.30–7pm). Reputed to have been founded by St Gregory the Great in the 6th century, the abbey was destroyed and rebuilt a number of times over the centuries. Now part convent, part school, it is known for its monumental staircase, monastic library and 18th-century paintings, including Marabitti's *St Martin and the Beggar*. The surrounding pine forests are a cool escape in summer.

A short distance away is **Montelepre** ❹, of which John Addington Symonds wrote in 1873: "The talk was brigands and nothing but brigands." This was especially true on the eve of World War II, when the tragic outlaw and local folk hero Salvatore Giuliano reigned over these desolate crags. If Mafia chroniclers are correct, this is still bandit country, and beyond the boulder-strewn countryside little seems to have changed since Giuliano's day. The medieval heart of Montelepre remains enmeshed by scruffy alleys and courtyards coiled around the Chiesa Madre.

Neighbouring **Partinico** is a byword for urban poverty. In the 1950s Danilo Dolci, known as Sicily's Gandhi because of his dedication to the poor, chose benighted western Sicily to set up his centres in an attempt to improve local conditions and expose the power of the Mafia. His work undimmed, he died unnoticed in poverty in 1997.

Piana degli Albanesi ❺, along the SS624, appears suspended above a lake. Lush pastures are encircled by hills, once home to 15th-century Albanian settlers. The community moved here in 1488 after Turkish troops invaded their homeland. Since then, generations have kept their customs and Orthodox faith in this cheerful town. Marriages and funerals, Epiphany and Easter are times for Byzantine rites leavened with enough folklore to draw visitors in. The community

speaks Albanian at home; signs are in Albanian as well as Italian. Local cuisine is a cultural stew: *stranghuie* (gnocchi), *brumie me bathé e thieré*, a filling bean casserole, or *dash*, castrated ram, Albanian-Greek style.

It was at Portella della Ginestra, just above the artificial lake of **Lago Piana degli Albanesi**, that Salvatore Giuliano gunned down 11 Piana citizens in 1947. Whether Giuliano was forced to shoot by the Mafia or was deceived by his own treacherous lieutenant is still unclear.

CORLEONE

Corleone ❻, perched along the rural SS118 and enfolded in desolate hills and high verdant plains, is dominated by the Castello, a rocky outcrop topped by a Saracen tower. A prison until 1976, it is now home to Franciscan friars who take their vow of poverty seriously. Below, the rooftops are stacked in a chromatic range of greys. At first sight, Corleone fails to live up to its infamous reputation as the cradle of the Mafia. It was from here, after all, that Mafia boss Toto Riina ruled before moving to Palermo where

☉ Fact

Two very different movies relate the story of the local bandit Salvatore Giuliano. Michael Cimino's 1987 *The Sicilian* embraces the romantic "Robin Hood" view. But Francesco Rosi's 1962 documentary-style *Salvatore Giuliano* offers much greater insight into the social and political forces of the late 1940s.

Monreale's cloisters.

⊘ Tip

Don't waste time in Corleone trying to follow in the footsteps of the Corleone clan in *The Godfather* movies. The town was too developed by the early 1970s for director Francis Ford Coppola's taste and the Sicilian scenes were shot in Sávoca (see page 241).

he went into hiding until his arrest in 1993. Bravely, the town has changed the name of its central piazza to Falcone-Borsellino, to honour the anti-Mafia magistrates gunned down by the Mafia. It also opened a **Mafia Museum** in 2000 – far more of a neutral documentation centre than a Disneyland experience (book a visit online: www.cidmacorleone.it). The town was established in 1237 and its **Chiesa Madre** contains 16th–17th-century wooden statues and stalls.

To the southeast lies the medieval town of **Prizzi** ❼ with its sloping chequerboard of rust-tiled roofs. The town is celebrated for its bizarre traditional Easter festival known as the *ballo dei diavoli* (dance of the devils). Dating back to Sicani times, the dance depicts the eternal struggle between Good and Evil, winter and spring, Christianity and paganism. The gap-toothed devil masks are primitive but menacing, while the atmosphere of ritualised violence appears to echo Mafia lore.

The neighbouring village of **Palazzo Adriano** ❽, 10km (6 miles) southwest, encapsulates the rivalries of these

provincial backwaters. Two sombre churches share the main square in mutual antipathy: the Orthodox **Santa Maria dell'Assunta** scorns the Catholic **Santa Maria del Lume**. Ironically, the square starred in the warmly evocative movie *Cinema Paradiso*. From here, the route back to the coast passes the hilltop village of **Mezzojuso** ❾, snug in the Ficuzza woods. Like many others, the village has mixed Albanian and Arab ancestry and religious frictions. **Annunziata**, the Catholic church, is overshadowed by the Orthodox **San Nicola**, home to lovely Byzantine icons.

Nearby, **Santa Maria delle Grazie** houses frescoes and the finest iconostasis in Sicily, while the adjoining monastery displays precious Greek manuscripts and miniatures. **Cefalà Diana** ❿, just north, is firmly in the Arab camp, with a tumbledown castle and the island's best-preserved Moorish bathhouse.

EAST OF PALERMO

From the capital to Cefalù, the coast curves past fishing villages and coves

View of Corleone.

to Capo Zafferano and the ruins at **Solunto** ⑪ (Tue–Sat 9.30am–5.30pm, Sun 9.30am–1.30pm; free the first Sun of the month). Set on majestic cliffs, the ruins are less impressive than the wild location. The solitary ruins were originally Solus, one of the earliest Phoenician trading posts on the island, until destroyed by Dionysius of Siracusa in 398 BC as he tried to clear Sicily of all non-Greeks. Later, it was taken by invading Carthaginians who invited Greeks to return, thus Hellenising the settlement. Then in the First Punic War, in 254 BC, it fell to Rome, only to be abandoned during the 3rd century AD. The highlights among the extensive ruins are the floor mosaics (including Leda and the Swan) and a luxurious villa dwelling with a colonnaded peristyle. From the agora there are stunning views of the Casteldaccia vineyards, an ancient castle and the coastal resort of Cefalù. Beyond the wizened olive trees and battered boulders are charming swimming spots near the lighthouse on the cape. **Porticello**, on the shore just below Solunto, is a straggling fishing village popular with Palermitans for a seafood Sunday lunch.

BAGHERIA

Just inland is **Bagheria** ⑫, 15km (9 miles) from Palermo, which developed during the *Ottocento* (19thcentury) vogue for ostentatious summer villas surrounded by orange trees but declined during the 20th century due to unbridled land speculation. These patrician villas are mostly in late Renaissance style, with grand staircases and a central body flanked by sweeping concave wings. The U-shaped lower wings were reserved for servants, with underground chambers (*stanze del scirocco*) used by the patricians as retreats from the humid summer heat. The villas were encircled by French formal gardens.

While views of cement works often mar the pastoral idyll, some villas are pitiful wrecks, others retain their grandeur. A fine example is **Villa Cattolica** (www.museoguttuso.com; Tue–Sun 9am–5pm, summer until 6pm). Built around 1737, it houses the **Museo Guttoso**, a bizarre collection of contemporary

Museo Guttuso.

Ruins at Solunto.

⊘ VILLA PALAGONIA

This villa, built in 1715 by Tommaso Maria Napoli, is famous for its crumbling interior with cracked mirrors and its garden full of grotesque statues of monsters, dwarves, tormented souls and fantastic animals. Most, it is said, were created by the surreal imagination of the wealthy Prince Palagonia and are said to represent his faithless wife's lovers. Beside the main entrance, two gargoyles with gaping mouths were used to extinguish the footmen's torches. A flamboyant double staircase ascends to the *piano nobile*, with the salon's mirrored ceiling representing the sky. Engraved over the door is the sobering message: "Mirror yourself in these crystals and contemplate the image of human frailty." For more information visit www.villapalagonia.it.

Stirring statue of Giuseppe la Masa in Términi Imerese.

Surreal statues at Villa Patagonia.

paintings and the tomb of Renato Guttuso (1912–87), one of Sicily's best-known modern painters. A sculptor friend made him a surreal blue tomb to match the sky, a capsule of kitsch among the cactus and lemons.

But the strangest villa of all is the **Villa Palagonia** (daily 9am–1pm and 4–7pm; www.villapalagonia.it) (see box).

TÉRMINI IMERESE

Further east, 8km (5 miles) outside Términi Imerese, is **San Nicola l'Arena** ⑬, a picturesque fishing village with a 15th-century crenellated castle overlooking the harbour. Now a private event venue, the castle belongs to aristocrats from Palermo. Beside it is a solid brick *tonnara* (tuna fishery), a reminder that the coast was devoted to tuna fishing until recently.

Términi Imerese ⑭ itself is an unfortunate jumble of industry, resort and classical ruins. However, the upper town remains fairly unspoilt, with a 17th-century **cathedral** (the statue of Jesus in one of the chapels has real hair) and the **Museo Civico** (Tue–Sat 9am–1pm, 4–6.30pm, Sun 8am–12.30pm), which has an art collection and archaeological finds. Just east of town is an impressive Roman aqueduct set in a wild olive grove.

Inland is **Cáccamo** ⑮, a dramatic 12th-century castle (www.castellodicaccamo.it; daily 9am–1pm, 3–7pm), one of the most important Norman strongholds in western Sicily and the province's best-preserved castle. It was the base of the local dukes of Cáccamo until sold to the Region in 1963. The towers, battlements and ramparts look convincingly medieval, even if parts were redesigned during the Baroque period.

There are collections of art and arms in its restored rooms, one of which, the **Sala della Congiura**, is where the duke and fellow nobles plotted to overthrow William the Bad in 1160. The coup failed; the duke died in the king's dungeon. The **Duomo** (remodelled in 1614) contains a 14th-century painted crucifix and many statues and sculptures.

HIMERA

The site of ancient **Himera** (Tue–Sat 9am–5.30pm, Sun 9.30am–1.30pm), founded as a colony of Zancle (Messina) in 648 BC, is nearby, east of Términi Imerese, in an industrial zone near Buonfornello. Himera was the scene of the 480 BC defeat of the Carthaginians by Theron of Agrigento and his brother Gelon of Siracusa, when the advance of the Carthaginian leader Hamilcar, determined to rid Sicily of all Greeks, was thwarted. Hamilcar perished in the defeat but in 409 BC his son Hannibal returned with a stronger force and devastated the city. There are ruins of a Doric temple and traces of houses, as well as an extensive museum containing findings from the site.

CEFALÙ

A return to the coast at **Cefalù** ⑯ is a chance to visit the province's great counterpoint to Monreale Cathedral (though both cathedrals became Unesco World

Heritage sites in the same year, 2015). Sitting snugly below the massive hill of **La Rocca**, Cefalù is the west coast's rival to Taormina. The consensus is that, although Taormina has better hotels, nightlife, sophistication and atmosphere, Cefalù is equally picturesque, but more peaceful, family-friendly and better-provided with beaches. What's more, the resort makes a safe haven from which to explore gritty Palermo.

The cathedral, or **Duomo** (http://cattedraledicefalu.com; daily Apr–Oct 8.30am–6.30pm, Nov–Mar 8.30am–1pm, 3.30–5pm, Sun 3.30–5pm; free), was built in 1131 by Roger II with a bold twin-towered facade and a triple apse with blind arcading. (The king confidently had a porphyry sarcophagus made for himself, but he and the sarcophagus are now in Palermo Cathedral as he died before this cathedral was completed.) Inside, a severe nave is flanked by 16 ancient columns with Roman capitals surmounted by Gothic arches. A sense of majesty is created by the concentration of other-worldly mosaics in the presbytery and over the altar. A superbly compassionate *Christ Pantocrator* in the apse holds an open book with Greek and Latin Biblical text (John 8:12): "I am the light of the world, he who follows me will not walk in darkness." Other highlights are the Norman font and the open-timber roofs which bear traces of the original Arab-Norman paintings.

Out of season, **Piazza del Duomo** is a delightful suntrap with a view of the cathedral at the foot of steep cliffs running up to the fortifications. The square is also framed by the Corso, a Renaissance seminary and a porticoed **palazzo**. Here, the Caffè Duomo (www.duomogelatieri.com) is the place for an *aperitivo* or a *gelato*. Cefalù's **old port**, tangibly Moorish and home to Tunisian fishermen, has been a backdrop in countless films, including *Cinema Paradiso*.

A warren of alleys leads west from **Corso Ruggero** and reveals Renaissance facades, Gothic parapets and mullioned windows overlooking tiny courtyards. An underground spring bubbles up in the arcaded Arab baths, sited at the bottom of curved steps. **Via Porto Salvo** passes battered churches and flourishing craft shops. In summer, the town is a delightful tourist trap with quaint craft boutiques selling ceramics and gold jewellery, matched by sophisticated restaurants. **Porta Pescare**, one of the surviving medieval gates, opens onto a creek, beach and boatyard. In the evening, the seafront, bastion and Corso become a parade devoted to the dual pleasures of a *passeggiata* and a *gelato*.

From Piazza Duomo, a steepish hill leads down to the **Museo Mandralisca** (www.fondazionemandralisca.it; daily 9am–7pm, in winter closed Mon). This is a dusty collection, except for several Madonnas and Antonello da Messina's *Portrait of an Unknown Man* (c.1460). The painting once served as a door to a pharmacy cabinet on the island of Lipari where an assistant, unnerved by the sneering expression, scratched the unknown man's face.

○ **Tip**

Cefalù makes an appealing base for exploring the Madonie Park on its doorstep, but for more of a sense of the mountains and the gentle pace of life, stay around Castelbuono.

Términi Imerese.

Cefalù Cathedral dominates the town.

Village perched on a ridge in the Madonie mountains.

From Corso Vittorio Emanuele sweeping steps lead to the charming medieval wash basins (*Lavatoio Medievale*), supplied with freezing water from the Cefalino river.

Above the medieval town is **Rocca**, where the original Arab town was sited, with sweeping views over Cefalù and the sea. After the Norman conquest in 1063, the populace left the looming crags for the port below. **Salita Saraceno** leads up three tiers of city walls to the restored fortifications of the crumbling stone castle, revealing traces of a pool, fountain, cistern and prison. Nearby is the so-called **Tempio di Diana**, *c.*4th century BC, built over an earlier cistern.

THE MADONIE MOUNTAINS

Cefalù is the gateway to the delightful Madonie mountains and their designated regional park, the **Parco Regionale delle Madonie** (tel: 0921 684 011; www.parcodellemadonie.it). Thanks to tourism based on outdoor pursuits like hiking and horse-riding, the Madonie region has largely escaped grinding poverty and rural emigration. In summer, well-signposted *agriturismi* (farmstays) make an appealing way of exploring the area.

Compared with the neighbouring Nebrodi mountains, the **Monti Madonie** range is higher (Pizzo Carbonara 1,979 metres/6,495ft), more accessible and more open to tourism. Unlike a lot of Sicily, the Madonie range has not been scarred by deforestation or urban blight. **Piano Cervi** and **Monte San Salvatore** are riddled with aqueducts and streams. Majestic firs have grown on these rugged ridges since the Ice Age and were used to create the roof of Monreale Cathedral. In the remoter regions, wild cats and eagles still roam.

Drives in the Madonie mountains tend to be off-the-beaten-track adventures to lofty medieval villages straight out of a Sicilian Spaghetti Western. Fortunately, the hairpin bends tend to end in a Slow Food inn or in the perfect spot for a picnic. Yet unlike most Sicilian regional parks, the Madonie are pretty accessible without a car, and trails are better marked than elsewhere, with buses running from Cefalù, Castelbuono and Petralia. Cefalù makes the best base for beach-lovers, but otherwise the Madonie villages are some of the prettiest in Sicily, and well-suited to pony-trekking too. But to explore fully, a car is best. For tours, contact the **Parco delle Madonie** directly.

RURAL ROUTE

After Cefalù, coastal olive groves give way to pine woods and valleys before the venerated sanctuary of **Gibilmanna** comes into view. The 16th-century **Capuchin monastery** contains an underrated museum of rural life and sacred art (www.fraticappuccini messina.org; Mon–Sat 11am–1pm and 3.30–6.30pm, Sun 10.30am–1pm and 3.30–7pm).

Isnello, 7km (4 miles) south, a winter ski resort, has a ruined Byzantine castle overlooking majolica-encrusted spires and limestone cliffs.

A vastly superior feudal castle towers over **Castelbuono** ⓱, 12km (7 miles) east, a civilised, prosperous, well-kept place that could be mistaken for Tuscany. Castelbuono lobbied successfully to be an exit point from the Palermo–Messina motorway. As such, it is reaping the benefits in the weekend influx of visitors drawn to the lively atmosphere, well-restored churches and welcoming restaurants. The 15th-century castle (www.museocivico.eu; mid-May–mid-Sept Mon–Fri 9.30am–1pm, 4–7.30pm, Sat–Sun 10am–1.30pm, 4–7.30pm, mid-Sept–mid-May Tue–Sun 9.30am–1pm, 3–6.30pm) is austere but with a pleasant chapel; it is home to the civic museum, with archaeological, religious and contemporary art collections.

The rural route follows the SS286 south to **Geraci Siculo** (22km/14 miles) and then winds up to **Gangi** ⓲, a tortoise-shaped town with a crumbling watchtower that is now a hard-working rural centre. On the second Sunday in August, in a custom dating back to the days of Demeter, sheaves of wheat tied with red ribbons decorate the streets for a harvest celebration, the *Sagra della Spiga*.

More surreally Sicilian is the sight awaiting unsuspecting visitors to Gangi's parish church. The **Chiesa Madre** now displays a crypt of the village's finest mummified priests (www.chiesamadregangi.it; summer Tue–Sun 10.30am–12.30pm, 4.30–6.30pm, winter Sat–Sun 10.30am–12.30pm, 4.30–6.30pm).

PETRALIA SOPRANA

Follow the SS120 west and the jagged skyline of **Petralia Soprana** ⓳ comes into view. This seemingly prosperous town, set on a spur, has covered passageways leading to a belvedere with bracing views, marred only by a vast car park on stilts. The **Chiesa Madre** was built in the 1300s by the Ventimiglia family. Half-hidden

⊙ Tip

A day trip offered by travel agents from Palermo and Cefalù visits mountain enclaves and fortified villages linked to the feudal Ventimiglia dynasty. There are also buses from Cefalù to the towns and villages. A car is best, however. For tours contact the **Ente Parco delle Madonie**, Corso Ruggero 116 (tel: 0921 684 011; www.parcodellemadonie.it).

Cefalù beach.

⊙ THE SICILIAN ALPS

Known as "the Sicilian Alps", the Madonie offer some of the island's more accessible walking country, matched by some of the best rural inns. Hiking through the foothills of the Madonie mountains means limestone trails scuffed by wild boar and views over vertiginous slopes to the Tyrrhenian Sea. Every inviting hamlet seems to have its own precipitous hillside, ruined Norman fortress and luminous Madonna. Walkers tread paths dotted with porcupine quills en route through woodlands of cork and holm oak, myrtle and beech. For company, there are grazing goats, soaring eagles, lizards on sun-baked rocks, peregrine falcons and wizened peasants in flat caps. The highest Madonie peak, Pizzo Carbonara, offers good skiing in winter.

Petralia Sottana rises out of the misty Madonie mountains.

down alleys are striking mansions and watchtowers.

Petralia Sottana (the lower town), nestling in the wooded hillside, also exudes a quiet ease. Now a mountain resort, this former Norman citadel has Romanesque, Gothic and Baroque churches. The **Chiesa Matrice** is perched on a *belvedere* and swathed in mist; inside is a precious Arabian candelabra.

Families might want to head to an exciting adventure playground nearby. Set in the Madonie, it's known as the **Parco Avventura Madonie** (Località Gorgonero, Petralia Sottana, tel: 0917 487 186; www.parcoavventuramadonie.it; summer daily 8.30am–6.30pm, year-round but call to book and check winter timetable).

The road west to **Polizzi Generosa** passes *masserie*, feudal farmsteads that were as self-sufficient as most villages. The **Chiesa Madre** has a 16th-century Flemish triptych and Venetian organ. Polizzi is a trekking centre which, in season, sustains walkers with pasta and asparagus (*pasta cu l'asparaci*).

In Castelbuono.

From here, the fast A19 returns to the coast, as does the winding route via the ski resort of **Piano Battaglia**.

USTICA

The lovely island of **Ustica**, 60km (37 miles) from Palermo, is connected daily to the city by hydrofoil and ferry services (1 hour and 2.5 hours respectively) and can be visited on a day trip. It is extremely popular with swimmers and nature-lovers, but serious divers or underwater photographers will choose to make the island their base.

Ustica is Sicily's best-established and best-preserved marine reserve. The rugged coastline is riddled with caverns and coves, partly accessible along coastal paths, and below its clear waters is an explosion of colour and life that includes corals, sea sponges and anemones as well as barracuda, bream, scorpion fish and groupers.

The volcanic, black, turtle-shaped island turns itself into a riot of colour in spring when wild flowers are abundant; true landlubbers can enjoy visits to the ruins of a Saracen castle (a long climb), the church of **San Bartolomeo** with its colourful ceramic saints and call in at a small **archaeological museum** (mid-June–mid-Oct daily 6–8pm, 10pm–midnight), which contains items excavated in the surrounding area. A walk around the island will take about four hours, covering 10km (6 miles).

One of the pleasures is an excursion from **Cala Santa Maria**, ideally on a glass-bottomed boat in order to view the marine reserve. There are 10 grottoes, too, mostly on the eastern side of the island, with the **Grotta Azzurra** as azure as it sounds, with its cave 10 metres (330ft) long.

For information about marine reserve sites contact **Area Marina Protetta Isola di Ustica** (tel: 091 844 8124; www.ampustica.it). For scuba information contact **Mare Nostrum Diving** (tel: 336 792 589; www.marenostrumdiving.it).

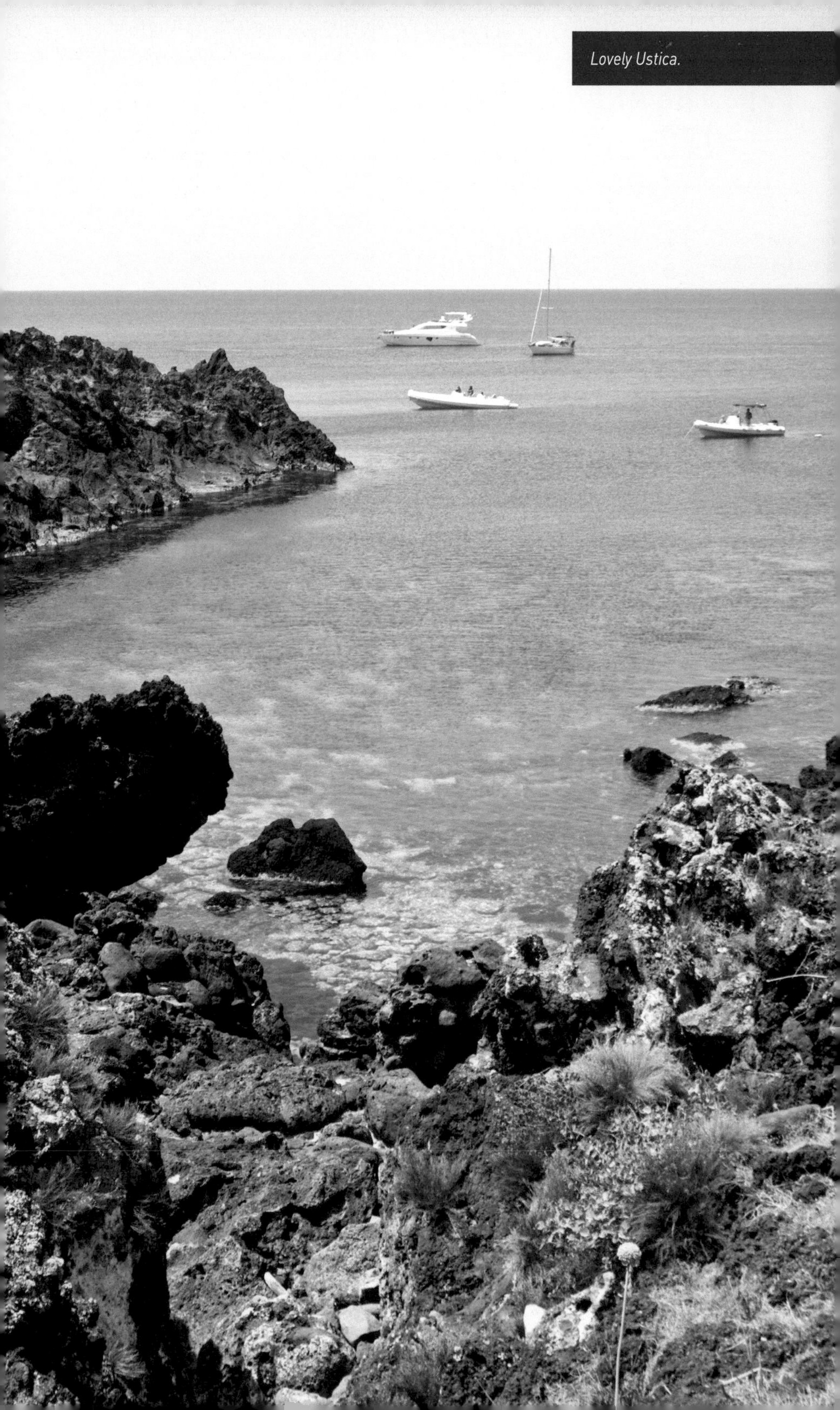

Lovely Ustica.

📷 THE ARAB-NORMAN LEGACY

Moorish domes, Norman cloisters, shimmering mosaics, honeycomb ceilings and fanciful geometry are just a few of the eclectic features that evoke Arab-Norman Sicily.

Arab-Norman rule coincided with Palermo's golden age, when the city was ringed by pleasure palaces such as La Zisa. Named after *aziz*, Arabic for splendid, this Moorish palace is a testament to Arabian craftsmanship, with stalactite vaults, latticework windows, a tiered fountain, and a wind chamber to protect the emir's family from the enervating scirocco.

Instead, the Cappella Palatina represents a Sicilian fusion of Byzantine, Arab and Norman civilisations. The ceiling is unique in a Christian church, a composition of ineffable oriental splendour. The Normans asked Arab craftsmen to portray paradise, and they obliged with naked maidens which the Normans prudishly clothed and crowned with haloes. Still, the roof remains a paradise of the senses: Persian octagonal stars meet Islamic stalactites.

Under Arab rule, the citizens of Palermo acquired a love of Islamic ornamentation that has never left them. Monreale Cathedral is also covered in a shimmering tapestry of mosaics, a tribute to a king whose world view embraced concubines, eunuchs and black slaves.

This fusion of styles is typified by Cefalù Cathedral: the raised choir represents an Oriental element whereas the gold firmament behind Christ is Byzantine. But a Norman font guarded by leopards symbolises King Roger's Hauteville dynasty.

In 2015, Arab-Norman architecture in Palermo, Monreale and Cefalù was awarded World Heritage status by Unesco.

The roof of San Pietro monastery in Marsala.

Cloisters at Museo Regionale Pepoli in Trápani, which ho an eclectic collection of Sicilian paintings and sculpture.

Norman soldiers depicted on the cloisters at Monreale Cathedral, one of the greatest examples of Norman architecture in the world.

Norman castle at Erice.

Norman Castles

The Normans planted their realm with castles in Romanesque and Gothic styles, inspired by Northern architecture, but often subverted by Moorish and Byzantine models, as in Palermo's Palazzo dei Normanni. From Cáccamo to Enna, Norman castles are one of the glories of Sicily. In the Arab-Norman citadel of Troìna, the loftiest town in Sicily, and the first Norman diocese, Count Roger and his wife were besieged by Saracens in 1064. The couple escaped by classic Norman cunning: while their enemies were lulled into a drunken stupor, the Normans scurried along secret vaulted passages that burrow deep under the castle.

But neighbouring Sperlinga is Sicily's finest Norman castle, dating from 1082. After the bloody Sicilian Vespers in 1282, Sperlinga became the Angevins' last stand. The castle was besieged but the French forces within held out for more than a year, protected by a system of trap doors that deposited invaders in underground pits. The only access is still a staircase hewn out of the rock. Switchback paths climb to the summit and crenellations with sweeping views. The castle has now reopened after a three-year closure following a major landslide (daily 10am–6pm).

The finest of them all: Sperlinga.

...alù Cathedral was built in 1131, just 40 years after the ...mans had conquered Sicily, and is a fine example of ...fusion of Arab and Norman styles. The Byzantine ...aics inside are stunning.

The red-domed San Giovanni degli Eremiti in Palermo was a Byzantine basilica converted into a mosque, so Arab squinches, filigree windows and Norman cloisters are all present.

Temple at Selinunte.

TRÁPANI PROVINCE

Western Sicily is the most seafaring part of the island, famous for its North African atmosphere, nature reserves, endless beaches and, above all, its remarkable ancient sites and treasures.

As the least definable yet most varied province, the Provincia di Trápani is a collection of contradictions. This seafaring region represents a swathe of ancient Sicily, from Phoenician Mozia to Greek Selinunte, medieval Erice and Arab Mazara del Vallo. The landscape spans saltpans, vineyards, woods and coastal nature reserves.

TRÁPANI

In ancient times Drepanon (hence Trápani) was the port of Eryx (Erice), famous in the Mediterranean for its wealth and magnificent temple of Venus, goddess of fertility. As a seafaring power, its history lay at the heart of the Mediterranean world.

As the capital of the province, **Trápani ❶** commands the commerce of the seas: its **Stazione Maríttima** (www. portotrapani.it) off Piazza Garibaldi is an embarkation point for the Egadi Islands and the remoter island of Pantelleria, as well as Sardinia and Tunis.

Trápani's traditional industries of coral, tuna fishing and salt production linger on, and it is said the town may also be a Mafia money-laundering centre – a rumour borne out by the city's countless small banks. Successful but culturally moribund was the consensus – until recently, when the citizens realised that, with careful restoration, the historic seafront could be the equal

of any city. And realised that pedestrianisation and revamped churches were not just good for the soul but good for business too.

Visually, Trápani is appealing from a distance: a patchwork of shallow lagoons bounded by thin causeways. In summer, drying in the sun, there are also heaps of salt roofed with red tiles. Close up, the promontory with the old town now has an easy charm, with its 11th-century Spanish fortifications matched by a regenerated seafront. The romantic promenade can certainly

Main attractions

Trápani
Erice
Riserva dello Zíngaro
San Vito Lo Capo
Segesta
Saltpans at Núbia
Mozia
Marsala
Mazara del Vallo
Selinunte
Cave di Cusa

Maps on pages 102, 110

Trápani harbour.

◎ Tip

The easiest and most picturesque way to get to Erice from Trápani is by cable car (www.funiviaerice.it; Mon 1–8pm, Tue–Fri 8.10am–8pm, Sat–Sun 9.30am–8.30pm, late June–early July and early Sept Mon 1–11pm, Tue–Fri 8.10am–11pm, Sat–Sun 9.30am–midnight) – it rises 703 metres (2,300ft) in just 20 minutes.

rival any in Sicily. The salty port also offers *cuscusu* (fish couscous) and lobster in boisterous fishermen's haunts.

After a snack of *arancini* rice balls at Bettina (Via di Torrearsa 110 or Via Garibaldi), stroll along the **Mure di Tramontana**, the ancient Spanish bastions. Literally overshadowed by the massive Tramontana walls, the once unsavoury fishing quarter has been transformed into an atmospheric promenade back into Trápani's seafaring past. From **Piazza Mercato del Pesce**, the former fish market, a leisurely walk leads along the sea walls to the **Bastione Conca**. En route to the bastion are views of both the bay and the fishermen's cottages. From here, the historic district comes into view, dwarfed by Monte San Giuliano looming beyond. If not tempted by the beach, reached via Porta Osuna, then carry on to the **Torre di Ligny** (Oct–Apr Tue–Sat 10am–12.30pm and 4–6.30pm, Sun 4am–6.30pm, May–Sept daily 10am–12.30pm and 5–7.30pm), a fortress built in 1671. The restored fortress overlooks the archaeological zone and

the open sea. Softly illuminated, it now makes a romantic evening stroll, a fac not lost on Trápani's young lovers.

The rest of Trápani's sights are no monumental but more than occupy a morning before taking a ferry to the outlying islands. Centred on Via Giudecca, the small Jewish Quarter has a faded charm epitomised by the **Palazzo della Giudecca** while on the tip of its promontory is the **Torre d Ligny** once more. **Via Torrearsa**, facing the grandiose Palazzo Cavarretta marks the start of a stroll taking in Baroque churches, palaces and inviting bars, including on lively **Via Garibaldi**, the main street. The cathedral area is now pedestrianised, while Baroque churches have been or are in the process of being restored. On Via Generale Giglio the church of **Purgatorio** (1683) boasts a fine dome and the 18th-century wooden statues of the **Misteri** that are borne aloft in a moving Good Friday procession.

Prosaically, the impetus for the city's resurgence is linked to the rise of low cost flights, but a new city pride is also

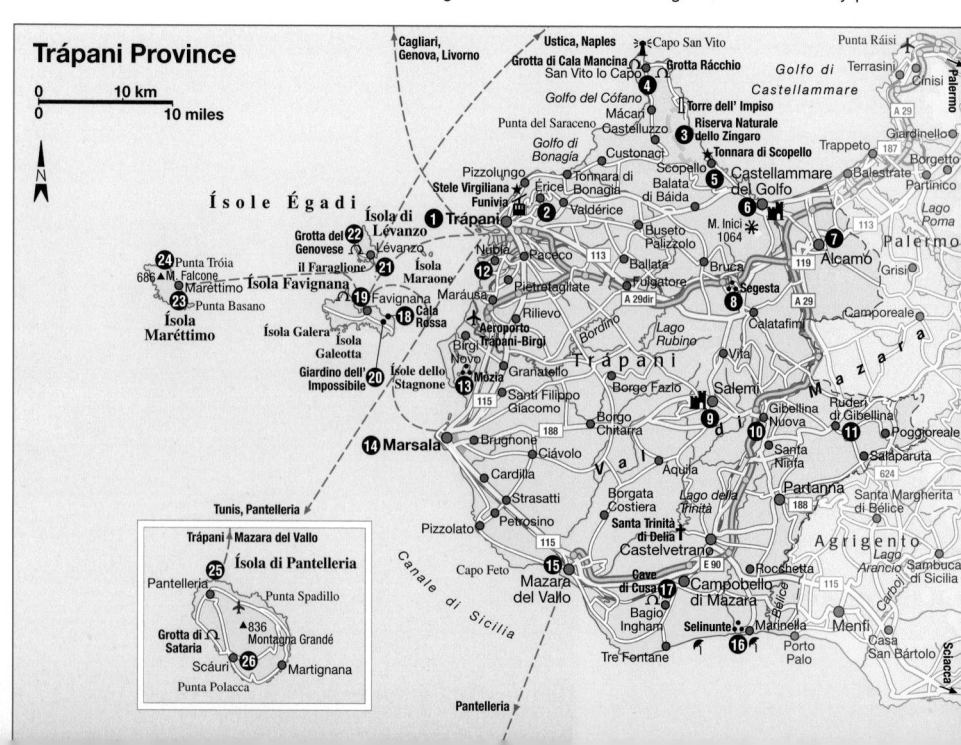

part of the story. Mercantile Trápani might yet become cultural Trápani.

SANCTUARY OF THE MADONNA

About 3km (2 miles) north of the old town is the **Santuario dell'Annunziata** (www.madonnaditrapani.it; daily 7am–noon, 4–8pm, winter until 7pm), a Carmelite church founded in 1315 but rebuilt in 1760. This sanctuary of the Madonna is considered Trápani's main monument. Its charms are a Baroque bell tower, a Gothic rose window and a doorway decorated in a zigzag pattern. Inside is a rococo nave and a cluster of exotic domed chapels. Dedicated to fishermen, the frescoed **Cappella dei Pescatori** (1481) embraces Byzantine and Moorish elements, as well as a Spanish diamond-point design. Behind the high altar is the lavish **Cappella della Madonna**, with sculptures by Antonino Gagini and the revered statue of the Madonna di Trápani by Nino Pisano, crowned in jewels. This venerated Madonna is credited with miraculous powers.

The **Museo Regionale Pepoli** (Tue–Sat 9am–5.30pm, Sun 9am–12.30pm) is the city's eclectic museum, housed in the former convent adjoining the cathedral. Off the cloisters lie Gagini sculptures, important Sicilian paintings and craftsmanship in the form of coral cribs and gilded figurines, enamelled Moorish lamps and majolica tiles. Gaudiest of all is a coral crucifix by Fra Matteo Bavera, with a salmon-coloured Christ against an ebony and mother-of-pearl cross.

ERICE

Just north is a more peaceful base than Trápani for exploring – and staying. In spring, the winding road climbs past views of acacia, wild gladioli and waxy lemon blossom to the legendary Mount Eryx (today's **Monte San Giuliano**). Swathed in seasonal mists or in a carpet of flowers, **Erice ❷**, perched at 750 metres (2,460ft), is an exquisite, tiny medieval walled town. The Carthaginian walls survive, rough-hewn slabs inscribed with Punic symbols, while nearby is the charming

An elaborately decorated Madonna (gold-plated copper, coral and pearl) dating from the 18th century at the Museo Regionale Pepoli, Trápani.

Trápani street scene.

⦿ GREEN TRÁPANI

Trápani Province has a reputation for being lethargic but, environmentally, it is often at the forefront. Trápani takes a stand against pollution, land speculation and the destruction of coastal saltpans. Here, both windmills and marshes are protected, as is the lagoon around Mozia, off Marsala, and the trailblazing reserve of Lo Zíngaro. It was Trapáni that launched *pescaturismo* (fishing tourism), offering visitors excursions with fishermen in order to discover aspects of the coast, its marine parks and the beguiling tuna fisheries here and on the Egadi Islands. Pescaturismo trips are organised by Cooperativa Trapani Pesca (www.cooptrapanipesca.it).

Erice bell tower.

View of Punta del Saraceno from Erice.

Quartiere Spagnolo, the 17th-century Spanish bastion.

As ancient Eryx, this mystical city was founded by the Elymni (Elymians), the mysterious settlers of Segesta who worshipped the Mediterranean fertility goddess known as Astarte to the Elymni and the Phoenicians, as Aphrodite to the Greeks and as Venus to the Romans.

The entrance to the town is **Porta Trápani**, a medieval gate leading directly to the **Chiesa Madre** (daily 8.30am–12.30pm, 3–6pm), with its 15th-century porch and a bell tower that began as a watchtower. Despite the profusion of churches within the walls, it is the views from the gardens of the **Villa Balio** on the summit of the hill that justify a pilgrimage. Below stretch ragged turrets, wooded groves and vineyards; a tapestry of saltpans and sea slip all the way to the turtle-shaped Egadi Islands and to Cap Bon in Tunisia. As the English poet Fiona Pitt-Kethley concluded: "If you want a good view, go up Eryx, not Etna."

On a rocky outcrop is the **Castello di Venere** (www.fondazioneericearte.org; daily Apr–June and Oct 10am–6pm, July and Sept until 7pm, Aug until 8pm). Inside the crenellated Norman walls is the site of the fabled **Tempio di Venere**, now the battered marble remains of a temple, beside a well. **Castello Pepoli**, with its neo-Gothic medieval tower, adds to the scene.

Virgil compared Eryx to Greece's Mount Athos for its altitude and spiritual pre-eminence. Not that Erice remains a sanctuary today. Its orphanages and convents have become ceramics and carpet shops or nightclubs and chic restaurants. Still, behind this public face lies a private Erice, one of wall-hugging cobbled alleys, grotesque Baroque balconies, votive niches and secret courtyards. In keeping with Arab traditions, such courtyards were where women and children could sit in private, working or chatting by the well. Erice is a paradox. In winter it resembles a windy Umbrian hill town, yet in summer it bursts with tourists and bijou boutiques recalling the Côte d'Azur.

⊘ SWEET INDULGENCE

Erice has a name for exceedingly sweet pastries based on almonds and dried fruits. As in Palermo with its *martorano* marzipan confections, *dolci ericini* were originally made by novice nuns in a closed convent. But in 1975 this convent closed, and locals lament that the sweets are not as home-made as they once were.

However, Maria Grammatico, who learnt her craft in the convent, vies for the title of Sicily's best bakery with her **Pasticceria Maria** (www.mariagrammatico.it) on Corso Vittorio Emanuele. (Her rival is Caffè Sicilia in Noto.) Apart from *pasta reale* (exotic marzipan treats), her sweets have such poetic names as *sospiri* (sighs) and *belli e brutti* (beauties and beasts). Also on offer are delicious jams made of local citrus fruits.

RISERVA DELLO ZÍNGARO

This coast was once noted for its rich tuna-fishing grounds, and surviving *tonnare* (tuna fisheries) are being restored, both here and on the Egadi Islands. The coastal road passes the traditional **Tonnara di Bonagia** before reaching the **Riserva dello Zíngaro ❸** (www.riservazingaro.it), a superb reserve set on a rocky headland pierced with sheltered coves and bays, and home to buzzards and falcons as well as palms, carobs and euphorbia. Many trails criss-cross the reserve, including the *sentiero della costa*, a coastal footpath that runs for 11km (7 miles) from Scopello to San Vito lo Capo, roughly a five-hour walk.

On the headland lies **San Vito lo Capo ❹**, a burgeoning resort noted for its fine coast, sandy beaches, fish restaurants and heady couscous festival. The northern entrance to Lo Zíngaro lies 11km (7 miles) southeast, just before the ruined Torre dell'Impiso. The coastal road south skirts the reserve, passing more ruined towers, primeval mountains, shepherds' huts, tuna fisheries and ragged rock formations at sea. The changing coastline continues to Castellammare, with the rugged journey made by boat, on horseback or on foot.

Scopello ❺, which is 10km (6 miles) before Castellammare, marks the southern entrance to the reserve and makes a lovely lunch stop in one of the rustic seafood trattorie. This fishing village is based around a *baglio*, an imposing medieval farmstead. Paths lead to the attractive bays of Cala Bianca, Cala Rossa and Baia Guidaloca and views dominated by the **Tonnara di Scopello** (www.tonnaradiscopello.com), the most scenic tuna fishery in Sicily. Beyond lies the bay and a shingle beach, topped by a couple of Saracen towers, designed to combat piratical invasions.

A leisurely four-hour marked trail begins in the south, beyond the **Galeria di Scopello**, and hugs the coast, passing coves and beaches, until it meets the road at Uzzo, in the northern end of the reserve.

CASTELLAMMARE DEL GOLFO

Castellammare del Golfo ❻, an overgrown fishing village, enjoys panoramic views across the gulf and, from the port, a boat ferries visitors to Lo Zíngaro nature reserve. The sweet, pastel-coloured cottages and idyllic harbour with its trattorie belie the town's bloody past as a Mafia haunt. In the 1950s, around 80 percent of the male population had been to jail and the internecine Mafia warfare led the port to become the chief embarkation point to the US.

Gavin Maxwell lived among the tuna fishermen in the 1950s, recording their destitution and illiteracy in his book *Ten Pains of Death* (1958). Even then, there was a clash between old and new lifestyles: "From my eyrie in the castle I watched Castellammaresi women come down to the sea to bathe and swim fully dressed in their everyday clothes, and to meet, while so floundering, bronzed visiting nymphs in bikinis and snorkels."

> **☉ Tip**
>
> In spring, the Riserva Naturale dello Zíngaro is a magnet for bird-watchers. Bird types include Bonelli's eagle, the Sicilian rock partridge, the peregrine falcon, the buzzard, the kestrel and the red kite.

Pasticceria Maria.

ALCAMO

From Castellammare consider a 13km (8-mile) detour east to **Alcamo** ❼, a confident, quietly prosperous wine town that provides a charming taste of small-town Sicily. After visiting the **Chiesa Madre**, call in to the medieval **Castello dei Conti di Modica** to see the castle's **Enoteca**, a wine museum and tasting centre. From here, wine-lovers can make their way to drinks at **La Barrique** (Piazza Mercato), lunch at **La Baita** or a wine and food pairing experience at the wonderful **Sirignano Wine Resort**.

SEGESTA

In rolling countryside south of Castellammare lies **Segesta** ❽ (daily 9am–one hour before sunset), one of the most romantic classical locations. The site can also be reached along the A29 from Trápani.

The vast, largely unexcavated city of **Egesta** (today's Segesta) is believed to have been founded by the Elymni in the 12th century BC. The settlers claimed to be refugees who escaped the fall of Troy, but some scholars believe them to

be an iconoclastic tribe of Iberian-Ligurian descent. Elymnian writings found at Segesta are in an unfathomable language nonetheless written in the Greek alphabet. However, the Trojan link could explain their hatred of the Greeks, an enmity that led to their role in the razing of their rival nation at Selinunte in 409 BC. (Segesta itself was sacked by Siracusa in 307 BC when nearly 10,000 residents were killed and the rest sold as slaves.)

Crowning a low hill on the edge of a ravine is a great Hellenic monument, the roofless **Doric temple** that lacks a *cella* (inner chamber) and fluting on its 36 columns, but is no less lovely for that. No one knows to which god the temple was dedicated, or if it was ever completed. It appears to have been abandoned, unfinished, around 420 BC.

A regular shuttle bus takes visitors to the next level on **Monte Barbaro** 3km (miles) away with its theatre built in the 3rd century BC. (Only the fittest should attempt the 30-minute climb on foot.) Well preserved, the theatre measures 63 metres (207ft) in diameter and has 2

Castellammare del Golfo.

ows of seats facing the fabulous view of the Golfo di Castellammare. Greek plays are staged here in summer.

THE EARTHQUAKE ZONE

In 1968 a major earthquake struck western Sicily, including Calatafimi, Salemi, Partanna and Gibellina. Over 50,000 people were left homeless and many still live in makeshift accommodation. The reasons for this are unclear but would appear to involve bureaucratic inefficiency and yet another curious disappearance of funds earmarked for the project. **Salemi** ❾, a benighted hilltop town, is the most intriguing of the earthquake spots, with its blackened medieval alleys and crumbling churches. Just east lies **Gibellina Nuova** ❿, a would-be futuristic new town built after the earthquake flattened the original city, 18km (11 miles) to the west. **Ruderi di Gibellina** ⓫, the rubble of a devastated city, has been left as it fell in 1968.

THE NORTH AFRICAN COAST

South of Trápani is the so-called North African coast, closer to Tunisia than to mainland Italy. It is known for its saltpans, reflecting an industry that has flourished since Phoenician and Roman times thanks to ideal conditions: low rainfall, regular tides and the absence of estuaries that would dilute the salinity. Salt was the mainstay of the local economy between the 14th and 17th centuries. Today's **Via del Sale** (the salt road) stretches from Trápani to the Stagnone Lagoon, embracing Mozia and Marsala. It takes in stretches of salt-pans and windmills, with the brackish lagoons home to wild ducks, grey herons, common puffins and African cranes. As a result, this coastal area has become a designated nature reserve dedicated to the workings of the saltpans and the passage of migratory birds.

SALTPANS AND LAGOONS

At **Núbia** ⓬, only 5km (3 miles) out of Trápani, is the **Museo del Sale** (www.museodelsale.it; daily 9.30am–7pm), a working museum which demonstrates the ancient salt industry in action. (In March sea water is drawn into the saltpans where it evaporates in the sun. By

Doric temple at Segesta.

July the salt is dry enough to be harvested into pyramids, covered with tiles, and allowed to dry out before being taken away for cleansing and packaging.)

Further south, a stretch of salt-pans and shallow lagoons embraces the marshy **Saline dello Stagnone**, the largest lagoon on Sicily's coastline. Poetic views across the shallow saltpans are intensified at sunset. On the coast is a newer, well-organised salt museum, **Mulina Salina Infersa** (www.salineettore-infersa.com; daily summer 9am–8.30pm, autumn and winter 9.30am–3pm, Jan–Feb by appointment only), housed in a converted windmill (mill operates July–Aug Wed and Sat 4–6pm).

MOZIA

From a small jetty here a ferry crosses the lagoon to the **island of Mozia ⑬**, Sicily's chief Punic site (www.ariniepugliese.com or www.mozia line.com; boats run 9am–6.30pm summer, until 4pm in winter). A submerged Phoenician causeway just below the surface links the island to the shore, but this is now impassable.

Ferry to Mozia.

Mozia, first known as Motya, looms on the far side of the Stagnone lagoon, its largest island. As Motya, it was established as a Phoenician colony in the mid-8th century BC, set within a ring of ramparts and towers, and protected by a landward bastion. When the Phoenicians founded a colony, Lilybaeum (Marsala), as their new home, Motya fell into total neglect. It was bought, centuries later, by the Marsala wine merchant Joseph Whitaker (1850–1936), who made the excavations his life's work. As Mozia was never again colonised, Whitaker discovered a secret city more complete than Carthage.

The ruins of Motya are still only partially excavated, but the remains of the city walls, cemetery and small man-made harbour, the **cothon**, are visible. There is also a **tophet**, dedicated to the goddess Tanit, where the Phoenicians reputedly sacrificed their first-born children. Ruins of mosaic-encrusted houses include the **Casa dei Mosaici** with a black and white pebble floor depicting lions attacking a bull. The well-restored **Whitaker Museum** (www.

ondazionewhitaker.it; Apr–Oct 9.30am–5.30pm, winter 9am–3pm) contains pre-Punic pottery and nearly 1,000 burial urns. One particular treasure is a remarkably fine Greek statue from the early 5th century BC of a sinuous youth, possibly a charioteer, known as *The Man in a Tunic*.

MARSALA

Marsala ⑭ occupies the next cape, 10km (6 miles) south, and takes its name from the Arabic Marsa-al-Allah, harbour of God. The view of Capo Boeo, the most western point of Sicily, was enjoyed by refugees from Mozia in 396 BC when it became Carthaginian **Lilybaeum**, the best-defended Punic naval base in Sicily, and the only city to resist Greek expansion westwards. (Marsala, in turn, has given its name to a famous dessert wine produced in the local vineyards.)

Marsala is an engaging place with a mix of chic wine bars and traditional seafood inns, reflecting its role as a cosmopolitan port. But overladen as it is with impressive Roman, Hellenistic and Punic remains, the faintly Moorish flavour is just one strand. In that, Marsala is quintessentially Sicilian.

In the heart of the old town is the **cathedral** dedicated to **St Thomas di Canterbury**, built on the site of a church dedicated to St Thomas à Becket. Close to the cathedral on Via Giuseppe Garraffa is the small **Museo degli Arazzi** (Tue–Sun 9am–1pm, 4–6pm), containing 18 richly coloured Flemish tapestries given to the church in 1589 by the Archbishop of Messina.

Spread over the promontory are the ruins of **Lilybaeum (Lilibeo)**, presented through Baglio Anselmi (a former distillery) in the **Museo Archeologico** (Tue–Sat 9am–7.30pm, winter until 6.30pm, Sun 9am–1.30pm). These historic Marsala warehouses display finds from Mozia and Lilybaeum, including Roman mosaics, striking Hellenistic funerary monuments and a superb **Punic ship** reconstructed after its discovery by English archaeologist Honor Frost and recovery from the Stagnone Lagoon in 1971. At 35 metres (115ft) long, the war galley was manned by 68 oarsmen. For

Pre-Punic pottery masks at the Whitaker Museum in Mozia.

Marsala Cathedral.

Garibaldi Gate, Marsala.

some unexplained reason its original iron nails have not rusted.

Close by are the remains of a Roman villa at the **Insula Romana di Capo Boeo** (by request only at the Baglio Anselmi, Tue–Sun 9.30am, 11.30am, 3.30pm, Mon 9.30am and 11.30am), a reminder that this was once the most important Roman city in Sicily, with ongoing excavations leading to the opening of new sites. One such is the **Ipogeo di Crispia Salvia** (Sat 9am–1pm, booked through the Baglio Anselmi or tel: 0923 952 535), an underground chamber frescoed with funerary banqueting scenes.

On the seafront is the **Cantine Florio** (www.duca.it; see box), one of the most typical of the Marsala distilleries, mostly set in *bagli*, imposing walled estates. The Florio are Sicily's greatest entrepreneurs, but the amber-coloured dessert wine was pioneered by British wine merchants. The Florio museum even flaunts the illicit bottles sent to the US during Prohibition, when Florio cunningly labelled the alcohol as seasoning or medicinal tonic.

MAZARA DEL VALLO

From Marsala, the coastal road passes saltpans and marshes north to Trápani or south to **Mazara del Vallo** Ⓕ, a place of moods rather than specific sights. The fishing port feels like a North African souk and indeed flourished under Arab rule. A ragged **Norman castle** overlooks the seafront and palm-filled park, while the **Norman cathedral** has been given a Baroque veneer and contains two dramatic Roman sarcophagi. The main portal depicts Count Roger vanquishing a Muslim infidel.

Yet Christian sights are underpinned by a Moorish sensibility, Sicilian-style, especially in the fishing quarter. Overlooking the port, the dilapidated Norman-Byzantine church of **San Nicolò Regale** boasts crenellations and Roman mosaics.

Since the town is now home to one of Italy's largest fishing fleets, the Mazaro river is packed with trawlers all the way to the fish market. **Via Pescatori** is full of Tunisian fishermen. Behind lies the Kasbah, the Tunisian Quarter, an intriguing den of arcaded, tapering

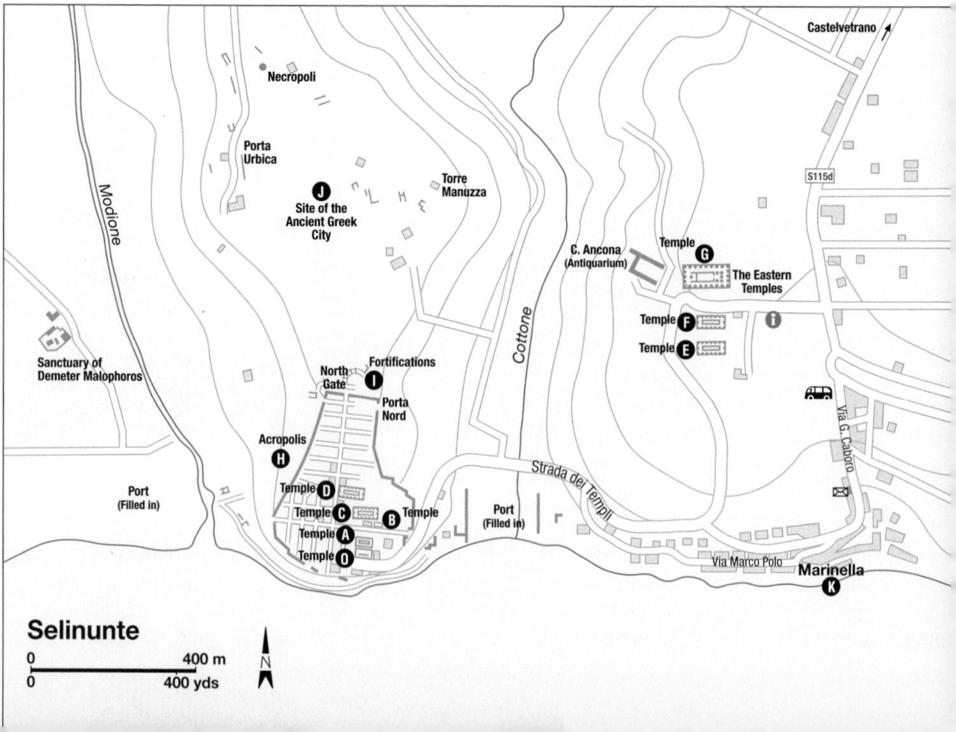

Selinunte

0 — 400 m
0 — 400 yds

N

alleys and backstreet charm. **Piazza Bagno** has a hammam with baths and massage. Nearby are a ritual butcher's and several Tunisian cafés with North Africans smoking *chicha* bubble pipes. The Tunisian trawlermen, the backbone of the local fishing fleet, are made to feel welcome. The mayor has made restoration of the Kasbah a priority, with courtyards increasingly decorated with colourful mosaics. But a Christian mood reasserts itself in the **Chiesa di San Michele**, a blaze of gold, and the adjoining **Convento di San Michele**, where nuns from a closed order make some of the best Sicilian pastries (ring the bell and speak softly through the grille).

A couple of squares south, on Piazza Plebescito stands the **Museo del Satiro** (daily 9am–7.45pm), a delightful museum dedicated to the *Dancing Satyr*, a Greek bronze dredged up by a Mazara trawler. Now restored, the young satyr is dancing himself into an orgiastic state for eternity.

The seafront is the mayor's next project, with a marina planned on one side and a proper beach on the other. Decent sandy beaches are currently a 10-minute drive away at **Tonnarella**.

SELINUNTE

As the most westerly Hellenic colony, 30km (19 miles) east of Mazara, **Selinunte**  was a pocket of Greece in the part of Sicily under North African control. Set in a richly arable plain on the edge of the sea, the ancient city was founded in 650 BC by colonists from Megara Hyblaea. It took its name from *selinon*, Greek for the wild celery that grew here in abundance. By the 5th century BC it had become a prosperous city with great temples and two harbours, where the rivers Modione and Cottone that then framed the site reach the sea. At that time Selinunte and the city of Siracusa were allied in their hatred of powerful Carthage (in today's Tunisia) but, in 409 BC, when

the Carthaginians attacked the city with the help of the people of Segesta, it was ransacked and destroyed. The city never fully recovered, and when in 250 BC it was again attacked, the population decamped and resettled at Lilybaeum (Marsala). However, an aerial view of Selinunte's collapsed columns reveals that they fell like dominoes, evidently the result of an earthquake, not man's destruction.

Surprisingly for Sicily, the huge **archaeological site** (https://en.visitselinunte.com; daily 9am–6pm, until 4pm in winter) is not overshadowed by building but left in splendid isolation, flanked by two rivers and the ancient ports, both silted up. The oldest temples, named alphabetically **A**, **B**, **C** and **D**, lie in the acropolis, while the main temples **E**, **F** and **G** were built on the eastern hill.

A curious entrance directs visitors from the ticket office and car park through tunnels in sandbanks to the reconstructed **Temple E** that was possibly dedicated to Hera (Juno) wife of Zeus, queen of heaven. Its

Fishmonger in Mazara del Vallo.

Selinunte is probably the most child-friendly classical site: the mystical setting and the sprawling ruins prompt enthusiastic scrambling over fallen pillars, with the electric train on hand for when tiredness sets in. Marinella beach lies beyond the ruins, perfect for parents to watch the children play while they tuck into a lobster lunch.

Temple in Selinunte.

lovely sculptures are in the Museo Archeologico in Palermo, much to the chagrin of locals who would like the *metopes* and friezes to return, especially the statue of the *ephebe*, a noble youth, which was unearthed by a local farmer.

Temple F, the oldest on the hill, is the most damaged of the trio, dedicated, perhaps, to Athena, goddess of war, while **Temple G**, probably dedicated to Zeus (Apollo), is now a vast heap of rubble with one restored raised column. Each column in this temple was built using stone drums weighing 100 tons and remained incomplete. Fragments of their painted stucco have been unearthed.

Sited within a walled enclosure, the **acropolis ⑭** retains some original **fortifications ⑮**. The 5th-century BC **Temple O** is barely visible, with only the *stylobate* (platform) remaining, while **Temple A** is equally elusive.

On the knoll of the hill is the conspicuous **Temple C**, dated at around mid-6th century BC. The largest temple of all, it appears to have been dedicated to Apollo, the great Olympian god. When the columns collapsed in an 8th-century earthquake, they flattened a Byzantine village that had grown around them. The columns were rebuilt into a towering colonnade in 1927. Only the platform remains of **Temple B**, while **Temple D** has its platform and some blocks from the columns.

North of the acropolis is the **Ancient City ⑯**, and on either side of it lies an unexcavated necropolis. Selinunte is a tragic yet hauntingly lovely spot. The sight and sound of the waves merge with squabbling magpies and fast yellow-back lizards. In cracks of the ruins grow aromatic wild fennel, parsley, mandrake, acanthus and beds of yellow flowers. It is deeply therapeutic.

A lengthy visit to the sprawling site can be followed by a swim along the sandy coast. Framed by temples, the seafront at **Marinella ⑰** is lined with lively restaurants.

ANCIENT QUARRIES

Between Selinunte and Castelvetrano a road leads to **Campobella di Mazara**, a wine-producing town. Further on are the **Cave di Cusa ⑰** (daily 9am–12.30pm), the ancient quarries that provided the stone to build Selinunte. Set 4km (2.5 miles) south of Campobella di Mazara, this charming rural site, overrun with wild flowers, is always open (daily, times vary). Huge column drums lie chiselled, as if ready to be transported to Temple G at Selinunte, 18km (11 miles) away, before being abandoned.

The fascination lies in the complex mechanics of construction. Old sketches show how half-carved capitals were levered and pillars were hauled to Selinunte in carts. The poignancy lies in the fact that all work stopped the moment Selinunte was destroyed. The vanquished city just disappeared under the sands. It is yet to be excavated.

Sheep grazing near Temple G at Selinunte.

The port at Maréttimo island,
a paradise for divers.

THE EGADI ISLANDS AND PANTELLERIA

As the easiest offshore islands to visit, the Egadi attract summer crowds, but out of season they offer peace and traditional charm. Much further south lies Pantelleria, Sicily's island close to the shores of North Africa.

As a short ferry ride from Tràpani, the archipelago of the Egadi Islands (Ísole Egadi) are deservedly popular. Set in a marine reserve, Favignana, Lévanzo, and Maréttimo are a paradise for sailors, scuba-divers and fans of tuna fish. Today, fishing and tourism keep the economy alive, and the restoration of the tuna fishery has given the island of Favignana a new focus.

CAVE DRAWINGS

The Egadi have 15,000 years of history, and the caves of Favignana and Lévanzo contain traces of the islands' prehistoric settlers. In Lévanzo, cave drawings in the Grotta del Genovese etched 12,000 years ago show bulls and deer as well as hunting men. It is thought the archipelago was once part of a land bridge linking Africa to Italy.

The islands were the springboard for the Arab conquest of Sicily and the great traders, the Phoenicians, then settled here and remained until despatched by the Romans. Over the centuries the Saracens and the Normans followed, then the Aragonese and, finally, the Genoese. The Normans and Aragonese fortified the Egadi, while the Spaniards encouraged the growth of a coral industry.

After Spain sold the islands to Genoese bankers in 1637, the economy took off and reached its peak under the

entrepreneurial Florio family in the early 19th century, when both tuna and tufa (volcanic rock) were exported.

FAVIGNANA

At 20 sq km (8 sq miles), **Favignana**, home to around 3,400 people, is the largest and most populous island. Ancient tufa-quarrying remodelled the landscape until it was brought to a standstill in the 1950s by the high cost of extracting and transporting the rock.

The island is a homage to stone, its slopes dotted with tufa houses. Even

 Main attractions

Tonnara di Favignana
Diving off Punta Marsala
Lévanzo boat tour
Grotta del Genovese
Walking on Maréttimo
Cycling on Favignana and Pantelleria
Pantelleria's dammusi houses
Moscato Passito wines
Mud baths

Map on page 102

Favignana, the largest of the Egadi Islands.

⊙ Tip

There is a variety of walking tours of Favignana available, enquire at the tourist office (Palazzo Florio, tel: 0923 925 443; www.welcometoegadi.it).

cliffs and caves represent a pleasing spectrum of ochre, russet and cream-coloured rocks. However, if cyclists heading for one of the coves stop to peer over the roadside stone walls, they will discover an abundance of sunken gardens. These sheer stone walls, overgrown with wild fennel and capers, give shelter from the sweeping sea winds to the orange and lemon trees, as well as the figs and tomatoes planted below on the floor of the abandoned quarries. Other quarries were carved at the very edge of the sea too, so that the tufa could be loaded directly onto the boats transporting it to the mainland. Stone from the maze-like **Cala Rossa** ⑱ helped build many cities in Sicily and North Africa. The chiselled walls and eroded geometry of the seaside quarries make Cala Rossa a popular spot for picnics and swimming.

In the bustling medieval town of **Favignana** ⑲, to one side of the ferry quay in the **port**, stand beautiful vaulted warehouses in which the big black-bottomed tuna boats, the long nets and huge anchors are stored during the winter. The still waters of the harbour

reflect the tiled roofs and stone smoke stacks of the **Tonnara di Favignana**, former tuna cannery, which closed i the 1990s (all processing is now car ried out in Trápani). Previously know as Tonnara Florio, this masterpiece c industrial archaeology has been con verted into a heritage museum coverin the tuna business (daily mid-Apr–Ma 10am–2pm, June until 5pm, July–Sep 10.30am–1.30pm and 5–11pm).

Palazzo Florio, built in 1876, was onc the home of the tuna tycoon Ignazio Flo rio. Today it contains the tourist offic (tel: 0923 925 443), town hall and a cul tural centre. The palazzo and the statu of Ignazio Florio in **Piazza Europa** reca the island's heyday. In Florio's time, day's catch could be as high as 10,00 fish. Today, it has shrunk to under 2,00 a month because of overfishing. Even so the tuna industry survives, with tradi tional techniques allied to hi-tech sona detection, used to spot the shoals.

If tuna is on your mind, call int **Sapori di Mare** (Via Roma 23) to dine o tuna prepared 50 different ways, from tuna *caponata* to sweet and sour tuna.

⊙ DIVING IN SICILY

Marine caverns, reefs, rainbow-coloured sponges, ancient wrecks and archaeological sites are all part of the Sicilian diving experience. Although Ustica is, by common consent, an experienced diver's first choice, all the offshore marine reserves offer good diving. The Egadi Islands' crystalline waters teem with marine life and are popular with snorkellers as well as divers. On the island of Favignana, snorkelling and scuba-diving enthusiasts appreciate the waters off Punta Marsala, Punta Fanfalo and Punta Ferro, including the underwater cavern between Scoglio Corrente and Cala Rotonda.

Serious divers or underwater photographers might wish to make the island of Ustica their base. As Sicily's best-established marine reserve, Ustica's waters reveal an explosion of colour, from corals, sea sponges and anemones to barracudas, breams, scorpion fish and groupers. Deep-sea archaeological excursions also explore wrecks and inspect amphorae in their original sites on the seabed. Among the best diving spots in the entire Mediterranean are La Scoglia del Medico (Doctor's Rock) and Secca della

Columbara. Contact Profondo (tel: 091 844 9609; www. ustica-diving.it) to dive in the area. Ustica can be visited on a day trip from Palermo.

But even the top resorts should be able to set up a customised diving or snorkelling experience. From Taormina, the most popular dives are around Isola Bella and reveal octopus, schools of fish and a selection of corals. The beautiful Blue Grotto dive (at a depth of 16 metres/52ft) showcases colourful corals and eels lurking in craggy walls and of course spectacular blue light effects. Far more challenging is the dive to the so-called "Roman temple" (at a depth of 26 metres/85ft), the result of a shipwreck over 2,000 years ago. These ghostly white marble columns were intended for a temple at Taormina until the Roman ship came to a sticky end off Capo Taormina. Two of the best dive centres near Taormina are Sea Spirit (Via Recanati 26, Giardini-Naxos, tel: 0320 867 3320; www.seaspirit.it) and Divesicily (Taormina and Giardini-Naxos, tel: 360 289 555; www. divesicily.com).

Also in town is **Forte San Giacomo**, a fortress built by Roger II in 1120, later converted into a Bourbon prison in 1837, and today housing a maximum-security prison for some of Sicily's finer mafiosi.

PALAEOLITHIC CAVES

Eastwards along the shore is **Punta San' Nicola**, awaiting excavation of its caves that were inhabited in Palaeolithic times, **Bagno delle Donne** (once the women's baths), and **Cala Rossa** where the sea was said to have turned red in 241 BC during a bloody battle between the Carthaginians and Romans. Also in the east, in the Bue Marina area, see the **Giardino dell'Impossibile** ⓴ (www.villamargherita. it; daily May–Oct, guided tours, booking necessary tel: 0389 804 8028) botanical and tropical gardens "impossibly" thriving in an ancient tufa-stone quarry.

LÉVANZO

The smallest island, and the one closest to the mainland, bears witness to the islanders' bond with the sea. Much of the coast is still inaccessible, except by boat. The port of **Lévanzo** ㉑ (or **Cala Dogana**, because the Customs offices are here) consists of a handful of houses with rooms to let, a couple of small hotels, several cafés and trattorie.

Its one tarred road turns into a dirt track as it leaves town and winds along a gentle valley between the peaks of the Pizzo del Mónaco and the Pizzo del Corvo. The stony slopes are covered with *macchia mediterranea*, arid-looking grey-green scrub that turns lush with the winter rains and blooms in spring.

At the head of the valley the track forks: the left-hand path zigzags down the steep coast towards the sea, leading to the **Grotta del Genovese** ㉒, a deep cavern overhanging the rocky shoreline. It is Lévanzo's greatest treasure. If the sea is calm and the wind right, you can reach the grotto by boat, combining a visit to see the ancient carvings with sailing and swimming (tel: 0923 924 032; www.grottadelgenovese.it; departures 10.30am–2.30pm).

View of the Egadi Islands from the mainland.

Cala Dogana, the port at Lévanzo.

THE GREAT TUNA MASSACRE

The cruel ritual is both a gory tradition and a gruesome spectacle that survives despite conservationists' concerns and the contravention of rules on driftnet fishing.

Tuna fishing is rooted in the Sicilian psyche. Nowhere is this more so than in Favignana, where it is considered the sea's ultimate challenge to man, as well as the island's traditional livelihood. The tuna's only predators are the killer whale, the Mako shark and man, and their ritual death here at the hands of fishermen is both gruelling work and a disturbing spectacle.

THE MATTANZA RITUAL

The season lasts from May to mid-June, with the ritual *mattanza*, the traditional method of tuna slaughter, as the inexorable fate of the passing

Dividing up the tuna.

shoals. The fast-swimming tuna hunt off the coast of Norway but spawn in the Mediterranean's warm waters. Shoals circle Favignana where they are captured in a system of huge chambered nets *(tonnare)* introduced by the Arabs in the 9th century. Buoys mark out a 100-metre (330ft) rectangle; up to 10km (6 miles) of nets are suspended between the floats. Halfway along lie five antechambers. The innermost section is the *camera della morte*, the death chamber 30 metres (100ft) deep.

At dawn, or when the winds are right, the helmsman leads the fleet in prayers, aided by an image of the Madonna. The 60-strong crew sings and chants the *cialoma* in guttural tones. Entreaties are uttered by the *rais*, a Moorish title given to the chief fisherman, who travels in a separate boat and constantly checks the entrance to the *camera della morte*.

The black boats encircle the nets. When the *rais* decides that the currents are right, the shoal is steered into the death chamber and the gate closed. As it fills with fish, the floating death trap sags, like a heavy sack. To the command of *"Tira, tira!"* (pull, pull!) the net is pulled tight. The *rais* chants the fateful battle cry. Each verse of this bloodthirsty sea shanty has a chorus of *"Aiamola, aiamola"*, perhaps derived from *Allah! Che muoia!* (Allah, may it die!).

THE DANCE OF DEATH

As the net is drawn in to the length of a football pitch, the fish circle frantically in the *sarabanda della morte*, the dance of death. The chanting stops and the slaughter begins. The frantic fish are harpooned and caught behind the gills with long pole-gaff hooks to be dragged onto the boats. Some of the tuna are man-sized and weigh over 200 kg (over 400 lbs).

As the silvery fish are pierced, the frothing water is stained red. It takes a frenzied 15 minutes and a sea of vivid red to slaughter about 200 tuna, although some die of heart attacks or over-oxygenation. With true Sicilian logic, the tuna's breeding grounds also become their tragic end.

The tuna's delicious red meat is much sought after by Japanese chefs especially to use in sashimi and sushi. The rising demand and resulting depletion of stocks have triggered restrictions that have put out many Sicilian tuna canneries out of business.

The **rock carvings** are prehistoric and were not found until 1949. Etched into the soft stone about 10,000 years ago, they include impressions of human dancers and wild animals in naturalistic poses. More recent ones of men, women and fish were created about 5,000 years ago.

Most of the rest of the island is inaccessible, and there are only a few inlets for swimming.

MARÉTTIMO

The most mysterious, mountainous and greenest of the Egadi Islands, Maréttimo lies to the west, separated from its sister islands by a stretch of sea rich in sunken treasure. Here lie the remains of the Carthaginian fleet destroyed by the Romans in 241 BC.

The little port of **Maréttimo** ㉓ has no hotel, but manages with a few serviced apartments and enthusiastic B&B arrangements. Peace and natural beauty are what draw visitors here. Scuba-divers come to explore the 400 caves and grottoes scattered along the coast; plant-lovers study the Mediterranean vegetation at its purest. The rest simply want to relax, swim in the aquamarine waters, or take three-hour trips in the brightly coloured traditional boats around the coast.

Ambitious visitors will climb up to survey the island from **Monte Falcone** (686 metres/2,250ft). An easier walk is an excursion to **Case Romane**, not houses but ruined Roman fortifications not far from the village. (From the port follow directions to Pizzeria Filli Pipitone.) Beside the ruins is a crumbling Arab-Norman chapel.

An alternative hike leads north along the cliffs and cuts across an isthmus to **Punta Tróia** ㉔, a rocky promontory dominated by a Saracen castle. Originally a watchtower, the castle was enlarged by Roger II and converted by the Spanish into its present form, with an underground cistern that later did service as a dreaded prison. But such

sombre thoughts quickly float away on this restful, thyme-scented island.

In summer, hikers should always carry bottled water with them. On these parched islands, water is more precious than wine.

PANTELLERIA

Pantelleria is closer to Tunisia's Cap Bon, 70km (44 miles) away, than to Sicily, which is 110km (68 miles) distant, and is reached on a six-hour ferry crossing from Trápani, or by air. At 83 sq km (247 acres), it is the largest island off Sicily, with a population estimated at around 7,700. The island's evocative name probably derives from the Arabic "daughter of the winds", after the winds that can buffet this rocky outpost, even in August. The island is dotted with *dammusi* – cube-like, low-domed houses – and surrounded by terraces used for growing capers or grapes; even the vines are trained low to protect them from the winds. The landscape is dramatic and relatively bleak but enlivened with hot springs, jagged rocks and coves

⊘ Drink

Pantelleria is famous for its sweet raisins and for its wines, especially *Moscato di Pantelleria* produced from its sweet moscato grape, Zibibbo. The wine made from raisins is *Passito*, usually highly scented with almonds.

Punta Tróia, Maréttimo.

instead of beaches. Many mainland Italians, especially from Milan (like fashion designer Giorgio Armani) have summer retreats here.

PANTELLERIA TOWN

Pantelleria town ㉕ was bombed heavily during the Allied forces invasion of Sicily in World War II, so charm is in short supply. But the island itself has a lively air as well as an exoticism encapsulated by the white-cubed houses and restaurants that serve fish couscous.

Pantelleria was originally founded as a trading post by the Phoenicians. Its small harbours provided excellent protection for the small ships of the day. The island was captured by Rome but eventually – after the Vandals and Byzantines – it was the Arabs who claimed it and introduced farming.

A rewarding hike or a bus ride from Pantelleria town to the port of **Scáuri** ㉖ on the southern coast passes the traditional domed, white-washed *dammusi* houses, framed by terraced vineyards, small settlements and expanses of blackened,

Dammusi house on Pantelleria.

lava-stone landscape. The dry-stone walls enclose citrus groves and often appear to have hardy, locally bred donkeys peering over them.

The route also passes strange Neolithic dome-shaped funerary monuments, known as *Sesi*, conceivably built by early settlers who arrived here around the 18th century BC. Little is known of the *Sesi* people; it is assumed they came from Tunisia on foot before the Mediterranean Sea developed. They built circular domed structures using the island's volcanic rock, similar in shape to the *dammusi*. At Mursia their village with *Sesi* structures was protected by walls. Its name, Alta Mura, means High Wall.

HOT SPRINGS AND MUD BATHS

The island's volcanic origins are visible in the presence of lava stone basalt rock, hot springs, *stufe* (volcanic steam vents) and a landscape pitted with small *cuddie* (baby spouts), which are extinct volcanic craters. On **Monte Grande** (836 metres/2,743ft), near the hamlet of Bugebera, lies a lake in an old crater full of warm, bubbling, sulphurously brown waters, known as **Specchio di Venere** (Venus's mirror) and used by local bathers to cure myriad ills. The water here can reach 50°C (122°F) because of a hot spring. **Bagno d'Acqua** is another small lake inside a former crater, and visitors are drawn to it too, in order to cover themselves with beautifying volcanic mud.

As for coastal scenery, the craggy shore is studded with coves, with rocks shaded from red through green and black. For swimmers and divers the absence of beaches is compensated for by the privacy occasioned by secluded coves and hot springs and by the quality of the underwater landscape, with sightings of ancient wrecks as well as sea sponges and coral. In fact, the great excursions on the island are a tour in a car or by boat. By boat is better.

The rocky coastline at Pantelleria.

Stairway to the Temple of Hera,
Valley of the Temples.

AGRIGENTO AND THE VALLEY OF THE TEMPLES

The classical splendour of the Valley of the Temples makes this Sicily's most visited ancient sight, overshadowing Agrigento itself.

Siracusa may have been the most powerful city in Greek Sicily but **Agrigento** (known as Akragas to the Greeks, Agrigentum to the Romans) was the most wealthy and luxurious, a city that reached from the acropolis high on the ridge down to the blue sea below. It was first settled by people from Gela in 580 BC, attracted there by the abundance of springs and the prospect of a dreamy, well-fortified site. It was Benito Mussolini who, in his campaign to unify Sicily and all Italy under one flag, changed its name to Agrigento.

EXPLORING AGRIGENTO

At first sight, little remains of the ancient splendour. Not that the "modern" city is wholly poor, or even modern. Beneath the charmless muddle is a fascinating urban mix. The medieval core is a maze of Moorish streets and substandard housing while, in contrast, the new quarter overlooks the temples in an attempt at bourgeois chic, but one that went horribly wrong when landslides, aggravated by overcrowding and shoddy building, killed many in 1966.

Even so, don't be dismayed. Restoration is under way in Agrigento, and the summer festival season is magical. Even the image of a parasitical city living off its past glories can be dispelled by a starlit night, a heady southern Sicilian wine and a dinner of grilled swordfish as an alternative to tuna.

If you are in the Agrigento area only for a day, head straight for the **Valle dei Templi** (Valley of the Temples) and restrict your visit to the town of Agrigento itself for dinner and an evening stroll. Parking problems, poor public transport, the scattered nature of the archaeological sites and their relative distance from the city, make

Main attractions

Chiesa di Santo Spirito
Santa Maria dei Greci
Catacombe (catacombs)
Tempio della Concordia
Tempio di Hera
Tempio di Castore e Polluce (Dioscuri)
San Nicola
Museo Archeologico Regionale
Hellenistic-Roman Quarter
Giardino di Kolymbetra

Map on page 124

Ruins of Castor and Pollux Temple with Agrigento in the background.

Agrigento's crest.

it inconvenient to combine the city and the temples, even for meals.

If not staying close to the Valle dei Templi, take a picnic lunch to avoid the coach party options on site. The **tourist office** is at Via Empedocle 73 (tel: 0922 20391).

CITY SIGHTS

Above Via Atenea, Agrigento's pedestrianised main shopping street as well as the entrance to the historic quarter, stands the **Chiesa di Santo Spirito** ❶ www.monasterosantospiritoag.org), the church of a fine Cistercian abbey founded in 1290. Often known as the **Badia Grande** it is the finest church in the city. It is a complex of cloisters, chapter house

and refectory in Chiaramonte style. The church has a Gothic portal and rose window, plus a panelled ceiling and Baroque interior with stuccoes attributed to Serpotta. The vaulted Gothic dormitory leads to a chapter house with mullioned windows and a bold portal, all emboldened with Arab-Norman geometrical motifs.

The sacristan in the house opposite will gladly open the church for a tip, while the Cistercian nuns sell sweet almond and pistachio pastries shaped like snakes, shells and flowers. Faced with such delights, the French writer Dominique Fernandez was torn between the "Baroque opulence" of the architecture and the "Arab unctuousness" of the cakes. The cakes won.

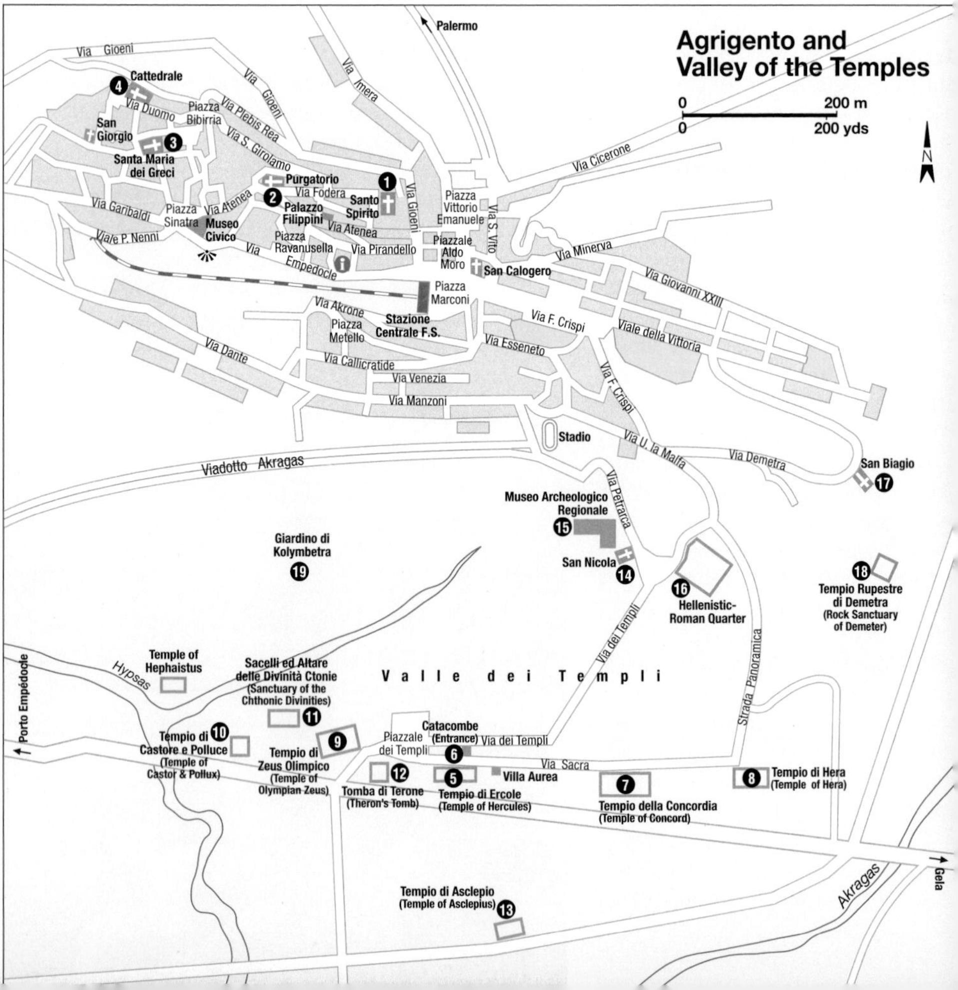

Agrigento and Valley of the Temples

0   200 m
0   200 yds

N

Palermo

Via Gioeni
Cattedrale
Via Duomo
Piazza Via Plebis Rea
Bibirria
San Giorgio
Via S. Girolamo
Santa Maria dei Greci
Purgatorio
Via Fodera
Via Atenea
Santo Spirito
Palazzo Filippini
Via Garibaldi
Piazza Via Atenea
Sinatra
Museo Civico
Via Atenea
Piazza Ravanusella
Via Pirandello
Viale P. Nenni
Via Empedocle
Piazzale Aldo Moro
San Calogero
Piazza Vittorio Emanuele
Via S. Vito
Via Cicerone
Via Gioeni
Via Imera
Via Akrone
Piazza Marconi
Piazza Metello
Stazione Centrale F.S.
Via F. Crispi
Via Esseneto
Via Giovanni XXIII
Via Minerva
Viale della Vittoria
Via Dante
Via Callicratide
Via Venezia
Via Manzoni
Via F. Crispi
Viadotto Akragas
Stadio
Via U. la Malfa
Via Demetra
San Biagio
Museo Archeologico Regionale
Via Petrarca
Giardino di Kolymbetra
San Nicola
Hellenistic-Roman Quarter
Strada Panoramica
Tempio Rupestre di Demetra (Rock Sanctuary of Demeter)
Temple of Hephaistus
Hypsas
Sacelli ed Altare delle Divinità Ctonie (Sanctuary of the Chthonic Divinities)
Valle dei Templi
Via dei Templi
Porto Empedocle
Tempio di Castore e Polluce (Temple of Castor & Pollux)
Tempio di Zeus Olimpico (Temple of Olympian Zeus)
Catacombe (Entrance)
Piazzale dei Templi
Via dei Templi
Via Sacra
Villa Aurea
Tomba di Terone (Theron's Tomb)
Tempio di Ercole (Temple of Hercules)
Tempio della Concordia (Temple of Concord)
Tempio di Hera (Temple of Hera)
Akragas
Gela
Tempio di Asclepio (Temple of Asclepius)

THE HISTORIC QUARTER

Dominating Piazza Purgatorio, off Via Atenea, is the 17th-century church known simply as the **Purgatorio ②**, built on an ancient sacred site, but better known for its riot of Baroque allegorical stuccowork by Serpotta.

To the left of the church, a stone lion guards an entrance to the ancient underground drinking water and drainage system. Created in the 5th century BC, these were known as one of the wonders of the ancient world. Linked to the underground chamber beneath San Nicola church, the system used conduits and cisterns to channel water to the city. There are plans to open the chambers to the public and create a copy of a Roman food store complete with a lava-stone grinding mill.

Further west is **Santa Maria dei Greci ③**, a Norman church set among Agrigento's alleyways, in the heart of the medieval quarter. A Chiaramonte Gothic portal leads to a Norman nave, a coffered ceiling and some Byzantine fragments. Below ground is the greatest surprise: the church is constructed around a 5th-century Greek temple dedicated to Athena. A narrow gallery contains the bases of six fluted Doric columns, the remains of the temple peristyle and stereobate. The sanctuary spans Greek and Christian cults: tradition has it that St Paul preached here.

On Via del Duomo is the 14th-century cathedral, the **Cattedrale ④** (www.cattedraleagrigento.com), which surmounts a ridge and incorporates Arab-Norman, Catalan-Gothic and Baroque elements, from Catalan blind arcading to a Norman bell tower. The Norman-Gothic nave boasts an inlaid, coffered ceiling while the graceful Baroque stuccowork in the choir contrasts with a severe Gothic chapel.

Further south, on Via Atenea, the restored Baroque **Palazzo Filippini** is a shining example of Agrigento's renewed commitment to culture.

Even more uplifting is the way the classical city stages open-air performances of drama in tribute to Persephone. The modern city responds with *passeggiate* along tree-lined Viale della Vittoria. From this road there are some excellent views

⊙ Fact

The Chiaramonte, the dominant feudal dynasty of the 14th century, gave its name to the Catalan-Gothic architectural style, in which fortresses doubled as palaces, with decorated facades, vaulted rooms and lavish painted ceilings. The best of these tower houses had an austere beauty.

The cathedral at Agrigento.

⊙ A LURID PAST

The city abounds in classical anecdote regarding its fabled wealth. For example, the tyrant of Akragas kept wine in reservoirs hacked out of solid rock; each giant cellar contained 4,000 litres (900 gallons). And returning Olympic heroes were welcomed by cavalcades of chariots drawn by white horses, which were legendary in the Greek world. The ancient poet Pindar wrote that "Akragas was the most beautiful city the mortals had ever built". But a cruel one, too. One ruler of this sybaritic city supposedly burned his enemies alive in a large bull made of bronze.

The people, it was said, "built for eternity but feasted as if there were no tomorrow". The city rivalled Athens in the splendour of its temples, but in its hedonistic lifestyle Akragas was the Los Angeles of the ancient world.

Temple of Hercules in the Valley of the Temples, built in 520 BC.

Temple of Concord, the best-preserved Greek temple in the world.

of the Valley of the Temples. At the far end is the medieval church of San Biagio and the Sanctuary of Demeter.

VALLE DEI TEMPLI

It is here, for a fleeting moment, that the classical world comes alive. The Valley of the Temples (www.lavalledeitempli.it) is not really a valley but a string of Doric temples that stand imposingly on a ridge south of the city facing the sea. An ideal first glimpse of the temples is by night, during a drive along the **Strada Panoramica** and **Via della Valle dei Templi**. The temples glow in the dark countryside, radiating a sense of cohesion, security and serenity. This crest of temples was designed to be visible from the sea, both as a beacon for sailors and to show that the gods guarded the sacred city from mortal danger.

An early start guarantees enough solitude to slip back into the classical world. But unless you plan to view the Tempio della Concordia (the Temple of Concord) from the elegant restaurant in Villa Athena, come armed with a picnic. Otherwise, the on-site snack

bar could bring you back to the presen times with a bump.

Piazzale dei Templi, the entrance t the main temples, was once the *agor* (market place) and is still alive to th ancient trading spirit. The local guide operate a monopoly, refusing to allo unauthorised rivals to present th archaeological park, and small boy often demand money to protect tourists cars from unknown dangers, a feature c many Sicilian sites. The archaeologica park falls into two sections: the **West ern Zone** (daily 8.30am–7pm; mid-July mid-Sept evening visits by request unt 11pm) and the **Eastern Zone**, (Mon–Sa 9am–7pm, Sun 9am–1pm), which is bes viewed in the early morning or late after noon – or perhaps from afar when it i floodlit at night.

THE EASTERN ZONE

The first treasure visible in the East ern Zone is the **Tempio di Ercole** (Temple of Hercules). Built in 520 B in Archaic Doric style, this is the oldes temple, second in size here to the Tem ple of Zeus and of roughly the sam

⊘ SAFEGUARDING SICILIAN TREASURES

Sicilian treasures are probably safer than they have ever been, with recent success stories all over the island. The Sicilian Ministry of Culture has instituted a long-term collaborative venture with California's Getty Museum to favour the exchange of priceless treasures. Agrigento is a prime beneficiary, lending its Greek marble *Kouros (The Agrigento Youth)* and another Attic masterpiece, in return for significant American loans and assistance. The Getty has also installed anti-earthquake protection in the Agrigento Museum.

Instead, Aidone has recovered its *Venus*, and other treasures, which ended up in the Getty Museum in Malibu. After incontrovertible proof linking it to Morgantina, the *Venus* returned to Sicily in 2010, and has set a precedent regarding the recovery of stolen treasures, including the drawing up of new anti-trafficking legislation (see page 162).

The picture is not so rosy at the Villa Romana (www.villaromanadelcasale.it), where the priceless Roman mosaics have suffered from flood damage, vandalism and political wrangling. Although damage and discoloration have occurred, the Unesco-listed mosaics are finally being restored in line with international curating standards (see page 159).

proportions as the Parthenon in Athens. It once had a gorgeous entablature emblazoned with lions, leaves and palms, but now it presents an almost abstract puzzle. Although much is in ruins, Alexander Hardcastle performed a truly Herculean task by re-erecting eight columns in 1924.

Villa Aurea, which is set in olive and almond groves beside the former Golden Gate, once belonged to Hardcastle, the Englishman who devotedly excavated the site. The grounds are riddled with catacombs and water cisterns, which run under rocks and orchards the length of the classical site. A path on the left leads to the **catacombs** ❻, which emerge in a necropolis on the far side of the villa. Now excavated and well lit, the passages cut through the rock and reveal a cross-section of tombs and fossilised bones.

Arches link circular rooms (tholoi) containing circular honeycomb cells stacked high with shelf-tombs. Though the oldest tombs here date from the 4th century BC, the main Roman necropoli lie just to the south, while Greek burial grounds are scattered around the city.

At the end of the Via Sacra lies the **Tempio della Concordia** ❼ (Temple of Concord), abutting ancient city walls. After the Theseion in Athens, it is the best-preserved Greek temple in the world. The pastoral surroundings are at odds with the temple's bloody history: on this bulwark thousands were slain in battle against Carthage. Dating from 430 BC, the temple was saved from ruin in the 6th century by being converted into a church. The peristyle was sealed by dry-stone walls, and the *cella* opened to form twin naves, although sadly the *metopes* and pediment were destroyed.

The tapering columns tilt inwards imperceptibly, creating an ethereal grace and airiness that belie the weighty entablature. A further refinement is that the fluted columns have different spacing, narrowing towards the corners. They were originally coated with glazed marble dust to protect the flaky sandstone, then painted with vivid polychrome scenes, predominantly bright blue or blood-red. Now lichen-coated,

> **◎ Tip**
>
> The Festival of Myth takes place in Agrigento in summer and features classical and pop concerts in the Valley of the Temples (tel: 0922 32888, www.ilsestante.net). In February the temples provide a striking backdrop for the annual Almond Blossom Festival (Sagra del Mandorlo; http://sagradelmandorloinfiore.com) and international folk festival. There are parades, shows, crafts exhibits and a chance to listen to anything from Filipino groups to Scottish pipe bands.

Temple of Concord at night.

the temple still represents sheer perfection in line. The only jarring image is the distant cityscape with its high-rise apartment buildings and cemetery but, seen though a heat haze, even that shimmers obligingly. The temple is transformed by light: locals say that one has not lived until seeing Concord changing with the seasons, at dawn and sunset, dusk and moonlight.

Restoration of the temples is ongoing, with the jury still out as to whether damaged sections of the temples should be replaced by replicas, and the originals moved to the city's well-designed archaeological museum. Even if certain sections have been moved, it might be the only solution.

Commendable cultural initiatives are under way, such as the evocative summer music festivals and contemporary sculpture exhibitions. Sculptors of the stature of Igor Mitoraj have been invited to display their works in the Valley of the Temples.

The **Tempio di Hera ❽** (Temple of Hera) surmounts a rocky ridge which formed part of the city ramparts.

Temple of Olympian Zeus ruins.

Known as Juno to the Romans, Her was protector of engaged and married couples. Fittingly, hers is held t be the most romantic of temples, se "high on the hill like an offering to th goddess". Yet Zeus's sister and wif was perceived as a bloodthirsty goddess, to be appeased by sacrifice at a altar beside the walls. Part of the *cell* and 25 columns remain intact alon with the drums of columns; the res fell over the hill during a landslide. Th stones bear reddish traces of fire dam age where they were singed by flames

THE WESTERN ZONE

After retracing your steps to th entrance, cross the road to the **Tempio d Zeus Olimpico ❾** (the Temple of Olym pian Zeus). Even at the peak of its golde age, the temple was unfinished. With th area of a football pitch, it was the larges Doric temple ever known. The U-shape grooves on the stone blocks represen primitive pulley marks formed durin construction. Today's fallen masonr is a challenge to the imagination: th best stone was plundered to build th

ort of Empédocle 9km (5.5 miles) way. A frieze on the east side depicted the battle between Zeus (known also to the Romans as Jupiter or Jove, that is, Giove), and the Giants, matched by the War of Troy on the western side.

The facade was supported by 38 telamons (columns carved as male figures) – a revolutionary concept for the time. In this way, the weight of the pediment was shared by the giants and by the columns of the peristyle. The telamons also had allegorical and aesthetic functions. They both broke up the uniformity of the peristyle and illustrated the war against Zeus; like Atlas, the defeated giants were compelled to carry the world on their shoulders.

A sandstone copy of a telamon lies on the ground, dreamily resting his head on his arms, and one of the originals is on display in the archaeological museum. On the temple, these male *giganti* (also known as atlantes, or atlas figures) alternated with female caryatids and represented the three known racial types of the time: African, Asian and European.

West of the Temple of Zeus is the most confusing quarter, dotted with shrines dating from pre-Greek times. The Via Sacra leads to the **Tempio di Castore e Polluce** ❿ (Temple of Castor and Pollux, or the Dioscuri), spuriously named after the twin sons of Zeus. Although it has become the city symbol, the building is theatrical pastiche, erected in 1836 from the remains of several temples. Even so, it is a graceful and evocative reconstruction. Locally, the temple is known as *tre colonne*, since only three of the four columns are visible from the city. Despite its name, the temple was first dedicated to Persephone and Demeter, Chthonic (Underworld) deities, along with Dionysus.

This theory is supported by the temples in the surrounding area. Known as the **Sacelli ed Altare delle Divinità Ctonie** ⓫ (Sanctuary of the Chthonic Divinities), the quarter conceals sacrificial altars and ditches, a veritable shrine to fertility, immortality and eternal youth. Pale-coloured beasts were offered to the heavens but black animals were sacrificed to the gods of

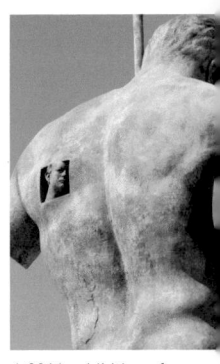

A 2011 exhibition of sculptures by Igor Mitoraj in the Valley of the Temples contrasted the contemporary with the classical in a dramatic setting.

Temple of Hera.

Facade of San Nicola.

Display inside Agrigento's archaeological museum.

the Underworld. The altars took the form of flat, concentric circles or deep, well-shaped affairs. Now bounded by a gorge and an orange grove, this sanctuary of death was also the fount of life, with lush gardens and a lake full of exotic birds and fish.

Close to Piazzale dei Templi lies **Tomba di Terone**  (Theron's Tomb), a tribute to Agrigento's benevolent tyrant. This truncated tower in Doric-Ionic style is essentially a Roman funerary pyramid, more a celebration of conquest than glory to a local hero. Outside the ancient walls is the isolated **Tempio di Asclepio** ⓭ (Temple of Asclepius), half-hidden in an almond grove. Dedicated to the god of healing, it lies between the River Akragas and a sacred spring.

From Piazzale dei Templi, a short drive along Via dei Templi leads to the **Villa Athena** with its restaurant (tel: 0922 596 288), the **museo archeologico**, the Hellenistic-Roman Quarter and a clutch of pagan shrines. En route are fortifications, a reminder that Agrigento was once enclosed by walls, towers and massive gates, of which the perimeter and craggy foundation remain. The sandy landscape is dotted with olives and pines. Subsidence ha created strange slopes and whirling patterns on the soil.

San Nicola ⓮ (daily 9am–7pm) on Via Petrarca is a Romanesque church with 15th-century cloister whose severe but grand facade i reminiscent of monuments in ancien Rome. This is not so far-fetched given that the church is built from Greek stone raided from the ruin and also purports to be a Roman temple dedicated to the sun god. chapel contains the **Sarcophagus o Phaedra**, an exquisitely carved scen of Phaedra's grief at the loss of he lover and stepson Hippolytus.

REGIONAL MUSEUM

Next door is the well-presente **Museo Archeologico Regionale** ⓯ (Mon–Sat 9am–7.30pm, Sun 9am– 1.30pm, combined ticket with the temples) incorporating a church courtyard and temple foundations The Graeco-Roman section is the cen trepiece, along with a Bronze Age ur from a Sican tomb and a three-legge *Trinacria*, the ancient symbol of Sicily Exhibits include a wealth of painte Attic vases dating from the 5th centur BC, Greek lion's-head water spouts, vibrant Roman mosaic of a gazelle and a controversial *ephebe* (classica youth). A poignant marble sarcopha gus depicts the death of a child amids weeping. The highlight is a telamo in all its massive glory accompanie by other powerful giant heads. Else where are votive offerings and statue associated with orgiastic rites: phal lic donkeys compete with a libidinou pygmy and a hermaphrodite.

The **Hellenistic-Roman Quarter** ⓰ (Thu–Tue 9am–1pm; Wed until 6pm lies opposite, an ancient commercia and residential area laid out on a gri system. Whereas the Greeks create the grid system, the Romans over-laid it with a rational arrangement of public and private space. The well-preserved remains of aqueducts, terracotta and stone water channels are visible, as well as vestiges of shops, taverns and patrician villas. The frescoed villas are paved with patterned mosaics protected by glass enclosures.

On the far side of Strada Panoramica is a stretch of Greek walls and **San Biagio** ⑰, a Norman church perched on a rocky platform. It is carved into an ancient temple to Demeter and Persephone. Two circular altars lie between the church and another tribute to the goddess of fertility. At the foot of the cliff is the **Tempio Rupestre di Demetra** ⑱ (the Rock Sanctuary of Demeter), the oldest sanctuary in the valley, dating from the 7th century BC.

When visiting Sicily in 1885, Guy de Maupassant was lucky enough to see the temples without tourists or modern desecration. The writer was struck by their air of "magnificent desolation; dead, arid and yellowing on all sides".

Yet with falcons hovering above, lizards scurrying at one's feet, the air heavy with the scent of blossoms, today's landscape throbs with life.

The **Giardino di Kolymbetra** ⑲ (www.fondoambiente.it/luoghi/giardino-della-kolymbethra; daily Mar–Apr, Oct 9.30am–5.30pm, May–June, Sept until 6.30pm, July–Aug until 7.30pm, Feb and Nov–Dec 10am–2pm) is the latest addition to the Valley of the Temples. This restored Greek garden, sandwiched between the Tempio di Castore e Polluce and the Tempio di Vulcano, began life as a vast pool, hence the name "*kolymbetra*" – Greek for pool. It was used for sacred rites and, conveniently, as a fish farm and irrigation system.

In the 3rd century BC the conquering Carthaginians buried it but created gardens instead, using sophisticated underground irrigation systems that still work perfectly. The Arabs cultivated sugar cane here, but today's gardens are an enchanting mix of orchards, citrus groves and evocative ruins.

Giardino di Kolymbetra.

Caltabellotta.

AGRIGENTO PROVINCE

This enigmatic province embraces everything from earthquake-struck towns to spectacular hilltop villages, from mineral spas and coastal forts to distant Moorish islands.

People from Agrigento are a mysterious breed, often referred to as *né carne né pesce*, neither fish nor fowl. Yet this elusive province has produced exceptional Sicilians: Empedocles, the pre-Socratic philosopher; Pirandello, the playwright; and Sciascia, the political novelist. All were gifted mavericks who shared a bitter-sweet relationship with their homeland. Empedocles committed suicide on Etna. Pirandello was the master of split personalities. Sciascia called his land a "wicked stepmother" yet rarely left, except to visit Paris.

Outside the capital, Agrigento is barely touched by tourism. There are no obvious sights in this low-key province. Instead, there are myriad chance discoveries of a lesser order: distinctive hilltop towns; deserted classical sites; coastal fortresses; remnants of former feudal estates; Arab-Norman ports; prosperous vineyards.

But weighed against this are: shabby towns; suburban sprawl; neglected fields; and the scars left by disused sulphur mines. Agrigento's additional drawbacks are extreme poverty, the lingering grip of the Mafia, and a torpor conditioned by centuries of failure. The province's insularity and lassitude make few concessions to visitors' demands for decent service, charming hotels and reliable roads.

Off to market on Lampedusa.

That said, the roads are improving, as is the wine around Menfi, while the opening of the luxurious Verdura Golf and Spa Resort has brought a glimmer of hope to the region.

AN EASTERN FORAY

The route into the hinterland east of Agrigento passes rugged hilltop towns of Arab origin which were fortified during the Muslim conquest and later. Many of these were sulphur-mining centres until the early 20th century and, despite a slight agricultural

Main attractions
Naro
The Leopard Literary Trail
Eraclea Minoa
Sciacca
Caltabellotta
Linosa

Map on page 134

revival or diversification into wine, have yet to recover from the collapse of the traditional industry.

Leaving **Agrigento** ❶ in the direction of Caltanissetta, follow the SS122 through the rolling countryside to **Favara**, a former sulphur centre, with a dilapidated Chiaramonte castle (rebuilt in 1488 from an original 1275 castle), two 16th-century churches, the **Purgatorio** and the **Rosario**, and an elegantly Baroque main square.

From here, choose the hilly road east to the neighbouring medieval hilltop town of **Naro** ❷, an important market town. It is an appealing place, with battlement walls (c.1265) enclosing a late 13th-century Chiaramonte castle and some impressive Baroque mansions.

PALMA DI MONTECHIARO

Follow the SS410 south to the sea: the rewarding 17km (11-mile) drive lined with olive trees and vineyards leads to **Palma di Montechiaro** ❸ with panoramic views over the coast. The town may strike a romantic chord with readers of Lampedusa's novel, Il

Gattopardo (The Leopard). It was established in 1637 by the Prince of Lampedusa, an ancestor of Giuseppe Tomasi di Lampedusa (1896–1957), who used much of the life in this town as his inspiration for the novel (his only one) which he wrote shortly before he died. The action takes place in Sicily in 1860 as the kingdom of Naples and Sicily is brought to an end by Garibaldi and his army invading Sicily in order to forge a united Italy.

Today, however, the town of Palma di Montechiaro conjures up a catalogue of Sicilian ills: Mafia intervention, disturbing images of poverty, unemployment, public indifference, despair and dogs. The once splendid late 17th-century **Palazzo Ducale** is crumbling and the town's only dusty glory is the **Chiesa Madre**, built above imposing steps between 1666 and 1703, decaying under the weight of civic inertia. To qualify for funding, the church steps must be restored in the same stone as before. However, the original quarry is closed, so Sicilian bureaucracy decrees that renovation is impossible.

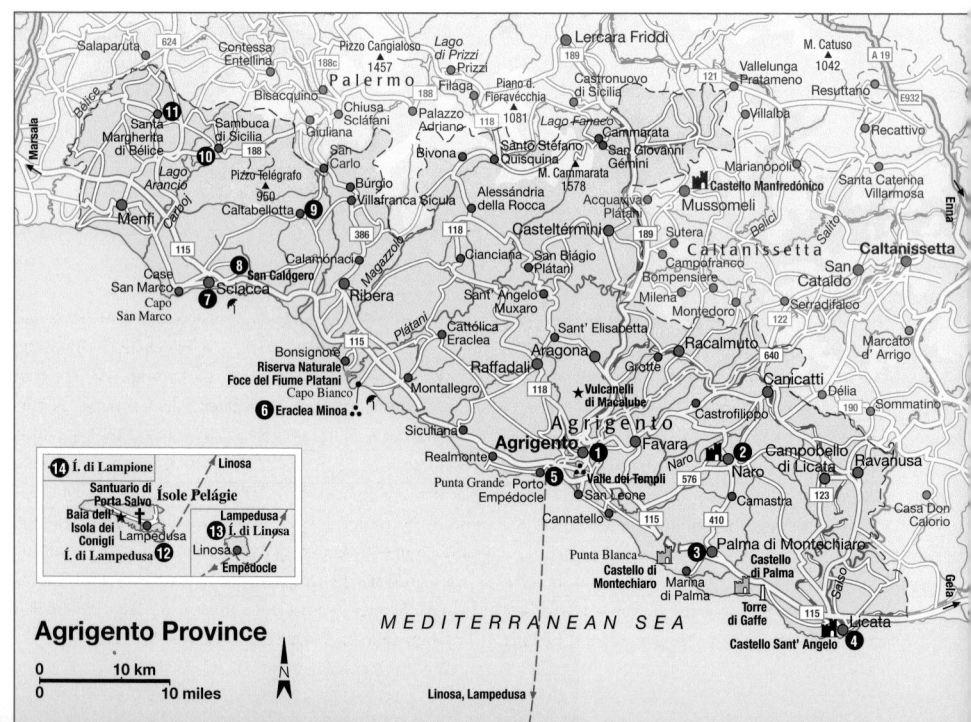

Agrigento Province

0   10 km
0   10 miles

About 4km (2.5 miles) south, the coastal road ends in the fishing port of **Marina di Palma**. From here, the S115 leads back to Agrigento. However, castle aficionados can follow the same road east to see the remains of a string of fortifications along the coast, notably the striking **Castello di Palma** and, just east, **Torre di Gaffe**.

Further east lies downtrodden **Licata ❹**, a working port that witnessed the Allied invasion in 1943. Licata also has a 16th-century castello, layers of palazzi, the 17th-century convent of **San Francesco** that is now a school, and a 17th-century church dedicated to **San Domenico**. The **Museo Archeologico** (Tue–Sat 9am–1pm, Tue and Thu also 4–6pm; free) has prehistoric and Greek period relics.

THE SOUTHWESTERN COAST

Just outside Agrigento city, the hamlet of **Caos** on the Porto Empédocle road is where Luigi Pirandello, one of Italy's greatest and most wide-ranging writers, was born in 1867. The irony of the village name was not wasted on Pirandello, who called himself a "son of chaos" (see box).

The traditional farmhouse in which the "master of the absurd" was born is now a small but pleasing museum (Tue–Sun 9am–7pm). In 1936, in accordance with his wishes, the playwright's ashes were buried in the countryside (access to the tomb 9am–one hour before sunset). Although this once idyllic spot now overlooks industrial sprawl, Pirandello, whose life was a lesson in defeat snatched from the jaws of victory, would have appreciated his posthumous fall from grace.

Just 7km (4.5 miles) south of Agrigento is **San Leone**, the city's pleasant but unexceptional seaside resort, which was a humble fishing village until the 1960s, and **Porto Empédocle ❺**, just west of San Leone, an unmitigated black spot, despite its illustrious past. The port authorities quarried the classical site for stone to build its harbour walls and, it would seem, in revenge the temple gods cursed it with ugliness. The benighted city can be avoided

⊘ **Fact**

Family loyalty extends to the village as a whole, especially when villagers face outsiders. It's not unusual to hear people refer to themselves first as members of a village – Sciaccatani, Caltabellotesi – and only then as Sicilians.

⊘ ON THE TRAIL OF THE LEOPARD

Giuseppe Tomasi di Lampedusa was a Palermitan prince born into a life of leisure in 1896, at his happiest ensconced in a café with a good book. In his own words he "was a boy who liked solitude, who preferred the company of things to that of people". Yet out of such glorious self-indulgence came The Leopard, an elegy to aristocratic Sicily, a complex novel covering immutability and nostalgia. Both a great aristocrat and discerning critic of his own class, he lost his first family palace in an Allied bombing raid in 1943.

In Palermo, follow in the prince's footsteps by passing **Palazzo Lanza Tomasi** (Via Butera 28), his last home, overlooking the sea. This was where the prince moved after losing his family home in the bombings, where he died in 1957, and where you can stay. You can even enrol in a cookery course organised by his daughter-in-law, the Duchess of Palma, which includes a morning trip to the Capo food market, a four-course lunch followed by a guided tour of the palace.

Cross lovely Piazza Marina towards the Teatro Massimo, stopping en route at the glorious Baroque **Oratorio di Santa Cita**, beside the ruins of the prince's first palazzo.

East of the Teatro Massimo, at Via Generale Magliocco 19, used to stand **Pasticceria Mazzara**, where The Leopard was largely written; sadly the patisserie has closed down.

Diehard Leopard fans can visit the prince's fictional summer palace, Donnafugata, inspired by his beloved ancestral palazzo in **Santa Margherita di Bélice**. Although ravaged by an earthquake in 1968, the palace shell has been restored. Even so, the family museum is overshadowed by the peaceful gardens and an overwhelming sense of pathos, typified by the melancholic cryptomeria trees which somehow survived the earthquake. The trail then takes in **Palma di Montechiaro**, the Lampedusas' feudal hilltop town, tarnished by urban sprawl yet redeemed by a Leopard-like twist – a taste of the almond cakes made by the local nuns – which sent the fictional prince into raptures. To appreciate the Leopard trail, book a tour through the Lampedusa Literary Park (tel: 091 625 4011, www.parcotomasi.it) or visit Lampedusa's palace in Palermo, Palazzo Lanza Tomasi (groups only, or stay overnight, or book a cookery course, 039 333 316 5432, www.butera28.it).

unless you are taking a ferry trip to the remote **Isole Pelágie**.

Fortunately, the SS115 soon passes through sparsely populated countryside leading to the province's most delightful, but isolated, classical site. En route are views of the coast, which borders a fertile valley and overlooks neat orange plantations and smoothly contoured fields.

ERACLEA MINOA

The classical site of **Eraclea Minoa** ❻ (daily Mar–Oct 9am–7.30pm, Nov–Feb 9am–4.30pm) squats on bleached soil alongside olive-covered slopes at the mouth of the River Platani. As one looks down from this idyllic headland, there is a view over the white cliffs of **Capo Bianco** encompassing a crescent of golden sands and pine groves. Eraclea was a satellite of Selinunte, but suffered a grim fate at the hands of the Carthaginians when it was depopulated and became a no-man's-land in Greek and Punic territorial disputes. The name Minoa suggests a Minoan settlement and evokes the legend of King Minos of Crete who pursued Daedalus from Crete to Sicily, but the connection is tenuous.

While the site is delightful and the atmosphere therapeutic, the excavations have been laborious and the results far from spectacular. So far, Eraclea has revealed substantial city walls, a Hellenistic theatre (4 BC), a necropolis and ruined villas dating from Greek and Punic times. Concerts and productions of classical drama take place in July and August (tel: 0922 846 005).

SCIACCA

Further along the coast is **Sciacca** ❼, a working fishing port and spa town with a population of nearly 41,000, many of Arab descent. The town was evangelised by San Calógero and prospered in Arab times thanks to its location, midway between Mazara and Agrigento. Its name derives from the Arabic *As-saqah* meaning "cleft" – a reference to the caves of Mount Kronion, whose thermal springs were to make the area an important spa. In the 16th century Sciacca was torn apart by two warring families, the

The coast at Eraclea Minoa.

Norman Perollo and the Catalan Luna, and it suffered a gradual decline until the revival of the port and mineral spa, aided by an injection of Mafia funds and its close links with North Africa.

Sciacca lacks great architecture, but some exhilarating sea views and an engaging ensemble of tawny, weather-beaten buildings justify a visit.

Corso Vittorio Emanuele, the main street, has sumptuous palazzi from all periods, including **Palazzo Steripinto** (1501), with its crenellated facade of diamond-shaped design, a rusticated style borrowed from Neapolitan architecture.

The terrace of **Piazza Scandaliato** is the bustling Baroque centre of both the town and the Corso. Its scenic balcony is perfect for drinking in the views of the sea over an *aperitivo*. On summer evenings, the square usually belongs to Tunisian hawkers selling exotic clothes and local ceramics.

The **Duomo** (daily 8am–noon and 4–7.30pm) presents a confused image, with Arab-Norman apses buried in a Baroque facade. It was built in 1656, replacing a church erected in 1108. It has considerable charm, as well as statues by Antonino and Gian Domenico Gagini.

Set in the neighbouring Palazzo Scaglione, the **Museo Scaglione** (daily 9am–1pm and 4–8pm) houses a quirky private collection of paintings, ceramics, sculpture and a much-admired 18th-century crucifix.

From Piazza Scandaliato, steps lead down to the port and numerous fish restaurants. After the slightly oppressive hinterland, visitors tend to appreciate this forthright, living town, noted for its sandy beaches, spa waters and seafood platters.

Sciacca's churches embrace all periods and styles. **San Calógero** and **San Domenico** are sober Baroque works, while the **Convento di San Francesco** combines clean lines with Moorish cloisters. The **Chiesa del Carmine** is a Norman abbey with a Gothic rose window and half-hearted Baroque restoration. Facing is a sculpted medieval gate and the Gothic portal of **Santa Margherita**.

Ceramic shop in Sciacca.

Sciacca city gate.

⊘ LUIGI PIRANDELLO

The playwright and novelist, born in Caos in 1867, won the Nobel Prize for Literature in 1934, two years before his death. His influence on European drama challenged the conventions of the day in their naturalism, personal relationships, disillusionment and reality, and his play *Sei Personaggi in Cerca di Autore (Six Characters in Search of an Author)*, written in 1921, is still in constant repertory around the world. His writings anticipated the works of Brecht, Beckett and O'Neill. His novel *L'Esclusa (The Outcast)* broke all society's rules when published in 1901, as it concerned a woman's desire for independence in Sicily's patriarchal society. Learn more about the life and work of the famous author at his home (Casa di Pirandello).

Basilica Santa Maria del Soccorso in Sciacca.

Filippo Bentivegna's heads carved from lava.

To the east is the ruined Romanesque **San Nicolò** church which contrasts with **Santa Maria della Giummare**, a Catalan Gothic church with crenellated Norman towers and a Baroque interior. Just within the walls is the Badia Grande, an impressive 14th-century abbey.

Set among almond and olive groves just 2km (1.25 miles) outside Sciacca, **Castello Bentivegna** (daily 9am–1pm and 4–8pm) is also called the "enchanted castle". It is a folly in stone created by a peasant sculptor, a forest of statues that is the work of one man. In 1946, after great personal tragedy, Filippo Bentivegna returned from the United States and bought a patch of land in his native town. Using the rocks at the foot of Monte Kronio as his material, he sculpted 3,000 primitive heads of devils, politicians and knights. Not content with his work above ground, the sculptor set about carving heads from olive wood and creating frescoed caverns in the mountain. Bentivegna died in 1967.

SPA CENTRES

Sciacca is also a noted spa centre with thermal spas close to town. Known to the Romans as Thermae Selinuntinae, the **Terme**, the Sciacca thermal spa (www.termesciaccaspa.it) is open from April to November. Used since prehistoric times and praised by Pliny, the spa's mud baths and volcanic vapours occupy a grand Art Nouveau establishment that proposes cures for rheumatic and respiratory conditions.

Just north is the **San Calógero** ⑧ spa on Monte Kronio that harnesses the powers of a "mini" volcano, with bubbling hot springs and vapour-drenched grottoes used as saunas. The galleries, seats and water channels were hollowed out in ancient times by the Sicani or, according to the myth-makers, by Daedalus. The place takes its name from the patron saint of the harvest.

Outside town is the famous **Verdura Golf and Spa Resort**, whose destination spa is helping to kickstart tourism in the province.

⊘ LEONARDO SCIASCIA

Sciascia (1921–89), born at Racalmuto, remained emotionally tied to Sicily all his life and said he had never left the island for more than three months (then generally to Paris). He was an intellectual and one of the greatest Italian writers of the 20th century, and his novels were infused with Sicilian life that revolved around the sulphur mines and the farms. His most famous novels include *Il Giorno della Civetta* (*The Day of the Owl*, 1961) and *A Ciascuno il Suo* (*To Each his Own*, 1966). In *The Moro Affair* he tackled the murky world of Italian politics in the 1970s and the murder of the former Italian prime minister by the Red Brigades. A Communist Party member of Palermo City Council, he later became a member of the European Parliament.

THE RUGGED WEST

From Sciacca, a circular route and winding road leads 20km (12 miles) inland, up to the mysterious mountain village of **Caltabellotta** , the height of this rural route, with its cluster of towers, churches, grey roofs and a population of 3,600. The commanding village is spectacular, whether seen through spring blossom or swathed in mist. On the highest level, below the hulk of the ruined castle, is the restored Norman **Chiesa Madre** with its original portal and pointed arches. In the level underneath is the lopsided **Piazza Umberto** and the handsome **Chiesa del Carmine**, which has also been restored. Below stretch shadowy mountain views from the spacious **Belvedere** and the white **Chiesa San Agostino**. The peace that brought the Sicilian Vespers to an end in 1302 was signed here. On the edge of the village lies the **Eremo di San Pellegrino**, an abandoned hermitage with stupendous views of a mountainside studded with necropoli. Legend has it that a dragon lived here which feasted on young maidens until it was killed by the saint.

Northwest of Caltabellotta, but linked by circuitous country roads, is **Sambuca di Sicilia** , an Arab-Norman town with its old centre near Piazza Navarro showing its Islamic antecedents. There is also a popular lake and facilities for watersports and barbecues. Amateur archaeologists are drawn to the neighbouring **Zona Archeologica di Monte Adranone**, (Mon–Sat 9am–4.30pm, first Sun of the month only 9am–1pm), where the remains of a Greek colony have recently come to light, as well as huts and burial chambers from an Iron Age village.

SANTA MARGHERITA DI BÉLICE

Further west still is **Santa Margherita di Bélice** , inextricably linked with *The Leopard*. In the novel, the fictional town of Donnafugata includes existing and easily recognisable places, including the **Palazzo Filangieri Cutò**, which belonged to the family of Lampedusa's mother. According to the information contained in a letter he wrote to his friend Baron Enrico di Merlo Tagliavia, "The palace at Donnafugata is one and the same as the one at Santa Margherita, while for the town as a whole, the reference is to Palma Montechiaro".

In recent times Santa Margherita has become better known as the epicentre of the earthquake zone. Between here and the coast lies **Menfi**, another earthquake-damaged town, and a centre for the province's winemaking.

ISOLE PELÁGIE

This remote, sun-baked archipelago of three islands lies amid strong currents off the North African coast, closer to Tunisia's Cap Bon than the Sicilian mainland. Although there are pockets of agriculture, the islands are unnaturally barren due to wanton deforestation, neglect, water shortages and strong winds that

Local life, Caltabellotta.

Collapsed volcanic crater in the small island of Linosa.

Swimming in a cove on Lampedusa.

have caused a virtual disappearance of the native olive groves and carob plantations. Fifty years ago, much of this lunar landscape was farmland bounded by dry-stone walls, but today the economy rests on sponge fishing, canning and tourism.

There are no outstanding cultural sites, but the translucent waters are as appealing as the local couscous. The rugged native character and cuisine are distinctly Tunisian, as are the Moorish *dammusi* houses.

LAMPEDUSA AND LINOSA

Due to its location, **Lampedusa** ⓬ used to be known as "a gift from Africa to Europe" but is now dubbed "the backdoor into Italy". The normal population of Sicilians and weather-beaten Tunisian fishermen has been usurped by waves of refugees from North Africa. Since the Arab Spring revolutions in 2011 and, more recently, the Syrian conflict, boatloads of illegal immigrants have overwhelmed the island, and crushed tourism for the immediate future.

Lampedusa port, with its ferry service to Porto Empédocle and Linosa, contains a rabbit warren of a kasbah that reeks of spices, sardines and anchovies. Indeed, the port is the best place for sampling pasta with sardines, sweet-and-sour rabbit or Sicilian candied fruit and spicy desserts.

Buses from the port are infrequent so, despite the rocky roads, bicycles and mopeds are a popular way of exploring the interior. At the centre of the island is the **Santuario di Porto Salvo**, a church in a lush garden surrounded by grottoes once inhabited by Saracen pirates.

A boat trip is the best way of appreciating Lampedusa's secluded grottoes, craggy inlets and sheer limestone cliffs. The island of Conigli, just offshore, is a nature reserve with the **Baia dell' Isola dei Conigli** (Bay of the Island of Rabbits), the island's greatest attraction.

Linosa ⓭ (pop. a little over 430) is the island closest to Sicily and can be reached on a day trip from Lampedusa, 42km (26 miles) to the north, as can uninhabited Lampione. Linosa, formed by the tips of three vast submerged volcanoes, is popular with scuba divers and sunbathers.

There is little to do here except rest, roast, swim, hike along dusty paths through vineyards or spot *dammusi*, the pastel-coloured cube-like houses with white window frames. These traditional Arab houses date back to designs created by the first Tunisian settlers. The domed roofs are designed to keep the interior cool.

About two hours by boat from Lampedusa, **Lampione** ⓮ is an uninhabited island, with a modest area of just 1.5 sq km (370 acres), scorched dry thanks to man's negligence. Its drama lies underwater: the translucent sea is unpolluted and rich in marine life, from sponge beds to basking sharks. Sicilian pleasures are notoriously double-edged.

📷 FESTIVALS SACRED AND PROFANE

Christianity and paganism, classical myth and memory, folklore and food, magic and music all combine in Sicily's frequent and fervent celebrations.

Many Sicilian festivals mark a historical event with an overlay of religious worship. Palermo's **Festa di Santa Rosalia** celebrates the saint reputedly saving the city from the plague in 1624 with a mixture of prayer and wild festivities. Similarly, Catania's **Festa di Sant'Agata** combines prayers, and processions with pastries made to honour the patron saint.

Other Catholic *feste* have pagan elements lurking just beneath the surface. Thus **Carnevale** (literally "farewell to meat") marks the beginning of Lent and a period of abstinence, but is celebrated in many places with a licentious abandon that echoes the ancient Saturnalia.

Easter *(Pasqua)* is the dominant Christian festival, but is celebrated in a variety of forms: processions of floats and *tableaux vivants* or holy relics, re-enactments of the Passion by chosen citizens, respects paid to the *Addolorata* (Our Lady of the Sorrows).

Celebrating the festival of Saint Agata, patron saint of Catania, who is believed to have saved the city from Mount Etna's lava.

On Easter Sunday in Prizzi, the Dance of the Devils (Abballu de li diavoli) has devils in grotesque masks tr to prevent the Madonna meeting the resurrected Chri It's a dramatic reworking of the Christian story, but al an unconscious echo of Lupercalia, a distinctly demo pre-Christian festival.

The Sagra del Mandorlo in Fiore, a celebration of spring with folk danci and music, takes place every year in the Valley of the Temples in Agrige

Fireworks in Trápani celebrate Easter.

Secular Celebrations

Not all Sicily's *feste* have a religious basis. Historical events are commemorated with equal gusto, including the Piazza Armerina's medieval pageant, the Palio dei Normanni, when the exploits of Roger II are recalled with flag-waving and jousting, Norman-style.

The first signs of spring are excuse enough for a festival in Agrigento, where, in February, the Sagra del Mandorlo in Fiore celebrates the almond blossom in the Valley of the Temples.

On the west coast, near Erice, San Vito lo Capo's September Couscous Festival is a multi-ethnic party where chefs from around the world compete to make the best couscous.

In the southeast, the most captivating autumn festivals are Módica's Chocobarocco chocolate extravaganza and the Ibla Buskers Festival, when Ragusa's atmospheric old town is taken over by jugglers, fire-eaters, magicians and mime artists.

...at featuring giant figures takes part in a carnival in ...cca. Thousands of people follow the procession which ... with the burning of the characters.

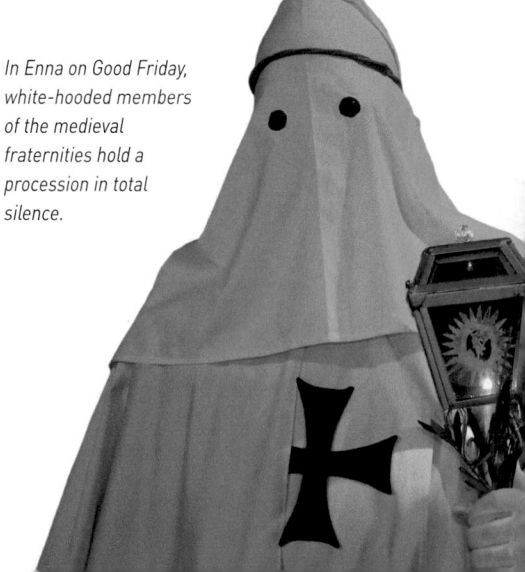

In Enna on Good Friday, white-hooded members of the medieval fraternities hold a procession in total silence.

CALTANISSETTA PROVINCE

At the heart of Sicily's west, this dramatic, often wild, landscape is a beguiling place with its craggy scenery, traditional customs and Mafia lore.

⊙ Main attractions
Abbazia di Santo Spirito
Wine-tasting on the
  Regaleali estate
Castello Manfredónico
Butera
Gela Archaeological
  Museum (Museo
  Archeologico)
Gela Greek Walls
Falconara

Map on page 146

The province of Caltanissetta is a place of subtle moods rather than specific sights. Although from the hilltop villages there are spectacular views of mountain ridges and purple canyons, abandoned farms and ruined Norman castles, the province is sparsely populated and the visitor is often alone with this beguiling scenery.

"This is ancient Sicily, the land of *latifundia* (feudal estates), sulphur mines, hunger and insecurity," wrote the French writer Dominique Fernandez, relishing the feeling o its desolation and lawlessness.

Caltanissetta occupies a centra position on a sulphur-bearing plain its yellowish soil scarred with dis used mines. Yet the province is fa from uniform. There is a differenc in character between the siege men tality of the bleak hilltop towns an the more accessible Greek flavour o Gela's coastal plains. This is a prov ince that feels betrayed by recen history: just as the sulphur mine brought hardship and a high mortal ity rate to the hinterland, so coasta industrialisation brought pollutio but not prosperity, and mass emi gration brought depopulation an despair. Although not the most pov erty-stricken province, Caltanissett is arguably the most aggrieved.

PROVINCIAL CAPITAL

Caltanissetta ❶, the provincia capital, is a harsh summation o the region's struggle for survival Its name reflects its cosmopolita past: Arab conquerors added th prefix *kalat* (Arab for castle) to th name *an-nisa*, meaning ladies. Th first documented reference to th city is dated 1086 when Conte Rug gero (Roger the Norman) took th region under the jurisdiction of th Catholic Church, conquered the for

Butera.

f Pietrarossa and established the bbey of Santo Spirito. As befits an ncient bastion on hilly ground, it s a closed city, its defences raised gainst outsiders.

Modern war damage means that nedieval monuments are restricted o the outskirts, along with the origial Greek settlements. Nonetheless, altanissetta is no mere market town ut the agricultural heart of Sicily's nterior, with grain and cotton long rown in the countryside. As the hisprical hub of Sicilian mining operaons, the city fell into decline in the 960s with the collapse of the sulhur industry. Potassium and magesium mining have now supplanted ulphur and the city has achieved nodest prosperity. Still, life here emains tough.

¶AFIA LORE

s the headquarters of the crimial justice courts, Caltanissetta is ntrusted with trying controversial ¶afia cases. Ironically, the province s itself tainted by Mafia association,

while local citizens have been reluctant to express the resurgence in civic values that characterises optimistic new Sicily.

In 1992, despite public dismay, the town was entrusted with the investigation into the murder of Judge Falcone, his wife and bodyguards (see page 43). Much to the astonishment of American FBI agents cooperating on the case, Caltanissetta magistrates hoped to compete with the Mafia without access to a computer. Despite its presumed probity, the city's magistrates court remains Sicily's most understaffed and overworked. Cynics may say that this is intentional, giving *mafiosi* suspects a head start.

CITY SIGHTS

Caltanissetta's heart, in so far as it has one, lies in Piazza Garibaldi. Here, the Baroque **Duomo** (1570–1622), flanked by bell towers, overlooks the ugly neo-Romanesque church of **San Sebastiano**, the Baroque Town Hall and a bronze

Easter fireworks in Caltanissetta.

⊘ THE SULPHUR MINES

At the height of demand for sulphur in the 19th century, more than two-thirds of all of Sicily's production came from sulphur mines in the Caltanissetta region. But aggressively marketed production from the United States destroyed its competitiveness and by 1945 the industry had effectively collapsed, causing widespread emigration. Today it is possible to visit a number of mines and see the long corridors where the dangerous extraction and processing were carried out. Many of the workers sent to the narrowest and deepest shafts were boys under 15. There are sites at Delia, Montedoro, Sommatino, Riesi and San Cataldo, but the region is putting its faith in the creation of new mining museums to attract more visitors.

A statue of Umberto I stands in front of the late Renaissance church of St Agatha, Caltanissetta.

statue of Neptune. The cathedral interior is an engaging explosion of kitsch, highlighted by sugary ceiling paintings by Wilhelm Borremans (1720) the Flemish painter. A triumphal angel and cherubs adorn a gaudy glass and gold coffin, a Sicilian disguise for a rotting corpse.

Behind the Town Hall, Via Palazzo Paterno leads to the nicely restored **Palazzo Moncada**. This was the home of the Moncada dynasty, the feudal rulers of the region from 1406 onwards. The Baroque mansion, emblazoned with snarling lions posing as gargoyles, now houses temporary exhibitions, a theatre and a cinema (www. moncadamultisala.com).

Corso Umberto, the main street, is lined with dark buildings and scruffy bars where wizened men drink Amaro, a reminder that Caltanissetta is the main producer of this famous *digestivo*.

AROUND THE CAPITAL

Fortunately, the disappointing provincial capital is a stone's throw from several significant medieval or prehistoric sites. **Santa Maria degl Angeli**, on the city's eastern outskirts, is a Norman church with richly carved Gothic porch. Almost next door is the stump of **Castell di Pietrarossa**, perched on a jagge spur, an Arab-Norman castle tosse into a pitiful heap by the 1567 earth quake. Further east, the **Abbazia d Santo Spirito**, established by Kin Roger I in 1153, is the region's fines Norman church. Commonly know as the Badia, this severe structur is reasonably well kept and house the **Museo Archeologico** (daily 9am 1pm, 3.30–7pm). On display here ar prehistoric and Greek remains from the area, including rock tombs, Atti vases, painted urns, and the earlies Bronze Age figures found in Sicily.

On the flanks of **Monte Sabbucin** lies a significant prehistoric necropo lis, even if the best finds are now i Caltanissetta's Museo Archeologico Take the SS122 road from Caltanis setta to Enna, leaving town throug the barren Terra Pilata. The roa crosses the Salso river at **Pont**

Caltanissetta Province

0   10 km
0   10 miles

MEDITERRANEAN SEA

apodarso, a delicate 16th-century Venetian bridge: 6km (4 miles) along the Enna road, a scenic route is marked to the archaeological park of Sabbucina ❷ (by appointment only: opricl@regione.sicilia.it; free). This Bronze Age settlement was later occupied by Hellenised Siculi (Sicel) tribes, who flourished here from the 6th to the 4th centuries BC. The Sicels lived within a square-towered fortress, parts of which survive.

THE WILD WEST

A sweeping circular route west passes a series of shabby but atmospheric hill towns. As for the fortresses, although feuding barons once inhabited these lofty strongholds, depopulation and desolation have turned many into virtual ghost towns. From such windswept eyries stretch views of ravines and deserted plains, sulphurous hills and abandoned mines.

Santa Caterina Villarmosa ❸, 20km (12 miles) north of Caltanissetta along the SS122 bis, is worth a cursory glance if you are interested in looking at lace and delicate embroidery, the town's main claim to fame.

Villalba ❹, about 35km (22 miles) west, just off the SS121, is a notoriously down-at-heel Mafia haunt, once held by Don Calógero Vizzini. Vizzini was the main Mafia boss from 1942 until his death in 1954, and as mayor he ran this scruffy town like a private fiefdom. His tombstone in Villalba cemetery laments the death of a gentleman and praises his Robin Hood status as a defender of the weak.

Even before the rise of the Mafia, Villalba was doomed to be milked by absentee landlords whose revenues from the production of wine and grain here provided them with a noble lifestyle in Palermo.

The local **Regaleali wine estates**, produced by Count Tasca d'Almerita, are heirs to this feudal system, but the dynasty can also take credit for not sitting on its laurels. Regaleali wines regularly outshine ones produced by Donnafugata and other reputable estates. Wine-tasting sessions and

Castello di Pietrarossa.

The castle at Mussomeli, a former Mafia stronghold.

traditional cookery courses are run on the estate (see box).

More than most surrounding market towns, **Mussomeli 5**, 20km (12 miles) south of Villalba, has suffered from Mafia mythology and emigration. New York received some of Mussomeli's finest Mafia members in the 1960s.

CASTELLO MANFREDÓNICO

Just east of town, on the Villalba road, stands **Castello Manfredónico**, named after Manfredi Chiaramonte, Frederick II's son, killed defending his kingdom against Charles of Anjou. Set on an impregnable crag, the lopsided castle blends into the rock. From the fortress are vertiginous views over the desolate valley below.

The country road zigzags south for 13km (8 miles) to **Sutera 6**, the first of several ragged towns set on rocky outcrops in old mining country around Caltanissetta. Beyond a series of acrobatic bends lies Sutera's shadow, **Bompensiere 7**. (From Sutera, follow the SS189 south for 4km/2.5 miles before taking the rural road east

towards Caltanissetta.) **Serradifalco 8**, 15km (9 miles) east, is another neglected hilltop town, linked across a ridge to Villalba. **San Cataldo 9**, nestling in wooded hills to the east, was once the administrative heart of a great agricultural estate, but is today noted for its crafts, especially terracotta pots and wrought ironwork. Nearby is the archaeological site of **Vassallaggi** (by appointment only: sopricl@regione.sicilia.it; free), where there are traces of Greek settlement.

SOUTH TO THE COAST

Sinuous upland roads link the craggy countryside with the Gela plains to the south. The higher peaks are covered in mountainous vegetation, but the wooded slopes soon give way to olives and almonds. The journey passes sleepy towns with populations reduced by emigration. They share a battered rural economy and dignified poverty. **Sommatino**, **Riesi** and **Niscemi** are typical of such spots, though the ruined castle at **Délia 10** helps distinguish it from its neighbours.

From Caltanissetta, the SS626 ridges the rugged hinterland and the coastal plains towards Gela. **Mazzarino 11** lies 10km (6 miles) east of the main thoroughfare, reached along the SS190. The town's modest reputation rests on Mafia lore and a ruined castle. Founded by the princes of Butera, the castle retains its original keep and some defensive walls.

Ragged palazzi and a couple of undervalued churches add to the atmosphere of gentle nostalgia. **Chiesa San Domenico** contains a touching Madonna by Paladino, while **Chiesa dei Carmelitani** houses an 18th-century marble tabernacle encrusted with ivory, ebony, coral and tortoiseshell.

BUTERA

Butera 12, a crumbling hill village perched on a chalky crest 18km (11 miles) south, is the most attractive in the province. The fief prospered under Spanish rule, held by the Branciforte family, the princes of Butera. Although currently closed, the battlemented 11th-century castle is fairly well preserved, with a powerful keep and mullioned windows. The **Chiesa Madre** has a Paladino Madonna and a Renaissance triptych. Nearby, the **Palazzo Comunale** (Town Hall) has an intricate 14th-century portal and panoramic views over the Gela plains to the coast.

Just east of Butera as the crow flies is **Lago di Disueri 13**, a dam with a late Bronze Age necropolis on its rocky shores.

Southeast of Butera, on the SS117 bis, the curious mound of **Il Castelluccio 14** presents a dramatic break in the fertile Gela plains. This tumbledown castle keep, jutting out of fields of artichokes and wheat, was built by the warlike Frederick II. Nearby is a modern **war memorial**, a reminder that these fields witnessed the Allied landing in Sicily in 1943. Il Castelluccio overlooks the fertile **Gela plain**, rich in grain, wine and olives as well as artichokes and oranges, lemons and cotton.

Gela 15, the gateway to this land of plenty, was an open invitation to the

Don Genco Russo, based in Mussomeli, was a Mafia capo di tutti capi after the death of Calógero Vizzini.

The keep at Butera.

Gela elders.

ancient Greeks, the first and most welcome wave of settlers. Devastation struck in 1943 when the Allies liberated Sicily and bombed Gela to smithereens. Unbridled industrialisation has been Gela's ultimate desecration, so only those with a passion for Greek archaeology will brave the polluted outskirts.

GELA'S GREEK TRAGEDY

Gela was renowned for its entrepreneurial spirit, inspired military architecture and artistic excellence. It became a Doric colony in 688 BC, settled by Greeks from Rhodes and Crete. However, the indigenous Sicani tribe transmuted the superior Greek culture into a unique shape. Exquisite coins, terracotta figurines, sculpted walls, and flourishing agriculture remain a testament to these times. From here, Hellenistic influence spread to the rest of Sicily. Yet Gela was sacked by the Carthaginians in 405 BC, a year after Agrigento's fall, and was eventually razed by the tyrant of Agrigento in 282 BC, who deported the entire

population. Since then, the ancient cit has been a symbol of an almost Gree Sicilian tragedy.

There is nothing between Gela' glorious Greek heritage and today' grim sprawl. Still it is worth sift ing through the industrial debri to reach the ancient city. The wall built by Timoleon, the good tyrant o Siracusa, are set amongst mimosa eucalyptus and pines; just beyon the sand dunes are futuristic dome and glittering pipes of modern powe generation.

The **Museo Archeologico** (Mon–Sa 9am–7pm), on Corso Vittorio Ema nuele, is built alongside the ancien **Molino a Vento** acropolis, with it recently excavated remains of Hellen istic houses open to inspection. Th museum itself displays painted Atti vases, coins, Ionic capitals and terra cotta sarcophagi. Gela terracotta wa renowned throughout Magna Graecia prized for its painted designs and th delicacy of the figurative work. Th star piece is a noble terracotta horse' head from the 6th century BC, part of

emple pediment. **Parco della Rimem-branza**, close by, is a park with a single Doric column, the remains of a temple to Athena.

CAPO SOPRANO

Outside the city, the 5th-century BC walls and the site of **Capo Soprano** (Mon–Sat 9am–1pm and 2–6pm; same ticket as for the Museo Archaeologico) are Gela's chief glory. Situated at the western end of town, on Viale Indipendenza, these romantic walls were covered by sand dunes, preserved in their full height and glory, until 1948 when excavation was begun. Running parallel with the sea, the battlemented ramparts were rebuilt by Timoleon after the Carthaginians razed the city. The thick walls are topped with angle towers and sentry posts, with the remains of barracks inside the northern sections. The **Greek baths**, the only ones to have survived in Sicily, date from the 4th century BC.

From here, you can turn east to Ragusa and Siracusa. West of Gela,

the sandy shore is littered with military pillboxes, relics of Gela's most recent defences and invasion.

FALCONARA

Falconara ⓖ, to the west, is a small resort with two appealing beaches, **Manfria** and **Roccazzelle**. The stretches of golden sands beckon invitingly. **Castello di Falconara** (www.castellodifalconara.it), the local castle, is set in lush grounds overlooking the sea. Built in sandy-coloured stone, the feudal castle has crenellations and a 14th-century keep. This atmospheric spot is used by Palermitan aristocrats for their summer residences.

If the oil-laden winds are blowing the wrong way, take the SS117 bus north across the plains, passing eucalyptus and cork plantations en route to Piazza Armerina and Roman Sicily.

These are Virgil's celebrated **Campi Geloi**, the plains in which the poet Aeschylus supposedly met his death (see margin). Archaeologists are still searching for the great tragedian's tomb.

Beach at Falconara.

Calascibetta.

ENNA PROVINCE

This elevated inland province possesses the island's greatest Roman villa and a succession of hill towns and strategic castles in its fertile landscape.

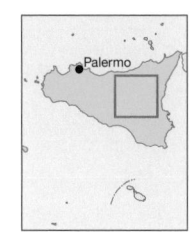

he desolate, sun-parched centre of icily is the only province without an utlet to the sea. Yet there is much o proclaim, from the Roman villa at Piazza Armerina, one of the wonders f the ancient world, to a hinterland tudded with hilltop towns and Norman astles. Around its historical sites is an gricultural province producing corn, lives, cheese, nuts and wine.

Enna **1**, known as Sicily's navel for ts central position 942 metres (3,090ft) bove the countryside, is sacred thanks o the cult of Demeter (the Olympian oddess of corn and sustainer of life) nd the myth of Persephone (Dem-ter's daughter by Zeus, carried off by Hades to be queen of the Underworld). Despite Persephone's gift of spring, Enna often feels cloaked in winter, hrouded above the plains in mist or lown by wintry gusts. However in ummer, while Sicily swelters, this levated position offers locals a refuge rom the heat.

CITY IN THE CLOUDS

Enna's sights are fairly compact, but f the mist falls, expect to cling to the ity walls between churches. Tradi-ion has it that the restored **cathedral** daily 9am–1pm, 4–7pm) was begun by leanor of Aragon in 1307, but a fire n 1446 swept away most of the treas-res. Nonetheless, the cathedral on

Inside Enna Cathedral.

Via Roma is a fascinating romp through Enna's mystical past. The elaborately carved white pulpit is encrusted with cherubs and rests on a Graeco-Roman base removed from a temple to Demeter, as does the marble stoup nearby. The quaint portico is matched by Gothic transepts and apses, while the wrought-iron sacristy gate once graced a Moorish harem in the **Castello di Lombardia**. There are works attributed to Paladino and the beloved 15th-century statue of the *Madonna della Visitazione* (the city's patron saint), which

Main attractions

Enna
Calascibetta
Sperlinga
Nicosia
Troina
Piazza Armerina
Villa Romana del Casale
Villa delle Meraviglie
Aidone
Morgantina

Maps on pages 154, 159

Tip

While in Enna, pay a visit to the nearby Floristella Grottacalda Mineral Park (www.enteparcofloristella.it), a geological open-air museum of 400 hectares (988 acres) covering the two abandoned sulphur mines of Floristella and Grottacalda.

is carried through the streets in procession on 2 July.

Enna's esoteric past would appear to make it susceptible to pagan magic. The black basalt base of the capitals incorporate sculptures of Hades and demonic symbols in an attempt to crush evil forces by fair means or foul. The adjoining **Museo Alessi** (currently closed) displays the contents of the cathedral's **treasury**, including the prized **Corona della Madonna** (Madonna's Crown), a sacred 17th-century enamelled diadem studded with precious stones.

Along bustling Via Roma lies a string of dignified mansions and churches, such as the Catalan-Gothic **Palazzo Pollicarini** and the Baroque **Chiesa San Benedetto**. Via Roma is pedestrianised for the evening *passeggiata* and contains a good *pasticceria* as well as cos restaurants. At the bottom are sweeping views from the belvedere and **Torre di Federico II**, a tumbledown octagonal tower built by Frederick II. The tower is linked by secret passageways to the **Castello di Lombardia** (daily 9am–8.30pm; free) at the top of the hill, in Piazzale Lombardia. As one of Sicily's largest medieval castles, this imposing fortress began as a draughty Byzantine keep but acquired towers with each wave of invaders, from the Normans to the Swabians. A series of three courtyards leads to the majestic eyrie of **Torre Pisano**, the tallest of the castle's six surviving towers, and views over the entire island.

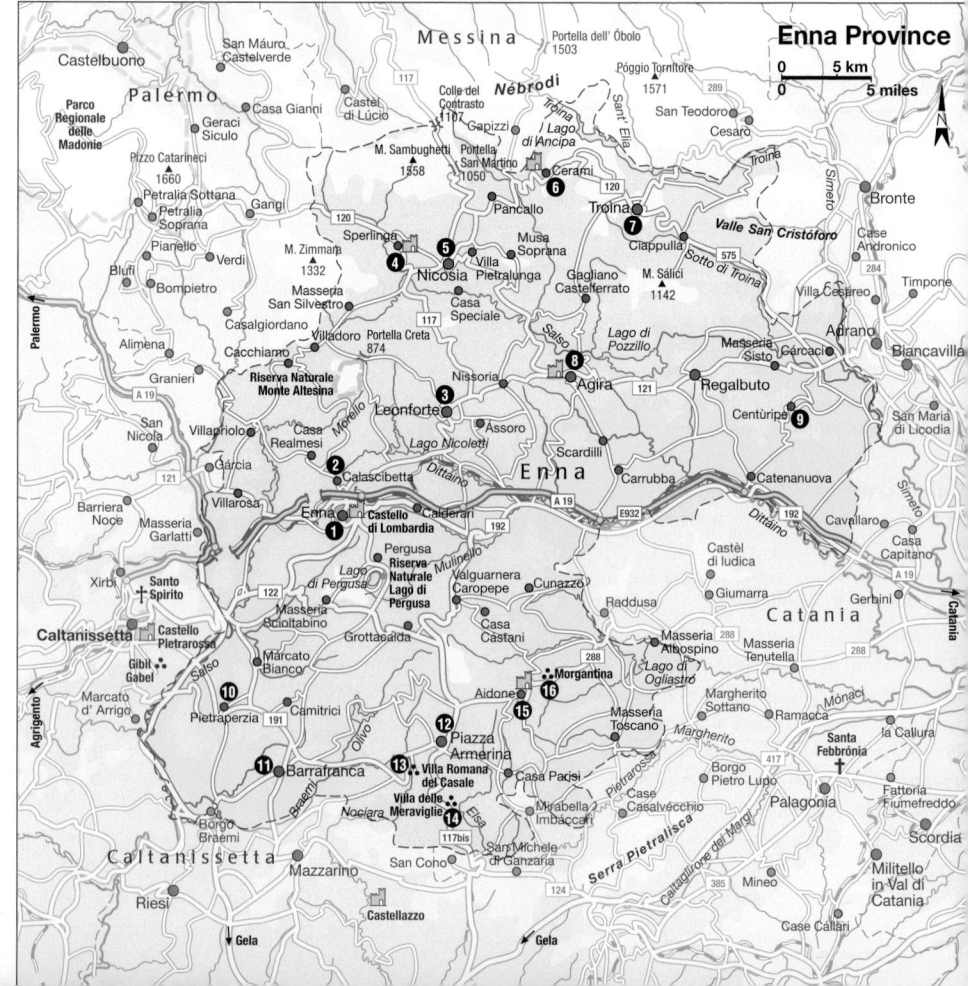

Just beyond the castle looms a mas-ive boulder on the tip of the plateau, the **Rocca di Cerere**, also known as the Tem-ple of Demeter. Legend has it that Deme-ter's daughter Persephone was abducted by Hades and swept off into **Lago di Per-gusa**, gateway to the Underworld.

CASTLES AND CITADELS

This circuitous route explores the cas-tle-studded landscape north of Enna. Facing the city is **Calascibetta ❷**, a decrepit but atmospheric hill village built by the Arabs while besieging Enna in 951. Rust-coloured buildings cling to the slopes, and the **Chiesa Madre** is perched on top of a blustery cliff.

From here, the SS121 winds north to **Leonforte ❸**, a 17th-century Bran-ciforte fiefdom best known for its col-ourful Good Friday procession and its **Granfonte**, a delightful fountain that is a testament to feudal largesse. Set on the edge of town, the graceful arched fountain fills troughs from 24 spouts.

Picturesque **Sperlinga ❹**, north of Leonforte, may well be Sicily's most intriguing castle, with battlemented Norman towers and bastions that reach to the bottom of the cliff. The castle (daily 10am–6pm) reopened in 2017 following a major landslide. Above ground, the village is a string of modest cottages; below the castle, the rock is riddled with chambers, a secret underground city. The rocky slopes are pitted with caves, some of which have been inhabited since Sicani times. The caves were occupied by Sperlinga's poorest peasants and their livestock until the 1980s (for more about the castle see page 99).

Nicosia ❺, 8km (5 miles) southeast of Sperlinga, is a charming medieval town set on four hills and ringed by rocky spurs. It has been a Greek city, Byzantine bishopric, Arab fort and Norman citadel. In the Middle Ages it was riven by religious rivalry between Roman Catholic newcomers from the north and the indigenous population who, in Byzantine tradition, followed the Greek Orthodox rite. After pitched battles, the matter was settled in favour of the natives.

The 14th-century **San Nicolò** tri-umphed as the city cathedral, with its 14th-century facade and lacy campanile. From the cathedral, which dominates the town, Salita Salamone climbs to **San Salvatore**, a Romanesque church that would look at home in Burgundy.

Piazza Garibaldi, the main square, is dotted with dingy bars and *circoli*, working men's clubs. Old men sit and chat in gallo-italico, a Lombard dialect stemming from northern settlers and shared with Aidone, Piazza Armerina and Sperlinga. Leading off Piazza Garibaldi are myriad *vicoli*, crooked alleys climbing Nicosia's hills. From here, the steep **Via Salamone** winds above the cathedral, passing dilapi-dated palazzi and convents encrusted with garlands or gargoyles. At the top is **Santa Maria Maggiore**, a Nor-man church rebuilt in Baroque style which faces a montage of bells that fell when the campanile came down in the last earthquake, in 1978. From the

⊘ Fact

Nicosia, isolated by the motorway, typifies the time-warp towns of the interior, where, between 1950 and 1970, half the adult population emigrated and have never returned.

View from Enna.

terrace, the tumbledown castle is visible, overgrown with cacti and thistles on a rocky spur.

The SS120, a meandering mountain road, leads 20km (12 miles) northeast to **Cerami** ❻, a jagged village dominated by a ruined castle. The wooded countryside is interspersed with orchards and lolling cattle.

Just north of the SS120 is the scenic **Lago di Ancipa**, a lake set in a lush wilderness. East of Nicosia are windswept views across the bleak Nebrodi mountains.

Further along the SS120 lies **Troìna** ❼, at 1,120 metres (3,674ft) the loftiest town in Sicily, which occupies an Arab-Norman stronghold on a solitary ridge. This citadel has declined into an austere hill town with a nest of churches crammed into winding medieval alleys. Tall, draughty convents look out over scruffy terraces and the makeshift houses of returning emigrants.

The grand Norman churches include the **Chiesa Matrice**, with its hulking bell tower, nave, crypt, tower and solid external walls. Inside, the fusty church has been revamped in Baroque style, complete with flaking gold leaf and late Byzantine art. Outside, an arched walk slopes under the bell tower and returns to the atmospheric Norman stronghold. On the belvedere, Troìna's youth gather to enjoy rugged windswept views over the distant blue-grey hills.

On the last Sunday in May, devotees gather to celebrate the **festa di San Silvestro**, patron saint of the village, wreathed in laurel leaves with processions and banquets.

AGIRA

Agira ❽, a tortuous 30km (19 miles) south of Troìna, is set on a hill surmounted by a Saracen castle and adorned with several fine churches, even if the designer shopping mall here is more of a magnet to young Sicilians. The slopes once housed a Siculi settlement but are now given over to olives, grapes and almonds. These hills saw heavy fighting during the Sicilian campaign in 1943, hence the Canadian war cemetery on the town outskirts.

Nicosia.

The churches contain several fine works of art. **Santa Maria Maggiore**, in the shadow of the castle, boasts a 15th-century triptych and sculpted Norman capitals, while the church of **Santa Maria di Gesù** contains a painted crucifix by Fra' Umile da Petralia. The Gothic **San Salvatore**, laden down by a 16th-century facade, has a treasury containing a bejewelled medieval mitre.

BALCONY OVER SICILY

Further east, past **Lago di Pozzillo**, an artificial lake, a minor road winds through orange and olive groves to **Centùripe ⑨**. The name supposedly comes from the Latin for steep slopes, justifying the town's tag used by Garibaldi in 1862, *il balcone della Sicilia* (the balcony over Sicily), with its magnificent valley views to Catania and Etna. In the heart of town is a pink and white 17th-century **Duomo**, contrasting with the town's modern, ugly buildings. Classical statues, terracotta and vases are visible in the **Museo Archeologico** (daily 9am–7pm; free).

On the outskirts of Centùripe, classical finds have been made at **Castello di Corradino**, the site of a clifftop Roman mausoleum. At the foot of Monte Calario are the ruins of a Greek villa and, in the Bagni Valley, the remains of Roman baths.

ECHOES OF ANCIENT ROME

The territory south of Enna has its fair share of crumbling hill towns, but the countryside is also home to several Greek settlements and Roman outposts, notably the magnificent Roman villa at Piazza Armerina.

Southwest of Enna are a couple of isolated hill towns, notably **Pietraperzia ⑩**, a market town stacked up on the slopes south of Caltanissetta, and **Barrafranca ⑪**, set on a spur in the **Monti Erei** (Erei mountains). These former feudal estates once provided a living for the landowning Barresi dynasty. Established by the Arabs, Barrafranca

was conquered by the Normans before being swallowed up by the Barresi clan in 1330. The Baroque **Chiesa Madre**, with its campanile and arabesque dome, comes a poor second to sampling the local produce, including olives, almonds and grapes. Further east are Piazza Armerina and the Villa Romana at Casale, Sicily's greatest wonder of the Roman world.

PIAZZA ARMERINA

Piazza Armerina ⑫ is upstaged by the Roman villa but still has a faded elegance all of its own. The closure of the sulphur mines cast a pall over the town, but low-key tourism is slowly reviving the *centro storico*, helped by a dynamic tourist board and ongoing restoration projects.

Surrounded by farmland and trees, the ancient settlement was favoured by the Romans, the Byzantines and the Arabs, but truly flourished with the arrival of the Normans. This event is celebrated on 13 and 14 August each year with the **Palio dei Normanni**, a heartfelt medieval pageant featuring

Drinks in this region are not for the weight-conscious.

An Easter procession in Pietraperzia.

costumed riders, recalling the trouncing of the Arabs and the Normans' victorious entry into the city.

Even if the Normans made their mark on Piazza Armerina, the town is rich in late medieval and Baroque monuments which merge together seamlessly, largely thanks to the rust-coloured local stonework.

In town, a series of flights of steps and alleys leads to the Baroque **Duomo** (8am–noon, 3.30–6.30pm), crowning the terraced hill. Erected in 1604 on the site of an earlier church, the cathedral balances a Baroque facade with theatrical staircases, accentuating the spacious belvedere. A Catalan-Gothic campanile (c.1490) with blind arcading remains from the original church and sets the tone for the bold interior.

Bordering the cathedral is **Palazzo Trigona**, a sober 18th-century counterpoint to the Baroque flights of fancy. The palace is being turned into the city museum. For a taste of how the noble Trigona family now lives, stay in their delightful Villa Trigona outside town (www.villatrigona.it).

The hilltop quarter radiates from Piazza Duomo and Piazza Garibaldi. In keeping with 13th-century urban design, this is in fishbone formation, with tiny alleys fanning out delicately along the contours of the slopes. The town clings to its traditional districts, with the lofty **Quartiere Monti** around the cathedral considered the noble district, and the former Moorish and Jewish section below. A stroll down the steep **Via Monte**, the medieval main street, reveals an evocative slice of history, passing palazzi dating from Norman and Aragonese times. From Via Monte the route leads past turreted mansions to Via Crocifisso, a turning on the right, and to the Gothic church of **San Martino**.

Once back at the cathedral, take Via Floresta beside Palazzo Trigona to the picturesque **Castello Aragonese**, the Aragonese castle. From here, Via Vittorio Emanuele II leads to Largo Capodarso and the **Convento dei Gesuiti**, a former Jesuit foundation which is now home to the **Biblioteca Comunale** (Mon–Fri 9am–1pm, Mon and Wed also 3–6pm), a remarkable public library encrusted in Baroque stuccowork.

Further north, the steep Via Castellina nudges the city walls and an old watchtower.

Just north of the compact hillside quarter is **Sant'Andrea**, a delightful Norman priory and the oldest church in town. The unadorned but delightful priory has a frescoed interior designed in a Coptic cross plan.

To visit the monuments, check opening times with the helpful **tourist office** (Via Generale Muscara; tel: 0935 68-814) as some churches, for instance, are only open for early morning Mass.

At night, moody lighting casts a soft glow over the *centro storico*, setting the scene for an inviting stroll from the cathedral square down the cobblestoned Via Monte, taking in **Piazza Garibaldi** and Largo Capodarso, ideally ending a rustic-style dinner in **da Toto** (Via Mazzini 29; www.ristorantedatoto.net).

Piazza Armerina.

r at **Trattoria Al Goloso** (Via Garao , Piazza Garibaldi) with its excellent alue-for-money Sicilian dishes.

'ILLA ROMANA DEL CASALE

Jestling among oak and hazel woods, the **illa Romana del Casale** ⑬ (www.villaro anadelcasale.it; summer daily 9am–7pm, vinter until 5pm, July–Aug Fri–Sun until 1.30pm) lies 5km (3 miles) southwest of 'iazza Armerina at **Casale**. The excellent unting in these forests was the bait that rew the villa's original Roman owners. It vas occupied throughout the Arab period ut destroyed by the Norman King Wil- am the Bad in 1160 and then covered y a landslide.

Now a Unesco World Heritage site, ne Villa's fluid, impressionistic mosa- cs may have inspired the Normans in heir designs for Palermo's Palazzo dei Jormanni. In splendour, the only rivals re Hadrian's villa at Tivoli or Diocle- an's palace at Split. But Sicily's mosa- cs better reflect the flux of Roman olitics, with the emergence of sepa- ate Eastern and Western empires. ne theory is that, after Diocletian

realised that the Roman world was too vast to be ruled by one mind and retired to his villa in Split, so Maximian withdrew to contemplation here.

Whether hunting lodge or country mansion, the villa disappeared under the landslide for 700 years but, after a hoard of treasure was found in 1950, serious excavations were begun. Much remains to be unearthed in the hazel- nut orchards, from the slave quarters to the water system.

The vaulting may be lost and the fres- coes faded, but the villa's magic lies in the 40 rooms covered in Roman-African mosaics. Their vitality, expressive power and free-ranging content set them apart from models in Tunisia or Antioch. The stylisation of these mosaics is under- cut by humour, realism, sensuality and subtlety. Above all, the mosaics' visual energy shines through.

EXPLORING THE SITE

The current path leads to a massive tri- umphal arch leading into an **atrium** ❶, surrounded by a portico of marble col- umns, then crashes down to earth in the

Visitors inspect the mosaics of hunting scenes at the Villa Romana del Casale.

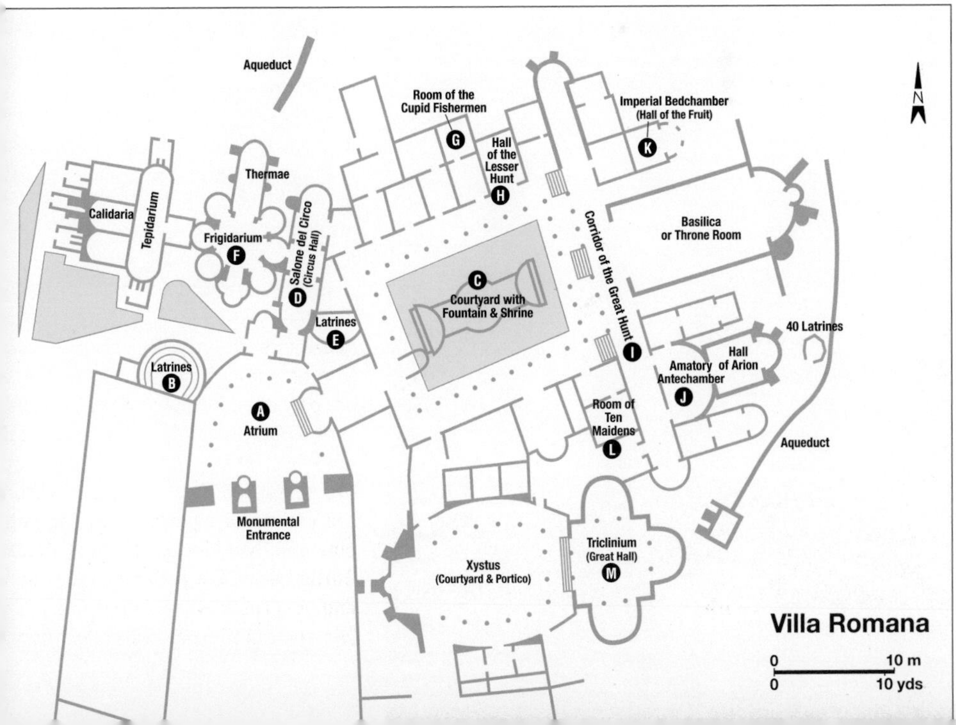

Villa Romana

Aqueduct
Room of the Cupid Fishermen
Imperial Bedchamber (Hall of the Fruit)
Thermae
Calidaria
Tepidarium
Frigidarium ❶
Salone del Circo (Circus Hall)
Hall of the Lesser Hunt ❶
Corridor of the Great Hunt
Basilica or Throne Room
❶
Courtyard with Fountain & Shrine ❶
Latrines ❶
❶
Hall Amatory of Arion Antechamber
40 Latrines
Room of Ten Maidens ❶
Aqueduct
Latrines ❶
❶
Atrium
Monumental Entrance
Xystus (Courtyard & Portico)
Triclinium (Great Hall) ❶

0   10 m
0   10 yds

Uncovered room in the Villa Romana del Casale, which has stunning Roman mosaics.

Detail of a mosaic in the Hunting Corridor.

male **latrines** **B** that were once lined with marble seats. Mosaics here feature a bestiary of Persian ass, ram and pouncing leopard. The villa's centrepiece is the **courtyard** **C**, with peristyle, pond and statue. The mosaics depict whimsical animals' heads framed in wreaths, from a fierce bear and tiger to a horse with a stunted nose. The design has a symmetry, pairing domestic and wild or male and female animals; a fierce ram thus sits beside a gracious deer.

The **Salone del Circo** **D** (Circus Hall) illustrates chaotic races at the Circus Maximus. These are the most extensive of their kind so far uncovered anywhere. Nearby, outside the **Thermae**, the thermal baths complex, are the small **latrines** **E**, with bidets for women. In the octagonal **frigidarium** **F** (leading to the warm and hot rooms) are vestibules and plunge baths adorned with tritons, centaurs and marine monsters, while in the anointment room next door, a man is depicted being massaged and perfumed by his naked servant.

Off the courtyard the **Room of the Cupid Fishermen** **G** depicts a naked mermaid clasping a dolphin in the presence of fishermen exposing their chests or bare buttocks. Nearby is the **Hall of the Lesser Hunt** **H**, with a frenetic deer hunt, the snaring of a wild boar, and a toast to a successful day's sport. To the Romans, hunting meant food, sport, sensuality, adventure and pleasure, preferably all at once.

Edging the courtyard is the **Corridor of the Great Hunt** **I**, the finest mosaic ever known, a gloriously animated work meant to be appreciated while walking. In this swirling mass of movement, chariots, lions, cheetahs, rhinos and huge swans merge in lovely autumnal colours. A mosaic sea separates Africa and Europe, echoing the division of the Roman Empire. Africa is personified by a tiger, elephant and a phoenix fleeing a burning house. The exotic, bare-breasted Queen of Sheba is being ogled by a tiger as well as by Romans.

Sport and erotica are often neatly entwined in the mosaics. The **amatory antechamber** **J**, part of the empress's suite, features Cupid fishermen netting a fine catch. The **Imperial** edchamber **K** is decorated with figs, rapes and pomegranates, snatching t Greek fertility symbols. The **Room f Ten Maidens L** presents prancing irl gymnasts in costumes that prove onclusively that the bikini was not vented in the 1950s.

Nearby, steps lead up to the **Tri- inium M** (Great Hall), the villa's mas- erpiece, 12 metres (39ft) square and ith deep apses, where the mosaic f the central pavement is a flowing ythological pageant based on the **10 abours of Hercules**. It is a symphony f pathos and poetic vision worthy of ichelangelo: the gods are threatened y chaos and decay; tortured giants rithe in agony; and a mighty nude Her- ules is glorified. Passion is present in erberus, the three-headed dog, and in e fierce Hydra, which has a woman's ce but snake-encrusted hair.

ILLA DELLE MARAVIGLIE

hen sated with Roman sights, consider icnicking in the surrounding pine and ucalyptus woods. Alternatively, visit an clectic villa-museum overlooking the

Villa Romana. **Villa delle Meraviglie 14** (daily 9am–7pm, until 5pm in winter; www.villadellemeraviglie.it) is owned by a baronial family who lived in the villa until recently. If you are lucky, you will be guided by Enzo Cammarata himself, both a classical scholar and Sicily's foremost authority on Greek and Roman coins. Even the grounds of this gracious 18th-century villa are dotted with clas- sical statuary. But beyond the majolica collection, Hellenistic busts and Greek- inspired paintings, this is a fascinating portrait of how the Sicilian landowning aristocracy once lived. Now a Unesco Heritage site, the glorious Villa Romana was unearthed on the Cammarata fam- ily estate, a fact which the Barone notes ruefully.

AIDONE

Aidone 15, 10km (6 miles) northeast of Piazza Armerina, represents a window on the Greek world. This warm, red- stone town boasts a ruined castle and a clutch of austere churches, including San Domenico, noted for its diamond- point facade. But the main attraction

Ancient bikinis in the Room of Ten Maidens.

⊙ A TEMPLE OF PAGANISM

All the scenes normally excluded from Christian art lie here, in the Unesco- listed Villa Romana. This entrancing Roman site depicts a kaleidoscope of everyday life, highlighting intimate pleasures such as child's play and youthful dancing, hunting, feasting, massage and lovemaking. A timeless quality also infuses the mosaics' undisguised eroticism: the female nudes may have odd-shaped breasts but they dance in pagan abandon. The more accomplished male nudes are studies in virility. The Romans wor- shipped heroism and masculine val- our, a vitality crushed by cool Christian art. In essence, this villa remains a temple of paganism and a celebration of everyday life that reverberates down the centuries.

Venus of Morgantina.

Aidone.

is the revamped **Museo Archeologico** (daily 9am–6.30pm), which contains one of the most magnificent Greek sculptures in Sicily (see box). Set in a restored 17th-century Capuchin monastery in the upper part of the village, the museum also serves as an introduction to the rural site of Morgantina, perhaps the most legible site in antiquity.

MORGANTINA

Morgantina (daily 9am–6.30pm; includes Museo Archeologico at Aidone), just 5km (3 miles) east, occupies a rural paradise worthy of Persephone, its slopes covered in calendula, pomegranate, pines and olives, and framed by grey-blue hills. Morgantina is divided into two sections by a deep valley, with Serra Orlando on the ridge to the west, and hilly Cittadella to the east. This huge ancient Siculi settlement was Hellenised in the 6th century BC and survived for 500 years, including under the Romans. Sometimes dubbed a Sicilian Pompeii, the site is not aesthetically beautiful like Piazza Armerina but is supremely clear, an exposition of a classical city in stone.

The polis (Greek city) reveals a civic and sacred centre bounded by commercial and residential quarters.

Cittadella, the hilly Bronze Age settlement, is pitted with chamber tombs. Visible Hellenistic sections include: the *macellum* (covered market), designed like a shopping mall; a schoolroom complete with benches; a gymnasium with an athletics track; the *bouleuterion* (Senate); a theatre, magistrates' chamber, granary and bakery. Several noble villas contain the earliest known mosaics in the Western Mediterranean, including a floor inscription saying welcome *(euexei)*, which is now in the museum at Aidone. Theatrical steps lead to the agora, complete with aqueducts and fountains. Nearby stands a temple with a *bothros*, a round well-altar once used for sacrifice.

Morgantina is a reminder that Enna marked the crossroads of Trinacria, ancient Sicily's three provinces. According to one historian, Enna is the hub of a giant geomantic chart, lying on ley lines spanning the island. This network of sacred spots supposedly provides the key to the region's occult power.

⊘ VENUS RETURNS HOME

A priceless Sicilian statue stolen by tomb-robbers and trafficked to the United States has finally found her way back to Sicily. The so-called *Venus of Morgantina*, a life-size Greek marble statue made in the 5th century BC, was stolen from a Greek sanctuary in Morgantina over 30 years ago and later sold to the Paul Getty Museum in Malibu for 10 million USD; the museum returned it to Sicily in 2011. Now fully restored and complete with anti-seismic protection, the statue is the showpiece of the classical collection in Aidone. But the debate continues: the Venus/Aphrodite figure is more likely to be Demeter/Ceres, the goddess of the harvest and fertility, than the goddess of beauty, although some scholars still see her as Persephone, Demeter's abducted daughter, whisked to Hades by Pluto.

RAGUSA PROVINCE

Currently Sicily's most flourishing region, Ragusa favours subtlety over drama. Rolling countryside framed by dry-stone walls gives way to classical sites by sandy beaches or cave settlements by Baroque towns.

◉ Main attractions

Ragusa Ibla
Chiaramonte Gulfi
Monti Iblei
Castello di Donnafugata
Camarina
Módica
Cava d'Ispica
Scicli
Montalbano Trail
Palazzo Arezzo (Ragusa)
Marina di Ragusa
  (in summer)

📍

Map on page 166

Discreet wellbeing is the keynote to the region. Novelist Gesualdo Bufalino proudly described his province as *"un ísola nell'ísola"*, an island within an island. Historically, this was home to a cave-dwelling population who for millennia felt more secure clustering in grottoes or ravines, a tradition that survived until recently, with caves around Ragusa, Módica and Scicli inhabited until the 1980s. It is perhaps not accidental that this earthy, community-minded province is an almost a crime-free haven, surviving beyond the Mafia's reptilian gaze. Here the typica conditions for Sicilian crime are absent

LOW-KEY TOURISM

Industry and tourism reached th province relatively late, with the resul that Ragusa has not concreted over it coast but cultivated low-key tourism in the same way that it tends the land selling itself as an off-the-beaten track destination. Unlike much of Sic ily, there is a civilised balance betwee ancient *cultura contadina* (peasant cul ture) and the creativity of the *borghesia* Class distinctions aside, the Ragusar are deeply hospitable, more open tha those in the mountainous interior.

The city of **Ragusa** was a Norma stronghold that became a fief of th Cabrera dynasty. However, the 169 earthquake reduced most of Ragusa t rubble. The merchant class responde by building **Ragusa Alta ❶** (sometime called **Superiore**), the new city on th hill. But the aristocracy refused t desert their charred homes, and rec reated **Ragusa Ibla ❷** (Lower Ragusa on the original valley site. The town only merged in 1926, so now Ragus is a hilltop town divided into two parts While Ragusa Ibla is an enchanting timeless pocket of Sicily, Ragusa Alt is the business centre, riven by gorges and redeemed only by several Baroqu mansions and churches.

Ragusa Ibla.

RAGUSA ALTA

In the upper town, **San Giovanni Battista** (www.cattedralesangiovanni. ; Tue–Sat 10am–1pm, 4–7pm, Sun 10am–1pm) is the city's theatrical Baroque cathedral, with an ornate facade and soaring, pretty **campanile**.

Nearby, Baroque mansions have wrought-iron balconies featuring sculpted cornices. One such is **Palazzo Bertini** on Corso Italia, with its grotesque masks representing "the three powers": a peasant, a nobleman and a merchant – a fair introduction to Ragusa's class concerns.

On Corso Vittorio Veneto is the crumbling Baroque **Palazzo Zacco**: a gap-toothed monster sticks out his tongue, mocking the church of San Vito opposite. The palazzo houses a small museum on farming (Tue–Fri 8am–2pm, 3–7pm, Sat 9am–1pm, 3–7pm), one way in to see the palace interiors. Just south is the gorge criss-crossed by three bridges, one of which was built by a friar who tired of the daily uphill trek to his parish. The **Museo Archeologico Regionale di Ragusa** (Mon–Sat 9am–6.30pm; free) on Via Natalelli is rich in finds from Camarina and Siculi necropoli, including prehistoric pottery and Greek vases. On the far side of the chasm lies densely packed Ragusa Ibla, now easily reached by shuttle bus along the scenic ring road, faced in subtle local stone.

Santa Maria delle Scale (Mon–Fri 4.30–6pm, Sat 3.30–7pm, Sun 10am–1pm), framed by parched hills, represents the gateway to Ibla, joining the old to the new. This Gothic church was remodelled after the 1693 earthquake. A medieval portal remains, as does the Catalan-Gothic nave, complete with Renaissance ornamentation. From this balcony over old Ragusa, 250 steps lead down into Ibla, offering a commanding view over the blue-tinged cupola of the cathedral below.

RAGUSA IBLA

In Ragusa Ibla, the Baroque city recreated on a medieval street plan, an old-world charm and intimacy prevails. Snapshot vistas of Ibla capture secret shrines, family crests and Baroque

Classic cars in Ragusa Ibla.

⊘ RAGUSAN DELIGHTS

Ragusa province is noted for its scented honey and robust cheeses, among the best in Sicily. Ricotta, mozzarella, provola and cacciocavallo are the main cheeses to sample, either in savoury or sweet dishes. Although caciocavallo has cow's milk as its base, goat's milk is added to give it a distinctive flavour. Its texture is smooth, with a sharp, smoky flavour. The economic revival as well as renaissance of the local cuisine have prompted the opening of specialised delis offering traditional local products made according to old recipes but in line with modern organic standards. To buy artisanal salamis, cheeses, local honey, preserves and wine in Ragusa, head to centrally located Food – Custodi di Sensi on Via Lombardia 76; www.foodcustodideisensi.com.

fountains. Shrines lurk in narrow alleys and on facades, representing a need for reassurance as well as an expression of faith and a superstitious belief in future miracles. Ibla is also oriel windows, tiny squares and showy staircases, tawny-coloured stone mansions and filigree balconies hung with washing, dark courtyards popular with ambling dogs, secret arches and yellowing palm trees.

Gentrification has reversed the neglect of Ibla in recent years. The crumbling mansions are being restored and cherished by young, middle-class couples returning to the old city. Easier access too has helped open Ibla up to citizens from the upper town without losing its sense of separateness or leisurely pace of life. Where once Ibla was deserted in the evening, its pedestrianised quarter is now the focus for Ragusa's low-key nightlife. Semi-hidden restaurants and bars have taken over historic palaces, with tasteful bohemian conversions coexisting with the clubby, patrician side of town.

BAROQUE DRAMA

Palazzo Nicastro, the Baroque chancery erected in 1760, sits astride the winding staircase linking old and new Ragusa. To the left is **Santa Maria dell'Idria**, a Baroque church owned by the Cosentini, one of Ibla's leading families. Given the narrowness of the alley, it takes time to gain a perspective on the robust bell tower and majolica-encrusted dome. Crushed between the church steps and Corso Mazzini is **Palazzo Cosentini**, an ancestral home adjoining the family church of Santa Maria. The sculpted Baroque balconies are a mélange of fantastic bare-breasted sirens and monsters with flaring nostrils. Leering faces proffer scorpions or serpents instead of tongues, a warning not to gossip.

On Piazza della Repubblica, the next square down, stands the **Chiesa del Purgatorio**, a dramatic Baroque church surmounting an elegant staircase. The bell tower is built on Byzantine city walls, visible from the steps of Salita dell'Orologio.

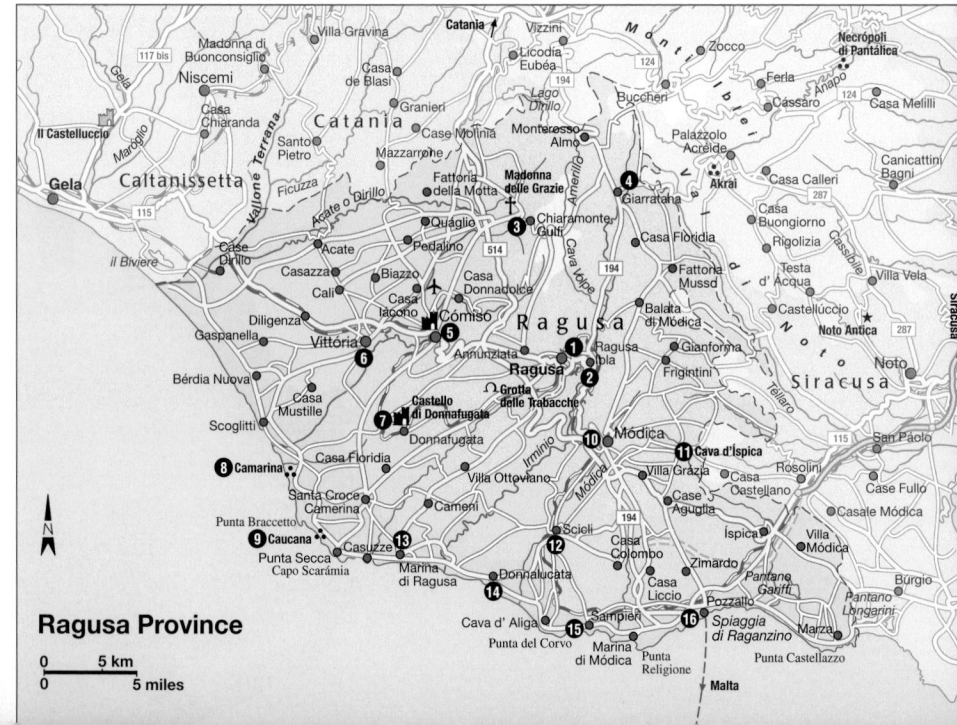

Ragusa Province

0 — 5 km
0 — 5 miles

PIAZZA DEL DUOMO

fter the cosy claustrophobia so far,
he spacious **Piazza del Duomo** below
omes as a shock. The square is lined
rith palm trees, Baroque mansions and
ristocratic clubs. The far end of the
iazza is dominated by Rosario Gagli-
rdi's cathedral dedicated to **San Gior-
io** (daily 10am–12.30pm and 4–7pm),
 masterpiece of Sicilian Baroque. As
he city centrepiece, completed in 1775,
his wedding-cake cathedral was pat-
onised by the nobility (St George was
onsidered the unofficial patron saint of
he Sicilian aristocracy).

The sandstone church occupies a
aised terrace and tricks one's eyes
p from its convex centre, seemingly
vrithing with statues, in a crescendo
o the balconied campanile, topped
y a blue neoclassical dome that is a
ity landmark.

Its smaller imitator on the Corso is
he church of **San Giuseppe** (Fri–Sun
am–noon and 3–7pm), which gains in
ubtlety what it lacks in theatricality.
he church facade is attributed to the
chool of Gagliardi.

PALAZZO AREZZO

Adjoining Piazza Duomo is Baron
Arezzo's arched **Palazzo Arezzo**,
whose facade is adorned with sculpted
hedgehogs, the family crest. The
Arezzo dynasty still owns much of the
province, from farmland to villas and a
castle. Given their credo of enlightened
paternalism, the family has endowed
local hospitals, parks and churches.
Ibla's nobles have always immortalised themselves in stone, linking grand
Baroque mansions to a graceful family chapel or even a gentlemen's club.
Today, Domenico Arezzo and his father
offer guided tours around the palace's
richly decorated halls and rooms, ending the tour with a tasting of local products (by appointment only, tel: 0392 820
7857; https://siciliaospitalitadiffusa.it).

Nearby is the **Circolo di Conver-
sazione** (ring for admission), a literary
salon founded by local noblemen. The
belle époque interior contains an allegorical *trompe l'œil* ceiling and busts of
Michelangelo, Galileo, Dante and Bellini, representing art, science, poetry
and music. Nor is the art of aristocratic

Duomo San Giorgio.

*Baroque decoration
inside the cathedral.*

⊙ Tip

Giardino Ibleo is the focal point of the Ibla Buskers' Festival each October, when performers from all around the world are offered free hospitality in return for entertainment.

conversation dead in sleepy Ibla: here, men sit amongst frescoed nymphs while chatting over news or playing cards.

The adjoining **Palazzo Donnafugata** was the nobles' private theatre, gallery and reading club until opened to a slightly wider membership. Sadly, the sculpted marble staircase, sumptuous salons and gallery adorned with old masters are only visible during private banquets, but you can visit the theatre (booking through the bar next door). Most symbolic is the heavily shuttered loggia on the *piano nobile*, a secret spot from which to view visitors.

ANCIENT JEWISH GHETTO

Behind the cathedral on Via Capitano Bocchieri is **Palazzo La Rocca**, an austere Baroque mansion transformed into the welcoming **provincial tourist office** (tel: 0932 675 111). The facade is enlivened by bizarre balconies depicting 18th-century aristocratic entertainment: a lute player and cherub blowing a hunting horn vie with gawky, naked lovers clinging to each other in gauche poses.

The alleys in the shadow of th cathedral are what Italians read ily term *suggestivo* (atmospheric This, the heart of the ancient Jewis ghetto and artisan quarter, is slow being restored and repopulated wit younger residents and craft shops. I the square of Largo Camerina, how ever, a traditional cabinet-maker sur vives, creating tables from olive, carob cherry, cyprus and orange wood. Mor typical of the reinvigorated quarter i Federico II (www.federicosecondo.info), a elegant restaurant housed in an ol palace close to Portale San Giorgio, o L'Antica Drogheria (www.anticadrogher iblea.it), on Corso XXV Aprile, a superio delicatessen selling Iblean honey an herbs, cheeses, salami and biscuits.

IBLEO PARK

The **Giardino Ibleo** (9am–10pm, Fri Sat until 1am), created in the 19t century around the church of **Sa Giacomo** (Fri–Sun 11am–1pm, 5–9pm is a charming landscaped park set o a spur at the eastern end of Ibla. I spring, the statues, palm trees an

Ragusa Ibla from Largo Santa Maria.

ool are complemented by daffodils,
broom and irises. Around the grounds
are three ruined churches, victims of
the 1693 earthquake, and a popular
café. The multicoloured majolica dome
of **San Domenico** overlooks Gothic **San
Giacomo**, built on the site of a pagan
temple, and the church of the **Cappuc-
ini**, a Baroque monastic church. On
the far side of the gardens on Via Normanni is the dilapidated 15th-century
Gothic doorway to the church of **San
Giorgio Vecchio**, with a relief depicting *St George and the Dragon*. Carved in
soft local stone, this is all that remains
of the original church destroyed in the
earthquake that devastated Ragusa.
From this uncharacteristically lush corner of old Ibla, both ancient locals and
young lovers take time to look out over
terraces and dry-stone walls to a valley
encrusted with ancient Siculi tombs.

Yet, despite its noble veneer, parts
of Ibla are still poor. Within view of the
heart of town are outlying quarters
riddled with blind alleys, abandoned
hovels and rock dwellings, side by side
with remains of medieval, Byzantine
and even pre-Christian Ragusa. Set
below the jagged landscape of modern
Ragusa, the ancient Siculi tombs now
tend to be used as storerooms, wine
cellars or even garages. The valley
floor is cut by a river that fed several
mills until the 1980s; the scene is one
of whitewashed cottages, steep steps,
pots of geraniums, and peppers dried
on walls Arab-style.

NORTH OF RAGUSA

Chiaramonte Gulfi ❸ was founded
in the late 7th century as Gulfi but
destroyed by the Angevins in 1299. It was
then revived by Manfredi I, the Count of
Módica, one of the Chiaramonte dynasty.
The town flourished until overtaken by
neighbouring Vittória which, as it grew
in size, gained in prosperity and power.
The citizens of Gulfi added Chiaramonte
to their town's name in 1881 to honour
its original benefactor.

The infamous 1693 earthquake
destroyed much of Chiaramonte's
small-town splendour, but the *centro
storico* has been preserved. Although
the **Arco dell'Annunziata** is the one
remaining medieval gateway, other
low-key attractions include several
lofty churches and a cluster of endearing museums, including a costume
museum, local history museum and,
best of all, an olive oil museum. Today
Chiaramonte Gulfi is famous among
Sicilians for its superb olive oil, country
food and hearty trattorie. A well-organised olive oil trail leads through the
scenic **Monti Iblei**, with opportunities to
stop for tastings at oil or wine estates
or to sample rustic meals at farmstays.

At about 2km (1.25 miles) away in
the countryside is the **Santuario dell
Madonna delle Grazie**, restored in
1710, but more a place for picnics than
religious devotion.

Giarratana ❹, sandwiched between
the Iblean mountains and the plains,
represents a rural Sicilian backwater, complete with ruined castle. After
the 1693 earthquake the town was

Balcony detail in
Ragusa Ibla.

Giardino Ibleo.

rebuilt on the sunnier adjoining hill, and produced a trio of impressive (but irregularly open) Baroque churches that survive today: the Chiesa Madre, Sant'Antonio and San Bartolomeo.

WEST OF RAGUSA

From Ragusa, the rural hinterland unfolds. On higher ground, olives, almonds and carobs abound but, in well-irrigated areas, greenhouse cultivation is gaining ground. Where there is enough water, on the coast or in river canyons, dwarf palms, holm-oaks, plane trees and Aleppo pines flourish. But on the plains, the view is of dust-coloured farmhouses, low dry-stone walls, endless fields, rugged limestone plains beaten to the colour of sandstone.

A dramatic descent from the Iblean hills leads across a vast plain to **Cómiso** ❺ (population just over 30,000), an attractive Baroque town that had the misfortune to become a NATO military base in the 1980s. Peace protests were the price residents paid for housing the last cruise missiles located on European soil. As a bonus, 7,000 American soldiers subsidised the local economy until the final removal of the missiles in 1991. Fortunately, Cómiso reopened as a low-cost airport in 2013.

Ruled by the Aragonese Naselli dynasty from the 15th to the 18th centuries, Cómiso still has a feudal castle. The restored 14th-century **Castello dei Naselli** retains its original Gothic portal and octagonal tower, converted from a Byzantine baptistery. Although shattered by the 1693 earthquake, fragments of classical Cómiso survive: Piazza di Munícipio contains **Fonte Diana**, a Roman fountain whose waters once gushed into the Roman baths now under the municipal offices.

In Piazza delle Erbe there is **San Francesco**, with the fine Antonello Gagini marble **mausoleum** and, just off the piazza, is the **covered market** (1871). Adding to the Baroque scenery is the vast domed **Basilica dell'Annunziata** and the slim-domed **Santa Maria delle Grazie**, a monastic chapel which offers the town's most gruesome sight: mummified bodies of monks and benefactors stacked in frightening poses.

Módica.

Vittória ❻, further west, is a wealthy vine-producing centre on the slopes of the Iblean hills. While perfectly safe for visitors, this neat city remains wealthy rather than healthy – as under the surface the Mafia maintains a toehold. Giuseppe Fava, a Sicilian journalist murdered by the Mafia, once dismissed Vittória as "a city built by those without the time, money, imagination or background to make anywhere better".

Even so, the elegant **Piazza del Popolo** contains the Baroque church of **Santa Maria delle Grazie** and the monumental **Teatro Comunale**, a fine example of neoclassical architecture.

On Piazza Libertà, amid the bland modernity are bourgeois mansions with grand courtyards. From the city gardens are views across the fertile valley to the sea, with flowers and peaches supplementing the traditional crops of olive oil and wine. The illustrious wine producer Florio has an important base here.

SOUTH OF RAGUSA

Castello di Donnafugata ❼ (Tue–Sun 9am–1pm, Tue, Sat–Sun also 2.30–4pm)

lies 20km (12 miles) southwest of Ragusa. Set in a carob and palm plantation, this modern Moorish pastiche feels authentically Sicilian. The castle dates from 1648 but was redesigned as a full-blown Ottocento fantasy by Corrado Arezzo, the baron of Donnafugata, in the 19th century, and remained in the family until the 1970s. Arezzo, a campaigner for Sicilian independence, created Donnafugata as his whimsical refuge from revolutionary politics.

The exterior is a Venetian palace transplanted by magic carpet to *The Arabian Nights*. The crenellated facade, inspired by an austere Arab desert fort, is softened by an arcaded Moorish balcony. Below the arched windows opens an amazing loggia in Venetian-Gothic style. The finest rooms include a picture gallery, billiards room, winter garden and a salon for conversation. The frescoed music room illustrates the noble pastimes of painting, *bel canto* and piano recitals.

Charmingly faded, this palace of 122 rooms is quietly being restored. But for now, the floating drapes, tarnished gilt,

○ **Tip**

Around Vittória there are several wine trails, to put you on the right track for Cerasuolo di Vittoria (www.stradadelvinocerasuolo-divittoria.it) and Nero d'Avola wines and producers. A wine route map can be picked up from the local tourist office.

⊘ CULINARY REVIVAL

Sicily's culinary renaissance is in the southeast of the island, and the Val di Noto, centred on Ragusa and Módica. Sicily now has everything from Slow Food organic eateries and creative trattorie to country-style restaurants and Michelin-starred establishments that are setting the agenda for *la cucina siciliana*, such as Ragusa's Don Serafino (www.locandadonserafino.it) and La Fenice (www.lafeniceristorante.com). The region is noted for rustic cheeses (ricotta, mozzarella, provola and cacciocavallo) and meats, so even the most celebrated chefs offer affectionate nods to the island's peasant traditions. For a memorable meal, choose Duomo in Ragusa or Locanda del Colonnello in Módica.

In Vittória's Piazza del Popolo.

The Castello di Donnafugata, a 19th-century palace built on the site of an Arab village, combines Venetian Gothic with Moorish whimsy.

Fonte Diana, the Roman fountain in Cómiso's Piazza di Município.

inlaid tables and dusty chandeliers conspire to create an atmosphere straight out of *The Leopard*. Unsurprisingly, the castle is a sought-after film set.

During World War II, the Luftwaffe commandeered the castle but respected Donnafugata, so all the baron's quirky touches remain, from the cute well and the children's maze in the garden to the artificial grotto and glorious parkland.

The ancient Greek site of **Kamarina** (in Greek or Camarina in Italian), the **Parco archeologico di Kamarina** (daily 9am–2pm and 3–7pm), lies on the coast just 12km (7 miles) southwest of Donnafugata. Founded in 598 BC, two centuries after Siracusa (the ferocity of the local Siculi tribes was a deterrent to earlier settlement), Kamarina is a sophisticated example of urban planning covering three hills at the mouth of the River Ìppari. But it was attacked, sacked and rebuilt many times until finally the city of perfect parallel lines was destroyed by the Romans in AD 258. The first excavations of the site were begun in 1896; then, after a

hiatus, excavations continued again i 1958 and are still in progress.

In the park are traces of the 6th century BC walls that stretched 7kr (4 miles) to encircle and protect a ci that was divided into distinct public civil, religious and residential areas.

Close to the **museum** (same openin times) lie the foundations of a **tempio c Athena** (temple of Athena). The museur contains objects retrieved from ship wrecks on this shoreline, including sar cophagi and amphorae as well as a Gree bronze helmet (4th century BC) and 1,00 coins found in a treasure chest. Nearby the **House of the Altar** has rooms radi ating from the central courtyard with battered mosaic floor. Other Hellenisti dwellings include a merchant's house confirmed by the presence of scales an measuring devices.

On the headland just south of Kama rina, at **Punta Secca**, is the Roman por of **Caucana** (by appointment, tel 347 697 4535). Now slowly being exca vated, the port was partly preserved b sand, as at Gela further down the coast The lush site is lovely but inscrutable, a uzzle compounded by the discovery of ellenistic amphorae, Roman coins and ewish candelabra. Amid the rubble, he clearest find is a Byzantine church with a colourful mosaic of a goat. It was t this port that the navy of Count Roger he Norman gathered in 1091 before he conquest of Malta.

OUTHEAST TO MÓDICA

eyond farmsteads and stone walls re two high road bridges that provide sudden, terrifying glimpse of a grey-rown town in the deep valley below. Módica ❿, the former regional capital, s perched on a ridge spilling down into he valley. Like Ragusa, it is two towns n one, high and low. At first sight, the etting is more prepossessing than the own, but Módica repays exploration, rom its mysterious alleys and mouth-watering food to its illustrious history s the most powerful fiefdom on the sland. Currently the wealthiest town in icily, unshowy Módica still boasts the egion's best shopping, chocolate and ourmet restaurants, as well as the ighest ownership of Ferraris in Sicily.

The prosperous Arab citadel of Mudiqah became a fief of the Chiaramonte family in 1296 and merged into the county of Módica. After succumbing to Spanish influence, it passed from the Caprera viceroys to the Henriquez, Spanish absentee landlords. Around town are the family crests of the three dynasties: respectively mountains, a goat, and two castles. Módica's charm lies in the complexity of the multi-layered town, with its tiers of sumptuous churches and shabby palaces stacked up on the hill.

At the entrance to the town is the **Convento dei Padri Mercedari**, which houses the municipal library and the **Museo Ibleo delle Arti e Tradizioni popolari** (daily 10am–1pm, 4–7pm), depicting local trades such as shoe-making and cart-making, along with farming and winemaking.

SAN GIORGIO CATHEDRAL

Above, perched precariously on the slope of the hill, looms the Baroque landmark of **San Giorgio** (daily 9am–1pm, 3.30–7pm). Set in Módica Alta (Upper Módica), against a backdrop

of rocky terraces, the church makes a bold statement and surmounts a daunting Baroque flight of 250 steps. Climb the stairs only if you are feeling fit: there is little to see in the church behind its ornate facade. Not that Gagliardi's masterpiece disappoints: its exuberance and inventiveness encapsulate Sicilian Baroque. This frothy concoction of flowing lines and curvy ornament seems barely rooted to the spot. The vision is one of Rococo splendour, shadowy recesses and a soaring belfry silhouetted against the sky.

CORSO UMBERTO I

After such spectacle, other churches play walk-on parts. However, on Corso Umberto I is the **Chiesa del Carmine**, with a marble group representing *The Annunciation*, attributed to Antonello Gagini. In the centre of town, where the Corso meets Via Marchesa Tedeschi, stands **San Domenico**, a church which was hit by two 17th-century earthquakes.

Just around the corner is the town hall, embracing the **Cripta del Convento di San Domenico** (key and guide from the tourist office on Vi Grimaldi). The Dominicans used thi mysterious medieval crypt as a bur ial chamber, but it was also a tortur chamber linked to the Inquisition.

Still on the Corso, reached by a the atrical staircase along which tiers o the 12 apostles welcome visitors muc like today's party greeters, is the grea San Giorgio's nearest rival, the opu lent church of **San Pietro** (built afte 1693). Gagliardi may have designe this church, too.

The Palazzo Della Cultura at Cors 149, a former Benedictine convent, no houses the **Museo Civico Archeolog ico** (Tue–Sun 10am–1pm and 4–7pm summer 10m–1pm and 5–8pm).

Close to San Pietro is the ancien church of **San Niccolò Inferiore** essentially a grotto displaying 11th century frescoes. Also on the Cors are the 16th-century church of **Sant Maria del Soccorso**, the 18th-centur **Teatro Garibaldi** and 18th-centur **Palazzo Manenti** with its balcony an Baroque embellishments.

Forza, an archaeological park outside Ispica.

Museo Campailla (Mon–Fri 10am–noon, Sat 3–7pm and by appointment, tel: 093 276 3990) is the most bizarre minor museum in Sicily: an early syphilis clinic founded by Tommaso Campailla, a 17th-century doctor and philosopher, and used until the early 20th century. The cure, a refinement on an 8th-century Arab practice, involved placing patients in the hot mercury chambers, heated by hot coals to produce a sauna-like effect, and subjecting sufferers to vaporous infusions. The eerie original chambers are still visible, surreally interconnected with rooms where city council workers go about their normal business.

Nearby, back on Via Marchese Tedeschi, is the 15th-century church of **Santa Maria di Betlem**, which appears to be four tiny churches converted into one. In the right nave, a magnificent portal opens into the late Gothic-Renaissance **Cappella del Sacramento** where a *Madonna and Child Enthroned* is painted on stone above the altar. The side chapel contains a **crib** (1882) adorned with terracotta figurines.

CAVES AND TOMBS

From Módica, it's a short drive south to Baroque Scicli and the coast, or southeast to the Ispica canyon and to Siracusa province. The **Cava d'Ispica** ⓫ (www.cavadispica.org; May–Oct daily 9am–6.30pm, shorter hours rest of the year; free first Sun of the month) is an 11km (7-mile) limestone gorge, typical of local gorges but on a giant scale, where ghostly galleries and caves have been inhabited almost continuously since prehistoric times. There are prehistoric tombs and medieval cave dwellings. The southern end of the narrow valley is overlooked by the **castello**, a castle-like rock which acted as a four-storey dwelling.

The better tombs are in the northern end of the gorge, close to the entrance to the site. The honeycomb of galleries conceal native Siculi oven-shaped tombs, Greek necropoli and early Christian tombs. Highlights include the **Larderia**, the most complete set of early Christian catacombs in southeastern Sicily, and the **Grotta di Santa Maria**, a rock chapel with wall paintings that

Interior of San Pietro, Módica.

Stone monster on a Scicli mansion facade.

Marina di Ragusa.

was inhabited until the 1950s. Sections of the site are often closed, but it's best to visit with a guide, in any case.

At the far end of the Cava d'Ispica gorge is the **Parco Archeologico della Forza** (May–Oct daily 9am–6.30pm, shorter hours rest of the year; free first Sun of the month), outside the small town of Ispica. The Parco too has its catacombs and traces of pre-historic settlements. Ispica was rebuilt after the great earthquake in a safer position. On Via XX Settembre is the Baroque church of **Santa Maria Maggiore**, while on the Corso, **Palazzo Bruno di Belmonte** (1906), now the town hall, is an Art Nouveau castle created by the great Ernesto Basile.

SCICLI

Southwest of the canyons is **Scicli** ⑫, a gorgeous Baroque gem that is coming into its own as a film set, thanks to an enlightened mayor and the worldwide popularity of the *Montalbano* detective films (see box). The Baroque centre is experiencing a revival, with an influx of young craftspeople and arty types as well as canny second-home-owners in search of a civilised but forgotten corner of Sicily. A sprinkling of boutique hotels and chic B&Bs now make Sicli a lovely touring base.

The road from Ispica reveals vistas of a grotto-encrusted hillside opening onto the restored remains of the church of **San Matteo**, part of a medieval settlement once on the slopes, now overlooking the Baroque heart of Scic on the valley floor below. Scicli's fust city churches and fantastic Baroque mansions seem out of place in the sleepy world. The ochre-coloured facades are decorated with sirens, monsters and fauns, part of the cavalcade of Christian and mythological creatures inspired by designs on Greek temples or Romanesque cathedrals.

Piazza Italia, the main square, opens with the Baroque 18th-century **Duomo**, the **Chiesa Sant'Ignazio**. Its gilded interior holds a painting of a historic battle for Scicli between the Turks and Christians in 1091, where the successful intercession of a bellicose Madonna supposedly brought victory, an event celebrated in Scicli's own festival in Ma

The most theatrical part of town around **Via Mormino Penna**, the best preserved Baroque street. Here stand the elegant church of **San Giovanni**, with its concave-convex facade and dazzling exterior matched by an equally impressive interior: the exuberantly stuccoed surface has a gaudy emerald and turquoise Moorish design. The church was previously the preserve of cloistered nuns, who sat in balconied splendour to watch processions on feast days.

Just south, **Palazzo Beneventano** has beautiful balconies, with fantastic corbels representing mythical beasts, Moors and ghoulish human masks. Almost as splendid is nearby **Palazzo Fava**, representing a riot of galloping griffins and horses ridden by cherubs. Just east, at the foot of the rock, looms the majestic cupola and domed apse of **Santa Maria la Nuova**, signalling

e start of Scicli's intriguing medieval quarter, dotted with alleys and steps verflowing with pot plants.

An attractive path that winds up to the p, where the ruined castle and Chiesa an Matteo overlook the town, has won vour as a popular summer stroll. rom here, secret passageways dating from the Saracen sieges reputedly ad out of town. The hill is pitted with rmer cave-homes that were inhabited ntil the 1980s but which now serve as ine cellars, garages and storerooms.

ESIDE THE SEASIDE

agusa province has some of Sicy's best beaches. Less than 10km (6 iles) from Scicli, the coastal landcape is wild and unspoilt. Sandy eaches await around the archaeologial site of **Kamarina**, with a secluded ocky beach on **Punta Braccetto**, the eadland beyond.

Heading eastwards, **Marina di agusa** ⓭, lined with inviting fish resaurants, contains the only managed eaches, equipped for windsurfing and arious other watersports. In summer,

this winter ghost town turns into a newly fashionable resort, popular with yachting types and families.

Just east is the wooded coastal reserve of **Fiume Irmínio**, with the broad sandy beaches of **Donnalucata** ⓮ beyond, a stretch of coast rapidly being swamped by greenhouses.

A 7km (4-mile) coastal drive leads east to the rocky headland of Punta del Corvo, and on to coastline that lies further south than Tunisia's northern coastline.

Sampieri ⓯ stands out for its self-consciously quaint atmosphere, a prettified fishing village popular with Ragusani out for a family romp in the sand dunes. Further along the coast, at the port of **Pozzallo** ⓰, the industrial complex is too close to the beach for comfort, although the beaches are perfectly acceptable further east, towards Siracusa province. Still, Pozzallo is a pleasant enough place to stay for a lunch of salted tuna or sardines, both caught and processed in the port.

From here, you can escape on a day trip to Malta by catamaran (see margin) or visit the Baroque masterpiece of Noto.

⊙ Tip

Sicily can be combined with Malta on a two-island holiday using Virtu Ferries (www.virtuferries.com). Fast catamarans run between Valletta, the capital of Malta, and Pozzallo in Ragusa province (90 minutes) or on the longer (three-hour) sailing from Valletta to Catania.

View over Scicli.

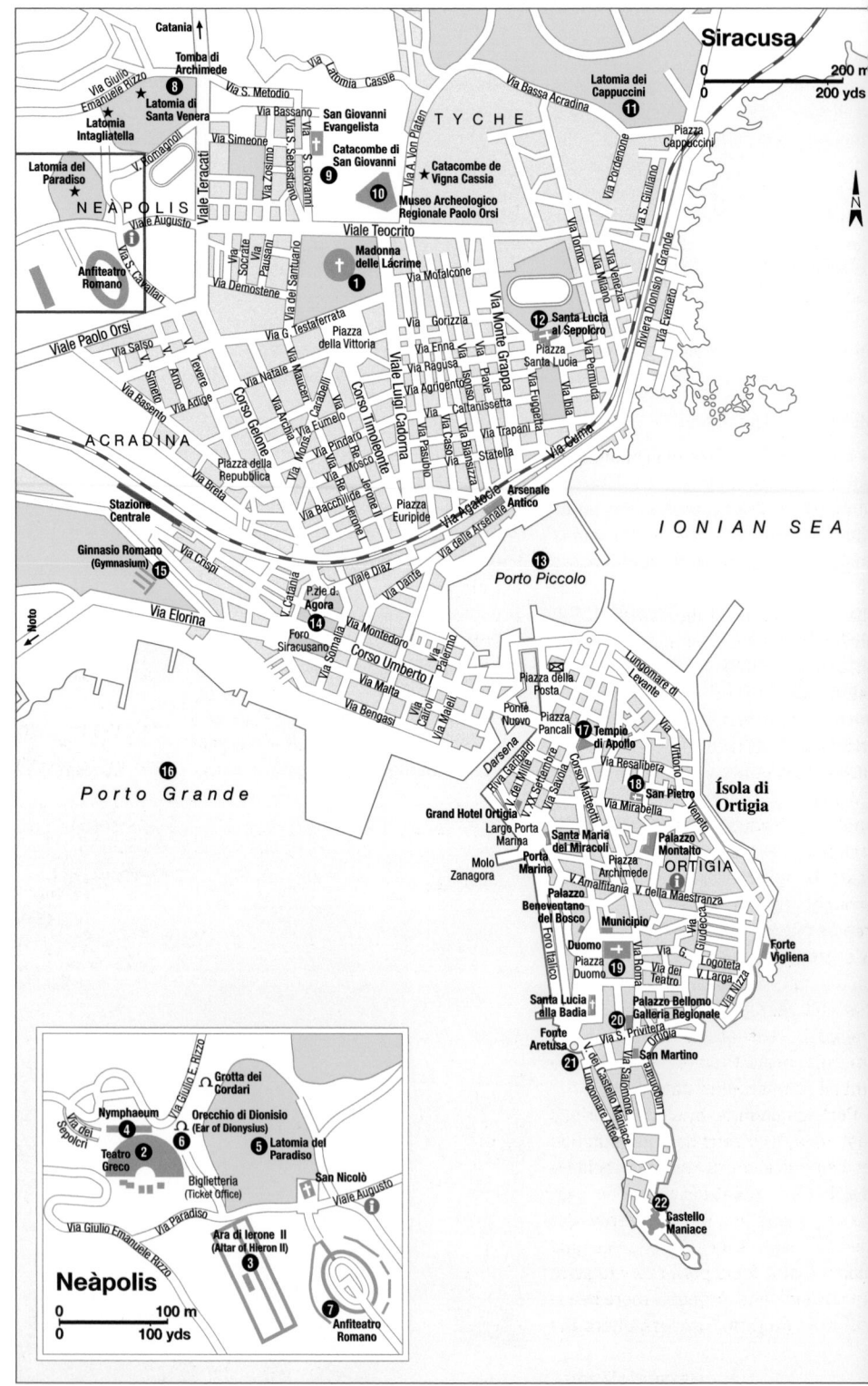

Catania ↑
Tomba di
Archimede
Via Giulio
Emanuele Rizzo
Latomia
Intagliatella
Via S. Metodio
Via Bassano
Via Simeone
Via Zosimo
San Giovanni
Evangelista
Catacombe di
San Giovanni
Latomia di
Santa Venera
8
Latomia del
Paradiso ★
N E A P O L I S
Anfiteatro
Romano
Viale Augusto
Via S. Cavallari
9
10
Catacombe de
Vigna Cassia
Museo Archeologico
Regionale Paolo Orsi
Via Latomia Cassie
Via Bassa Acradina
T Y C H E
Latomia dei
Cappuccini
11
Piazza
Cappuccini
0   200 m
0   200 yds
Siracusa
Viale Teocrito
Madonna
delle Lácrime
1
Via Mofalcone
Via Gorizzia
Piazza
della Vittoria
Via Testaferrata
Via Enna
Via Ragusa
Santa Lucia
al Sepolcro
12
Piazza
Santa Lucia
Viale Paolo Orsi
Via Salso
A C R A D I N A
Corso Gelone
Piazza della
Repubblica
Via Brea
Via Agrigento
Via Caltanissetta
Via Trapani
Statella
Via Celme
I O N I A N   S E A
Stazione
Centrale
Ginnasio Romano
(Gymnasium) **15**
Via Crispi
Viale Diaz
Piazza
Euripide
Arsenale
Antico
Via della Arsenale
13
Porto Piccolo
Via Elorina
P.zle d.
Agora
14
Foro
Siracusano
Via Montedoro
Corso Umberto
Via Malta
Via Bengasi
Piazza della
Posta
Piazza
Pancali
17 Tempio
di Apollo
Lungomare di
Levante
16
P o r t o   G r a n d e
Ponte
Nuovo
Darsena
Riva Garibaldi
Via XX Settembre
Via Savoia
Corso Matteotti
Via Resalibera
18
San Pietro
Via Mirabella
Ísola di
Ortigia
Grand Hotel Ortigia
Largo Porta
Marina
Porta
Marina
Molo
Zanagora
Santa Maria
dei Miracoli
Palazzo
Beneventano
del Bosco
Foro Italico
Via Amalfitania
Piazza
Archimede
Via della Maestranza
Palazzo
Montalto
ORTIGIA
Municipio
Duomo
19
Piazza
Duomo
Via Roma
Via dei
Teatro
Via G.
Logoteta
V. Larga
Forte
Vigliena
Santa Lucia
alla Badia
Forte
Aretusa
20
21
Palazzo Bellomo
Galleria Regionale
San Martino
Lungomare Alfeo
22 Castello
Maniace

Grotta dei
Cordari
Nymphaeum
4
Via dei
Sepolcri
Via Giulio E. Rizzo
Orecchio di Dionisio
(Ear of Dionysius)
6
Teatro
Greco **2**
Biglietteria
(Ticket Office)
Latomia del
Paradiso **5**
San Nicolò
Viale Augusto
Via Giulio Emanuele Rizzo
Via Paradiso
Ara di Ierone II
(Altar of Hieron II)
3
7
Anfiteatro
Romano
Neàpolis
0   100 m
0   100 yds

SIRACUSA

Alluring, civilised and sleepy, Siracusa is less dynamic than Catania, less sultry than Palermo, yet somehow charmingly steals most visitors' hearts as the capital of sheer indulgence.

Cicero called the island of Ortigia, part of the city of Siracusa today but separated from the mainland by a narrow channel, the loveliest city in the world, and, like Siracusa itself (Syracuse in English-speaking countries), Ortigia's name resounds in academic circles abroad. Siracusa is the summation of Sicilian splendour, with an emphasis on Greek heritage. It was this cultivated city that supposedly witnessed the birth of comedy in its Greek theatre and now boasts the only school of classical drama outside Athens.

Apart from tales of Artemis and Apollo, Siracusa gave the world architectural beauty with a Baroque heart: Ortigia has facades framed by wrought-iron balconies that are as free as billowing sails. In fact, as Sicily's greatest seafaring power, Siracusa indulged an affinity with the sea that still pervades city myths and art. The city's sensual sculpture of Venus emerging from the breeze-swept sea embodies this cult of water.

Perhaps daunted by such a glorious past, today's citizens have a reputation for being dreamers and underachievers, better at wallowing in the past than at preserving it for posterity. But the end result is a city of such languid charm that it feels pernickety to point out such failings. Arguably more beautiful than Ragusa, Siracusa offers the marine nonchalance Ragusa Ibla lacks, while urban regeneration in the island heart of Siracusa is making the city lovelier than ever.

CLASSICAL GLORY

The city was founded in 733 BC, a year after Naxos, by Corinthian settlers who maintained links with Sparta. Although it was ruled by a succession of cruel but occasionally benevolent tyrants, Siracusa rose to become the supreme Mediterranean power of its age under Dionysius the Elder. The decisive battle

Main attractions

Neàpolis
Teatro Greco
Catacombe di San Giovanni
Museo Archeologico
Porto Grande boat trip
Ortigia
Duomo
Palazzo Bellomo (Galleria Regionale)
Fonte Aretusa
Lungomare di Levante
Castello Maniace

Map on page 178

Marriage in Siracusa.

⊙ Tip

Although Ortigia would be a perfect spot for cycling, all the new bicycle ranks have been permanently vandalised, so visitors are restricted to lovely walks or to the tourist train which covers the city's main sites (picked up in Piazza Archimede, and operational until mid-October).

was Siracusa's defeat of Athens in 415 BC at sea. During a despotic 38-year rule, however, Dionysius personified Sicilian tyranny (see box).

CITY SECTORS

Siracusa is a diffuse, segmented city whose ancient Greek divisions still resonate deeply with residents. **Ortigia**, the cultural island at the heart of the Greek city, remains true to its vocation: despite a grand Baroque and Catalan carapace, this beguiling backwater feels intimate, informal and quietly cultured. This is where the locals while away the long summer evenings.

By contrast, **Tyche**, the northern quarter on the mainland, can feel like the city of the dead: studded with ancient catacombs. Tyche lay beyond the bounds of Roman Syracuse and thus remains a testament to the impact of early Christianity. **Acradina**, bordering Ortigia, remains the commercial quarter, complete with railway station, while **Neàpolis**, to the northwest, though no longer "new", still embodies the ancient Greeks' notion

of public and sacred space, rangin from theatres to sanctuaries.

Both as a useful landmark and as a antidote to classical beauty, the ug modern **Santuario della Madonn delle Lacrime ❶** signals the way t the archaeological zones of Neàpoli and Tyche. Visible from most of th city with its statue of the Madonna o top, this popular pilgrimage centr (www.madonnadellelacrime.it; daily 7am 1pm, 3–8pm) commemorates a mod ern miracle: in 1953 a statue of Mar reputedly cried for five days and th spot became a shrine in the shape of giant teardrop.

To the west, Neàpolis, the ancier quarter, is synonymous with it sprawling archaeological park, **Parc Archeologico della Neàpolis** (dai 8.30am–7.30pm), containing rough hewn quarries, grandiose theatre and tombs. Although set among shad fir trees and olive groves, the site ca be sweltering in summer. But it's eas enough to avoid the tawdry stalls sell ing painted papyrus scrolls and me into the spacious Greek ruins.

⊙ DIONYSIUS'S LEGACY

Dionysius was a megalomaniac, a military strategist, a monumental builder, an inspired engineer and an execrable tragedian. The ancients didn't think highly of him and said he was the worst kind of despot – cruel, suspicious and vindictive. He presided over Siracusa's golden age, with the grandest public works in the Western world. After the sun set on ancient Greece, Siracusa became a Roman province and was supposedly evangelised by St Peter and St Paul on their way to Rome. It became the capital of Byzantium, albeit briefly, in the 7th century and produced several popes and patriarchs of Constantinople. After being sacked by the Arabs in AD 878 and the Normans in 1085, the city sank into oblivion but quietly prospered under Spanish rule.

Darsena, the docks at Siracusa.

EATRO GRECO

n the park, a stroll to the **Teatro Greco** ❷ asses the rubble of the **Ara di Ierone II** Altar of Hieron II) ❸, a sacrificial altar nce decorated by imposing *telamones* giants). Surrounded by trees, the vast pen theatre seats 15,000 and is often alled the masterpiece of ancient Greece.

This astonishing accomplishment ates from 474 BC, although much was ltered in the 3rd century BC. Carved nto the rock, the *cavea* (horseshoe of ered seats) is divided into two by a *iazoma* (corridor), and vertically cut into ine blocks of seats bearing inscriptions o deities and dignitaries. A satisfying limb to the top provides striking views ver modern Siracusa and the sea. On he terrace is a **nymphaeum** ❹, a com- lex of waterfall, springs and grotto that nce contained statues and niches for otive offerings.

In the Roman era, the theatre became n amphitheatre, with water dammed nd diverted to flood the arena for mock aval battles or gladiatorial combat. But, mong the Greeks, it was a stage that vitnessed the first performances of all

Aeschylus's tragedies. The theatrical tradition is maintained today, with the dramas of Sophocles and Euripides played on a stage once viewed by such notables as Plato and Archimedes.

Although partially closed, above the theatre, **Via dei Sepolcri** is a path of tombs, offering glimpses of tombs and carved niches at the upper level, while the lower level leads down to the *latomie*, giant quarries that were also used as prisons in classical times. A wooded path slopes behind the back of the Greek theatre to a secret rocky arch and the lush **Latomia del Paradiso** ❺. These ancient quarries were once vaulted but are now open to the sun, bursting with olive and citrus groves or overgrown with cacti and ferns.

Here, too, is the cavernous **Orecchio di Dionisio** (Ear of Dionysius) ❻, man-made and in places 47 metres (154ft) high, with excellent acoustics. It was given its name by Caravaggio after its resemblance to an ear. The poetic painter fancied that this echoing, dank, weirdly shaped cave was used by Dionysius to eavesdrop on his prisoners.

The Ear of Dionysius, a man-made cave named by Caravaggio.

Teatro Greco.

THE EUREKA MAN

Archimedes was no mere theoretician but an intensely practical inventor, master engineer and scientist when Siracusa was the most inventive place on earth.

The image of Archimedes leaping from his bath with a cry of *Eureka!* (Greek for "I have found it") is, despite the efforts of generations of physics teachers, not based in fact. While testing a gold crown suspected of being a mere alloy, Archimedes realised that the mass of water displaced by an object reveals its volume, and the mass of the object divided by its volume gives its density. The crown was found to be a fake as its density was less than that of solid gold. This discovery became known as Archimedes' Principle: the principle of specific gravity and the basis of hydrostatics.

Born in 287 BC, Archimedes worked for Hieron, the tyrant of Siracusa. While watching the tyrant's

Gold coin featuring Archimedes.

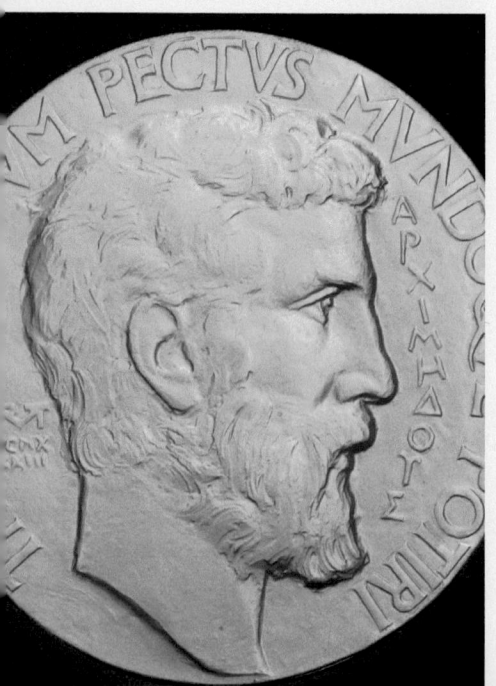

marine engineers, he devised theories worth a *Eureka!* each. His greatest discoveries were the formulae for the areas and volumes of spheres, cylinders and other shapes, anticipating the theories of integration by 1,800 years.

Dionysius's think-tank devised the long-range catapult which saved Siracusa from the Carthaginian fleet. Archimedes built on this tradition with the Archimedean screw, still used for raising water, and with siege engines that did sterling service against the Romans. Polybius says the Romans "failed to reckon with the ability of Archimedes, nor did they foresee that, in some cases, the genius of one man is more effective than any number of hands."

Archimedes is often quoted as saying "Give me a place to stand and I will move the world," implying that he understood the principles of leverage. It is unproven that he anticipated the laser beam by arranging magnifying glasses to set fire to the Roman fleet at long range, but he did produce a hydraulic serpent contraption that enabled just one man to operate a ship's pumps.

He also played a part in the construction of Hieron's remarkable 4,000-ton ship. Enough timber to build 60 conventional ships was used for the hull. It had three decks, one of which had a mosaic floor depicting scenes from the *Iliad*. The upper deck had a gymnasium, a garden and a temple to Venus paved with agate. The state cabin had a marble bath and 10 horses in stalls. Yet this was no pleasure craft. It carried a long-range catapult fitted to the masts which swung out over an attacking vessel and disgorged a huge rock, supported by a "cannon" that fired giant arrows. It was then loaded with corn, jars of Sicilian salt fish and 500 tons of wool and despatched to Ptolemy in Egypt as a gift.

Keen to exploit Archimedes' genius, the Roman commander Marcellus wanted him taken alive when the Romans occupied Siracusa. But, as legend has it, a Roman soldier came across an old codger apparently doodling in sand. Archimedes was working on his latest brainwave, so protested sharply when the soldier unwittingly stepped on his drawing. The soldier drew his sword and casually killed one of the greatest men in the world.

The adjoining **Grotta dei Cordari** is scored with chisel marks, because it was here that rope makers (*cordari*) stretched out their damp strands and tested their ropes for stress. A tunnel links Latomia del Paradiso with **Latomia Intagliatella**, and a rocky arch leads on to **Latomia di Santa Venera**, lemon-scented quarries which are pitted with votive niches.

It is hard to imagine that these lush gardens were once torture chambers. After Siracusa's decisive victory over Athens, the prisoners of war were lowered by rope into these pits. There was no need to mount guard: keeping captives alive involved no more than lowering a slave's half-rations and a drop of water. After 10 gruelling weeks, the non-Athenians who had survived were hauled out and sold as slaves. Athenians were branded with the mark of the Siracusan horse and also sold as slaves.

ROMAN AMPHITHEATRE

A separate entrance (but the same ticket) leads to the **Anfiteatro Romano** ❼, the Roman amphitheatre (partly closed for restoration) ringed by trees and overgrown with vegetation. While this tumbledown affair is not comparable with, say, the amphitheatre in France, at Nîmes, the site has charm. A path lined with stone sarcophagi leads to the imposing theatre carved by master craftsmen. Below a parapet circling the arena is a corridor where both animals and gladiators made their entrances for the spectacles.

Between the Greek theatre and Roman amphitheatre is San Nicolò, a Romanesque church concealing a Roman cistern. A circuit along **Via Giulio Emanuele Rizzo** reveals a cross-section of the classical city, including an aqueduct and the tomb-studded Via dei Sepolcri.

ANCIENT TOMBS

Further uphill lie the **Necrópoli delle Grotticelli**, a warren of Hellenistic and Byzantine tombs, including the supposed **Tomba di Archimede** (Tomb of Archimedes) ❽, framed by a dignified Roman portico. The Romans insisted that Archimedes' death was accidental, despite his creation of diabolical death traps used against them during the city's

◉ **Tip**

The Papyrus Museum may be closed, but Egyptian papermaking techniques linger on in Siracusa. Various studios throughout the city offer to reproduce anything in papyrus, from old masters on papyrus to holiday snapshots on parchment.

Roman amphitheatre.

Exhibition at the Museo Archeologico Regionale Paolo Orsi.

The Catacombe di San Giovanni.

siege. This quarter forms part of ancient Tyche, characterised by labyrinthine catacombs that often follow the course of Greek aqueducts.

The **Catacombe di San Giovanni** (San Giovanni Catacombs; www.secretsiracusa.it; summer daily 9.30am–12.30pm and 2.30–5.30pm, July–Aug 10am–1pm and 2.30–6pm, winter Mon–Sat 9.30am–12.30pm and 2.30–4.30pm) provide entry to the persecuted world of the early Christians. Escorted by a friar, visitors view early Christian sarcophagi, a 4th-century drawing of St Peter and a mosaic depicting Original Sin. The galleries open into space-creating rotundas decorated with primitive frescoes and arcane symbols, including a mysterious fish-headed boat or dead dove bound by an alpha and omega. Could this be a secret Christian code? Or a pagan transmigration of souls? Academics disagree.

In the wild garden outside is the shell of **San Giovanni Evangelista**, with its rose window and sculpted door often masked by monastic underwear drying in the sun. This modest church was Siracusa's first cathedral and is dedicated to St Marcian, the city's earliest bishop. Crooked steps lead down to **Cripta di San Marziano** and more catacombs. Light filters in on faded frescoes of St Lucy, sculpted cornices and an altar supposedly used by St Paul. Amid Greek lettering and crosses are primitive depictions of a phoenix and a bull.

MUSEUM OF ARCHEOLOGY

Probably the finest archaeological collection in Sicily lies in Villa Landolina, fittingly built over a quarry and pagan necropolis, in the **Museo Archeologico Regionale Paolo Orsi** (www.regione.sicilia.it/beniculturali/museopaoloorsi; Tue–Sat 9am–6pm, Sun 9am–1pm) on the neighbouring Viale Teocrito. The well-organised museum reveals a succession of superb collections, prehistoric and Greek, coming from Siracusa and its colonies, including finds at Gela and Agrigento. In the prehistory section, the stars are reconstructed necropoli, earthenware pots from Pantalica, and depictions of Cyclopes and dwarf elephants.

In the classical sections, the tone is set by two strikingly different works: the "immodest modesty" of the headless **Venere Anadiomene** (known also as **Venus Landolina** because it was unearthed here where the villa stands) and an Archaic sculpture of a seated fertility goddess suckling her twins, found in Megara Hyblaea. Elsewhere, the collection bursts with beauty and horror: lion's-head gargoyles, Aztec-like masks, a *Winged Victory*, a terracotta frieze of grinning gorgons and a Medusa with her tongue lolling out. Away from the horrors, smoothly virile marble torsos of *kouroi* (heroic youths) await. Beauty, both pure and sensual, lingers in the Roman sarcophagus of a couple called Valerius and Adelphia and in fragments of frieze from Selinunte and Siracusa.

Off the adjoining Via Augusto Von Platen are the **Catacombe di Vigna Cassia**, catacombs with 3rd-century tombs and frescoed chambers which lead on to **Latomia dei Cappuccini** , the most

icturesque quarries, alongside a for-mer Capuchin monastery. Set on the oast, these huge honeycombed pits are natched by sculptural vegetation, but urrently they can only be viewed from ia Acradina above. From the adjoining iazza Cappuccini are stirring views of ne rocky shore.

Further south again, near the sports tadium, are a series of catacombs Mon–Fri summer 11am–5.30pm, win-er until 4.30pm; guided tours only, tel: 931 64694) surrounding the church of anta Lucia al Sepolcro ⑫, a Byzantine hurch founded by San Zozimo, the first Greek bishop of Siracusa, and dedicated o St Lucy, the city's virginal patron saint vho was martyred here. Next door, con-ected by an underground passage, is ne octagonal **Cappella del Sepolcro**, vhich was constructed in 1630 as a aintly sepulchre.

ORTO PICCOLO TO PORTO GRANDE

On the banks of the **Porto Piccolo** ⑬, the mall harbour, are the scant remains f the city's ancient arsenal. Nearby

stands the Byzantine **bath-house**, where legend has it that Emperor Con-stans was assassinated with a soap dish in AD 668. On **Piazzale del Foro Siracu-sano**, just behind the port, is the original **Greek *agora*** ⑭ of Acradina. This was the commercial centre of the Greek city but sadly suffered bombing by both the Allies and the Luftwaffe in 1943. At its centre is a war memorial.

Further west lies the ruins of the **Ginnasio Romano** ⑮, the Roman gym-nasium (Mon–Sat 9am–1pm; free), a 1st-century theatre and shrine occu-pying a picturesquely flooded spot. Although its origins are obscure, the shrine was conceivably dedicated to ori-ental deities. The raised portico is well preserved and shimmers obligingly.

Nearby, the **Porto Grande** ⑯, where Dionysius defeated the Athenian navy in 415 BC, has become a busy mercan-tile harbour and pleasure port, with a new yacht marina.

ORTIGIA

A stroll across the main bridge, Ponte Nuovo, leads past bobbing boats and

⊘ Tip

One excursion worth considering is a short cruise from Porto Grande around Ortigia, following the coastline and fascinating fortifications. Several boat companies on Porto Grande ply their wares but, as in classical times, remember that bargaining is a Sicilian art form.

Outside Siracusa's Duomo.

⊘ ORTIGIA'S REAWAKENING

After decades of neglect, Ortigia is slowly returning to its ancient splendour. The most charming part of Siracusa is already awash with waterfront bars and cosy restaurants, but now the locals are moving back, turning Baroque palaces into boutique hotels and upmarket B&Bs. Creeping gentrification is taking place everywhere, attracting a more enlightened generation, particularly young professionals in search of urban charm.

The transformation is far from complete. Despite EU funds earmarked for Ortigia's restoration, the city's bureaucratic lethargy and lobbying by vested interest groups mean that many projects remain stalled. But rather than grumbling, entrepreneurial citizens are exerting pressure for urban renewal, with the waterfront promenades a success story in the making. Even if parts of the Lungomare di Levante are still to be restored, this moody promenade makes a glorious seafront stroll in any season. Exploring the medieval lanes on foot is the best way to discover this pic-turesque part of the town. The classic stroll leads to the restored Castello Maniace, now a museum and events centre, and winds its way round to Fonte Aretusa and the promenade of Lungomare di Ponente on the west-ern side of Ortigia. The evening *passeggiata* (walk) is best enjoyed with a cooling gelato or granita in hand.

Temple of Apollo.

Cheerful Siracusians.

pastel-coloured palazzi to the **Darsena**, the inner docks. This is the tiny but atmospheric island of Ortigia, jutting into the **Mare Ionio**, the Ionian Sea. Rivalled only by Ragusa as a centre of aimless wandering, this largely pedestrianised island is the place for leisurely lunches, summer promenades and dreamy ruminations amid crumbling history.

Graced with two natural harbours, fresh springs and the blessing of the Delphic oracle, this seductive island was dedicated to the huntress Artemis, with the chief temple known as "the couch of Artemis". In Christian times, the goddess fused with St Lucy, the city's patron saint, and her cult is still venerated in city festivals.

Heralding the entrance to Ortigia is the **Tempio di Apollo** ⓱ (Temple of Apollo), sunken and dishevelled but still the oldest city temple in Sicily. This Doric temple was built in 565 BC and discovered by chance in 1862. It is dedicated to Apollo, whose name is legible on the steps of the base. The squat temple has accrued Byzantine and Norman remains, and is thought to have functioned as both a church and a mosque.

In the maze of streets behind the temple is **San Pietro** ⓲, supposedly founded by St Peter before being converted into a Byzantine basilica. The 8th-century apses and blind arcading are incorporated into a 15th-century shell. Just west, Via XX Settembre contains tracts of the massive Greek walls. Dionysius was an indefatigable builder and the immense wall, 5km (3 miles) in length, was built in 20 days by 60,000 men on double time, and is still visible in other parts of the town.

ORTIGIA'S CENTRE

From the temple, it is a short stroll along Via Roma to Piazza Archimede, the grandiose centre of Ortigia. This Baroque stage set, adorned by a decorative fountain, is home to dignified mansions and open-air cafés. On the next square awaits the magnificent **Duomo** ⓳ (www.secretsiracusa.it; daily Apr–June and Sep 9am–6.30pm, July–Aug 9am–7pm, Oct–Mar 9am–5.30pm). This 5th-century temple to Athena was converted into a Christian cathedral in AD 640. Classical columns bulge through the external walls in Via Minerva, a sign that the temple has only been encased in a church since the 7th century. Before then, the temple was a beacon to sailors, with its ivory doors and a gold facade surmounted by the goddess Athena bearing a glinting bronze shield.

The exterior conjures up a unique spell: a rich Baroque facade (1754) with dramatic chiaroscuro effects, including an inside porch boasting twisted barley-stick columns. Yet the cool, striking interior betrays its Greek origins; the worn but lovely fluted Doric columns set into the outer walls belong to the Temple to Athena. Notwithstanding a Greek soul, the temple also glorifies later conquerors. A Greek baptismal font rests on Norman bronze lions; above is a medieval wood-panelled ceiling; a Baroque choir and Byzantine oses strike newer notes; only the rab presence is missing. The apses ere slightly damaged in the 1991 arthquake, but the Greek sandstone uted columns survived. In the side hapel, **Cappella del Crocifisso**, is a ainting of *St Zosimus* by Antonello da Messina, and one of *St Marcian* attributed to the school of Antonello, also elieved to have painted the 13 panels the **Sagrestia** (Sacristy).

Virtually next door is the church of **anta Lucia alla Badia**, which is now ome to Caravaggio's masterpiece *The urial of St Lucy* (1608). Also in Piazza el Duomo is the Palazzo Vermexio 633), the **Municipio** (Town Hall), built n the ruins of a small Ionic temple ossibly dedicated to Artemis.

Just a short distance away, on Via apodieci, stands **Palazzo Bellomo** ⑳, he loveliest Catalan-Gothic mansion Ortigia, and the city's compact art allery, **Galleria Regionale** (Tue–Sat am–7pm, Sun 2–7.30pm).

Inside, an elegant courtyard leads to he intimate gallery housing Antonello a Messina's remarkable *Annunciaon* (1474) and the grandiose **funerary onument** for Eleonora Branciforte 'Aragona by Giovan Battista Mazzolo. ther highlights include 14th- to 18thentury works, from Byzantine icons Catalan and Spanish paintings, 'enaissance tombs and important ieces in gold, silver, coral, ceramics nd terracotta.

'ONTE ARETUSA

t the southern end of Via Capodieci is **'onte Aretusa** ㉑, a freshwater spring hat is the symbol of Siracusa. Legend as it that the nymph Arethusa, a folower of great Olympian deity Artemis Diana), was loved and pursued by the iver god Alpheius after she bathed in is waters in the Peloponnese.

As she fled from his embrace to Sicy, she prayed to Artemis for help and, n reaching Ortigia, was changed by rtemis into a spring called Arethusa (Aretusa). Alpheius, however, did not give up. He flowed below the sea and mingled his waters with hers. Whether this was rape or the uniting of lovers, Siracusani continue to disagree.

After a 17th-century earthquake, however, the spring is supposed to have mingled with sea water but, in reality, Ortigia has an abundance of fresh water coming from the Iblei mountains through a peculiar geological land fault. Many houses have serviceable wells.

In any case, ducks make the clumps of reedy papyrus plants in spring water a romantic love nest. At night, the fountain sees a parade of Siracusa's youth, accompanied by flirtation and the obligatory stop for a water-ice nearby. In 1798 Admiral Nelson's fleet drew water at the fountain before proceeding to Malta and then on to the battle of the Nile.

From Fonte Aretusa, the panoramic terraces of **Passeggio Adorno** lead back to the Porto Grande quays via the **Porta Marina** archway, one of the city gates created in the 15th-century

Strolling at Fonte Aretusa at night.

Spanish fortifications. Known as the **Lungomare di Ponente**, this charming promenade makes a lovely stroll. The triumphal archway itself leads to the Catalan-Gothic Quarter, centred on **Santa Maria dei Miracoli**. Set off Via Savoia, this finely sculpted 15th-century church is a prelude to lunch at one of the seafood inns tucked into the side streets.

LUNGOMARE DI LEVANTE

The other side of the island is skirted by the **Lungomare di Levante**, the atmospheric eastern waterfront, easily approached via the Temple of Apollo. The waterfront borders the Arab Quarter, with its tortuous, narrow streets designed to create breezes and keep homes cool even in summer.

You can also get to the Lungomare from Piazza Archimede, along **Via della Maestranza** and the old guilds' quarter, graced with Spanish palaces that have been reborn as gracious B&Bs or bohemian bars. Amid the sombre courtyards and swirling sculpture, local *pasticcerie* literally

represent the icing on the cake There is a vegetable and fish market on the Lungomare on weekday mornings.

On the southernmost tip of Ortigia the fortified hulk of **Castello Maniace** ㉒ (www.comune.siracusa.it; daily 8.30am–12.30pm) dominates the promontory and once served as protector of Siracusa's two shores. Constructed in 1239 by Frederick II, takes its name from the Byzantine general Giorgio Maniace, who was in charge of the city's defences. Even largely empty, the Swabian castle is a magnificent monument in terms of ambition and scale. By the northwest tower is the castle's secret freshwater supply, the Bagno della Regina, a chamber fed by a freshwater spring which was fundamental to the siting of the castle here.

Until 2001 the fortress was an army base, but is now open to the public, apart from one section that houses Italy's art police, responsible for recovering (or safeguarding) national treasures.

Puppet workshop.

While the castle was a major military base, the troops stationed here played an important role in anti-Mafia campaigns in the 1990s. Temporary exhibitions and summer concerts are also staged here.

GREAT ESCAPES

Close to the city are sandy beaches and two unique spots, a Greek castle and a dreamy riverscape of papyrus plantations. Alternatively, to sample Siracusa's funky urban beach, you can join the locals on the Ortigia pontoons built over the waterside at **Forte Vigliena** (see page 196).

South of Siracusa, off the SS115 (the route to Noto and Módica), lie popular beaches at the small resorts of **Arenella**, **Ognina** and **Fontane Bianche**. Although Siracusa's beaches tend to be full of golden bodies rather than golden sands, a more atmospheric swimming spot is 20km (12 miles) north of Siracusa, past Augusta, at **Brùcoli**. It is a rocky beach set around a Spanish castle that enjoys views of Etna on clear days.

In ancient **Epipolae**, 8km (5 miles) northwest of Siracusa, is the **Castello Eurialo** (variable hours, call tel: 0931 711 773; follow signs to Belvedere). The fort represented the fifth component of the Greek pentapolis and was the most magnificent of Greek military outposts. Designed by Dionysius, the castle protected Siracusa's most exposed flank, the conjunction of the northern and southern city walls.

Apart from amazingly solid masonry and moats hewn out of the rock, the castle had labyrinthine passageways and a keep surrounded by five towers. As a final security measure, the sole entrance was concealed by a patchwork of walls. When Dionysius was in residence, he would not allow his wives into his bed unless they were first searched. According to legend, his bed was surrounded by a moat, and his wives reached it across a little wooden drawbridge, which he then drew up.

FONTE CIANE

South of the city, after 5km (3 miles) is **Fonte Ciane** (Spring of Ciane), a picturesque spot close to the ruined Temple of Olympian Zeus. (Follow signs to Fonte Ciane.) Ciane is the mythical spring and pool dedicated to the water-nymph Ciane (Cyane), who dissolved into her own pool with grief as she wept, having failed to prevent the rape of Persephone by Hades who had risen from the Underworld through the pool.

Canoes, easily rented from the tiny riverside marina from March onwards, are a way to explore the relaxing rivers, framed by canopies of lush foliage. The bohemian boutique hotel of Caol Ishka is on the neighbouring Anapo river and can book trips for guests, as well as gourmet dinners.

The Ciane weaves through groves of papyrus with tendrils as delicate as cobwebs. The origins of this wild plant are obscure: it was either imported from Egypt or native to Siracusa. Either way, its habitat is endangered, but it flourishes in this idyllic backwater.

Tip

For many visitors Siracusa is the place for market shopping. Best bets are the markets (daily except Sunday) on Ortigia, on the Lungomare close to the Tempio di Apollo, and the larger, rambling general market, La Fiera, on the outskirts, on Via Algeri. Coaches bring in the crowds from the surrounding towns and villages, so you will not be alone.

Castello Maniace.

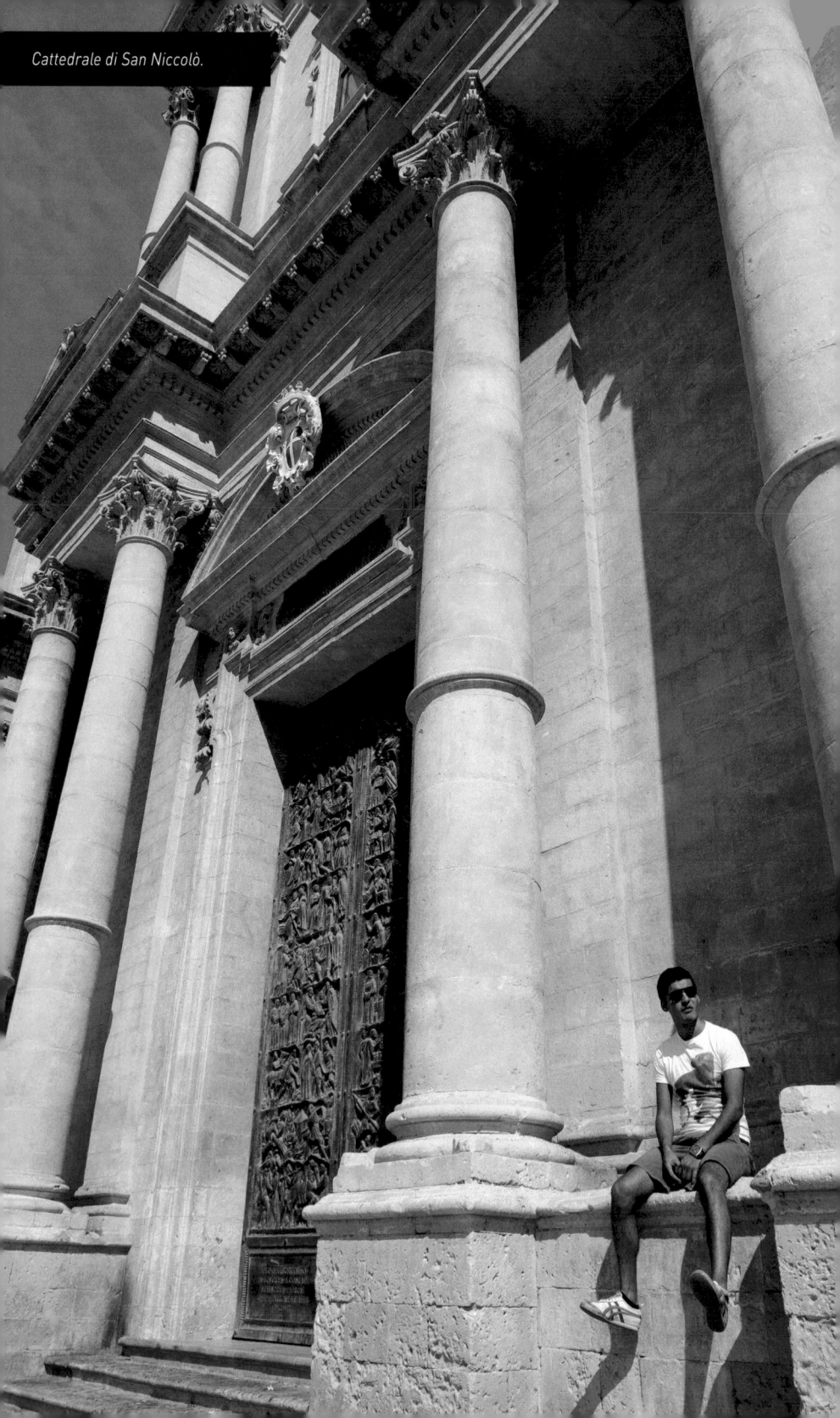

Cattedrale di San Niccolò.

SIRACUSA PROVINCE

Outside the city, this southeastern province offers a cross-section of Sicily: Baroque, classical and prehistoric blended with a leisurely way of life.

The Greeks colonised this area two centuries after settling the rest of eastern Sicily. Since then Siracusa has rested on its laurels, parading its Greek heart and Levantine soul with the effortless superiority of a born aristocrat.

The province has been shaped by the cataclysm of the 1693 earthquake. Although all Norman castles were razed to the ground, the region responded by building some of the greatest Baroque architecture in Sicily, notably in the newly restored town of Noto.

FARMING COUNTRY

The journey southwards from **Siracusa ❶** passes gentle farming country dotted with olive and almond groves, citrus orchards and low-slung farms. Just inland of the flat coastal strip and sandy beaches, the farmland is interspersed with rugged terrain spanning limestone escarpments and rocky gorges.

At **Cassibile**, south of Siracusa, surrounded by grand sweeps of land cultivating citrus, almonds and cereals, is the spot where, on 3 September 1943, US general Bedell Smith signed the Allied terms of surrender with the Italian general, Castellano. From that day onwards Italy's army was no longer in World War II. The event is commemorated by a stone plaque on the SS115 route south.

Street scene in Noto.

Further south is the flourishing market town of **Avola**, whose prosperity stems from its role as Italy's almond capital. Avola is merely the prelude to the Baroque setting of Noto, stacked up on a hill. On Piazza Umberto I, in the heart of this hexagonally shaped town, is the **Chiesa Madre**, built after the 1693 earthquake.

NOTO

Then there is **Noto ❷**, the finest Baroque town in Sicily, one that is both blatantly theatrical and deeply rational.

Main attractions

Siracusa (Syracuse)
Noto
Palazzo Nicolaci di Villadorata
Eloro
Vendìcari wetlands
Marzameni
Capo Pàssero
Necrópoli di Pantálica
Akrai

Map on page 192

◎ Eat

In Noto, **Caffè Sicilia** (Corso Vittorio Emanuele 125; tel: 0931 835 013) celebrates sweet Sicilian classics, including *cannoli* (pastries stuffed with sweet ricotta and candied fruit) and *cassata* (a ricotta, chocolate, candied fruit and marzipan treat), as well as recherché but less calorific concoctions, such as mulberry sorbet.

With justification, visitors praise its proportion, symmetry, spaciousness and innate sense of spectacle. Sicilians simply call it a garden of stone. For many years much of it lay crumbling and neglected, but with restoration in hand, this Unesco World Heritage site is rapidly returning to its former glory. Noto is now one of Sicily's most delightful towns, best seen in the late afternoon when the sun strikes the golden facades and the chic cafés confirm the impression of walking in a stage set.

After the original Noto, known now as **Noto Antica 3**, was destroyed in the 1693 earthquake, it lay buried under rubble, abandoned ruins nestling in the foothills of the Iblean mountains, the phoenix that never rose from the ashes. It was a complex city full of classical foundations, Romanesque and Baroque churches, convents and mansions, a home over the centuries to Romans, Arabs and Normans as it grew into a flourishing medieval city. All this was obliterated in 1693.

Ten years later a new site on safer ground 10km (6 miles) away was selected by the inhabitants and headed by Giuseppe Lanza (duke of Camastra) and Prince Giovanni Landolina, new Noto was planted on the flanks of a distant hill. The city was composed around three parallel axes running horizontally across the hillside, with straight streets and three squares to create interest, each enlivened by a scenic church as a backdrop. The whole design was clothed in warm, golden limestone, with monumental flights of steps to enchant with tricks of perspective. The project was entrusted to Gagliardi and Sinatra, gifted local architects closely associated with masterpieces in Ragusa province.

Despite the beauteous architecture, the glowing limestone buildings are inherently fragile and susceptible to erosion and pollution. The city faced its greatest crisis in 1996 when the cupola and roof of the Cathedral of San Niccolò collapsed after a heavy thunderstorm. Since then, civic pride and impressive restoration have brought Noto to life once more.

Noto at night.

CORSO VITTORIO EMANUELE

The monumental gateway **Porta Reale** (1838) at the end of the tree-lined public gardens leads to **Corso Vittorio Emanuele**, Noto's stately main thoroughfare. Broken by three equally monumental squares, this processional avenue is dotted along its length with inviting cafés and kiosks for ices and *granita*. To the left, the town slopes downwards; to the right, it rises graciously to meet **Noto Alta** (Upper Noto).

The first building on the right, on **Piazza dell'Immacolata**, gives a fine idea of what is to follow. At the top of a theatrical, grand flight of stairs (only for the fittest), the church of **San Francesco** (daily) looks like the backdrop for a film set. Built between 1704 and 1745 by Rosario Gagliardi and Vincenzo Sinatra, it has a pleasant facade and simple, stucco interior. The **Seminario**, once the Benedictine monastery of **San Salvatore** (1706), sits alongside the church, facing it across the steep incline of Via Zanardelli. It has a fine 18th-century facade attributed to Rosario Gagliardi. Also on this piazza is the richly decorated church of **Santa Chiara** (daily 10.30am–1pm and 2.30–4pm), containing Antonello Gagini's marble statue of the *Madonna and Child*. Pay a small fee to climb the church's panoramic *terraza* for wonderful views of the town. The adjacent former Benedictine convent houses the **Museo Civico** (daily 9.30am–1.30pm and 3.30–7.30pm, Aug 9am–midnight) including archaeological findings from Noto Antica and a contemporary art section.

The Corso sweeps onwards to **Piazza Municipio**, the second square, Noto's stage set. The golden grace of the buildings matches the majestic proportions of the design. On the square is the **Palazzo Ducezio**, (daily 10am–1.30pm and 3–6pm), the elegantly grand town hall designed by Vincenzo Sinatra in 1746. The *pièce de résistance* is the **Sala degli Specchi**, an oval, mirrored reception room designed in Louis XV style.

Opposite is the splendid towering **Cattedrale di San Niccolò** (entrance on Via Cavour; daily 8am–1pm, 4–8pm). The cathedral boasts a theatrical staircase, wide 18th-century facade,

Madonna and Child in Santa Chiara.

cupola and cool pastel interior, with the restoration story recounted in the adjoining museum.

Next to the cathedral is the **Palazzo Landolina**, the Bishop's Palace that was once the home of one of Noto's benefactors.

The Corso progresses to **Piazza XVI Maggio**, graced by gardens of palms, monkey puzzle trees and a fountain of Hercules taken from Noto Antica. (The helpful tourist office is in this garden; tel: 0931 573 779.) Dominating the shady garden lies the well-restored church of **San Domenico**, a curvilinear Gagliardi masterpiece with a beautiful facade influenced by Roman and Spanish Baroque.

Facing it is the restored, ornately gilded 1850 **Teatro Vittorio Emanuele** and the **Collegio dei Gesuiti**. On the downwards slope, where Via Ruggero VII meets Via Ducezio, stands **Santa Maria del Carmine** (daily 9am–7pm), created by Gagliardi's assistant, Vincenzo Sinatra. Its concave doorway is guarded by two *putti* (cherubs), the symbol of the Carmelite order.

Cattedrale di San Niccolò steps.

PALAZZO NICOLACI DI VILLADORATA

Leading uphill from Piazza Municipio Noto's pride and joy, the **Palazzo Nicolaci di Villadorata** (daily 10.30am–1p and 3–5.30pm). Set on Via Nicolaci a named after the noble Nicolaci dynas this Baroque jewel has finally be restored to its former glory.

Don Giacomo Nicolaci, a patron of t arts, donated part of his huge libra to the town, but the palace itself no belongs to Noto citizens too. Arou the windows are ornate balconies a friezes of mythical monsters, a snarli parade of griffins, sphinxes, sirens a cherubs. Arabesques climb the wall clashing with crested cornices and b lowing wrought-iron balconies. T sloped courtyard was designed for ca riages and includes an access ramp that the prince could ride directly in the *piano nobile*. The palatial interio convey the opulence yet intimacy aristocratic life in Noto, from the fre coed ceilings to the antique ceram floors and the views over Baroque No

Palazzo Nicolaci plays a starring r in the city drama away from the Cors but secondary characters should be overlooked, especially in conven churches and cafés. Around the co ner, on Via Nicolaci, call into **Canti Módica di San Giovanni** (www.vinidino it) to see the private museum of Ale sandro Módica while sampling Mo Iblei cheeses, salami and wine fro this young baron's wine estate.

On Via Cavour, parallel to the Cors is the church of **Montevergine** (1748–5 with its concave frontage, while Via G vanni XXIII, behind San Niccolò, revea ornate niches, sculpted cornices a bulging "goose-breast" balconies.

Paradoxically, the higher the lev the lower the class of the resident Even so, the two-tiered city loo entirely homogeneous. The spacio lower town was originally only f the clergy and aristocracy. On the h above the grandiose public face

oto rises the *popolare* district, clustered around the hilly Piazza Mazzini, ominated by the **Crocifisso**, a domed hurch attributed to Gagliardi that has portal flanked by Romanesque lions escued from Noto Antica. Inside is Francesco Laurana masterpiece, *Madonna della Neve* (Madonna of the now, 1471), a serene sculpture amid ne frenzy of Baroque.

The massive building with an attracve facade stretching from Via Trigona o Piazza Mazzini is the former monstery, **Monastero di San Tommaso** 1720), now a prison.

The **Giardino Pubblico** at the eastern nd of the Corso is a peaceful end to ny visit to Noto.

HE SOUTHERN COAST

outheast of Noto are well-signposted andy beaches that become busy only n July and August. Visitors in search of istinctiveness will prefer the Vendìcari ands and wetlands to the unassuming each resorts of the **Lido di Noto** and **Lido d'Avola**, which essentially cater to icilian families.

Eloro ❹ is a classical site on the unpolluted stretch that leads south to Capo Pàssero. Now in ruins, the Siracusan city of Elorus (visits by appointment only, tel: 0931 450 811) was founded at the end of the 6th century BC. Well-preserved turreted walls survive, as do porticoes, a pair of gateways, the *agora* and a Sanctuary of Demeter. Just outside the site stands the **Colonna della Pizzuta**, a curious Hellenistic funerary column that looks like a chimney stack. In the neighbouring hamlet of **Caddeddi**, a villa from the same period has been unearthed, along with mosaics depicting hunting scenes.

OASI VENDÌCARI

The 6km (4-mile) journey south to the deserted **Vendìcari wetlands** ❺ (Riserva Naturale Oasi Faunistica di Vendìcari; www.riserva-vendicari.it) passes citrus and almond groves. The Vendìcari salt marshes appeal to both beach-lovers and birdwatchers, as this haven for flamingos, storks and egrets also embraces a sweeping crescent of sand. Invigorating walks

Ceiling fresco at the Palazzo Nicolaci di Villadorata.

Church of San Francesco.

⊘ Tip

Siracusa boasts several fine beaches in the south of the province. In Ortigia itself, visitors can sunbathe or swim from the bathing platform erected over the sculpted rocks at Forte Vigliena. South of the city, off the SS115 to Noto, lie popular sandy beaches at the small resorts of Arenella, Ognina and Fontane Bianche. However, discerning locals prefer to travel to the wilder shores of the Vendicari nature reserve further south.

and marked trails run through the salt marshes, with medieval water channels cut to reach the saltpans. The site also includes battered medieval fortifications, a Swabian tower, Byzantine catacombs and an abandoned 18th-century *tonnara*, one of the tuna fisheries that made Sicily's fortune. Although sun-worshippers will prefer summer, birdwatchers and walkers should opt for autumn and spring, when waders and ducks share the waters with the flamingos. (Bring a picnic as there are virtually no facilities in the reserve.)

MARZAMEMI

Further down the coast lies **Marzamemi ❻**, the most appealing fishing village in the province. As a former feudal domain, the village retains a crumbling noble palace, adorned with the Villadorata family crest. Despite becoming a small-time summer resort and summer marina, at heart Marzamemi remains a working fishing village, complete with lobster pots and the obligatory fishing nets drying in the sun. *Cernia* (grouper), like *pesce spada*

Marzamemi harbour.

(swordfish), is a prized Mediterranean fish, but mullet, mussels and tuna are also on local menus.

In summer, Sicilians also flock to **Pachino ❼** and the sandy beaches around Capo Pàssero. The pillboxes littering this stretch of coast are a testament to troubled times. In July 1943 the Allied invasion of Sicily took place on these shores. While General Patton and the American forces landed near Gela, General Montgomery and the British 8th Army landed between Pachino and Pozzallo. Giuseppe Tornatore's film *Malena* includes a dramatic re-enactment of the landing on Pachino's beaches. Nowadays, Pachino is a quiet tomato- and wine-producing centre with a faded Baroque heart.

Beyond is **Capo Pàssero ❽**, the southernmost tip of the province and home to several low-key seaside resorts that were, until recently, entirely dependent on tuna fishing. Today, only one tuna fishery remains, run by Don Bruno di Belmonte. Energetic visitors can rent a boat to row to Isola di Capo Pàssero and the other island rocks here.

NORTH OF SIRACUSA

Swimming is not advisable on the northern stretch of coast, in the **Golfo di Augusta** between Siracusa and Augusta, except at Brùcoli, just north of Augusta, where the Golfo di Catania begins. As the coastline reputed to have Europe's highest concentration of chemical effluents, this area is an ecological disaster. Petrochemical plants based around Augusta have destroyed 48km (30 miles) of beach. At night, however, this stretch has a savage, futuristic beauty of its own, with its glittering towers, gargantuan oil tanks and livid smokestacks.

The classical sites of Thapsos on Penisola Magnisi and neighbouring Megara Hyblaea are too close for comfort to the belching fumes. Acrid fumes threaten to engulf the important site of

Megara Hyblaea ❾, one of the earliest Greek cities in Sicily, founded in 728 BC. Cypresses shield it in poetic desolation, but industrial blight is tangible. A wall and a group of sarcophagi front the ramparts of a Hellenistic fortress. Beyond are the foundations of an archaic city, as yet unexplored.

As a smaller mirror image of Siracusa, **Augusta** once had charm and prestige. However, while its islet setting, double harbour and faded Baroque centre remain, so does rampant industrialisation.

THE ANCIENT INTERIOR

The rocky, wild, sparsely populated interland is one of Siracusa's charms. The summer-parched slopes and odd mounds conceal several significant classical sites. The desolate countryside generates an austere appeal that is matched by the dusty Baroque country towns along the route. This is Sicily with its roots laid bare, a prehistoric and Siculi land that predates Siracusa city by centuries. The rocky tableland is home to **Pantálica**, the region's

foremost prehistoric site. The drive to Pantálica skirts the bleached white or pale-green Iblean hills before reaching the lush **Anapo Valley**.

Dedicated hikers with a full day to spend in Pantálica will choose the northern entrance, reached through Palazzolo. However, for less walking, choose the southern route through **Sortino**, following signs for Pantálica Sud. This rural drive passes country villas, citrus groves and dry-stone walls.

Despite their importance, the **Necrópoli di Pantálica ❿** (daily 9.30am–sunset) are off the beaten track. However, Siracusani have long been drawn to the lush gorges, a verdant paradise remote from the barren image of the Iblean hills. Apart from the loveliness of this sprawling site, Pantálica offers a slice of Sicily's earliest history: this Siculi necropolis contains rock tombs dating from the 13th to the 8th century BC. As the largest Bronze and Iron Age cemetery in Sicily, it contains over 5,000 tombs carved into the sheer cliffs of a limestone plateau, not to mention cave dwellings.

Pachino, the site of the Allied invasion of Sicily in 1943.

Capo Pàssero.

⊙ Fact

The sandy beaches around Pachino are where the British 8th Army landed in July 1943 to reclaim the island from the Germans.

Although Pantálica's history is shrouded in mystery, tradition claims it as Hybla, the capital of the Siculi king who allowed Greek colonists to occupy Megara Hyblaea. Certainly, some of these gaping holes are 3,000 years old.

The tombs lie at the end of a gorge carved by the River Anapo and studded with citrus trees and wild flowers and prickly pears. In this secret garden lie tiered rows of tombs, a honeycomb-pitted surface of jagged rectangular openings cut into the pale rock. Mule tracks and marked paths follow the river towards a disused railway line, with easier paths marked "A", and more challenging ones marked "B". Walkers are rewarded with discreet picnic spots, as well as views of sheer rock faces and deep ravines. Apart from the tombs and dwellings, there remains a Byzantine rock chapel, and early Christian frescoes. In spring this sacred chasm is a beauty spot bursting with snapdragons, asphodel and daisies.

A country drive leads southwest to **Palazzolo Acrèide ⓫**, a sleepy Norman town surprised to discover that outsiders should stray so far. The Baroque centre displays several theatrical set-pieces, whose charms are only slightly diminished by the air of abandon. The town's rough-hewn charms are apparent in the Palazzo Zocco on Via Umberto, with its chaotic Baroque ornamentation, and the early Baroque **Chiesa Annunziata**, with a portal guarded by Spanish barley-shape columns. However, many rewards are low-key: the occasional gargoyle, carved doorpost or billowing balcony. Palazzolo Acrèide is also known for its traditional carnival and its marvellous feast day that celebrates San Sebastiano. The pork sausage from **Casa della Salsiccia** (Piazza Liberazione 2; tel: 0931 882 410; closed Wed pm) are much favoured too.

AKRAI

A signposted road for **Teatro Greco** leads to the Classical city of **Akrai ⓬**, a Greek site set on high, windy moorland. The attractive walled park (daily 8am–6.30pm) encloses quarries and temples founded in 644 BC by Siracusa, and a Greek theatre (3rd century BC, but then also used by the Romans) built on a grand scale.

The confusing site contains stone carvings, votive niches, a necropolis, catacombs and the remains of a Temple to Aphrodite. The most impressive views are of the deep quarries framed by dry-stone walls, firs, bay trees and wild olives. The lovely site suffers from poor management, with temples and sculptures arbitrarily locked. Across the hillside are the Santoni (Holy Ones), a series of 12 crudely carved sculptures made in honour of the goddess Cybele, the Magna Mater whose esoteric cult originated in Asia. These precious finds lie a few fields away, and a visit there requires a custodian's presence.

Leading out of town, the **Strada Panoramica** circling Akrai lives up to its name, offering fabulous views across the Greek settlements towards Ragusa province.

Pantálica.

The bucolic setting of the Pantálica necropolis.

THE ART OF PUPPETRY AND PAINTED CARTS

Flamboyant manifestations of the nation's folklore, puppets and carts portray Sicily's history in brash primary colours.

The travelling puppet show has provided entertainment in Sicily for centuries, telling tales of saints, bandits or heroes, but most commonly the Paladins, the knights of Charlemagne's court, and their battles against the Saracens.

The Christians traditionally strut on the left of the stage, the turbaned, baggy-trousered Saracens on the right. The audience knows all the characters – the knights Orlando and Rinaldo, the beautiful Angelica and the wicked traitor Gano di Magonza – and identifies with them as characters in a familiar soap opera.

The great writer Carlo Levi said of the tradition: "The Paladins are actual idols, we delight in their victories and cry at their deaths." Not so long ago, watching a puppet show was an evening ritual for many Sicilians. Now it is more of a beloved folk memory, even if the tradition is still kept alive in Palermo, Catania and Siracusa. Puppetry was even added to the Unesco World Heritage List as a recognition of its unique place in Sicilian life.

The artists who decorate these traditional painted car raid motifs from their multiracial heritage: Arab adornment and arabesques; chivalric legends and Bib epics; the Crusades and the Napoleonic wars.

A puppet show at the Teatro dei Pupi, Siracusa; metal wires move the hands and a thicker bar turns their he

Old puppets at the Puppet Workshop and Museum in Siracusa.

Santo Stefano ceramics.

Exhilarating Pottery

Traditional Sicilian ceramics display the same vivacity and vibrant use of colour as the island's puppets and carts. Even if pottery is far more usual, some of the greatest Sicilian palaces will have decorations, even floor tiles, made by Caltagirone craftsmen.

Thanks to the inexhaustible deposits of clay surrounding the town, Caltagirone had a reputation for pottery even before the Arabs introduced local craftsmen to the glazed polychromatic colours – particularly blues, greens and yellows – that have become typical of Sicilian ceramics.

As well as functional items such as vases, bowls and jugs, Caltagirone craftsmen also produce decorative tiles, medallions and figurines in the same lively colours.

Santo Stéfano di Camastra is the second great ceramics centre on the island. On the Messina–Palermo road, the small town seems overwhelmed with its pottery: tiers of dishes, tureens and bowls line both sides of the road. The traditional style here has a rustic look and feel, often featuring fish designs. The other local speciality is tiles decorated with smiling suns and saints.

...corative plate from Santo Stefano.

...amics maker in Santo Stefano.

Painted clown pottery figure from Sciacca.

CATANIA

As Sicily's second city, Catania is a slow burn, both a bold Baroque affair bustling with commerce and the natural springboard to Mount Etna.

Main attractions

Piazza del Duomo
Palazzo Biscari
Teatro Romano
Opera at Teatro Bellini
Via Crociferi
Villa Bellini
Castello Ursino
La Pescheria

Map on page 203

Catania is a city of contradictions: brash, belligerent and beleagured yet also vibrant, cultured and resilient. It is a commercial success as well as a showcase of Sicilian Baroque. But the city has an edginess, not least because its 315,000 people live permanently in the southern shadow of Mount Etna, a volcano that can seem menacing, glowing red in the night sky. The approach to Catania along the *circonvallazione* (ring road) reveals the extent of nature's wrath. Etna's recent volcanic flows are visible between the grim tenements or piled like black slag heaps by the roadside.

In keeping with its volcanic temperament, Catania celebrates a vibrant arts scene, offering *bel canto* opera in the homeland of Bellini, as well as classical music, live jazz and blues. The city also boasts the best night life in Sicily, with a profusion of cool galleries, bars, restaurants and clubs tucked away in the historic centre. As an energetic university city, Catania offers events ranging from pop-rock spectaculars to open-air summer festivals. The venues vary from converted refineries to cosy clubs in the city centre.

CITY SIGHTS

Visually, Catania seems the most homogeneous Sicilian city. From 1730 it was stamped with the vision of one man, Giovan Battista Vaccarini, an architect from Palermo influenced by grand Roman Baroque. His work has a sculptural quality allied to a native vigour. Billowing balconies, sweeping S-curves and a taste for chiaroscuro are intermixed. Until your eyes adjust, the dark colour of the volcanic stone can seem oppressive, but the chromatic effects are skilful.

Piazza del Duomo ❶ is the Baroque centrepiece, a dignified composition on a grand scale. The buildings in

Locals doing a deal near Catania's fish market.

e square make use of flat facades, strained decoration, elegant windows and huge pilasters. At the centre the city's famous symbol, Vaccarini's delightful **Fontana dell'Elefante**, a lack lava-stone elephant supporting towering Egyptian obelisk taken from e Roman circus.

The **Duomo ❷** (www.cattedralecatania.it; ww.museodiocesanocatania.com; Mon–Sat 30am–noon and 4.30–7pm, Sun 7am–pon and 4–7pm, museum Mon–Fri am–2pm, Tue and Thu also 3–6pm, Sat am–1pm), the cathedral dedicated to ant'Agata, was begun by Count Roger 1092 and rebuilt by Vaccarini after the 593 earthquake. It is a magnificently onfused summation of Catanese history: Roman theatres were raided for ranite columns to adorn the lugubrius Baroque facade, and the interior onceals vaulted subterranean Roman aths and a Romanesque basilica under e nave.

Roman and Byzantine columns line e transepts. St Agata's chapel, a audy shrine of multicoloured marle, is where St Agatha's relics are displayed on feast days. At other times, the locals content themselves with pistachio pastries inspired by the patron saint's breasts, available from Savia.

The tombs of the 14th-century Spanish rulers of Sicily are sited in the nave, including the graceful tomb of Costanza d'Aragona, wife of King Federico III, and the Roman sarcophagus containing the ashes of other Aragonese royals. The tomb of Catania's famous composer, Vincenzo Bellini (1801–35), is here, too.

Across Via Vittorio Emanuele II is the church of **Sant' Agata** with its grand dome, and on the piazza itself are the **Municipio** (1741) with its decorated windows, and **Porta Uzeda**, an archway (1696). This leads into a small, popular park where pensioners while away time and also to **Porto Vecchio**, Catania's port. On weekdays a colourful fish market fills the neighbourhood streets.

In Via Museo Biscari is the **Palazzo Biscari ❸** (www.palazzobiscari.com), the most accomplished Baroque mansion in Catania, still partly owned by the Moncada family, the Biscari

The Baroque mansion of Palazzo Biscari.

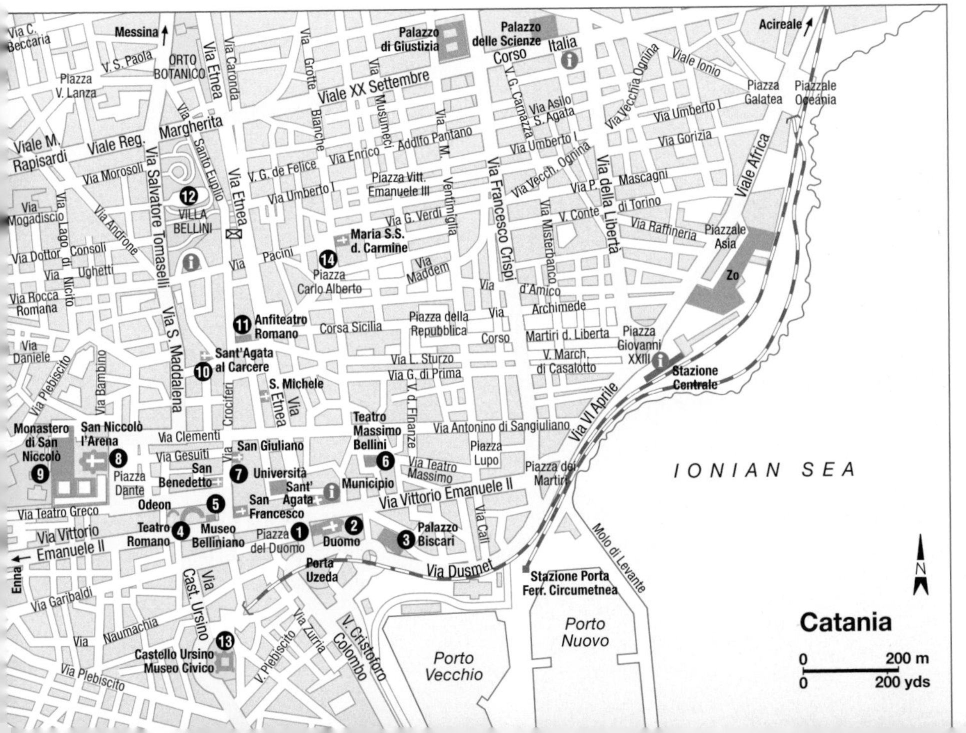

descendants, who have even turned their private theatre into a restaurant.

Via Dusmet offers the best view of the facade, with its frolicking cherubs, caryatids and grinning monsters. Ideally attend a concert in the *salone della musica*, a Rococo wonder, with a grand staircase, minstrels' gallery and allegorical ceiling. Otherwise, book a palatial tour (tel: 095 715 2508) and visit the adjacent **Marella Ferrera** fashion museum (Tue–Sun 10am–7pm).

As for dinner, it is possible to arrange traditional banquets with waiters and classical music. You can even stay in this Baroque masterpiece.

ANCIENT REMAINS

The city's ancient remains are unlike the spacious marble theatres or golden sandstone temples found elsewhere. Instead Catania offers cramped, low-lying monuments in sombre black lava stone. If you traipse down unpromising alleys, the rewards are worthwhile. While most classical remains enjoy splendid isolation, Catania's are fully integrated in the urban fabric,

Catania's Duomo.

generally in dilapidated parts of tow[n] where every second turning reveals th[e] odd Roman column, tomb or hypocau[st] (underfloor heating, Roman-style).

A good example is the **Teatro Gre[co] Romano** ❹ (daily 9am–5pm; free fir[st] Sun of the month), with its entrance [at] 266 Via Vittorio Emanuele. The theat[re] was built on the site of a Greek theatr[e] but has Roman underground passag[es] and *cavea* as well as some of the *sce[na]* and orchestra. The original marble fa[c]ing was plundered by the Normans [to] embellish the cathedral. Next door [is] the semicircular **Odeon**, used for orato[ry] and rehearsals. The building materia[ls] were chosen for their contrasts: volcan[ic] stone, red brickwork and marble facin[g].

TRIBUTES TO BELLINI

On Piazza San Francesco is the wel[l-] restored Baroque church of **San Fran[c]esco** (daily 9am–8pm) and the **Muse[o] Civico Belliniano** ❺ (Mon–Sat 9am[–] 7pm, Sun 9am–1pm), with a shabb[y] Baroque facade concealing a museu[m] of musical memorabilia and origin[al] scores of the composer's work. Th[e]

me ticket is also valid for the Museo milio Greco.

The father of *bel canto*, Bellini is uried in the cathedral, but he is also mmemorated in the richly decorated eatro Bellini ⑥, which opened in 1890 ith Bellini's opera *Norma*.

A CROCIFERI

eyond the arch of **San Benedetto** 777) leading off Piazza San Franc- sco is **Via Crociferi**, Catania's most harming street, with its succession monumental 18th-century Baroque hurches, convents and noble palazzi. xcavations have brought to light signs a Roman city beneath the street. orth along the street stands Vacca- ni's church of **San Giuliano** ⑦ (1739–), distinguished by a graceful loggia nd elliptical interior.

From here, Via Clementi leads to azza Dante, with the monumental hurch and Benedictine monastery of an Niccolò l'Arena ⑧ (Mon–Sat 9am– m). It resembles a grim religious ctory rather than a church complex. s the largest church in Sicily, this 16th-century work was conceived on a colossal scale but never completed because its sheer size would be unable to withstand an earthquake. It has an eerie, amputated look, with truncated stumps of columns framing the door like elephant tusks. Inside is a Hol- lywoodesque folly, Sicily's first clas- sical staircase. After a long period of closure, the church is being restored, especially the vast cupola, 62 metres (203ft) high.

The adjoining **Monastero di San Niccolò** ⑨ (www.monasterodeibenedettini. it; daily 9am–5pm, Aug 11am–6pm; guided visits of monastery and library) was the Benedictine monastery and now houses Catania University's Fac- ulties of Arts and Philosophy. The original monastery was almost totally destroyed in the 1693 earthquake, then rebuilt on an even grander scale after 1703. Long-term archaeologi- cal excavations are under way in the entrance courtyard, but beyond lie the charming former cloisters, complete with a battered garden and a curiously decorated folly.

Inside Chiesa San Benedetto in Via Crociferi.

Teatro Romano.

⊘ CATANIA'S NEW FACE

While Catania's architecture is less ebul- lient than that of Noto or Siracusa, this is still trail-blazing Baroque, a city with spacious streets and sinuous churches. However, as Sicily's commercial power- house, modern Catania stands accused of selling its soul to property speculation and neglecting its Baroque heritage. Until recently, the city centre was under- valued and dilapidated, the province of students and the poor, at least after nightfall. But a new city dynamism has seen the cathedral restored, Baroque palaces cleaned and the restoration of churches and classical sites under way. There are more than 150 historic build- ings dating from the 18th to the 20th cen- tury. With art galleries and cool cafés increasingly sited in restored palaces, the future is looking promising.

Castello Ursino, a Swabian castle, is now an art museum and exhibition space.

North along Via Crociferi is the church of **Sant'Agata al Carcere** ❿ (St Agatha in Prison; Tue–Thu, Sun 10am–noon, Fri–Sat 10am–noon, 4–6pm). According to legend, and supported by graffiti on these Roman walls, it was here that St Agatha was imprisoned before her martyrdom. Although the site was converted into a fortified church in the 12th century, the 3rd-century crypt remains. More impressive is the Romanesque portal, moved from the cathedral after the 1693 earthquake. Sculpted with griffins and glowering beasts, the door conjures up suitable horrors of the church's original function as a prison.

Further on, adjoining Via Etnea lies the **Anfiteatro Romano** ⓫ (Tue–Sat 9am–1pm, 2.30–5pm; free), the battered remains of the largest amphitheatre in Sicily, dating back to the 2nd or 3rd century AD and able to seat 16,000 spectators. This is where St Agatha supposedly met her fate and where earthquake ruins were dumped in 1693. Ancient necropoli stretch north and east of this site and are visible in

Police in Villa Bellini.

many spots, including below the Rina cente store in Via Etnea.

VIA ETNEA

The grandiose **Via Etnea**, the main ci thoroughfare, runs parallel to Via Cr ciferi and climaxes in a stunning vie of Mount Etna. Busy throughout th day, the street is particularly popular night when the Catanesi indulge in th evening *passeggiata*, parading past ch shops selling fashion, jewellery, shoe fruit sorbets and nougat ice cream.

The most elegant, richer, section the street lies between Piazza Duom and **Villa Bellini** ⓬, not a palazzo b public gardens. This delightful ar well-kept public park represents retreat from Catania's constant bustl One part is named *labirinto* after th maze of paths, all leading to aviari and an oriental bandstand. Betwee the fig trees and palms are snow capped or smouldering views of Etna

To the south of Via Etnea, on Piazz Federico di Svevia, is the **Castell Ursino** ⓭, a restored Swabian cast built on a steep bastion. It comman

☉ A SHARP CITIZENRY

The people of Catania, the *Catanesi*, have long had a reputation for being sharp operators with a flair for commerce. This entrepreneurial spirit is traced back to the citizens' Greek ancestry, presenting a counterpoint to the more indolent, aristocratic "Arab" temperament prevalent in Palermo. This ancient Siculi settlement was colonised by settlers from Naxos in 729 BC and, by 415 BC had become a significant Athenian base. As an ally of Athens, Catania incurred the wrath of Siracusa and after Dionysius conquered the city in 403 BC, the *Catanesi* were sold into slavery. By contrast, after the Roman conquest in 263 BC, the new regime ushered in a degree of prosperity.

In modern times, Sicily's second largest city has produced many of the island's best engineers and entrepreneurs – as well as many of the Mafia's most active leaders. By the 1960s Catania won plaudits for being commercially vibrant, the Milan of the South. But several decades later the corruption in both Milan and Catania gave the praise a hollow echo. Since then, the city administration is no longer so compromised and Catania, if not quite enjoying a resurgence, is at least demonstrating resilience and dynamism (particularly strong in the electronic, small enterprises and tourist sectors), not to mention a booming nightlife.

view of what was once the harbour: the moat was filled in by the lava flow of 1669, which also left the castle marooned inland, and deposited a large lump of lava outside the walls. Now an art museum and exhibition space, it was the Aragonese seat of government in the 13th century and became a palace under the Spanish viceroys. The courtyard displays a cavalcade of Sicilian history, featuring fine Hellenistic and Roman sculpture. The **Museo Civico** (daily 9am–7pm) on the upper floors contains a wide-ranging art gallery.

FISH MARKET

South of the Duomo, sandwiched between the cathedral quarter and the port, is **La Pescheria**, the noisy morning fish market (Mon–Sat). On slabs of marble lie sea bream and swordfish, mussels and sea urchins, squirming eels and lobsters. The area is centred on **Porta Uzeda**, the monumental Baroque city gate connecting the port with the public city. Beyond the adjoining park of Villa Pacini, the colourful portside area encircling Via Dusmet is given over to fishermen and traders.

Not far away is **Zo** (tel: 095 816 8912, www.zoculture.it), a futuristic cultural centre housed in an ex-sulphur refinery. It hosts concerts, events and exhibitions. Nearby congressional and cultural centre Le Criminiere is home to a small cinema museum (Tue–Sun July–Aug 10am–6pm, Sept–June 9am–5pm) and a museum dedicated to the Allied invasion of Sicily in 1943 (Tue–Sun July–Aug 10am–6pm, Sept–June 9am–5pm).

A visit to the scruffy but appealing **Fera o Luni** market (daily except Sun) on **Piazza Carlo Alberto** ⓮ creates an appetite for Catania's varied cuisine, including *pasta alla Norma* (made with aubergine/eggplant), named after Bellini's opera. Framed by two churches and hemmed in by backstreets, the rectangular square is a sea of bright awnings; below lie displays of lemons, garlic and herbs, with clothes, household goods and leatherware on the far side. The Sunday antiques market here sells everything from junk to Sicilian ceramics and country-style furniture.

Catania's fish market.

MOUNT ETNA AND CATANIA PROVINCE

Although the province embraces a popular coastline crowded with lidos, beaches and quaint fishing villages, at its heart is the glowering volcanic hinterland of Mount Etna.

Map on page 210

Sicilians are always concerned that one day there may be a "big one", an earthquake or eruption that will reverberate down the centuries. Until then, however, they are happy to live the good life, enjoying the wines and crops that thrive in the volcanic soil. More than 20 percent of all Sicilians live on the flanks of the volcano. Farmers are enticed there by the fertile soil, while wealthy city residents have constructed villas on the mountain's slopes for the views, cooler summer climate and opportunity for skiing in the winter.

Coastal Catania, however, turns awa from the volcanic hinterland with ata vistic spirit and peasant culture. Th is commercial Sicily, profiting from i ancient entrepreneurial roots estab lished when it was a Greek trading co ony. From Catania the economic rippl reach the rest of the province, as do th effects of a healthy public administra tion allied to the native entrepreneuri spirit. Catania University's noted Eng neering Faculty provides the impetu for Italy's microelectronics and te ecommunications industries. To dub Silicon Valley, as the locals sometime do, is a wishful overstatement, but tou ism is thriving, thanks to the increasir popularity of Etna's natural wonderlan

SOUTH OF CATANIA

The southwest is dominated by th Piana di Catania, a dullish plain th comes a poor second to Mount Etna attractions north of **Catania ❶**. Th plain was reputedly the abode of th mythological race of man-eating giants, the Laestrygonians, who appea in Homer's *Odyssey*, but is now hom to little more than giant citrus grove **Militello in Val di Catania** is unde whelming despite its medieval quarte ruined castle and Baroque churches.

By contrast, the hilly souther interior has considerable charm

The Scalazza, a dramatic staircase in the heart of Caltagirone.

pecially Caltagirone, Sicily's ceramics capital.

Grammichele , approached via e SS417 from Catania, is a bizarre aroque town, a champion of bold wn planning after the 1693 earthuake. Within a hexagonal design, ads radiate from the central square ke the spokes of a wheel. The Chiesa adre and town hall epitomise the ty's rigorously Baroque image and ean geometric design. However, the inical effect is mocked by the down-:-heel population.

ALTAGIRONE

urther along the SS417, spread over ree hills, **Caltagirone** ❸ is charming. s name derives from the Arabic words r castle and cave, but the town was eviously settled by the Greeks. Like cireale and Noto, hilly Caltagirone els like a bold Baroque theatre, with oacious squares, majestic mansions nd monumental churches, often enlivned by ceramic decorative touches.

The upper town is surprisingly grand, ith imposing public buildings clustered around the **Duomo**. The cathedral contains a *Madonna and Child* attributed to the school of Antonello Gagini (1594).

Close by is the **Corte Capitaniale**, a dignified mansion decorated by school of Gagini sculptures and, beyond, the **Scalazza**, a staircase of 142 steps leading up to the church of **Santa Maria del Monte**. This stunning staircase links the old and new districts. Each lava-stone step is decorated with majolica tiles depicting mythological scenes. On 24–5 July, the feast of **San Giacomo** is celebrated with "the tapestry of fire", featuring a costumed procession and carpet of light. Illuminating the staircase are 5,000 tiny oil lamps, covered by delicate paper cylinders called *coppi*.

On the other side of the long piazza, on Via Roma below the cathedral, the **Museo Civico** (Tue, Fri–Sat 9.30am–1.30pm and 3.30–6.30pm, Mon, Wed–Thu 9.30am–1.30pm; Sun 9.30am–12.30pm and 3.30–6.30pm; free) was once a fearsome Bourbon prison and still retains its barbaric, spike-studded metal doors. The museum contains Greek and Roman

Plate-maker in Caltagirone, where ceramics have been produced for centuries.

The town hall clock, Caltagirone.

The dramatic staircase leading up to Santa Maria del Monte in Caltagirone.

finds and prized Renaissance ceramics. Off Via Roma is **San Francesco d'Assisi**, a Gothic church remodelled in Baroque style after yet another earthquake.

Signs of Caltagirone's thriving ceramics trade abound; workshops display decorative majolica vases, tiles and objets d'art; ceramics adorn city niches, window-ledges, balconies and bandstands. Ceramic flowers even grace the **Ponte San Francesco** (1626–66), the bridge close to San Francesco church. The **Giardino Pubblico**, the municipal gardens below Piazza Umberto, were modelled on English public gardens and boast balustraded terraces, a charming ceramic-decorated bandstand and a belvedere (1792). Predictably, the gardens are

home to the **Museo Regionale del Cerámica** (daily 9am–6.30pm), whic showcases Sicilian pottery from pr historic times to the present day, pro that terracotta and glazed ceramic have been produced in Caltagiron since time immemorial.

THE COAST OF CYCLOPS

Heading north from **Catania** is a we come release: sea breezes sweep awa images of Catania's scruffy outskirt The province hugs the Ionian coa towards the hillside resort of Taorm ina, and the Coast of Cyclops, name after the Homeric myth, presents spectacular seascape. The **Faraglio dei Ciclopi** (Cyclops) are jagged lump jutting out of the sea just off the coa

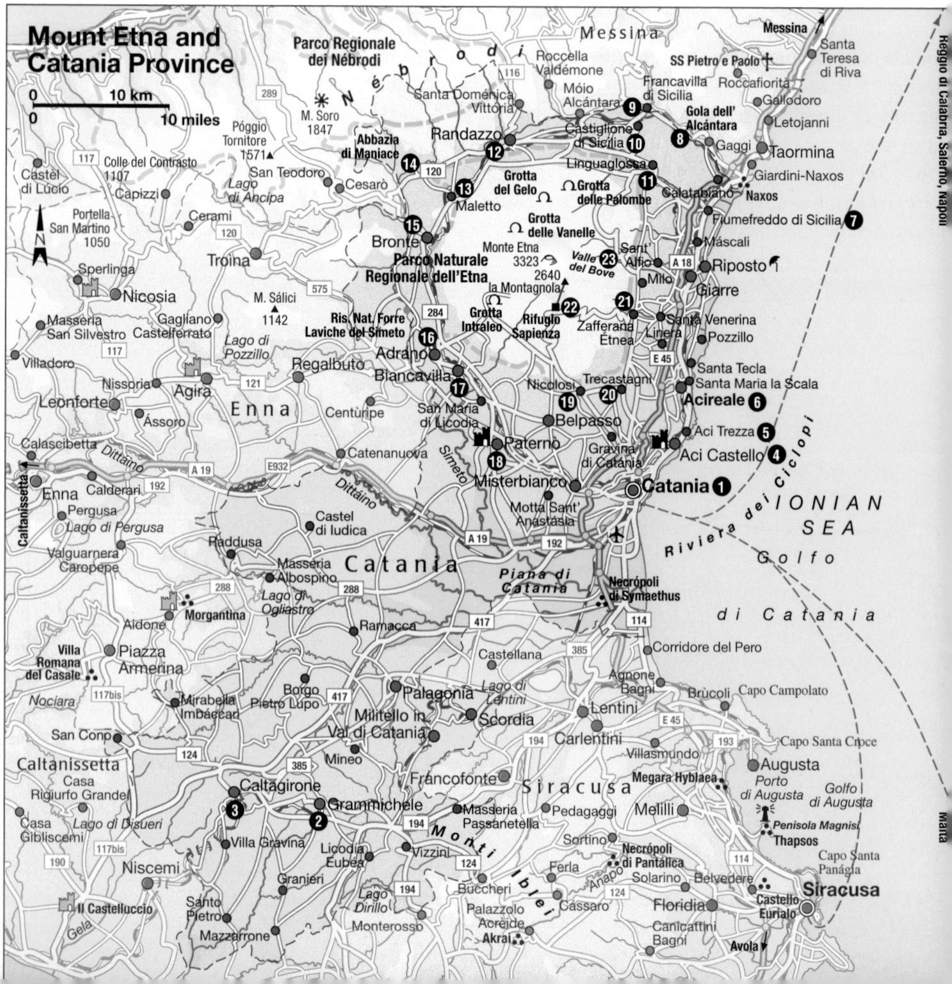

Map: Mount Etna and Catania Province

0   10 km
0   10 miles

Reggio di Calabria, Salerno, Napoli

Messina
Messina
Santa Teresa di Riva
Roccella
Valdémone
SS Pietro e Paolo
Francavilla
di Sicilia
Roccafiorita
Galodoro
Parco Regionale dei Nébrodi
Castiglione
di Sicilia
Gola dell'
Alcántara
Letojanni
Santa Doménica
Vittória
Móio
Alcántara
Randazzo
Gaggi
Taormina
Póggio
Tornitore
M. Soro
1847
Abbazia
di Maniace
Linguaglossa
Giardini-Naxos
Colle del Contrasto
1107
San Teodoro
Grotta
del Gelo
Grotta
delle Palombe
Naxos
Castel
di Lúcio
Cápizzi
Lago
di Ancipa
Cesarò
Maletto
Fiumefreddo di Sicilia
Portella
San Martino
1050
Cerami
Grotta
delle Vanelle
Máscali
Sperlinga
Troina
Monte Etna
Parco Naturale
Regionale dell'Etna
3323
Valle
del Bove
2640
Sant'
Alfio
Riposto
Nicosia
M. Sálici
1142
la Montagnola
Giarre
Masseria
San Silvestro
Gagliano
Castelferrato
Ris. Nat. Forre
Laviche del Simeto
Grotta
Intráleo
Rifugio
Sapienza
Zafferana
Etnea
Santa Venerina
Linera
Villadoro
Lago di
Pozzillo
Adrano
Zafferana
Etnea
Pozzillo
Nissoria
Agira
Regalbuto
Biancavilla
Nicolosi
Trecastagni
Santa Tecla
Santa Maria la Scala
Leonforte
Ássoro
San Maria
di Licodia
Belpasso
Aci Trezza
Calascibetta
Dittaino
Enna
Centúripe
Paternò
Gravina
di Catania
Aci Castello
Enna
Calderari
Pergusa
Catenanuova
Misterbianco
Catania
IONIAN
SEA
Lago di Pérgusa
Castel
di Iudica
Motta Sant'
Anástasia
Valguarnera
Caropepe
Raddusa
Catania
Piana di
Catania
Golfo
Aidone
Morgantina
Masseria
Albospino
Lago di
Ogliastro
Ramacca
Necrópoli
di Symaethus
di Catania
Villa
Romana
del Casale
Piazza
Armerina
Castellana
Corridore del Pero
Nociara
Mirabella
Imbáccari
Borgo
Pietro Lupo
Palagonia
Lago di
Lentini
Agnone
Bagni
Brúcoli
Capo Campolato
San Conp
Militello in
Val di Catania
Scordia
Lentini
Villasmundo
Capo Santa Croce
Caltanissetta
Casa
Rigiurfo Grande
Mineo
Francofonte
Siracusa
Megara Hyblaea
Augusta
Porto
di Augusta
Golfo
di Augusta
Casa
Gibliscemi
Lago di Disueri
Caltagirone
Grammichele
Masseria
Passanetella
Pedagaggi
Melilli
Penisola Magnisi
Thapsos
Niscemi
Villa Gravina
Licodia
Eubéa
Vizzini
Sortino
Necrópoli
di Pantálica
Capo Santa
Panágia
Santo
Pietro
Granieri
Lago
Dirillo
Búccheri
Ferla
Anapo
Solarino
Belvedere
Siracusa
Il Castelluccio
Mazzarrone
Monterosso
Palazzolo
Acréide
Akrai
Cássaro
Floridia
Canicattini
Bagni
Castello
Eurialo
Gela
Avola

Aci Trezza. Legend has it that these basalt rocks were flung at the fleeing Odysseus by the enraged, blinded Cyclops Polyphemus. The scenic rocks are now used as an oceanography station by Catania University.

In summer, the seafood restaurants are full and flotillas of fishing craft double up as pleasure boats. But essentially the character of the local fishing villages remains unchanged: the daily markets display catches of anchovies and sardines.

Aci Castello ④, on the Riviera dei Ciclopi near Catania, is memorable for its dramatic castle perched on a rocky crag overlooking the sea. The crenellated Norman **fortress**, built on a site used for defensive purposes since Byzantine times, is well preserved despite frequent eruptions and a fierce attack by the Aragonese. A charming garden of local plants has been created on the roof terrace. From the castle, which houses the **Museo Civico** (daily 9am–1pm, 3–5pm, until 8.30pm in summer) containing trophies found at sea, locals potter on the rocks or wander down to the fish restaurants along the gnarled coast.

Aci Trezza ⑤, a fishing village hoping to become a resort, is celebrated for its connection with Catania-born novelist and dramatist Giovanni Verga (1840–1922). His finest works reflect life at the poorer social levels and his novel, *I Malavoglia* (translated as *Under the Medlar Tree*, 1881), was inspired by this seafaring community. The novel depicts the benighted lives of a fishing family, a theme echoed by Visconti's film, *La Terra Trema (The Earth Quakes)* which was shot nearby. Verga was only too aware of the precarious nature of the fishermen's existence: "Property at sea is writ on water."

Close to the harbour is the **Casa del Nespolo** (daily 9.30am–1pm, 5–9pm), a tiny fishing museum linked to Verga's novel.

ACIREALE

Acireale ⑥ is the most important of the seven Etna towns with the prefix Aci. Legend has it that Aci (Acis) became the lover of sea-nymph Galatea, and when

A decorative tile on the Ponte San Francesco.

Rocky beach at Aci Castello.

he was killed by a jealous rival she turned him into a river here. (The river, of course, vanished in an earthquake.)

The town is proud of its appellation *Reale* (royal) and stands aloof, both from the over-commercialised resorts and the rural hinterland. As Akis, it was a Greek settlement that fared badly in the face of eruptions and earthquakes. However, thanks to the continuing ravages of Etna and the talent of local craftsmen, today's town is predominantly Baroque. Compared with most coastal resorts, Acireale is a proper town, admired for its carnival, quality of life, spas and sweet pastries.

The **Duomo** occupies centre stage, its 17th-century grandeur somewhat marred by the addition of a pseudo-Gothic facade. In compensation, the grand Baroque portal is adorned with statues of the *Annunciation* and saints, while the vaulted interior displays *trompe l'œil* decoration and bold stuccowork. The inlaid marble floor contains an appealing 1848 Meridian Line.

The **Palazzo Comunale** represents the first flowering of Catanese Baroque

with its elegant, graceful facade and delicate wrought-iron balconies. On the same square, set among the city cafés and grand churches, stands the restored white Baroque vision of **San Pietro e Paolo**. In Piazza Vigo further down is the **Basilica di San Sebastiano**, an exuberant Baroque feast, with the facade a riot of cherubs.

In the compact historic centre, the grandiose Baroque buildings are gathered around Piazza Duomo, presenting a contrast between the spacious public squares and the secretive side of town beyond. Yet even the dark alleys yield rewards in the form of pastry shops such as **Castorino** on Corso Savoia, famed for its ice cream, *cassata* and *pasta reale* – decorated marzipan confections. The city is even credited with inventing sorbets, aided by a profitable monopoly on snow held by the local archbishop until modern times.

Acireale is surrounded by citrus groves, a source of wealth that continues to sustain the local landowning class. From the public gardens stretches a fine view over the Coast

Market stalls, Acireale.

Cyclops, with the rocky shore riven by coves.

At the south entrance to the town, the **Terme di Santa Vénera**, a spa, exploits the healing properties of Etna's radioactive waters. Hot sulphurous lava mud baths (20°C/68°F) have been considered beneficial here for rheumatism and skin conditions since Roman times.

Just below Acireale is the quaint fishing hamlet of **Santa Maria la Scala**, with its lava-stone shore, beached boats, watchtower and simple inns. (The road, the SS114, follows the coast, and is slow-going, passing through Santa Tecla, Pozzillo and Riposto, compared with the A18 *autostrada*, which cuts through the countryside en route to Taormina.) **Riposto** is home to both a yachting marina and a flourishing fishing port where fishermen bring their daily catches.

Fiumefreddo di Sicilia ❼, just north, is named after a cooling river that flows through thick clumps of papyrus. This feudal town functions both as a calming interlude before the volcanic hinterland and as the springboard to chic Taormina.

Fiumefreddo has a tumbledown Phoenician tower and two castellated mansions. **Castello degli Schiavi**, the stranger of the two villas, has sculpted stone slaves leaning over an 18th-century parapet. Apart from coastal views and clean beaches, the area also draws families to the **Etnaland theme park** (see box).

MOUNT ETNA

Etna is the dramatic volcano where the heart of Catania province should be. The volcano munches Messina and the countryside too, with new lava mouths opening all the time. Locals joke that not even the Mafia can close Etna's myriad mouths. Mongibello or Muncibeddu, the Sicilian name for Mount Etna, comes from the Latin and Arabic words for mountain (mons and gibel). It is one of the most active volcanoes in the world – its last eruption was in March 2017 – and, since 2013, a Unesco World Heritage site.

The sense of appeasing the mountain gods still survives in **Zafferana Etnea**, a hiking village and ski resort that found itself in the path of the 1992 volcanic

Cathedral statuary, Acireale.

⊙ VOLCANIC FAMILY FUN

Families keen to explore Etna can do so the exciting way (see page 221) or the easy way. The **Circumetnea train** (tel: 095 541 111; www.circumetnea.it), in existence since 1894, is the single-track rail route around Etna, a leisurely 110km (68-mile) journey from Catania, taking in Adrano, Bronte and Randazzo, returning to the coast at Giarre-Riposto, convenient for Taormina. Depending on the timetable and the sections open, you can stop off at a couple of stations en route before carrying on your journey.

Younger children will probably prefer **Etnavventura**, one of Sicily's best adventure playgrounds (Contrada Serra la Nave, Ragalno, mob: +333 151 5904; www.etnavventura.it; May–Aug). Set on the southern flanks of Mount Etna, it is close to the Rifugio Sapienza cable car, so it works well in tandem. You can even call ahead to request a picnic of local cheeses and ham. Instead, at Fiumefreddo, **Etnaland** (tel: 095 791 3334; www.etnaland.eu; Apr–Sept) is Sicily's first theme park, complete with wave pools, miniature volcanoes and simulated eruptions, as well as less obviously Etna-related attractions such as the Dinosaur Park and Crocodile Rapids. Alternatively, head for Monti Rossi Adventure Park (tel: 388 755 3812; www.montirossietnaadventurepark.it; June–Sept) where there are several rope courses for beginners and experts.

THE WRATH OF MOUNT ETNA

Etna's smouldering or snow-capped cone will already be a familiar, perversely friendly presence – to the Sicilians it represents an uneasy, distinctly double-edged relationship.

Leonardo Sciascia, the Sicilian writer, called Etna "a huge house-cat that purrs quietly and awakens every so often". However, when Etna calls in her dues, the cat spits fire. And when Sicily's famous volcano erupts, the results are always unpredictable. As local resident Giovanni Giuffrida says: "Lava is like a mole; it takes cover, burrows and reappears where you are not ready to catch it." In terms of duration, an eruption can last 10 minutes or – like the outburst of 1614 – 10 years.

Over centuries, the Catania coastline has receded or advanced in response to Etna's major lava flows.

Eruption of Mount Etna, February 2012.

Even the 1908 earthquake, which razed Messina and claimed over 60,000 victims, did not change the coastline. But lava flows from Etna have often redrawn the map, most recently in 1978–9 when lava spilled into the sea, and reached the chapel doors at Fornazzo, a village on the coast. A miraculous intervention was claimed after the molten lava was halted by a statue of the Madonna.

Historically, two of the most catastrophic eruptions occurred in 1381 and 1669, with lava flows that engulfed Catania and destroyed Nicolosi. In modern times, significant eruptions demolished the villages of Gerro and Mascali in the 1920s. Randazzo was narrowly spared by an eruption in 1981, which reached the town walls and destroyed surrounding vineyards. Closer to the volcanic heart, the 1983 eruption destroyed most of Refugio Sapienza and neighbouring property, lifts and roads.

During the 1992 eruption, the Americans were called in to save the resort of Zafferana Etnea, on Etna's eastern slopes. A US Navy and Marine task force, armed with the world's largest helicopters, made daring forays to the mouth of the crater, dropping blocks of concrete into the seething river of lava, and managed to stem the flow.

In the year 2000 the southeastern crater split into two, with fireballs and eruptive matter tossed into the air to a height of 600 metres (2,000ft).

Intense eruptions have continued sporadically ever since, especially in 2011 and 2012, with spewing of lava and loud detonations heard in villages and towns all around Etna. In 2014 the volcano witnessed a flank eruption, the first in a decade, and yet again started spewing lava. A year later the volcano became active again sending fireballs into the sky and pouring lava into Valle de Bove and in 2017 it was erupting again.

Every few years, Etna's glittering red cone is visible from Catania during the day, while tourists as far away as Taormina can see nightly firebombs shooting out from a secondary cone.

Given that major eruptions occur, on average, every 300 years, and that the last catastrophic volcano and earthquake were in 1669 and 1693 respectively, simple calculations suggest that doomsday could be nigh. Not that Sicilians who choose to live on the slopes of an active volcano see it like that, of course.

ruption. Before abandoning his farmhouse to the volcano, Giuseppe Fichera left bread, cheese and wine to satisfy the tired and hungry mountain". Even gods of destruction need food and rest.

The circular journey around the volcano is a game of light and shade. From the Ionian coast to the fertile Etna foothills is a feast of glistening citrus and live groves, orchards and nut plantations. But clinging to Etna's flanks are dark volcanic villages and ruined Norman castles. It is a strange trail from green slopes to the moonscape above. From Taormina, a scenic railway runs to Randazzo, travelling along the valley floor, crossing a bridge made of lava rocks and even disappearing inside a lava cutting. But to appreciate Etna's grandeur, drive around the base or follow a similar route on the Circumetnea railway (see box).

AROUND THE VOLCANO

The best drive is the circular tour of Etna, around the **Parco Naturale Regionale dell'Etna** (www.parcoetna.it). Leave the coast at Fiumefreddo di Sicilia for a foray into the Alcántara Valley, starting with the **Gola dell'Alcántara** ❽.

This delightful gorge was discovered in the 1950s when a Taormina film director was so enchanted with the prospect of a secret gorge that he had a tortuous path built down to the river. He was the first of many to capture Alcántara on film. Seen from above, the view is of wooded crags descending to a weirdly pitted river canyon. The bed is rocky, the remains of a prehistoric lava flow that created the peninsula of Capo Schiso. The canyon was created not by erosion but by the splintering collision of volcanic magma and the cooling water of the river. The impact threw up lavic prisms in monstrous shapes: these warped black basalt boulders resemble a cross-section of a fossil.

Now the centre of a well-organised nature reserve, **Gole Alcántara Botanical and Geological Park** (daily 8am–6pm; www.golealcantara.com), with its botanical walk, numerous hiking paths, nature museum, permanent farmers' market and the gorge itself, makes for one of the most popular day trips from

Farmer, Castiglione di Sicilia.

Taormina. The gorge can be explored in several ways, but especially by wading. A waterfall with a sheer drop is a barrier to further exploration of the gorge for anyone not wearing a wetsuit and on a canyoning trip. A lift leads down to the grey-green river and the so-called beach where, in summer, low water levels mean you can either paddle in the chilly waters or, more adventurously, hire waders and explore further. Beyond are fast-flowing currents in ever-narrowing tracts, deceptive rapids that can only be explored on a guided body-canyoning adventure, one only open to those over 16. The popularity of the gorge means it's best avoided on Sundays in August.

Francavilla di Sicilia ⑨, just west along the SS185, is set in a fertile valley of citrus plantations and prickly pears. Founded by King Roger, Francavilla prospered under Spanish rule. Roger's **ruined castle** occupies a lone mound in the valley and once guarded the route to Randazzo. The other Norman relic is the hermitage of **La Badiazza**, perched atop a rocky platform

and victim of the 1693 earthquake. The **Chiesa Madre** has a Gagini *Madonna* matched by the sculpted Gagini fountain in Piazza San Paolo. The **Matrice Vecchia** has a Renaissance door with a vine-leaf motif. The finest sight is the **Convento dei Cappuccini**, a 16th-century monastery on a lovely hillock protected by Spanish sentry boxes and marble parapets. Inside is a profusion of *intarsia* work and carving, created by 17th-century monks.

CASTIGLIONE DI SICILIA

Castiglione di Sicilia ⑩, set on Etna's northern flank just south of Francavilla, is one of the most atmospheric Etna villages and is also a burgeoning wine-producing centre. Perched on a crag, this ancient bastion possesses Greek ramparts but is better known as a Norman fiefdom. Narrow medieval alleys wind to the crumbling lava-stone church of **San Pietro** and the grander **Santa Maria della Catena**. The **Norman castle** dominating the valley, with its jagged lookout tower, walls and roofs, houses a regional wine-tasting centre (May–Oct

Castiglione di Sicilia nestles below the mountains.

r by appointment, tel: 0942 980 348). his rocky citadel compels respect, s do the ominous views of rubble and ebris trailing from Etna's summit.

Linguaglossa ⓫, 18km (11 miles) outheast of Castiglione, is a popuar stop on the scenic Circumetnea ail route and doubles as a simple ski esort at 550 metres (1,800ft). It also makes a workaday hiking base, with reks leading through pine forests to **rotta del Gelo**, a lava-stone cave with eird light effects, and up Etna itself. In own, the Baroque **Chiesa Madre** pays ibute to the forests, with 18th-century hoir stalls and a coffered ceiling, while he village's lava-stone pavements ttest to its proximity to Etna.

RANDAZZO

Vest of Castiglione, **Randazzo** ⓬ is he most atmospheric and coherent medieval town on the northern slopes f Etna, and the one closest to the olcano craters. Much of the town is uilt using blocks cut from the dried ava streams. Originally settled by reeks fleeing from Naxos, it reached its apogee under the Normans. During Swabian rule, Randazzo was a summer court and retreat from the heat of Messina. It remains a self-contained market town with crenellated churches and sturdy 14th-century walls.

For a town in the jaws of Etna, Randazzo has survived magnificently. The 1981 eruption threatened to engulf the walls and blocked surrounding vineyards, roads and railway lines, leaving a lava flow visible today. But nature is not to blame for damage to the medieval core: Allied bombing in 1943 destroyed the enemies' last stronghold in Sicily, including the fortress and finest palazzi.

Until the 16th century, competition for supremacy within the walls was fuelled by the presence of three rival communities talking different dialects. Each parish church took its turn as cathedral for a three-year term: the Latins were centred on the church of **Santa Maria**, the Greeks at San Niccolò and the Lombards at San Martino. The churches were fiercely battlemented and ostentatious. Ultimately, the Catholics triumphed and the church of Santa Maria on Piazza Basilica is

View of Randazzo.

now the cathedral. Built between 1217 and 1239, it is a much-remodelled grey lava-stone church in Norman-Swabian design, with Norman apses and walls and side portals in Catalan-Gothic style. Its odd interior contrasts Satanic-looking black columns and altar with a pure Gagini font.

Porta San Martino, one of two surviving city gates, marks the entrance to the walled medieval town. The elegant Piazza San Martino is the heart of the damaged Lombard Quarter, set against the city walls. Appropriately, **Chiesa San Martino** has a 13th-century banded lava and limestone Lombard bell tower matched by an early Baroque facade in grey and white stone. Virtually next door is the **Castello-Carcere**, a medieval castle and Bourbon prison, now the **Museo Archeologico Paolo Vagliasindi** (daily 9am–6pm; free), an archaeological museum. Beside the lava-stone windows is an inscription to Philip II and bullet holes that attest to the military skirmishes in August 1943. A puppet museum, **Museo dei Pupi Siciliani** (9am–1pm, 4–7pm), is here too.

Countryside around Maletto.

Via Umberto contains symbols Randazzo's past role as a royal cit including the **Palazzo Reale**, the seve Swabian summer palace. Via Umbert ends in spacious **Piazza Municipi** a bustling square dominated by th **Palazzo Comunale**, the well-restore town hall. But leave the crowds by turn ing down the arcaded **Via degli Arch** to Piazza San Niccolò and the Gree Quarter, and the impressive Greek **Sa Niccolò**, with its original 14th-centur apses, huge Baroque lava-stone facad and tapering campanile. Inside th church are several Gagini sculpture including, appropriately, a St Nicholas

THE ADMIRAL'S ESTATE

Between Randazzo and Bronte extend a wooded, volcanic landscape south t **Maletto ⑬**, noted for its wine and straw berries. Maletto marks the highest poir on the Circumetnea railway line (1,20 metres/ 4,000ft) and offers views c recent lava flows. From Maletto, take right fork to Admiral Nelson's castle a Maniace or continue south to Bronte. Fol lowing signs to Castello di Nelson lead to the **Abbazia di Maniace ⑭** (closed fc restoration at the time of writing), on and the same. Set in a wooded hollov the fortified abbey was founded by Coun Roger, with the chapel commemoratin a Saracen defeat in 1040. With Norma help, the Byzantine commander Mani akes routed the Arabs and regained Sic ily for Constantinople. But the estate i better known as the fiefdom of Admira Horatio Nelson, duke of Bronte.

The title and estates were presente to Nelson by Ferdinand IV in gratitud for the Admiral's part in crushing th 1799 rebellion in Naples. Nelson' descendant, Viscount Bridport, onl relinquished his Sicilian seat in 1981 when the 12,500-hectare (30,000-acre estate was broken up and the orchards nut plantations and dairy farms sold Nevertheless, Nelson memorabili remains, from paintings of sea battle to the Admiral's port decanter.

Inside the castle compound, the best part of the Benedictine abbey owes nothing to Nelson. The late Norman chapel has an original wooden ceiling, doorway and statuary. The original castle is unrecognisable, thanks to the 1693 earthquake and heavy anglicisation. It resembles a gracious Wiltshire manor from outside, an image confirmed by the genteel English cemetery. Even the gardens are home to neat hedges, as well as cypresses and palms.

Between Maletto and Bronte are subtle shifts in scenery. Walnut and chestnut groves on the higher hills are dotted with jagged volcanic clumps, including the lava flow of 1823. Around Bronte, the slopes are covered with small nut trees, a reminder that 80 percent of Italy's pistachio crop comes from these well-tended terraces.

BRONTE

Bronte ⓯, at 760 metres (2,500ft) and with a population of around 20,000, was founded in 1520 by Charles V and is an ill-planned town sandwiched between two lava flows on the western slopes of Mount Etna. Legend says it was founded by the Cyclops Brontes, son of Uranus, who was known as The Thunderer and whose forge was in a cavern beneath the mountain. Devastated three times by eruptions, Bronte hangs on as the administrative and agricultural centre of the region.

Pistachio nuts are exported worldwide from here, and each year a pistachio festival takes place on the first 10 days of October. Bronte is resolutely shabby, its dingy charm residing in the neglected late Renaissance churches with crenellated towers. The church of **l'Annunciata** (1535) has a polychrome marble group attributed to Antonello Gagini that, local lore says, has miraculous powers and on many occasions has been able to stem the flow of molten lava.

South of Bronte, the pistachio plantations cede to scruffy, cacti-strewn slopes, with lumps of lava interspersed with white lava-coated trees. The makeshift mood reflects a region devastated by the 1985 eruption: everything built in haste but, given Etna's whims, with no time to repent at leisure.

Drink

One of Sicily's greatest successes is the creation of *granita* (water ices) made from fresh fruit and served in a tall glass accompanied by a brioche – a delightful mixture, especially on a hot day. Flavours change with the season. Watermelon *granita* is a summer favourite, and so are peach, apricot and grape.

The steep slopes of Bronte.

THE FERTILE FOOTHILLS

Adrano , set on Etna's southwestern slopes, is a shabby market town with mythical roots. On the outskirts are the remains of a grander past: the Greek city of Adranon was founded here by Dionysius I in the 4th century BC. In antiquity, the city was celebrated for its sanctuary to Adranus, the Sicel god of fire. Still today, during the bizarre August festival, a child dressed as an angel "flies" along a cord linking the old city powers: the castle, town hall and a statue of the god of fire himself. So far, Adranus has kept his city safe from fiery Etna.

Its battered charm lies in the busy **Piazza Umberto**. Like Randazzo, wizened old men gather in the clubs clustered around the main square. Here, too, is the austere **Norman castle** (Tue–Sat 9am–7pm, Sun 9am–1.30pm), sitting on its squat Saracen base. This powerful bastion was rebuilt by Roger I in the 11th century and remodelled by the Aragonese. The interior, once a Bourbon prison, houses an **archaeological museum** with minor Greek sculptures. On the floor above is Queen Adelaide's chapel, a mysterious room decorated with purplish lava-stone capitals by Roger's third wife.

Beside the castle, the **Chiesa Madre** a Norman church disfigured by clumsy restoration in 1811. The heavy basalt columns conceivably came from the Greek Temple to Adranon that once occupied the site. Plutarch records a dramatic eve-of-battle appeal to the god; in response, a bronze statue of Adranus suddenly quivered into life. A fina twinge of nostalgia for ancient Adranc is evoked by the **Greek city walls**, lying the end of Via Buglio.

Biancavilla , built on a basal escarpment 5km (3 miles) south Adrano, was founded by Albanian refugees in 1480. The sole Albanian link the *Madonna of the Alms*, an icon brough over by the first refugees and visible the comically grandiose Chiesa Madre.

If Biancavilla is best known for it prickly pears, **Paternò** , halfwa between Biancavilla and Catania, famous for its oranges, Sicily's juic est. Set on a hilly volcanic site, th scruffy Baroque town has a strikin Norman **castle** (for hours tel: 095 79

Adrano elders in conversation.

12) founded in 1073 by Count Roger. The severity of the 14th-century lava-zone keep is echoed by the Great Hall and frescoed chapel. Frederick II died here while journeying to his favourite fortress of Enna.

Nearby is the **Chiesa Madre**, a Norman church with a Gothic facelift containing a majestic 17th-century wooden Crucifix, and the ruined Gothic church of **San Francesco**. In World War the German forces used this hill as an observation post and drew heavy allied fire, leading to the death of 4,000 people. Known as **Rocca Normanna**, the castle quarter now enjoys happier associations: in summer, visitors can attend concerts, sample the stuffed aubergines, or simply drool over terraces glistening with orange groves.

ATEWAY TO ETNA

Nicolosi ⑲, northeast of Paternò, is both charmless ski resort and the southern gateway to Etna's terraced wine and walking country, covered in oak, pine and chestnut trees. Lying east of the wooded Monti Rossi twin craters, the town has

been reborn after repeated eruptions. Today it marks the start of bracing treks to Rifugio Sapienza and affords a fine view of Etna's active central crater and numerous secondary ones.

Just east, along the road to **Trecastagni ⑳**, the lava beds of 1886 and 1910 are visible. Once a medieval fiefdom, Trecastagni is noted for the **Chiesa Madre**, a Renaissance church attributed to Antonello Gagini, and for the Lombard-Romanesque **Sant'Antonio di Padova**, with its 17th-century lava-stone cloisters. Also take the time to appreciate traditional Etna craftsmanship: the local workshops are dedicated to Sicilian carts, wrought ironwork and colourful ceramics, as well as Etna carvings in lava stone or gnarled olive wood. Nor are Trecastagni's almond biscuits, sorbets and red wines to be sniffed at.

From here head for Acireale and follow *autostrade* signs to return to Fiumefreddo the quick way.

ASCENDING THE VOLCANO

Circling the volcano is intriguing and safe, but an ascent requires caution.

The Norman castle in Adrano was built of black volcanic rock by Roger I. Once a Bourbon prison, it now houses a museum of Greek and Bronze Age artefacts.

⊘ EXPLORING MOUNT ETNA

An exciting volcano has become yet more exhilarating with the creation of new adventures, from hiking and mountain-biking to quad-biking, skiing and helicopter tours. To explore the craters and summit of Mount Etna, the largest volcano in Europe, always trust the local guides. Memorable hikes start from the foothills or closer to the summit, such as Bocca Nuova and Cratere del Piano, along the western flank of Etna. The intrepid can hike to the underground lava caves of Grotta del Gelo and Grotta del Lampone, but winter hiking in high areas is not possible due to snow and bad visibility.

Local guides in Linguaglossa include **Etna Trekking** (tel: 368 663 453, www.etnatrekking.com) and **Guide Etna Nord** (tel: 095 777 4502, www.guidetnanord.com; prices from €70 per person for a full-day trek). Another good option is **Etna Moving** (tel: 377 980 4142; www.etnamoving.com) run by a passionate geologist and offering half-day, full day as well as trekking tours around Etna. It also offers accommodation in Trecastagni. Mountain-bikers can opt for the Pista Altomontana Etnea, which links Nicolosi and Linguaglossa,

passing dramatic lava flows and brooding crags. Equally exciting are trail-bashing jeep ascents over basalt-encrusted slopes, past gaping gullies, to the volcanic waste-land close to the summit. Instead, for a rollicking quad-bike experience on Mount Etna, riding through a lunar land-scape, contact **Etna Quad Adventure** (tel: 339 587 5145, www.etnaquad.it). **Etna Experience** (www.etnaexperience.com) organises all kinds of activities around the volcano, including wine and trekking tours (also in winter).

Etna also has two ski resorts, the larger Rifugio Sapienza (north slope) and the smaller, prettier Piano Provenzana (south slope). The former is better (and more crowded) as it offers a gondola, a chair lift and three ski lifts as well as five pistes ranging from beginners to intermediate. You can also ski down the northern flank through beech and birch, or indulge in off-piste snowboarding over lava bumps on the treeless upper slopes (www.parcoetna.ct.it). A new fad for thrill seekers has been skiing on the cold lava covered with fine volcanic ash at dazzling speeds. Consult www.etnasci.it for up to date weather and volcanic activity forecasts.

⊙ Tip

Below the murmuring summit of Etna is a vast depression, an area created by violent eruptions. Between Monte Rinatu (1,569 metres/5,147ft) and La Montagnola (2,640 metres/8,660ft), the Valle del Bove has deep lava walls that can reach 1,000 metres (3,280ft). A desolate, unreal silence fills the valley. One way to see this extraordinary phenomenon on foot is to start at Zafferana Etnea and follow the paths.

Depending on the season and Etna's mood, the menu may include a mere mass of clinker, a spent cone, a smoking cone, or even a seething lava front. When it works, it is wonderful, with sulphurous vapours, heat coursing through the soles of your shoes, and sightings of spitting fireballs.

An organised group trip is the sensible, relatively inexpensive way of experiencing Etna, but for sheer extravagant adventure, a private guide is recommended. Without a guide, suitably clad explorers can clamber about at their own risk up to a certain altitude, currently 3,000 metres (9,850ft), 323 metres (1,060ft) short of Etna's great height. Even so, it is essential to get advice on routes from local guides, unless you are taking the simplest option of the cable-car ticket that also includes a guided drive and walk to the summit.

At the cable-car summit, just outside the bar, suitable footwear and warm clothing can be hired, if needed. From here, reinforced minibuses ferry passengers to the different departure points, according to the chosen rou and the level of volcanic activity.

Once driving in the volcanic foothi or national park, follow signs for Et Sud, the main southern access poi reached via **Zafferana Etnea** ㉑. S on Etna's eastern slopes, this unpr possessing mountain resort hit t national headlines in 1992 when Etr threatened to engulf the village. Th resort had barely recovered from th 1984 earthquake, when the Baroqu Chiesa Madre became the focus fervent prayers as the local vineyar and citrus groves were swallowe up. The path of this eruption has no been landscaped into a strange garde memorial, signposted Colata Lavic 1992 (Lava Flow 1992). Since Zaffe ana is only 500 metres (1,650ft) fro the crater on Monte Serra Calvarin landslides and eruptive activity ar still common.

From here, a road leads to the **Rift gio Sapienza** base camp and an asce of Etna. As one climbs the scenic **Cas Cantoniera** road, citrus groves an wooded slopes give way to a wastel land of lava flows, bare slabs of brow rubble half-covered by snow. Even deepest winter, snow is unevenly dis tributed because of heat generated the volcano.

RIFUGIO SAPIENZA

The base camp of **Rifugio Sapienz** ㉒, situated at 1,800 metres (5,900ft includes a refuge (www.rifugiosapienz com) run by the Italian Alpine Club. Lik much on Mount Etna, the centre live dangerously, and was rebuilt after a eruption in 1983, an event depicted lurid technicolor inside. Before takin the cable car to the top, glance at th spent cone just in front of the refuge.

A winter **cable car** trip may b made in the company of skiers com paring eyewitness accounts of Etna most recent devastation. En route ar grim views of a burnt-out cable ca destroyed in the 1983 eruption, alon

Hiker climbing Mount Etna.

ith the wreckage of a ski lift and e original mountain refuge, buried y lava in 1971. At the summit, most sitors set off by minibus, leaving the ss adventurous simply to admire the nowcapped views, best in the morning at sunset, before sloping off to the ountain bar.

Torre del Filósofo, Empedocles' o-called observation post, wrecked a past eruption, currently marks e highest point one can go with a uide, close to the southeast crater. mpedocles did not live to tell the tale: e Greek philosopher allegedly leapt to the main crater in 433 BC trying prove that the gases would support s body weight. The charitable inter-etation is that it was also a quest for vine consciousness in death. But, as s sandal was found on the edge, per-aps he merely slipped.

The view from the top will depend n volcanic activity and the prevail-g winds: it is vital to avoid the gases nd burning volcanic matter emitted om active craters. Blue smoke indi-ates the presence of magma, while a

corona, a halo of sulphurous vapour, is a rare event. At most, you may see an active crater belching out sul-phurous fumes or exploding *bombe*, molten "bombs", or the bottom of the misty cone bubbling with incan-descent lava. In periods of intense seismic activity, the volcano spits out molten rock or fireballs, a dramatic sight, especially at night.

On the summit, many guides enter-tain visitors with a demonstration of the forging of black Etna ashtrays from molten lava. In exceptional cir-cumstances, you might be taken to see a lava front some distance away from the volcano. Usually bathed in mist and emitting a stench of sulphur, the lava front sounds like the clinking of china cups or the hissing of some chained animal.

The descent of Etna may not be an anticlimax if you can visit a lava front with a guide. **Valle del Bove** ㉓, best seen from **Milo**, was the most dramatic of recent lava fronts, hence its eerie, barren surface, devoid of vegetation: Etna at its most primeval.

Fertile ground around Mount Etna.

Tourist bus on the volcano.

FUNIVIA DELL'ETNA

Strolling on Piazza IX Aprile.

TAORMINA

As Sicily's foremost resort, Taormina has a languorous reputation, seductive hotels and a *dolce vita* image it proudly strives to maintain.

Taormina is Sicily's most dramatic resort, a stirring place celebrated by poets from classical times onwards. Goethe waxed lyrical about the majestic setting: "Straight ahead one sees the long ridge of Etna, to the left the coastline as far as Catania or even Siracusa, and the whole panorama is capped by the huge, fuming, fiery mountain, the look of which, tempered by distance and atmosphere, is, however, more friendly than forbidding." D.H. Lawrence was equally enamoured, calling Taormina the dawn-coast of Europe".

THE SICILIAN ST-TROPEZ

Today this elemental site has been domesticated into a safe, sophisticated, un-Sicilian pocket. A century of tourism has toned down the subversive native spirit, effaced poverty and displaced undesirables. French visitors liken Taormina to a Sicilian St-Tropez, stylish but unreal. Still, after Sicily's chaotic major cities, or the wariness of some of the islands' remote mountain villages, who wants reality? May, September and October are the loveliest months in Taormina, when the city enjoys a semblance of solitude combined with the pleasures of a mild climate.

The terraced town was once a wintering place for frustrated northerners and gay exiles. Today, this safe haven appeals to romantic couples, sedate shoppers and the cultured middle classes. As a resort, Cefalù, near Palermo, is Taormina's only serious rival. But Taormina scores in terms of sophisticated hotels, sheer professionalism and an enlightened, if rampantly commercial, approach to tourism.

Local gossip has it that the town is uncontaminated by corruption because even the Mafia likes a crime-free holiday haunt. Yet despite

Main attractions

Corso Umberto
Naumachie
Teatro Greco (Greek theatre)
Piazza IX Aprile
Cattedrale
Giardino Pubblico
Castelmola
Isola Bella
Mazzarò

Map on page 226

View from the Teatro Greco.

One of the top places for granita (water ices) on the island is Bam Bar (55 Via di San Giovanni, off Corso Umberto). The Sicilians eat granita at any time of day, including coffee granita and a brioche for breakfast.

designer glamour and hordes of blasé cruise-liner passengers, the site's majesty is not manufactured. Nor is the heady decadence and timeless charm.

Taormina started as a Siculi settlement at the foot of Monte Tauro. It was an outpost of Naxos until the Greeks fled the first colony for Taoromenion in 403 BC. Under the Romans, the city acquired a garrison and the new name of Tauromenium. The town also prospered in medieval times and became the capital of Byzantine Sicily in the 9th century. It was the last Byzantine stronghold to fall to the Arabs, destroyed in 902. But it was rebuilt almost immediately, and captured in 1078 by the Norman Count Roger d'Altavilla, under whom it enjoyed a long period of prosperity. Aristocratic leanings later drew Taormina into the Aragonese camp and support for the Spanish, with the Catalan legacy reflected in the town's array of richly decorated palazzi.

The main entrance to the town is the medieval gate of **Porta Messina ❶**,

close to the bus terminus on V Pirandello where the cable car *(funivi* takes you down to the resort beache of **Mazzarò** on the coast below. Outsic the gate is the tiny church of **San Pa** **crazio**, built over a temple to Isis.

CORSO UMBERTO

Corso Umberto, the pedestrianise main street, leads through the tow from Porta Messina to Porta Cata nia, revealing 15th-century palaz converted into craft shops, boutique and bars. On display are piles of can died fruit, marzipan animals and fres kumquats. These jostle for attentio with majolica tiles, traditional puppet cut-glass chandeliers and reprodu tions of classical statuary.

Just off the Corso lies the **Nauma chie ❷**, a hybrid construction secon only to the Greek theatre in impo tance. Originally a vaulted cistern co nected to the city baths, it evolved int a Hellenic nymphaeum and Roma gymnasium. The atmospheric arche buttress walls remain, propping u the Corso. For lunch, the restaura

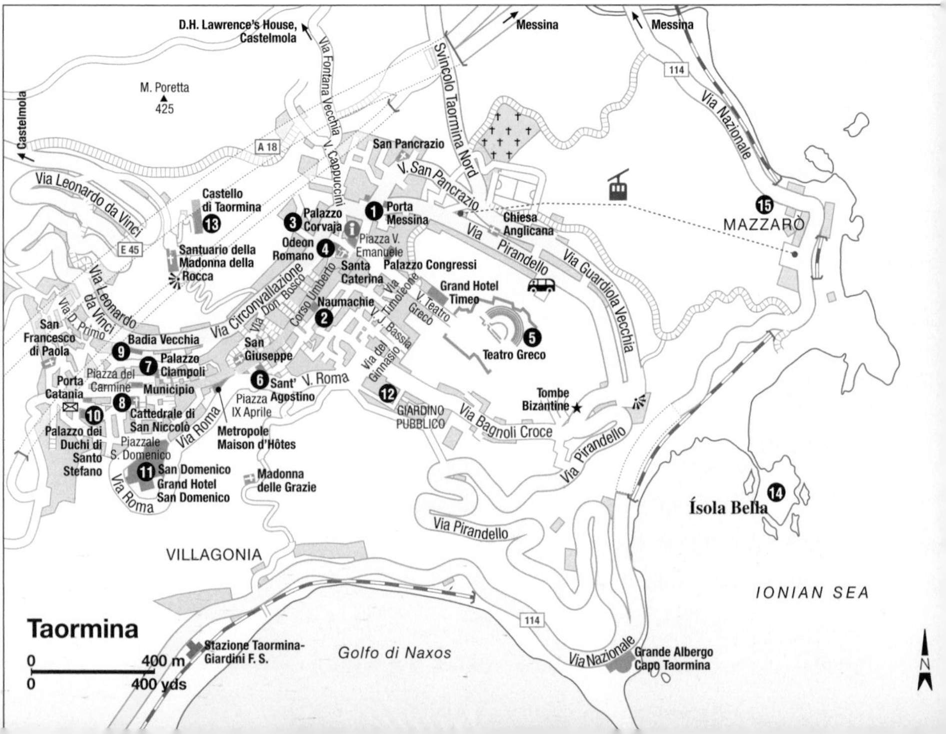

rraces of the adjoining Via Nauma-
ia beckon.

On **Piazza Vittorio Emanuele II**, the
ain square, is **Palazzo Corvaja** ❸,
historic mansion where the Sicilian
rliament met in 1411. Now a tourist
ffice for Taormina and the Alcántara
orge, this eclectic building incorpo-
tes a crenellated Saracenic tower, a
cluded courtyard, sculpted parapet,
d Catalan-Gothic decorative details
ound the doorway and windows. It
so contains the small **Museo Sicili-
o di Arte e Tradizioni Popolari** (Tue–
n 9am–1pm, 4–8pm; free) with local
ppets, carts, Christmas cribs and
ramics.

Next to the palazzo is the charm-
g church of **Santa Caterina
Alessandria**, constructed in the
th century on part of the remains
the **Odeon Romano** ❹, or Teatrino
omano, a Roman concert auditorium
rtly hidden by the church.

EATRO GRECO

ow we come to Taormina's *raison
être* on Via Teatro Greco (just follow
the crowds). This is the majestic **Teatro Greco** ❺ (daily 9am–7pm, closes
4 or 5pm in winter). It is a setting that
is pure drama, with the *cavea* (horseshoe of tiered seats) hewn out of the
hillside.

In Greek theatres, sea and sky were
the natural backdrop; the Romans
preferred proscenium arches. Where
the Greeks worshipped nature, the
Romans tried to improve on it. The
Hellenistic theatre was built under
Hieron in the 3rd century BC and
enlarged by the Romans in AD 2. Like
Tindari's Greek theatre, Taormina's
was turned into an arena for gladiatorial combat. Roman theatrical
conventions caused the view to be
obscured by arches. By adding a double portico and colonnades behind
the stage, they showed insensitivity
to the natural setting.

Romantics side with the Olympian
gods in seeing Roman grandiosity as
no match for the timeless character of
Greek art. However, Roman erudition is
evidenced in the well-preserved *scena*
(the construction behind the stage that

⊙ Tip

Getting around by car is
not advisable, as the
resort is virtually
pedestrianised. If booked
in a hotel, you are
allowed to arrive by car
and park there.
Otherwise head for the
multi-storey car park
below Porta Catania and
take the lift up to town.
The cable car *(funivia)*
links Mazzarò and
Taormina's Porta
Messina entrance.

Teatro Greco.

Get your portrait drawn on Piazza IX Aprile.

served as a backdrop and also storage area). But in the 19th century, the granite columns and Corinthian capitals were wrongly repositioned on the site. Still, Greek purists are delighted to see the Roman *scena* crumble, the better to appreciate the Greek atmosphere.

Not that the cats sunning themselves on the ruins distinguish between Greek marble and pinkish Roman brickwork. In high season, the theatre is best explored early in the morning or near closing time, to avoid the crowds. Views from the terraces above the *cavea* and *parascenia* (wings) reveal a perfect fusion of the elements. The writer Vincent Cronin likened the theatre to a seagull suspended between sky and sea. The scene is shrouded in mystery by a smouldering volcano or snow-capped peak. Citrus groves carpet the slopes, while the cliff face is a tangle of cacti and orchids. Make sure to climb to the very top for views of the craggy coastline, bay and the romantic islet of Isola Bella.

The passeggiata on Piazza IX Aprile.

The theatre is still used today, not just for performances of classical plays, as at Siracusa, but also as th venue for an international arts festiva Taormina Arte, which presents dram cinema, ballet and music from June August (tickets and information fro the tourist office in Palazzo Corvaj Piazza Santa Caterina; www.taormin arte.com).

PIAZZA IX APRILE

Halfway down the Corso, **Piazza Aprile ❻** offers glittering views of Etr and close-ups of preening poseu at classic cafés such as Wunderba **Sant'Agostino**, the forbidding 15t century church on the square, ha been converted into a cosy library ar art gallery, confirmed by the cluster caricaturists and street artists sketc ing outside. The other church fee more like a social than a spiritual ce tre: **San Giuseppe**'s Rococo interi overflows after a Sunday service; aft much handshaking, the congregatio spills into the cafés.

The Corso continues beyond th Porta di Mezzo, a clock tower markin the city's medieval quarter. Steps lea

the Catalan-Gothic **Palazzo Ciam-
li** ❼. After admiring its Aragonese
ttlemented facade and mullioned
ndows, call in for a sweet Sicilian
stry at Bar Saint Honoré before
imbing Via Venezia, a charming
ey by the Corso, or strolling further
the cathedral.

AZZA DEL DUOMO

azza del Duomo is a central meet-
g place. At sunset, or at the first
gn of spring sun, children fetch their
otballs, the *jeunesse dorée* pose, and
ormina's perma-tanned lounge liz-
ds, not a dying breed, search for for-
gn prey. Matrons still swan around in
eighty furs: in Taormina, the fur-coat
arade lasts until March.

The Duomo itself, the **Cattedrale di
an Niccolò** ❽ (daily 9am–8pm) draws
owds to its winter cycle of classi-
al concerts. The crenellated stone
cade has a severity that survived
enaissance remodelling but is sof-
ned by the Baroque fountain on the
quare, which sports sea horses, cher-
bs and a podgy female centaur. This

weird mythological creature is the city
symbol, confirmed by a stone centaur
unearthed on the Greek site.

Opposite the fountain, steps lead
to Piazza del Carmine and the **Badia
Vecchia** ❾, a battlemented 15th-cen-
tury abbey (Tue–Sat 9am–8pm; free).
Although over-restored, the abbey still
has Trecento flourishes, Gothic arched
windows, fretwork and friezes. Set on a
lower level, **Palazzo dei Duchi di Santo
Stefano** ❿ is a gracious ducal palace
and Taormina's loveliest medieval
building. Highlights are the Norman-
Gothic windows, delicate lava-stone
cornices and the lacy frieze of *intarsia*
work (decorative wood inlay), a Saracenic legacy.

From here, Via del Ghetto winds
down to **San Domenico** ⓫, a 15th-
century monastery converted into a
gorgeous de luxe hotel. During World
War II, it was Marshal Kesselring's
headquarters and suffered bomb damage, although the cells and cloisters
were spared. The Corso ends at **Porta
Catania**, the archway that matches the
Porta Messina entrance gate.

> **⊙ Tip**
>
> The Corso is dotted with
> travel agencies offering
> adventurous day trips to
> Mount Etna, to the
> Aeolian Islands or to the
> Alcántara Gorge. For a
> complete list, or for
> advice on tackling
> Mount Etna, visit the
> helpful tourist office in
> Palazzo Corvaja.

San Domenico Palace.

⊙ CHIC LIVING

As Sicily's glitziest resort, Taormina is
sophisticated fun, so join the chic set
over cocktails at San Domenico or Gran
Timeo. But even the poseurs are really
here for the artful simplicity of balconies
bedecked with bougainvillea and secret
gardens adorned with lemon trees.

At night, the Catalan-Gothic facades
are illuminated, and the squares seem
tinged pink in the moonlight. From the
belvedere, Etna's fiery cone glitters
before dissolving into the sea, stars and
smoky peaks. Those wanting to escape
the crowds should head for the Giardini
della Villa Comunale offering shade and
splendid views over the coast.

Solitary walkers climb Salita Ibrahim
to the Carmine, a tranquil monastic spot,
while dreamers take Via Caruso to the
Badia Vecchia and bay views.

Castelmola is dramatically perched on a limestone peak.

ENGLISH CONNECTION

It is a short stroll to the **Giardino Pubblico** ⑫, a lush park on Via Roma bequeathed to the town by an eccentric Englishwoman in the 1920s. Florence Trevelyan adorned her hanging gardens with pagoda-style follies and observation towers for bird-spotting (she was a keen amateur ornithologist). The tiered gardens are linked by mosaic paths and wind past tropical plants, from spiky cacti and lilies to dull English hedges.

St George's Anglican Church also dates from Trevelyan's time. Her contemporary D.H. Lawrence lived for a few years in a villa in Via Fontana Vecchia, part of which has been renamed Via David Herbert Lawrence. When King George V visited, Lawrence was the only British resident to ignore him. Undeterred, the king called on the writer and helped water his garden. In Taormina, the sickly Lawrence chose to live a solitary life, writing of sensuality. His former home is still a private house, marked by a plaque: "D.H. Lawrence, English author, lived here 1920–23."

Folly in the Giardino Pubblico.

On the north side of town, perche on **Monte Táuro**, is a tumbledow medieval **Castello** ⑬ (currently und restoration). It can be reached by half-hour ascent up a steep, windin path that passes by the clifftop **San tuario della Madonna della Rocca.** is a strenuous climb, which shoul not be attempted in high summe but the panoramas from the top ar worth the effort.

CASTELMOLA

Via Leonardo da Vinci climbs circ tously from Taormina to **Castelmol** above, a hamlet perched on a lime stone peak (there is a bus servic from Piazza San Pancrazio). Fror this natural balcony over the se there is a sense of what Taormin used to be. Out of season it is hom to craftsmen and part-time potter but in summer becomes a boisterou evening outing, with trinket shop and bars lining the alleys below th ruined castle. The best known is **Ba Turrisi** (tel: 0942 28181), a bizarr place decorated in honour of Pria pus, and strewn with phallic symbol Here, the eccentric owner plies fun loving visitors with his sweet "aphro disiac" almond wine.

DIPPING AND DIVING

Below Taormina, sheer cliffs drop the tempting islet of **Isola Bella** ⑭ which is now a marine reserve and good base for diving and snorkelling.

From Via Pirandello, the cable ca (check fares and timetable at www taorminaservizipubblici.it) links the cit to the pebbled beach at **Mazzarò** ⑮ Nearby are entrances to underwa ter caverns, where scuba-diver spot shrimps, red starfish, perch scorpion fish and sea urchins. If yo prefer your fish on a plate, leave th sea for the grey and pink cliffs abov Taormina. For details of beache close to Taormina, see Giardini Naxos (see page 242).

GAY TAORMINA

From the *belle époque* to Edwardian times, Taormina was, along with Capri, the quintessential homosexual haunt and still relishes its (undeserved) racy reputation.

When Harold Acton pronounced Sicily "a polite synonym for Sodom", he was really referring to Taormina. The town was founded during a period of Greek decadence and has always lived down to its debauched reputation. In this, it has been helped by its theatrical foreign residents.

SHEPHERD MODELS

The gay resort was first publicised by a trio of Germans: a poet, a painter and a photographer. Goethe pronounced Taormina a "patch of paradise on earth" in 1787. Otto Geleng, a landscape artist, settled there nearly a century later. The Prussian's paintings of the scenery drew gasps when they were exhibited in Paris salons. Although married to a Sicilian, he was a firm believer in the dictum of girls for procreation, boys for pleasure. His younger friend, Wilhelm von Gloeden, arrived in 1880 and stayed until his death 50 years later. The exiled blond baron photographed nude Sicilian shepherd boys whose beauty elevated them to the status of Greek gods. His lithe peasants, draped in panther skins or photographed against sunsets, soon entranced jaded Berliner high society.

Oscar Wilde often helped in the compositions, crowning the boy models with laurels or posing with pan pipes. Von Gloeden swooned over Wilde, declaring the poet "beautiful as a Greek god". Wilde returned the compliment, at least artistically, but preferred his "marvellous boys" as companions.

THE HOLLYWOOD ERA

A later voluptuary with showbiz connections was the Bavarian Gayelord Hauser, the Hollywood dietician to the stars. In the 1940s, such luminaries as Gloria Vanderbilt, Marlene Dietrich, Rita Hayworth and Joan Crawford danced until dawn at his parties. But while most of Taormina's male population ogled the screen goddesses, Hauser was more enamoured of the local gods.

Truman Capote and Tennessee Williams were regular guests at the wild parties at Villa Hauser. Both worked in Taormina before alcohol and drugs wreaked havoc with their writing. Capote accused Williams of "hiring boys for the afternoon", but both were often picked up drunk in bars on the Corso. Drunk or sober, Williams singularly failed to live up to his "lone wolf" reputation in Taormina. Somerset Maugham was a familiar figure on the Taormina scene, indulging in "the Disneyland of sin". Inspired by gossip about gay Taormina, the poet Jean Cocteau also came to see "the boys with almond eyes".

BRITISH RESERVE

All this was seemingly at odds with Taormina's air of twee Edwardian gentility, not to mention the mores of the English expatriate community. Douglas Sladen's book on *fin de siècle* Sicily confessed: "Nobody goes about naked, as might be imagined from the photographs." Thus reassured or disappointed, the British turned Taormina into a cosy hillside resort.

Still today, Taormina remains Sicily's most gay-friendly resort, beloved as much for its aesthetic allure as for its low-key scene (for more information on gay-friendly tourism consult the website of the Open Mind Catania LGBT centre: http://openmindcatania.ilcannocchiale.it).

A shepherd boy poses for von Gloeden.

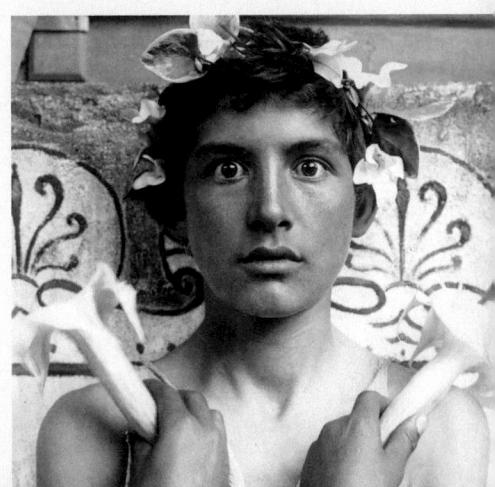

MESSINA PROVINCE

Where Sicily meets Italy, the province offers popular coastal resorts, a seemingly remote, mountainous hinterland waiting to be explored – and seaways to the Aeolian Islands.

⊙ Main attractions

Messina
Milazzo
Beaches from Oliveri to
  Cefalù
Tindari
Oliveri lagoon
San Fratello
Monti Nebrodi
Taormina
Sávoca
SS Pietro e Paolo d'Agro

Map on page 235

The province of Messina's slogan is *Monte e Mare*, mountains and seas. Certainly, the province delivers rugged mountain ranges and contrasting coastlines. The Tyrrhenian coast, the northern coastline leading to Palermo, is one of rocky inlets, saltwater lakes, sand dunes and dry gravel-beds; citrus groves are fringed by myrtle, broom and prickly pear. The Ionian coast is a gentler but equally exotic coastline as far south as Taormina, with sandy shores and resorts. Both coasts offer classical sites, stumpy castles, seafood dishes and an enticing hinterland.

MESSINA, THE CITY

Messina ❶, settled by the Greeks in 730 BC, was a thriving seafaring power but one beset by calamities in modern times. The 1908 earthquake killed 84,000 people in 30 seconds, while in 1943 the wartime port represented the Germans' last stand: the city was devastated and 5,000 people died during Allied bombing. As a result Messina, completely overshadowed by neighbouring Taormina, is designed on a modern grid system and intersected by wide boulevards. Although not instantly appealing, the bustling port, sunken treasures and lively bars make Messina an engaging stop before catching a ferry or touring the coast. The city is poised to learn whether the building of a suspension bridge over the Strait will ever be resumed (see box).

The protectress of the port is the *Madonna*, the tall statue surmounting the ancient harbour walls of the 16th-century fort, **Forte San Salvatore**, which protects the inner harbour. Curved around the sickle-shaped harbour is the neglected **Cittadella**, the 16th-century Spanish bastions and the naval base. The harbour welcomes grey NATO warships docked in deep water and long-prowed *feluccas* in pursuit of swordfish.

Fountain detail.

ver-present are the coastguard boats, scouring the Straits for illegal immigrants and drug smugglers. Despite the bustle, the overwhelming feeling is of space and sweeping views.

Just above the port, the **Cattedrale** (daily 7.30am–12.30pm and 4–7.30pm) symbolises the city's survivor mentality: this Norman cathedral has witnessed medieval fires, earthquakes and wartime American firebombing (1943). It is set on a lower level than the surrounding streets that were redeveloped after the 1908 earthquake, when the cathedral was shattered, its 26 granite columns reduced to rubble and its ceiling collapsed. The sculpted main portal and part of the Gothic facade are original, while the harmonious interior features a painted wooden ceiling, 14th-century mosaics in the semicircular apses, glittering Renaissance altars and a Gagini statue of *St John the Baptist*.

An amusing curiosity is the freestanding **campanile** outside, which houses the world's largest astronomical clock; at midday, folkloristic mechanical figures, including a flapping cockerel, ring the bells to the roar of a flag-waving lion. There is even Jesus coming out of a tomb and the Madonna presenting a letter to the burghers of Messina to sounds of Schubert's *Ave Maria*. The **Tesorio** (treasury; Mon–Sat but times vary greatly so tel: 090 675 175) displays silverware, reliquaries and a 14th-century *Madonna* surrounded by saints and archangels. The **Orion Fountain** (1547) in Piazza del Duomo is a surviving Renaissance masterpiece. It is a tribute to Orion, a mythical city founder, and also a celebration of the first aqueduct to supply the city with water. Human figures represent the rivers Tiber, Nile, Ebro and Camaro.

Piazza Antonello, just north, houses a cluster of Art Nouveau buildings leading to the vaulted Vittorio Emanuele gallery. In a neighbouring square is the small **Chiesa Annunziata dei Catalani**

(Mon–Sat 9.30am–12.30pm), a sunken Arab-Norman church with Byzantine echoes. Built over a temple to Neptune, this eclectic church has Norman arches, blind arcading, 13th-century portals and honeycomb apses. The mellow stonework is often festooned with flowers: as Messina University chapel, it is much in demand for academic weddings.

Due to the earthquakes and war damage, the city churches are a wayward mixture of restoration and invention. However, **Santa Maria degli Alemanni**, a few blocks south of the cathedral, is an authentic Gothic ruin, founded by the Order of Teutonic Knights.

Messina's magpie approach to architecture is illustrated by the neoclassical Town Hall, mock-Renaissance Chamber of Commerce, Fascistic Tribunal and Art Deco Prefecture. Contemporary churches can be Rhenish, Bavarian, Spanish or, like San Giuliano, a Byzantine pastiche. Even genuine relics are given a contemporary twist by an incongruous setting: San Francesco, a Gothic fortress of a church, overlooks a frothy ice-cream parlour.

Messina's Fountain of Neptune.

In Piazza Unità is Montorsoli's **Fountain of Neptune**, but the original Renaissance sculpture lies in the **Museo Regionale** (Tue–Sat 9am–7pm, Sun 9am–1pm), on Via della Libertà 465. The museum mostly displays art salvaged from the 1908 earthquake, including works by Caravaggio and Antonello da Messina (1430–78), Sicily's master painter and southern Italy's greatest Renaissance artist. His moving polyptych of the *Madonna with Saints Gregory and Benedict* blends Flemish technique with Italian delicacy and a Sicilian sense of light. The best-preserved panel is the *Madonna and Child*.

Writer Rodolfo de Mattei likened the city to "a sailing ship, low in the water, ready for a night cruise". Indeed, mercantile Messina looks romantic at night, its lights glittering along the harbour front. Summer strollers take a *passeggiata* from the seafront to the lively *cafés* on Piazza Cairoli. After dinner, under-age lovers enjoy the scenic drive up Viale Umberto to the botanical gardens.

LIDO DI MORTELLE

In summer, city life shifts to **Lido di Mortelle**, a youthful resort 10km (6 miles) north of Messina. En route, the coastal road passes the **Ganzirri lake**, once famed for its mussel beds, now a popular place for dinner in summer, and the lighthouse of **Torre del Faro** on Capo Pelaro, guarding the **Stretto di Messina**, the narrow Straits of Messina separating Sicily from Italy's toe. This peninsula was once graced by a temple of Neptune whose columns ended up, shattered, in Messina Cathedral. Today's view is sadly marred by gigantic pylons and power cables that supply Sicily with electricity.

Over-popular Lido di Mortelle, just around the cape, offers sandy beaches and fish restaurants. As a result, the air is heavy with a peculiar combination of petrol fumes and grilled swordfish.

THE TYRRHENIAN COAST

To get from Messina to Milazzo 41km (26 miles) away – where ferries sail to Strómboli and Lípari – either take the fast route on the *autostrada* A20, or for the best scenery, follow the SS113

Milazzo.

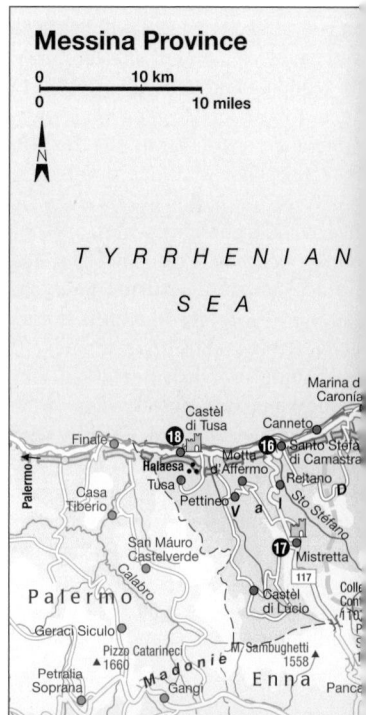

Messina Province

the old Roman road. The first stretch climbs the **Monti Peloritani**, winding past pine groves, broom, oleanders and geraniums. But even from the motorway are dazzling glimpses of azure inlets through the pines. On the way out of town are views of three ruined forts and apricot-coloured churches in the hills.

Tunnels thread through pine and olive groves to **Milazzo ❷**. The vision of this verdant peninsula is slightly marred by the presence of an oil refinery. Compensations lie in the welcoming breezes and dramatic castle, with views of the jagged green spit stretching towards the Aeolian Islands. While waiting for a ferry, be tempted to sample the local swordfish or *bottarga* (tuna roe).

Head for the walled city, passing the Baroque palaces that adorn the lower town, particularly along Via Umberto I. Here too, the **Duomo Nuovo**, the new cathedral, is memorable for its Renaissance paintings in the apse. **Salita San Francesco**, a steep stairway, climbs through the Spanish Quarter to the impressive medieval citadel, its flanks

encrusted with churches. The 17th-century **San Salvatore** belonged to a Benedictine abbey whereas **San Rocco** represents an older, fortified church. **San Francesco di Paola** is a frescoed 15th-century shell with a Baroque facelift. Don't miss the Antiquarium (Via Impallomeni 16, Mon 9am–2pm, Tue–Sat 9am–7.30pm, Sun 2–7pm; free). Located in a historic 16th-century building, it features priceless Neolithic, Greek, Byzantine and Roman exhibits illustrating the rich history of the area.

Facing the castle is the **Chiesa del Rosario**, once a seat of the Spanish Inquisition. This Dominican church is studded with stuccowork, an oddly fluffy vision for the rigorous interrogators.

The **Castello** (Mon 8.30am–1.30pm, Tue–Sun 8.30am–1.30pm and 4.30–6.30pm), perched beside a rocky precipice, occupies the site of the Greek acropolis. Erected between 1237 and 1240 and originally Arab-Norman, the citadel later fell into Hohenstaufen, Aragonese and Spanish hands. The castle's finest hour was in July 1860,

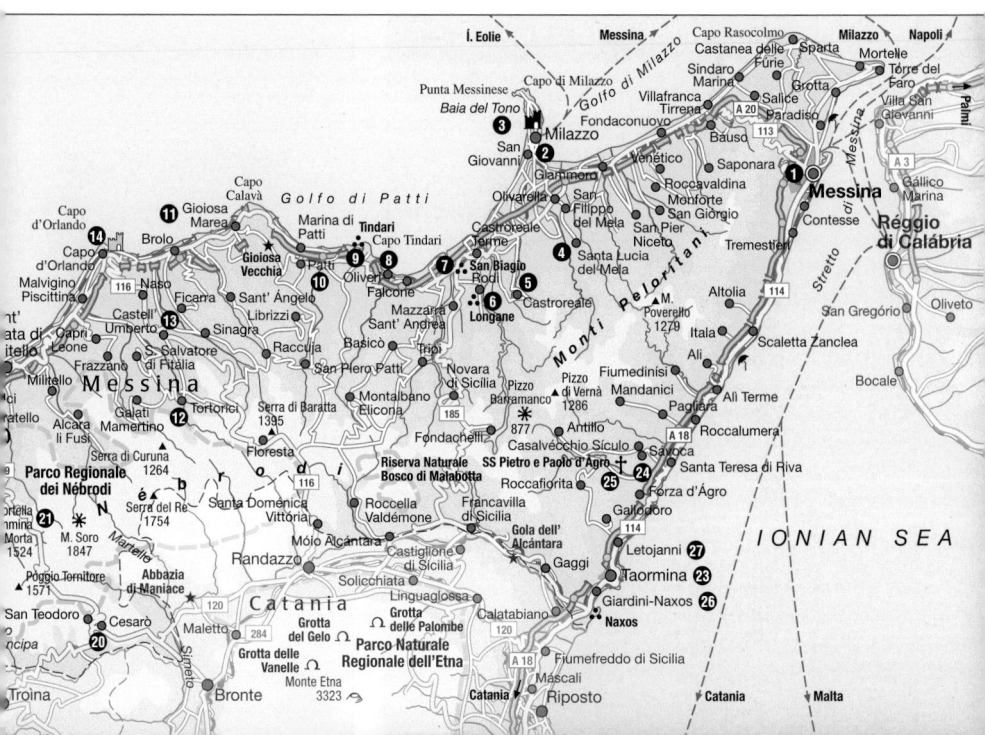

> ### ☉ Tip
>
> In Milazzo, a stroll along the Al Faro promontory from the lighthouse to Capo di Milazzo leads through lush vegetation to the cape. For the energetic, a climb to the heights of Monte Trinità provides a view towards the Aeolian Islands.

when its seizure by Garibaldi's forces spelt the rout of the Royalists and the Republican conquest of Sicily. The surviving fortress is of 13th-century Hohenstaufen dynastic design with Aragonese walls. A Gothic gateway leads to the keep and parliamentary Great Hall. Also within the castle walls is the Baroque **Duomo Vecchio**, and the ruins of the 14th-century Palazzo dei Giurati.

Boat trips to the **Baia del Tono ❸** visit reefs, coves and grottoes, including favoured swimming spots such as the Baia San Antonio or Baia la Renella. Near the Baia del Tono is **Grotta di Polifemo**, Polyphemus' cave, where Odysseus blinded the Cyclops. The 7km (4-mile) boat trip around the peninsula from **Al Faro** (the lighthouse) to Baia del Tono affords views of Sicily's two active volcanoes, Etna and Strómboli.

INLAND EXCURSIONS

If the hinterland beckons, then **Santa Lucia del Mela ❹**, 20km (12 miles) inland from Milazzo along a winding

Messina Cathedral.

rural road, is a Saracen village with a Norman castle once on the Lombard silk route. The Norman cathedral contains a Gothic portal and an Antonello Gagini statuette of St Lucy.

Back on the SS113, take the turning south for another foray into the hinterland. **Castroreale ❺**, a shabby upland village, was founded by the Siculi in the 8th century BC. Although the settlement flourished as a medieval barony, a ruined tower is all that remains of Frederick II's summer home.

The fertile coastal plain around Castroreale abounds in vineyards, olive plantations and orange groves, while the neighbouring coastal town of Castroreale Terme appeals to thermal spa enthusiasts. An inland road from **Castroreale Terme** leads to the archaeological site of **Longane ❻** (9am–one hour before sunset), near **Rodi**. Set on the edge of the Peloritani mountains, this megalithic and Sikel settlement was razed by Messina in the 5th century BC. The remains of a turreted fort are visible, and there are Bronze Age cavity tombs in the nearby necropolis.

☉ THE BRIDGE OVER THE STRAITS

The dream of building a bridge across the 3km (2-mile) Messina Straits separating Calabria from Sicily is currently just a pipedream. The Messina bridge, which would be the longest in the world, was the pet project of Silvio Berlusconi, but despite two false starts in 2010 and 2013, the project is currently on hold. While bridge supporters see it as a boost to the Sicilian economy, ferryboat operators, seismologists and environmentalists have long been against it, as are cynics who say the funds would only be siphoned off by the Mafia on both sides of the bridge. What's more, given the undeveloped nature of Sicily and the South, controversy rages over the wisdom of investing so much public money in a single engineering feat, with its six traffic lanes and two railway lines, when the money could be better spent on basic Sicilian infrastructure, especially roads and railways. Even on technical grounds, the project is fraught with doubts: the bridge will span a busy shipping lane and must also withstand high winds and earthquakes. Dozens of millions of euros were spent on studies and field works as well as on compensations before the project was eventually scrapped. As a result, it looks as if the Messina bridge, the final step in the unification of Italy and an unfulfilled dream since Roman times, is still some way off.

rom Rodi, join the SS185 as if return-
g to the coast.

Just before Castroreale Terme lies
he Roman site of **San Biagio ❼**, a
coman villa built in the 1st century
Mon–Sat 9am–7pm, winter until 4pm;
ee). The baths feature a black and
vhite mosaic of fishermen and danc-
g dolphins.

The SS113 takes you westwards to
Iliveri ❽ and a chance to exchange
hurches for seafood and excellent
eaches. Between here and Cefalù
s arguably the cleanest stretch of
oastline on the island. Oliveri itself
s a standard Sicilian resort with a
Norman-Arab feudal castle and sandy
eaches. On the seafront is a converted
onnara, the traditional tuna fishery, a
eminder of life before tourism.

Oliveri is on the **Golfo di Patti**, a
vilder spot than the Gulf of Milazzo,
tretching west to the rocky ridges of
apo Calavà. Its bays are framed by
he moody Nebrodi mountains. The
oastal road crosses fiumare, wide, dry
orrent-beds, and overlooks World War
  pillbox defences.

TINDARI

Dominating the Capo Tindari headland
is **Tindari ❾**, formerly Tyndaris, one of
the last Greek colonies established in
Sicily, founded by Dionysius in 396 BC.
Pliny records that in AD 70 much of the
city slipped into the sea. Despite subsidence and earthquake, the Graeco-
Roman city prospered until razed by
the Arabs in 836.

The **Santuario della Madonna Nera**
(summer 6.45am–12.30pm, 2.30–8pm,
winter 6.45am–12.45pm, 2.30–7pm;
free) stands on the site of an ancient
acropolis. The glittering sanctuary is
revered all over southern Italy as a
shrine to a black-faced Byzantine icon
with miraculous powers. The seated
16th-century *Madonna Nera* bears the
motto: *Nigra sum, sed hermosa* (I am
black, but beautiful). Among other
miracles, she is credited with causing
the sea to withdraw to provide a magic
mattress of sand to cushion a child's
fall over the cliff.

The **archaeological park** (daily
9am–one hour before sunset) is pleas-
ingly wild. Italian visitors, of course,

*Santuario della
Madonna Nera.*

The Trinacria, the symbol of Sicily, represents the three capes of the island (which was once called Trinacria). The Medusa denotes the protection of Athena, Sicily's patron goddess.

Santo Stéfano di Camastra ceramics.

are more impressed by the sacred *Black Madonna* housed in the church bordering the park. The Greek city covers a Bronze Age site and has left its mark in impressive **boundary walls** (3rd century BC) and assorted public buildings. The **Graeco-Roman theatre** cannot compare with Taormina's but enjoys a superb natural setting overhanging the bay. Classical drama, concerts and opera are now performed here in summer. A wide thoroughfare, one of three original *decumani*, links the theatre to the vaulted **basilica**. This Augustan basilica was once a grand entrance to the *agora*, a ceremonial space for meetings and festivals. Nearby are the remains of Roman baths, villas, workshops and taverns. One villa is adorned with geometrical mosaics, while the thermal baths enclose mosaics of dolphins, bulls, warriors and the *Trinacria*, the symbol of Sicily. The on-site **antiquarium** displays sculptures, ceramics, a tragic mask and a bust of Augustus.

Below Cape Tindari is the **Oliveri lagoon**, one of Sicily's loveliest natural havens. Migratory birds, includin grebes, coots and egrets, are draw to the pale-green saltwater pools an wide beaches of translucent grey peb bles. The lagoon's sands are a sublim spot for a picnic of fresh bread an local *caciocavallo* cheese.

Patti ⑩, set on a low hill facing th sea, was damaged in the 1978 earth quake but the medieval quarter, link ing Via Ceraolo and the cathedral, ha a quiet charm and several art-fille churches. The remodelled **cathedra** is home to remarkable treasures: subtle *Madonna* by Antonello da Salib and the Renaissance **sarcophagus** c Queen Adelasia, Roger I's wife, com plete with the original Norman effigy.

Sadly, this historic hill town is ringe by a jagged necklace of new develop ment. Even so, Patti unearthed it greatest attraction, a **Roman vill** (daily 9am–one hour before sunse at **Marina di Patti**. This sumptuou late Imperial villa was destroyed by a earthquake in AD 4 but restored an then occupied until Byzantine time After centuries of oblivion, it was redis covered during the construction of th motorway in 1973. The gracious room lead off a porticoed peristyle, look ing incongruous beside the motorwa flyover. The mosaics display geometric animal, figurative and floral motifs often of African inspiration. But Pat suffers from wilful neglect.

After a surfeit of art and architec ture, picnic among the poppies, as th Roman aristocracy did, or retreat to th beaches of Marina di Patti.

FORAYS INLAND

On the road from Patti to Cap d'Orlando are a cluster of resort fighting a battle against coastal rib bon development and Mafia influence currently losing the former but win ning the latter. On the Capo's prom ontory, reached by a hard climb, ar the remains of a medieval castle and

e sanctuary of **Santa Maria di Capo Orlando**, erected in 1598.

From the sandy resort of **Gioiosa area** ⓫, walk up to the ghost town **Gioiosa Vecchia**, abandoned after a 18th-century landslide. Brolo, just est, has a crenellated Saracen tower nd crumbling city walls, but Sicil-ns come here for the fish soups, quid dishes and salami from the hills ehind **Brolo**.

A rural foray inland visits Raccuja, rtorici and Castell'Umberto, a case the journey being more pleasurable an the destination. Citrus groves give ay to pine forests and steep ridges, ith stunning views from the hilltop llages to the Aeolian Islands. A tor-ous inland road leads from Brolo **Raccuja**. In winter, continue south ong the SS116 to the ski resort of oresta. Heading back to the coast om **Floresta**, turn off left to visit a uple of villages before returning to apo d'Orlando. **Tortorici** ⓬ is tradi-nally associated with the Mafia, but s several fine churches and school Gagini sculptures.

About 10km (6 miles) north along itchback roads is **Castell'Umberto** ⓭, former feudal domain with a long ominican tradition. Constant land-ides persuaded the citizens to aban-n the *centro storico*, even if it still has whimsical charm, with its ruined cas-e and vine-hung churches.

APO D'ORLANDO AND WEST

apo d'Orlando ⓮ is a windswept head-nd subject to sudden storms. Set on e edge of a fertile plain, this sprawl-g resort offers a sandy beach strewn th whale-shaped boulders, or a climb the ruined medieval castle and church rched on the cape.

Sant'Agata di Militello ⓯, the st significant resort west of Capo Orlando, is known for its prom-ades, popular pebbled beach and afood, with the local castle turned to a restaurant.

Pottery fans can follow the SS113 west to **Santo Stéfano di Camastra** ⓰, one of Sicily's main ceramics centres (see page 201). Lining the roadside, the piles of pottery make purchase a mere formality.

From here, the enchanting SS117 road leads 16km (10 miles) inland across the Nebrodi range to **Mistretta** ⓱, a rust-coloured town commanding a ridge. With its ruined feudal castle, sculpted **Chiesa Madre** (1630), red-tiled houses and cobbled streets, the town has a faded charm.

Castel di Tusa ⓲, which borders Palermo Province, is noted for its ruined castle, rocky beach and eclectic avant-garde hotel, the Atelier sul Mare (tel: 0921 334 295; www.ateliersulmare.it).

Inland is the pretty town of **Tusa**, and access to the Greek site of **Halaesa** (daily 9am–7pm), a city founded in 5 BC. Remains include the *agora*, bound-ary walls, theatre and temple.

MONTI NEBRODI

A rural drive through the wooded hin-terland of the **Nebrodi** mountains takes you into remote, rugged hill-walking

⊘ EXPLORING MONTI NEBRODI

The rounded silhouettes of the Nebrodi offer vistas of rocky outcrops or rolling hills covered in oak and beech woods or rough pasture. Compared with the Madonie range, the Nebrodi mountains are less accessible: exploration is necessarily slow, since the lack of east–west roads frequently means retracing one's steps to the coast. Before **Cesarò**, as you climb the range, Portella Fèmmina Morta offers a detour on foot or with an off-road vehicle to **Monte Soro**, the highest point in the Nebrodi at 1,847 metres (6,060ft), with fabulous views, a lake, thick woods and wildlife that includes falcons, eagles, herons, or even wild cats and wolves. Near fresh water, look out for wild fowl, the Sicilian marsh tit, and the wonderfully named *Tachybaptus ruficolis*. The name means "fast-bathing red stomach", an apt description of the little grebe. As a base, the most typical Nebrodi village is arguably the strange **San Fratello**. Covering an area of 86,000 hectares (212,500 acres), **Parco dei Brodi** (www.parcodeinebrodi.it) is the largest protected natural area on the island. Its verdant forests and picturesque lakes are at odds with the cliché sunburnt and dry Sicilian interior. Here, the once abundant indigenous wolves and bearded vultures became extinct long ago; instead the park houses rare wildcats and martens as well as Sicilian tits, buzzards and kestrels.

Reception at Atelier sul Mare, Castel di Tusa.

country. For an adventurous trail, try the circuit around the **Parco Regionale dei Nebrodi** (www.parcodeinebrodi.it), starting anywhere between Patti and Sant'Agata di Militello, where road signs indicate the Parco and San Fratello.

San Fratello ⑲, 18km (11 miles) from the coast, is one of the most evocative Nebrodi villages and is particularly colourful during its famous demonic Easter festival, the Feast of the Jews, **Festa dei Giudei**, a shrieking costumed chase. It is not so much anti-Semitic as Sicilian, hence a sacrifice of subtlety to spectacle. This scenic mountain village has a Norman church and a 15th-century Franciscan monastery. Horse-breeding has always played a big part in community life here, and each September Arab horses are put through their paces in the village.

Further along, the SS289 snakes through rugged terrain to **Cesarò ⑳**, where on 15 August they, too, celebrate horses in the Palio dei Nebrodi. This village of shepherds also has a ruined castle, destroyed during a battle between feuding dynasties in 1334.

From **Portella Fèmmina Morta ㉑** before Cesarò, hikers can reach th lofty **Monte Soro**, the highest point the Nebrodi at 1,847 metres (6,060f or adventure-seekers can opt for a off-road tour. Here, too, is the **Lag Biviere di Cesarò**, an ancient lake th turns bright pink with algae in the ho ter months, and a spot popular wi migratory storks and the marsh turtl

At **Cesarò** an appealing detour 20km (12 miles) along the SS120 lea to **Troìna ㉒**, at 1,120 metres (3,675 the highest town in Sicily. This pan rama of hills and valleys was on enjoyed by prehistoric man. Still vi ible are the remains of ancient Gree walls, while the **Chiesa Madre** has fine 16th-century campanile and med eval *Madonna and Child*.

To complete the Nebrodi circu from Cesarò the SS120 leads to **Abb zia di Maniace**, Admiral Nelson's hom (see page 218) and on to Randazz (see page 217), where the Sunda morning market displays Nebro crafts; then to **Floresta**, and aft some breathtaking bends, back dow

Patti and the coast. The complete circuit is about 230km (143 miles).

MESSINA'S IONIAN COAST

This narrow coastal strip is characterised by a contrast between the barren slopes of the Monti Peloritani (highest point 1,374 metres/4,500ft) facing the shore and the wooded slopes facing inland. As you travel south, there are architectural contrasts between the Baroque or modern coastal towns and the medieval settlements in the hilly hinterland.

From Messina, the motorway hugs the shore south for 52km (32 miles) from the narrow Straits of Messina to **Taormina** ㉓ (see page 225), hemmed in by mountains.

If travelling on the A18 motorway, at **Santa Teresa di Riva** leave the coastal crowds for mountain air and curious hamlets. Despite the proximity of Taormina, this is timeless Sicily, as remote as anywhere on the island. The scenery is stark: skeletal peaks and brooding ravines; mountains gouged by winter torrents and scorched brown in summer. Such fierceness is softened by sweet-scented scrub and the curves of Moorish monasteries.

SÁVOCA

Just inland is the battered mountain village of **Sávoca** ㉔, best known for its macabre mummies, embalmed in a crypt by local monks, and for its associations with *The Godfather* (see box).

The catacombs of the **Cappuccini monastery** (variable hours, tel: 0942 798 769; www.conventocappuccinisavoca. com) contain 32 ghoulish mummified corpses dating from the 17th century. At a time when corpses were thrown into the communal ditch, genteel mummification was a tradition among noble families. The bodies were drained, sprinkled with salt and left to dry for a year before being washed in vinegar, aired and then dressed in their original clothes. These gruesome, wizened faces and shrunken puppet-like forms are mummified abbots, lawyers, noblemen and priests. Now run by a religious association, this spartan former monastery accepts guests in its un-ghoulish rooms.

Sávoca.

After this macabre scene, leave the monastery for the evocative medieval village, a former Saracen stronghold. Sávoca's name derives from *sambuca*, not the famed Italian liqueur, but the elder trees that still perfume the hills. A paved path climbs cacti-dotted terraces and olive groves to the village, a scene embracing churches overgrown with prickly pear, a tumbledown dovecote, and terraces slipping into the sea. The church of San Niccolò lost its choir in a landslide but kept its dignity, while the **Chiesa Madre** retains the charm that caught Coppola's eye for *The Godfather*. This solitary church, on a narrow ridge overlooking the sea, was renovated with film money. The scruffy Bar Vitelli, immortalised in Michael Corleone's wedding banquet, comfortably hosts peasants and *borghesi*, united in their thirst for a cool *granita di limone* (lemon sorbet).

Casalvécchio Sículo, charmingly set above Sávoca, is livelier but less complex, with a gilded parish church and windswept views over terraces. On the outskirts of the village, take the first turning left, a steep road signposted SS Pietro e Paolo d'Agro ㉓, a monastic church down in the Val d'Agro. Despite its desolate location on the bank of the dry Agro river, this is the most significant Arab-Norman church in eastern Sicily. The twin-dome exterior is reminiscent of a Turkish mosque. A banded facade combines red brick, black lava, cool limestone and grey granite. Restored in 1171, the church is a synthesis of Byzantine and Norman styles. Moorish roundness and decorative flourishes compete with Norman verticality and austerity.

GIARDINI-NAXOS

Before ascending to Taormina, consider neighbouring **Giardini-Naxos** ㉔, Sicily's first Greek colony. It was founded (as Naxos) on an ancient lava flow by Euboeans in 735 BC and became a springboard for colonisation of Catania and the east coast. But after supporting Athens against Siracusa, the colony was destroyed by Dionysius in 403 BC.

The archaeological site (daily 9am-one hour before sunset) occupies the promontory of **Capo Schiso** (follow signs for *scavi*, excavations). A stretch of Greek lava-stone city walls remains, but the elusive **Temple of Aphrodite** is still being excavated, as are some villas. The small museum displays Greek, Roman and Byzantine finds, including a head of Silenus, god of fertility and wine.

Lemon groves are giving way to ribbon development, for Giardini-Naxos is Sicily's fastest-growing beach resort, as is neighbouring **Letojanni** ㉕. Still, for the young crowd there are compensations: cheap and cheerful trattorie, wide beaches fringed by volcanic rocks and a riotous nightlife that Silenus might have enjoyed. Moreover, unlike Catania province, this stretch of coast offers sandy, rocky or pebble shores, with an abundance of free and private beaches.

Giardini-Naxos.

Boats moored in Giardini-Naxos and Mount Etna in the background.

View from Vulcano.

THE AEOLIAN ISLANDS

Although two of the Isole Eolie still have active volcanoes, the archipelago is characterised by a sleepy charm and elemental landscape.

he setting is beguiling. Arching out rom the north coast of Sicily lies an nderwater volcanic ridge 200km (125 miles) long, from which rise the rocky slands of the Aeolian chain. But it is he exotic atmosphere and elemental majesty that make the Aeolians (Isole Eolie) unique.

Lípari is the largest island and the gateway to the archipelago, while Panarea is the most polished, Salina he dreamiest, Vulcano the most smouldering, and Filicudi and Alicudi he least developed. For adventure-lovers, the Aeolian Islands are argu-ably the most dramatic in Sicily, and he most brazenly beautiful, shaped by volcanic eruption and wind erosion.

Even by Sicilian standards, the Aeo-lians have seen cavalcades of settlers on their shores. Seven of the islands are inhabited today, as they have been since before the Bronze Age. The remains of Iron Age villages and Roman sites vie for attention, along with the Greek graves within the Span-ish walls of an ancient citadel. And that's just Lípari, the largest island.

There is also a lyrical quality to the Aeolian Islands, with their clashing colours, mysterious light and mythi-cal resonance, especially on Salina. It is this light, this wind that gives the sense of what the islands felt like in Homer's day.

Bar in Lípari town.

LÍPARI

Home to just over 12,000 of the total Aeolian population, Lípari is the lively hub of the archipelago, and the most interesting in terms of history and cul-ture. Part of the appeal of Lípari is also its blinding brightness, contrasting white pumice, black obsidian and the glittering sea, with the seabed scoured white by pumice.

As the boat approaches, the crowded roofs of **Lípari town ❶** come into view, dominated by a citadel, the Castello, set on a small hill, with the massive

Main attractions

Parco Arch. Diana (Lípari)
Museo Arch. Eoliano (Lípari)
San Calógero (Lípari)
Santa Marina di Salina
Pollara (Salina)
Gran Cratere (Vulcano)
Mud baths (Vulcano)
Yachting villages (Panarea)
Calcara beach (Panarea)
Strombolicchio (Strómboli)
Grotta del Bue Marino
(Filicudi)

Map on page 246

Lípari harbour.

Spanish bastion enclosing the cathedral and the 17th-century bishop's palace. Hydrofoils dock at **Marina Corta** on the southern side of the citadel, ferries on the north side at **Marina Lunga**. The two are linked by the main shopping street, Corso Vittorio Emanuele. The main sights are all within a short stroll of the harbour within the **Castello** walls. These include the cathedral, museums and an archaeological park.

From the Castello you can look down on the whole town, a cool vantage point among the pines. This also provides the best views of the main classical sites, the **Parco Archeologico Diana** and the **necropolis**, both to the west of Corso Vittorio. The excavations of the earliest stronghold unpeel the historical layers, illustrating the settlement on Lípari, beginning 2,000 years before the Romans.

The citadel is also home to a heavily remodelled Norman cathedral and the superb **Museo Archeologico Eoliano** (www.regione.sicilia.it/beniculturali/museolipari; Mon–Sat 9am–1.30pm, 3–6pm, Sun 9am–1.30pm, in winter by appointment), containing one of the finest Neolithic collections in Europe. This sprawling museum spans prehistoric and Roman times, with displays of prehistoric funerary urns, obsidian blades, Neolithic pottery, Roman amphorae and Greek masks. This is in addition to the re-creation of a Bronze Age burial ground and a big section on marine archaeology, complete with displays of wrecks.

If you are reeling from the Castello, retreat to the maze of backstreets off **Via Garibaldi**. Ringing the landward side of the Castello, these picturesque alleys will clear your mind and prepare you for your first taste of the Aeolians. Barbecued fish or pasta with tomatoes and capers will help.

CANNETO

A reliable road rings Lípari, linking the eight main villages, and a taxi tour provides a sensible introduction to the island. **Canneto ➋**, 4km (2.5 miles) north of Lípari town, has a long pebble and black sand beach and bustling

Aeolian Islands

0 — 10 km
0 — 10 miles
N

Napoli

I. Strombolicchio
Strómboli
Sciara del Fuoco **13** I Vancori
12 Ginostra 924
Ísola Strómboli

Ísola di Basiluzzo
Ísola Lisca Bianca
San Pietro **10** **11**
Villagio Preistorico Ísola Lisca Nera
Riserva Naturale Punta Milazzese Drauto
Montagna delle Felci e **Ísola Panarea**
Monte dei Porri

Í s o l e   E o l i e   o   L í p a r i

Ísola Filicudi
Fossa Felci
15 Grotta del ▲773 **6** Malfa
Bue Marino Filicudi-Porto **14** **7** Pollara Capo Faro
Pecorini **Ísola Salina** Santa Marina di Salina **5**
Filo dell' Arpa **8** Rinella M. Fossa d. Felci
▲675 Villagio 962
Alicudi Porto **16** Preistorico Lingua salina
Ísola Alicudi della
3 Quattropani Acquacalda
Canale ▲602 **Ísola Lípari**
Pianoconte Canneto **2**
Terme di San Calógero **4** Lípari **1**

Punta Crapazza Bocche di Vulcano
Porto di Ponente Porto di Levante **9**
Testa Grossa Gran Cratere
▲391
Ísola Vulcano Piano
Punta Bandiera
Gelso

T Y R R H E N I A N   S E A

Cefalú, Palermo

Milazzo Messina

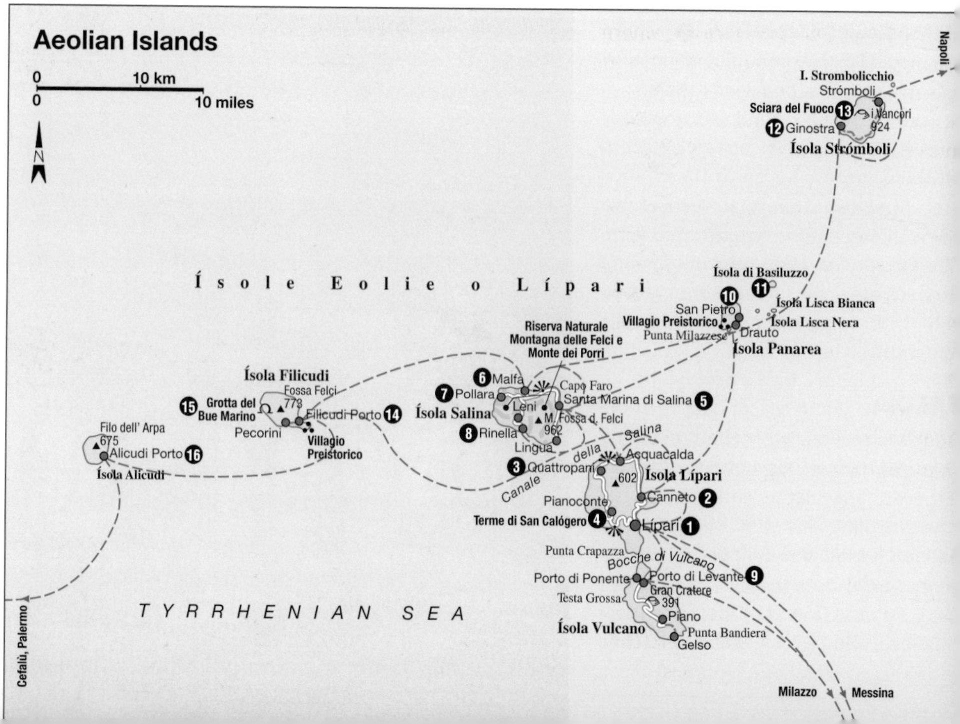

ars and trattorie. About 1km (1,100 ards) further you can take a winding ath down to **Spiaggia della Papesca**, sandy beach whitened by pumice ust. It is this dust that turns the sea n extraordinary turquoise all along to orticello, about 2km (1.25 miles) to he north. Pumice used to be quarried ere, and turned into building blocks, osmetics and fertiliser, but you can ick up small pumice stones all along he beaches.

Continuing the circuit of the island or 2km (1.25 miles) or so, you come o the northernmost village, **Acqua-alda**, on the slopes of **Monte Chirica**, t 602 metres (1,806ft) Lípari's tallest mountain, with pebbled beach views of alina across the narrow straits. From cquacalda the road winds up past the **Puntazze** rocks, overlooking Strómboli nd Alicudi, and continues through green countryside for 5km (3 miles) o **Quattropani** ❸, the site of a pretty hurch. Another 6km (4 miles) on, past everal small hamlets, is **Pianoconte**, home to Lípari's largest vineyards. Just outside the village, down a narrow road towards the coast, are the thermal baths of **San Calógero** ❹, where you can explore the ancient site and splash yourself with the hot therapeutic waters that come out of the ground n a domed chamber dating from the Mycenaean period.

Back on the main road, the circular route winds back down another 4km (2½ miles) to Lípari town, passing **Quattrocchi** where the belvedere provides a resting place and views across o Vulcano.

SALINA

Beguiling Salina represents the changing face of the islands. As with Panarea, the mellow island now welcomes a few hedonistic retreats. But Salina's boutique hotels are often surpassed by its boutique wine estates. Yet the verdant island also feels the most timeless, with quiet beaches matched

by volcanic peaks thickly wooded with conifer, sweet chestnut and oak.

Boats arrive at **Santa Marina di Salina** ❺, halfway along the island's east coast. The pretty village is an Aeolian blend of simplicity and sophistication, with chic shops and hearty inns that take in the comings and goings on the quayside. About 2km (1.25 miles) along the rocky palm-lined coast lies **Lingua**, its tiny lighthouse marking the southern tip of the island, and behind it a lagoon previously used for salt extraction, which gave the island its name.

The main town of **Malfa** ❻ is 7km (4.5 miles) from Santa Marina, its small harbour backed by a steep jumble of picturesque old boatsheds and crumbling fishermen's houses. Everywhere are signs advertising Malvasia, a sweet golden dessert wine made from sun-dried grapes. Also sample the distinctive wines produced by Carlo Hauner's boutique estate (www.hauner.it) or treat yourself to lunch at the chic Capofaro (http://capofaro.it). It will probably feature capers, which grow here in abundance.

⏲ **Drink**

No visit to Salina is complete without sampling the fine, honey-coloured Malvasia wine that leaves a slightly sulphurous aftertaste.

Street scene, Lípari.

Tip

A trip around Vulcano by boat views the island at its dramatic best, and the passage through the narrow Bocche di Vulcano channel that separates Vulcano from Lípari is exhilarating. Fishermen will offer a trip in summer.

Lunch is best followed by a fig *granita*, a Sicilian take on a sorbet.

From Malfa, the road winds steeply for about 6km (4 miles) to the small village of **Pollara** ❼, perched on one side of a half-submerged crater. For ever associated with *Il Postino*, which was filmed here, the delectable fishing village boasts two beautiful beaches, reached by a small path 20 minutes' walk from the bus stop by the church. To the right is a tiny beach ringed with boathouses carved into the cliff. To the left the path leads down to a black sandy beach backed by huge white cliffs. In the summer canoes and pedaloes can be hired for exploring the dozens of coves and inlets.

Behind the church is the path up to **Monte Fossa delle Felci**, the highest point on the islands at 962 metres (3,156ft). The ascent is shaded by mixed woodland, and well signposted, culminating in a rocky scramble and fabulous views. Depending on the route you take, the walk is between four and six hours. The steep path down to Santa Marina is very slippery and has to be taken slowly.

From Val di Chiesa, the roa descends steeply through the hamle of **Leni** and twists 3km (2 miles) dow to **Rinella** ❽, a pretty fishing por where most of the ferries and hydro foils make a second stop.

VULCANO

Vulcano is the smelliest island. It i enough to dock at the small port to b overwhelmed by sulphurous odour and steaming fumaroles, a reminde of the looming presence of the menac ing volcano. Known as **Gran Cratere** the great volcano on the island of Vul cano rises behind its smaller cousin **Monte Vulcanello** (123 metres/404ft perched on the north of the island which erupted from the sea in 18 BC. As the ferry arrives in **Porto d Levante** ❾ you can smell the sulphu fumes, and the lime-green, yellov and red rocks add to the extraordi nary experience. Porto di Levante' **beach** is popular despite the smell and immediately to the south of it behind a huge multicoloured rock, ar the famous therapeutic mud bath

THE AEOLIANS TODAY

The mineral-rich volcanic rocks of the Aeolians provided the basis of their early wealth: obsidian, a black, glass-like rock used to make cutting tools, was mined in Lípari and traded all over the Mediterranean more than 5,000 years ago, and pumice works survive on the island. But the overall decline of mining still led to a mass exodus, from a population of over 20,000 in 1911 to around 12,600 today. Many resettled in Australia in the 1950s, and you will hear returned émigrés talking with a Queensland twang. There is even a Miss Eolie competition in Sydney.

Today, tourism has turned around the fortunes of the Aeolians, though not without an eco dimension. Amid fears for the future of the islands, a tourism tax is now levied, but it is still tokenistic and serves to safeguard the future of these volcanic specks. Strict environmental controls, the designation of nature reserves and the relative remoteness of the islands ensure that even in high summer you can find an empty beach. Only Lípari has not been declared a nature reserve.

The islands have prospered, with volcano tourism taking off on Vulcano and Strómboli, cultural tourism boosting Lípari, wine tourism raising the spirits on Salina, and elite tourism transforming Panarea into an Italian St Tropez. Much tourism is sustainable or an extension of the traditional way of life, from the growing of capers to fishing, winemaking and walking holidays. Helped by the lack of decent roads (except for Lipari, Volcano and Salina which have a reliable bus service), visitors happily don hiking boots or take to boat trips round the islands. The largest island, Lipari, is a transport hub that makes for a good base to explore the rest of the archipelago. Main attractions include an atmospheric old quarter and a nearby pumice quarry. Tourists flock to the spectacular natural wonders of Volcano and Stromboli, the latter being the only in the world known to be continuously active throughout recorded history. Until a modern, environment-friendly desalination plant was opened in 2014 in Lipari, the islands struggled with severe water shortages that restricted its development. Thanks to the investment, some 36,000 litres of diesel a day (in peak season), which had to be burnt to operate the previous evaporation system, are saved.

anghi). After a bath you can wash off in the thermally heated sea, taking care to test the water, as some areas are scaldingly hot. Fumaroles (fissures of escaping volcanic gases) cause the sea to bubble.

Ten minutes' walk across the island's isthmus is the beautiful curve of black sand at **Porto di Ponente**, on the western coast, dotted with bobbing boats. Sunset illuminates the jagged forms of the Pietralunga and Pietra Menalda rocks off the coast. Just north, the road leads to Monte Vulcanello and, about 1km (1.25 miles) away on the northeastern edge of the island, to the **Valle dei Mostri** (Valley of the Monsters), a bizarre collection of sculptures created by lava eruptions in 1888 and erosion since; they are particularly evocative in the evening, when shadows create the impression of wild beasts.

Despite concerns that the influx of visitors is destroying the island's fragile habitat, any visit to Vulcano would be incomplete without a study of the volcano itself. Environmentalists suggest a boat tour of the island is sufficient, but you can still climb to the active Gran Cratere.

PANAREA

Northeast of Lípari is Panarea, Sicily's prettiest and most fashionable island. Here poseurs can preen on yachts, retreat to bougainvillea-clad villas or take helicopter tours of the islands. Decidedly chic compared with its countrified neighbours, Panarea's tiny harbour fills up with a flotilla of yachts when it welcomes the summer smart set. The three villages of **Ditella, San Pietro and Drauto** form a huddle of pretty cottages and tiny lanes along the eastern coast. The ferries dock at **San Pietro ⑩**.

From Drauto it is an easy stroll to the sandy beach at **Punta Milazzese**, a beautiful rocky headland with the remains of a *villagio preistorico* (prehistoric village). The finds are displayed in the museum in Lípari. A path from Drauto also leads up to the highest point on Panarea, **Timpone del Corvo** (382 metres/1,254ft), with a wonderful view of Strómboli and its smoking volcano.

Panarea cat.

Walkers on the volcano on the island of Vulcano.

⊘ GRAN CRATERE

On Vulcano, visitors have to weigh up a passion to explore the volcano against the disapproval from environmentalists. Climbing the Gran Cratere is the goal. Although only 391 metres (1,125ft) high, the ascent takes an hour and, though it's hot and exposed, can be undertaken by anyone reasonably fit. The smell of sulphur intensifies as the path zigzags up the slope, over black sand and crusty volcanic rock, passing deep furrows hewn by previous eruptions. At the top you are greeted by an otherworldly scene of the massive bowl of the crater, hissing and steaming and encrusted with yellow and red crystals. Take water and wear stout shoes and don't be tempted do climb down into the crater where poisonous gases accumulate.

Just past the headland is the tiny bay of **Cala Junco**, with excellent swimming. By boat it is also possible to see the caves and other tiny coves along the cliffs.

A steep signposted path leads from Cala Junco up into the high western side of the island, and back down to San Pietro, a fairly stiff but enjoyable three-hour walk. To the north of Ditella is **Calcara beach**, where a fumarole emits jets of gas and steam from fissures in the rock, coating the surface with yellow, white and green minerals and causing patches of sea to be decidedly warm.

From San Pietro you can get a boat trip out to **Basiluzzo** ⑪, now uninhabited, though a Roman jetty lies submerged and scraps of mosaic can be seen on its rocky heights, and to the tiny islets of **Datillo**, **Bottaro** and Lisca Bianca, where the swimming is superb.

STRÓMBOLI

Even those who have never heard of the Aeolian Islands have heard of Strómboli. The climb to its crater, blasting red-hot rock into the sky, is an unforgettable reminder of the powe[r] below the earth's crust. **Strómbol[i] town** is a lively spot, where you ca[n] relax while planning your 924-metr[e] (3,000ft) ascent. Ascents are no[w] only permitted when accompanied b[y] a volcanologist guide. If that sound[s] too daunting, then retreat to the long flat beaches, black sand to the nort[h] of the jetty, stone and shingly sand t[o] the south.

Strómboli and Vulcano are sti[ll] active volcanoes, though the last majo[r] eruptions – as opposed to continuou[s] emissions of steam or smoke – wer[e] in the 1880s. Even so, a minor erup[-] tion on Strómboli in 2007 proved unset[-] tling and provoked a rethink about th[e] advisability of exploring independently[.]

Tiny **Ginostra** ⑫ on the southwest sid[e] of the island is accessible only by sea.

Boat trips are also possible t[o] **Strombolicchio**, a tiny island of dra[-] matic coloured craggy rock topped wit[h] a lighthouse, and round to the base o[f] **Sciara del Fuoco** ⑬, the fiery slop[e] where lava from the craters flow[s] down to the sea. This is particular[ly]

Beach on Panarea.

xciting at night, when the booming
xplosions are matched by sightings
f the glowing lava, lit up against the
ark sky.

ILICUDI

eeply undeveloped, Filicudi is popuar with families, divers and anyone
n search of simplicity. Four hours by
erry westwards from Lípari, or an
our on the speeding hydrofoil, Filicu-
i's smooth whale-humped shape lies
uietly in the clear water. The locals
sed to earn their living by diving for
oral, but since coral is now protected,
ponges are collected instead.

Filicudi Porto ⑭ is the gateway to
n island of rugged beauty, explored
long criss-crossing paths. A boat
rip reveals the sheer northern side,
ne Grotta del Bue Marino ⑮, a cave
where Mediterranean monk seals
ised to live, and La Canna, a natural
belisk towering 70 metres (230ft) out
f the sea.

Given the shrinking population,
own to around 200, many houses
re ruined tangles enveloped by giant
chi d'India (prickly pear cactus). On
apo Graziano, the tail of the island,
urther along from the port, are the
emains of the oldest settlement on
he Aeolians, a Bronze Age village
ating from the 18th century BC. Also
n this southern coast is the seaside
illage of Pecorini, linked to the port
y the only road on the island. It is a
ood place to hire a boat for a tour of
he island.

LICUDI

t the western end of the chain is the
east visited island of the Isole Eolie,
licudi, a near-perfect green cone,
cattered with pink-and-white homes
nd terraced fields right up to its peak
t Filo dell'Arpa (675 metres/2,025ft);
ere are the remains of the old set-
lements, secure from mauraud-
ng pirates, carpeted with gorse and
eather. All the 200 or so residents

live on the eastern side of the island,
around the port, Alicudi Porto ⑯.
(This population shrinks to around 30
out of season.) The western side of the
island, too steep for houses, is a nature
reserve, the Riserva Naturale.

For the energetic visitor it is possible to circumnavigate the whole island
on foot, but the 7km (4 miles) entails a
scramble and two short swims around
impassably steep sections. Allow six
or seven hours and take water and
a picnic. A boat trip round to see the
twisted colourful strata and black lava
flows offers a less strenuous option.
There are two small shops and a hotel
(summer only). Otherwise, this is Sicilian life as it was for centuries.

The tiny 17th-century church of San
Bartolo perches high above the sea,
looking down the steep slopes of Scor-
bio to the small plain of Bassina round
the coast to the east. The lapping of the
water on the rocky beaches and the
sound of birdsong in the olive groves
are the only sounds to be heard. Alicudi
remains more interested in catching
lobsters than tourists.

*Waiting to board the
ferry at Lípari.*

A Palermo backstreet.

SICILY

TRAVEL TIPS

TRANSPORT

By Air

Sicily currently has four international airports: **Palermo** (Falcone-Borsellini), **Catania** (Fontanarossa), **Trápani** (Birgi) and **Cómiso**, formerly an American base, which opened in 2013 to help boost Ragusa's already thriving tourist industry. The first three have also been expanded due to the increase in budget flights.

Travellers for Messina use the **Reggio di Calabria airport** on the Italian mainland, just across the Straits of Messina. The bridge over the Straits project, potentially linking Messina and Calabria, has already been cancelled twice, but would transform the tourism scene if it ever were to come to pass.

Lampedusa and **Pantelleria**, two of the small islands with their own airports, are linked by services from Palermo or Trápani, but tourism to the former has stalled due to the influx of refugees from North Africa.

Scheduled flights for Alitalia, the national airline, and other major international airlines are usually routed, with transfers, through Milan, Rome or Naples. The major airlines include British Airways, Lufthansa, Air Malta, Air Italy, KLM and Air France. A number of low-cost airlines like Ryanair and EasyJet also run regular services into Sicily. Blu Express flies only to Lampedusa.

Palermo

All major airlines use Palermo's Falcone-Borsellino airport (www.gesap.it), 30km (19 miles) from the city at **Punta Raisi**.

Bus services run every 30 mins, linking the airport with **Stazione Centrale** and the general bus terminal at **Piazza Cairoli**. Timetables vary according to the season and are displayed at both the airport and the station. The first journey to the airport departs at 4am, and the last leaves at 10.30pm. From the airport, the first bus is at 5am, and the last leaves at quarter past midnight. The journey takes about an hour. The last bus usually waits for the final flight of the day. Bus ticket: €6.30 (€11 return).

The airport is also linked by the **Trinacria Express** train every 30 mins to and from Stazione Centrale, 5am to 8pm. Allow an hour for the journey. Fare: €5.80. At the time of writing, the service is suspended due to major track work so check for updates at www.trenitalia.com.

A taxi will charge about €45 for the trip to/from Stazione Centrale. **Flight information**: tel: 091 702 0111 – or call toll-free 800 541 880, a line which occasionally functions. See also the Palermo airport website: www.gesap.it.

Catania

All flights arrive and depart from Catania's airport, **Fontanarossa**, just 5km (3 miles) south of the city. There is an Alibus (toll free 800 018 696) service into town, 5am to midnight, departing every 20 mins for **Stazione Centrale** (railway station). Tickets can be bought from tobacconists. A metered taxi costs about €30.

Fontanarossa airport enquiries: www.aeroporto.catania.it.

Trápani

Trápani (Birgi) airport (www.airgest.it) is about 15km (9 miles) from Trápani, reached on an AST shuttle bus (www.astsicilia.it), with connections to Palermo, as well as to Segesta, Agrigento and Marsala (check shuttle timetables at www.trapaniwelcome.it/orari_aeroporto_ast.php). A taxi ride from the airport to the city centre costs €30 (fixed rate).

Messina

Air travellers coming to or passing through Messina usually use the **Reggio di Calabria** airport on mainland Italy or arrive via Catania or Palermo. A hydrofoil shuttle service links Messina and Villa San Giovanni, a short distance away from Reggio di Calabria's airport. Hotels and travel agents usually arrange a taxi or coach link.

Airport information, Reggio di Calabria, tel: 0965 640 517: https://reggiocalabriaairport.it.

By Sea

If you wish to avoid air travel, a long car drive or, indeed, the train journey through Italy, ferries (traghetti) are an excellent alternative. They link Sicily with **Naples, Genova** (Genoa), **Salerno** and **Civitavecchia** in Italy, with **Cagliari** in Sardinia, and with **Ustica** and the **Isole Eolie** (Aeolian Islands). There is also a link with **Tunis**, Tunisia, and **Malta**. Hydrofoils (aliscafi) also link Sicily to its smaller islands. Sicily can be combined with Malta on a two-island holiday using Virtu Ferries (www.virtuferries.com).

You can now book all ferries (traghetti) and hydrofoils (aliscafi) to and from Sicily, including all the islands (Aeolian, Egadi, Pelagie, Ustica e Pantelleria) through www.traghettilines.it. Ferry companies in Sicilian waters include: Siremar, Liberty Lines, Tirrenia, and Grandi Navi Veloci (GNV); and those linking Sicily and the Italian mainland: Tirrenia, GNV, Grimaldi Lines and Virtu Ferries. Timetables still need to be checked on the individual ferry websites.

Ferry prices tend to be low. Remember that sailing schedules are prone to change, and the small islands are often cut off during bad weather.

Palermo

Palermo's port is central, on Via Francesco Crispi. Cruise ships, ferries and hydrofoils embark and disembark passengers on one of the busy quays of the Stazione Marittima. Taxis are on hand to greet arrivals. **Ferries link Palermo** with Cagliari in Sardinia, with Naples, Genova (Genoa) and Civitavecchia on the Italian mainland, with Ustica and the Isole Eolie (Aeolian Islands) and with Tunis, Tunisia. All travel agents and hotels can arrange ticketing. Sailing schedules are prone to change.
Cagliari; twice weekly; Tirrenia; tel: +49 611 14020 (reservation centre for Europe); www.tirrenia.it.
Civitavecchia; one weekly; Grandi Navi Veloci: tel: 010 209 4591; www.gnv.it.
Genoa; daily; Grandi Navi Veloci.
Naples; daily; Grandi Navi Veloci and Tirrenia.
Tunis (Tunisia); twice weekly; Grimaldi: tel: 081 496 444; www.grimaldi-lines.com; and Grandi Navi Veloci.
Ustica and Isole Eolie; daily; Siremar: tel: 090 364 601, toll free: 800 627 414; www.siremar.it; and Liberty Lines, tel: 092 387 3813; www.libertylines.it.

Messina

All ferries and the train link to mainland Italy go through the Porto. The quay is on Via Rizzo.

By Rail

The Italian mainland is linked to Sicily by train, with Milan, Rome and Naples the best connecting stations to the south. Unfortunately, the great improvements in the Italian rail system do not extend to Sicily, and the fastest service from Sicily to northern Italy (Milan) takes 14 hours (with one change). Tickets cost about €150.

Always book a seat for long-distance travel. Credit-card booking can be made online (www.trenitalia.com), or go through any local travel agent – easier than the endless queues at railway stations.

There are several daily services between Rome and Palermo, Catania and Siracusa.

The crossing from Villa San Giovanni to Messina is an experience in itself: the train carriages are literally (and time-consumingly) shunted into the ferry, and then shunted off again at Messina. If you arrive on an overnight train, your first view of Sicily from the ship's deck may be of early morning sunlight on the sea and the mountains.

Palermo

The main station is **Stazione Centrale** (www.grandistazioni.it). Toll-free information tel: 892 021. All principal destinations are linked to Palermo with daily services to and from Rome, Naples, Florence and Genoa.

By Coach

Palermo

Autolinee (coaches) run by various companies leave **Piazza Cairoli** (near the central railway station) daily. There are services not only to Sicily's main towns but also to Bologna, Florence, Parma, Modena, Rome and Siena. Timetables change, summer and winter, and coaches may not run on public holidays.

GETTING TO THE ISLANDS

Aeolian Islands

Ferries and hydrofoils run frequently from Milazzo (near Messina), which is reached by train from Messina and Palermo, and by bus from Messina and Catania airport.

In the summer, there are several hydrofoils a day to **Lípari, Vulcano**, and **Salina**. There are direct ferries to the islands several times a week, but all can best be reached through Lípari. The ferry takes about 2 hours to Lípari and the hydrofoil about 45 minutes.

Ferry details: Siremar: tel: 090 364 601, toll free: 800 627 414. Call centre open Mon–Sat, 8am–8.30pm; www.siremar.it and Liberty Lines: tel: 092 387 3813; www.libertylines.it

Egadi Islands, Pantelleria

Ferries and hydrofoils from Trápani run several times a day to **Favignana**, **Lévanzo** and **Maréttimo**. The ferry trip to Favignana takes 45 minutes; the daily ferry to **Pantelleria** takes 7.30 hours.

Ferry details: Siremar: tel: tel: 090 364 601, toll free: 800 627 414. www.siremar.it and Liberty Lines: tel: 092 387 3813; www.libertylines.it

Ustica

In summer both ferries and hydrofoils run daily between Palermo and Ustica. In the low season, there are ferries only. The operators are Siremar and Liberty Lines.

Pelagie Islands

By Air

Flights to these islands via Trápani Birgi, information, tel: 0923 610 111 and Palermo Falcone e Borsellino airport (tel: 091 704 3028).
Lampedusa. Daily flights, to and from Palermo, Milan and Rome. Information, Alitalia, tel: 89 20 10; 066 5649; www.alitalia.com
Pantelleria. Daily flights to and from Trápani. Information, Alitalia, tel: 89 20 10; 066 5649; www.alitalia.com

By Sea

Summer hydrofoils or overnight ferries (cabin advised) run from Porto Empédocle to Lampedusa, stopping at Linosa on the way. The operator is Siremar.

GETTING AROUND

By Car

A car in Sicily is a great help for exploring, even though the island is well served by coaches and the many excellent tour agencies arrange visits to distant sites. In cities like Palermo or Siracusa where the traffic is so hectic and the sights so close to each other, it is easier to use public transport or taxis.

If you intend bringing your car to Sicily, the fastest crossing from the mainland is the 20-minute shuttle ferry service to and from Messina to Villa San Giovanni, in Calabria.

You will need a current driving licence and valid insurance. You must carry your driving licence, car registration and insurance documents with you at all times when driving.

Fuel and *autostrada* tolls can be paid with cash or credit card. The *Autostrada del Sole* south of Salerno leading to the Reggio di Calabria crossing point is free.
Car hire: Major hire companies include: Avis, Europcar, Hertz and Sixt. You'll find offices in the main airports, but it's usually cheaper to book ahead

through major travel websites or specialists such as www.autoeurope.co.uk.

By Taxi

In cities, taxis are best telephoned or found at taxi ranks. Licensed taxis are white, with a Taxi sign on the roof, and have a meter which should be turned on at the start of a journey.
Palermo: To phone for a taxi:
Autoradio Taxi, tel: 091 513 311, 091 8481.
Cooperativa Radio Taxi Trinacria, tel: 091 6878.
Catania: Radio Taxi, tel: 095 330 966 or 095 8833.

By Rail

Catania

Catania is well linked with other major cities. Trains depart and arrive at Stazione Centrale, Piazza Papa Giovanni XXIII.
The narrow-gauge train, **Ferrovia Circumetnea** (www.circumetnea.it), that calls at all villages around Mount Etna on a circular route (see page 213) leaves from Corso delle Province.

Messina

Messina is well linked to both Palermo and Catania, and all trains to Italy pass through its port in order to cross the Straits of Messina by ferry. Trains depart and arrive at Stazione Centrale, Piazza Repubblica; the boat trains at neighbouring Stazione Marittima.

By Coach

Fast buses link Sicily's main towns and offer relatively speedy access to the interior and the south. Generally speaking, coaches are more reliable and quicker than trains, but they cost more. The Palermo–Messina

Mopeds in Noto.

train route has improved, but the Catania–Palermo route takes twice as long by train as it does by coach.
The following lists the key routes on the island and the coach/bus company which runs them.

From Palermo

SAIS, Piazza Cairoli
Tel: 091 616 6028
www.saisautolinee.it
Buses go to Catania, Caltagirone, Enna, Piazza Armerina, Messina.
Cuffaro, Via P. Balsamo 13
Tel: 091 616 1510
www.cuffaro.info
Buses go to Agrigento, Canicatti, Favara, Racalmuto, Grotte, Comitini.
Interbus, Via P. Balsamo 26
Tel: 091 342 055
www.interbus.it
Buses go to Siracusa.
Segesta, 3 Via Turati (Politeama)
Tel: 091 304 106
Buses go to Trápani.
Salemi, Via Rosario Gregorio
Tel: 0923 981 120
http://autoservizisalemi.it
Buses go to Castelvetrano (near Selinunte), Marsala and Mazara del Vallo.

From Trápani

City buses and those for the rest of Trápani Province leave from Piazza Umberto.
AST, Piazza Malta
Tel: 0923 21021
www.aziendasicilianatrasporti.it
For Palermo and Agrigento, buses start from Piazza Garibaldi.

From Agrigento

City buses leave from Nuova Omnibus, Piazzale Fratelli Rosselli. Main bus companies:
SAIS, Piazzale Fratelli Rosselli
Tel: 092 226 059
www.saistrasporti.it
S. Lumia, Via Pindaro 3
Tel: 0922 20414
www.autolineelumia.it

From Enna

SAIS, Viale Diaz
Tel: 0935 500 902
www.saisautolinee.it
Buses leave from Piazza Scelfo in the lower town and connect with Piazza Armerina, Catania, Palermo, Caltanissetta and Caltagirone.

From Ragusa

All buses stop outside the railway station. Destinations include

Catania, Messina, Siracusa, Caltagirone and Piazza Armerina.

From Siracusa

AST
Tel: 0931 462 711
www.aziendasicilianatrasporti.it
Buses go to Lentini, Catania, Cómiso, Ispica, Módica, Noto, Gela and Ragusa.
Interbus
Tel: 091 342 055
www.interbus.it
Destinations include Catania, Noto, Pachino, Palermo and Taormina.

From Catania

The bus terminal is in front of the central station.
AST, Via Sturzo 220
Tel: 095 746 1096
www.aziendasicilianatrasporti.it
Buses connect with Acireale, Etna Rifugio Sapienza, Caltagirone, Modica, Noto and Siracusa.
SAIS, Via d'Amico 181
Tel: 095 536 168
www.saisautolinee.it
Buses go to Messina, Enna and Palermo.

From Messina

Giuntabus
Via Terranova 8, Milazzo
Tel: 090 673 782
www.giuntabus.com
Buses go to Milazzo and Pellegrino.
SAIS
Piazza della Repubblica 11
Tel: 090 771 914
www.saisautolinee.it
Buses connect with Catania and Palermo.

A–Z

A

Accommodation

Sicily has plentiful accommodation, with prices similar to the mainland. The choice ranges from grand hotels in Palermo, Catania and Taormina and stylish boutique hotels to simple B&Bs and rooms on farms. Accommodation in the interior is thinner on the ground, although there is a swathe of special hotels in and around Siracusa, Ragusa, Módica and Scicli. Book ahead for popular resorts such as Taormina, Cefalù and Siracusa, especially during Easter and summer. The same applies to hotels on the offshore islands. Many resorts close in winter; some hotels and *agriturismi* insist on half or full board during high season.

Agriturismi or farm stays have improved dramatically and are generally delightful and good value. Some of these might be rural estates, country houses or rural apartments rather than farms.

If you want to make an early morning start up Etna, Rifugio Sapienza (tel: 095 915 321) is a simple chalet with direct access to the cable car. Set up at 1900m (6,230ft), it can be cold, but these days the *rifugio* has decent heating, plus a café and restaurant. Tourists arrive for the cable car mid-morning, but by this time you'll be way ahead of the pack. Villa rental is now big business thanks to foreign villa owners and design-conscious locals.

Admission Charges

Museum and gallery charges vary, but the average is between €5 and €15, while some churches now charge too. Most state and civic galleries offer free entrance or special rates to EU citizens under 18 or over 65. A document of proof of age is often asked for.

B

Budgeting for Your Trip

Prices generally match those in Italy; the island is not much cheaper except, perhaps, for eating out and shopping in food markets. Food, wine and clothes remain good value.

Mid-range hotels charge around €150 a night for a double room, and you can pay more than €400 at a luxury hotel. But there are good bed and breakfast establishments, and the spread of *agriturismo* provides inexpensive farmstay accommodation (but only accessible by car).

In touristy areas you'll find a three-course dinner with wine will set you back €40–50 a head, but simple trattorie with equally delicious food and wine charge much less.

Fuel costs have risen in line with rising costs across Europe, but public transport remains comfortably inexpensive, even if train travel is painfully slow.

C

Climate

Sicily is renowned for its sunshine, with July to August hottest (averaging 28°C/85°F) when high temperatures are intensified by a rise in humidity and lack of rain. The coldest month is February (10°C/50°F). Along the coasts, winters are short and generally mild. The Etna ski resorts are usually open December to March. Temperatures remain comfortable into May or June, but the landscape begins to brown.

Clothes to Bring

You will need light clothing during the hot summer months. But remember that many churches and cathedrals will not admit visitors with bare legs (i.e. no short skirts or shorts) or bare shoulders (cover with a scarf or shawl). In spring (April and May) and autumn (October and November), you will need light clothes but also a summer jacket or sweater for evenings. Between December and March, bring warmer clothes since winter, particularly in the mountainous central areas, can be cold. Hotels and houses tend to be less well heated than is usual in northern climates: indoors is sometimes chillier than out. Mount Etna is often snow-covered in winter, and its lava-based rock requires strong footwear in any season.

Crime and Safety

The main problem for tourists is petty crime: pickpocketing and bag-snatching (by young criminals known as *scippatori* or *scippi*), together with theft from cars in Palermo, Catania and the historic centre of Siracusa.

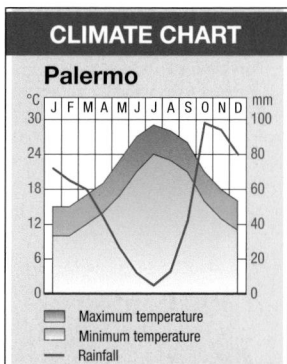

CLIMATE CHART

Palermo

- Maximum temperature
- Minimum temperature
- Rainfall

The resorts of Taormina and Cefalù are normally very safe. Elsewhere, use common sense and don't flaunt valuables.

Expect the police to have a casual attitude to petty crime and a slightly suspect attitude to a woman on her own. Expect, also, to have to prove who you are and where you are staying before even beginning to embark on your tale of woe. In the event of a serious crime, contact your consulate or embassy as well as the Carabinieri. Following that, try the Sicilian approach: summon the most influential Sicilian you know and request advice. Having friends in the right places helps.

If you are robbed, report it as soon as possible to the local police. You will need a copy of the declaration in order to claim on your insurance.

Danger Zones: Palermo, Catania and big-city backstreets are the most likely places for *scippi*. Avoid the station areas of Palermo and Catania, and also the myriad unlit backstreets of Palermo's historic centre after dark. La Kalsa in Palermo is fairly safe during the day, but should be avoided by night. Be wary of the San Cristoforo area of Catania (behind the castle) and in the portside fish markets. In Siracusa, by all means visit the characteristic restaurants, but steer clear of the Via Nizza port area late at night unless there are plenty of people about. In Mazara del Vallo, explore the Moorish Kasbah, but ideally in company (with a local guide) and not at night.

Driving: Always lock car doors when driving, and keep valuables hidden. Unfortunately, roads are often poorly signposted, especially in Palermo, Marsala and Mazara del Vallo, as well as in much of inland Sicily. If you're lost, stop and ask someone, and don't be surprised if they offer to escort you to your destination: that's Sicilian hospitality.

Driving tips: To save time on long journeys across the island, take the A19 *autostrada* between Palermo and Catania, or use the A20 which runs along the Messina coast. The A18 Messina to Siracusa is another fast route. In the Catania area, take the RA15 (Tangenziale Catania) to bypass the centre of Catania.

Customs Regulations

For European Union citizens: provided goods obtained in the EU are for your personal use there is no further tax to be paid.

For non-EU citizens: the duty-free allowances are 200 cigarettes, 50 cigars, or 250g of tobacco; 1 US quart of alcoholic beverages and duty-free gifts worth up to €430 (air and sea travellers).

If you plan to import or export large quantities of goods, or goods of exceptionally high value, contact the Italian Consulate and your own customs authorities beforehand to check on any special regulations which may apply.

The customs authorities are quite active in Sicily, partly to combat smuggling from North Africa, and partly because of the level of Mafia activity and the associated movements of goods and money.

D

Disabled Travellers

Sicily remains a challenging holiday destination. Most churches, museums and sites have steps, inside and out. Little has been done to create wheelchair access. Some trains have access arrangements (but check first) and seats reserved for disabled passengers.

Given the challenges in Sicily, it is wisest to book through a specialised tour operator or travel agency. These will offer customised tours and itineraries for those with disabilities. Recommended tour operators are **Flying Wheels Travel** (www.flyingwheelstravel.com) and **Accessible Journeys** (www.accessiblejourneys.com). In the UK travellers can contact **Holiday Care** (www.holidaycare.org.uk) to access travel resources for disabled and elderly people. The **European Network for Accessible Tourism (ENAT)** (www.accessibletourism.org) provides accessibility links for a multitude of European destinations.

E

Eating out

Where to Eat

Restaurants are usually referred to as *trattoria* or *ristorante*, and though the terms have come to denote establishments of similar character, in principal at least they are quite different. A trattoria is casual, serving home-style fare in an informal setting; a ristorante implies smarter décor, more polished service and more elaborate, more expensive cuisine. Some of the more formal establishments in Palermo and Taormina affect the ambiance of the latter, but most Sicilian eateries are of the family-run *trattoria* variety.

Bars in Sicily and elsewhere in Italy are not just places to drink alcoholic beverages. They sell wine and spirits, as well as soft drinks, mineral water and coffee. They also serve light fare: pastries (*cornetti* or brioche) both of which are croissants filled with jam, custard, or chocolate in the morning, little sandwiches (*tramezzino*) and filled flat rolls (*panini*) or other light dishes throughout the day. All these foods are usually displayed on the counter, you need only point to what you want. Many Sicilians will stop by their local bar several times a day for a quick coffee and chat, and you should find one you like and do the same – there's almost no better place in which to observe the engaging drama of day-to-day Sicilian life.

Yet another type of eating establishment is the *tavola calda* or *rosticceria*, both of which are cafeteria-style eateries where several selections of hot dishes are prepared daily and served from a counter. You generally pay in advance and take the receipt to someone behind the counter, who prepares a plate for you. Pizzerias appear in every Sicilian town, and often prepare their pizzas in traditional wood-burning ovens.

Sicily has a long tradition of street food, especially in Palermo and Catania. Food markets are the best sources. Look out for chickpea fritters (*pannelle*), potato croquettes with anchovy and caciocavallo cheese (*crocche di patate*), fried rice balls with chopped meat and peas (*arancini*) and beef spleen or tripe roll (*pani cu'la meusa*).

A *caffè* and its kindred *pasticcerie* usually serve pastries and other sweets (often ice cream, or gelato) and sometimes light meals, accompanied by coffee, tea, or a glass of wine. An establishment or two like this grace the main piazzas of most towns in Sicily.

One more essential stop when travelling in Sicily is a *gelateria*, a shop that sells only *gelato* (ice cream) and *sorbetto*, which is usually made with fresh fruit. Some distinctive Sicilian flavours are jasmine *(gelsomino)*, mulberry *(gelsi)* and pistachio *(pistacchio)*. When choosing a *gelateria*, look for queues of locals (who usually know where to find the best *gelato* in town) and for a sign that says *produzione propria*, which means 'made on the premises'. No trip to Mondello, the seaside retreat near Palermo, is complete without a stop at Renato, a famous *gelateria* in the centre of town on Piazza Mondello.

What to Eat

In Sicily, lunch is from 12.30pm to 3pm, and dinner from 7.30 or 8pm to 10.30pm. A restaurant will occasionally keep later hours, but rarely past 11pm or so. Most establishments close one day a week and occasionally for lunch or dinner immediately preceding or following the closing – so a restaurant that is closed on Monday may also close for Sunday dinner or Tuesday lunch. In the resorts, however, many restaurants keep longer hours in summer, and some close from November to March. Cafés are usually open from 8am to 11pm; bars tend to keep longer hours, especially in busy resort towns, from 7am or so until as late as 2am.

Most restaurants in Sicily include a service charge in the bill (usually 10–15 percent of the total), and many add a small *coperto* (cover charge) as well.

Electricity

Standard: 220 volts AC, 50 cycles. Connections are either two or three round-pins. Adaptors can be found locally, but it is wiser to carry an international adaptor.

Embassies & Consulates

In Rome

Australian Embassy
Via A. Bosio 5
Tel: 06 852 721
www.italy.embassy.gov.au
Canadian Embassy
Via Zara 30
Tel: 06-854 443 937
www.canada.it

Irish Embassy
Via Giacomo Medici 1
Tel: 06-585 2381
www.ambasciata-irlanda.it
New Zealand Embassy
Via Clitunno 44
Tel: 06 853 7501
www.nzembassy.com/italy
UK Embassy
Via XX Settembre 80a
Tel: 06 4220 0001
www.gov.uk/world/organisations/british-embassy-rome
US Embassy
Via Vittorio Veneto 121
Tel: 06 46741
https://it.usembassy.gov

In Naples

US Consulate
Piazza della Repubblica
Tel: 081 583 8111

Emergencies

Police: 113
Carabinieri: 112
Fire: (*Vigili del fuoco* is the fire brigade) 115
Ambulance/Medical emergencies: 118
Breakdown/road assistance: 116

Etiquette

Italians are generally friendly and will appreciate efforts to speak Italian. Any attempt to rush or pressurise them, however, will be regarded as the height of bad taste, and whatever you want will take longer.

Festivals

January–April

Carnival (pre-Lenten): the best are in Sciacca and Acireale.
Catania: Feast of Sant'Agata, the patron saint (3–5 Feb).
Easter festivals: Sicily-wide, including Trápani and Prizzi.
Agrigento: Almond Fair (Sagra del Mandorlo, Feb), **Palermo:** Opera season, Teatro Massimo
Caltavuturo: Madonie Food Festival (Apr)

May–June

Siracusa and Segesta: classical comedies and tragedies in the Greek

theatres. The season runs until end of summer.
Taormina: Taormina Arte: cinema, music, opera, ballet in the Greek theatre (June until end Aug) www.taormina-arte.com
Palermo: Beach festival in Mandolo.

July–August

Summer festivals in Catania, Cefalù, Enna, Erice, Siracusa, Ragusa and Taormina.
Caltagirone: Scala Illuminata (Staircase of Light, July) www.lascalailluminata.it
Palermo: Feast of Santa Rosalia (patron saint, July)
Enna: Summer concerts in the city castle.
Piazza Armerina: Palio dei Normanni (medieval pageantry, Aug)
Castelbuono: Jazz Festival (Aug)
Trápani: Luglio Musicale Trapanese. Summer Music. www.lugliomusicale.it
Taormina: Taormina Film Fest. www.taorminafilmfest.it
Palermo: Saint Rosalie; processions, plays, festivals and fireworks.
Cefalù: Night boat procession.

September–December

Etna villages: food and wine harvest festivals.
San Vito lo Capo: Couscous Festival in Sept, www.couscousfest.it
Ragusa: Ibla Buskers Festival (Oct, www.iblabuskers.it)
Catania: Concert season in Teatro Bellini.
Monreale & Palermo: Sacred Music Festival.
Módica: Chocomodica (chocolate festival, Dec), www.chocomodicaofficial.it
Siracusa: Feast of Santa Lucia (patron saint, Dec)
Palermo: opera season (Teatro Massimo) runs until May.
Cefalù: sorbet and ice cream festival.

Health & Medical Care

European Union residents are entitled to the same medical treatment as Italians, as long as they obtain a European Health Insurance Card (EHIC) before they travel. This covers medical treatment and medicines, although you will have to pay a percentage of the costs. Note that the EHIC does not provide for repatriation in case of illness.

In many areas in summer, there is a *Guardia Medica Turistica* (tourist emergency medical service), which functions 24 hours a day. Telephone numbers are available from hotels, chemists, tourist offices and local papers.

The *Guardia Medica* or *Pronto Soccorso* (first aid) for the area can also help in an emergency.

Lists of duty pharmacists are published in the daily papers (*Giornale di Sicilia* for Palermo and the west *or La Sicilia* for Catania and the east). In Palermo and Catania some are open late at night. The duty pharmacists will often speak some English.

General emergencies: 113.

Mosquitoes: If you are bothered by them, buy the small electrical devices which plug into a standard socket. Mosquito repellents are available in supermarkets.

Thermal spas: Many islands and resorts offer the chance to wallow in mud baths or take water cures. These are available at Sciacca (Agrigento Province), Castellammare del Golfo (Trápani Province) or on the Egadi and Aeolian Islands.

Water supply: Tap water is safe to drink in most places, but Italians generally prefer to drink mineral water, and this will usually be offered in restaurants. In some places the water supply becomes erratic in summer. Water supplies marked *Non Potabile* should never be used for drinking.

I

Internet

There are more and more Internet cafés as well as Wi-Fi hotspots in hotels, B&Bs, restaurants, shops and public spaces, but Sicily still lags behind the more developed regions. Ask for *un punto internet.* The best option is generally your (upmarket, modern, or business) hotel or a smartphone. Because of Italian anti-terrorism laws, to use an internet café you will need to show a passport or EU Identity Card.

Tourist information: Sicilian websites are improving and many are very good, though often still only in Italian (see page 262).

L

LGBTQ Travellers

There is little of an organised gay scene in Sicily, but attitudes are fairly relaxed and gay magazines are sold at most newsstands. Taormina is still the focus for the native and foreign LGBTQ community. Its gay bars come and go. Consult Arci-gay, a gay national organisation (www.arci-gay.it), or contact the Palermo branch (tel: 344 012 3880; email: palermo@arcigay.it). To access bars and clubs, you need to join the association, with a special membership card for foreigners.

M

Maps

The Sicilian tourist offices can supply maps which may be adequate if you are staying in one place. For touring, detailed maps are produced by the Touring Club Italia (TCI). One of their maps covers the whole of Sicily together with the islands. For general purposes, *Insight FlexiMap Sicily* is laminated for ease of use and durability and contains useful facts and travel information as well as clear cartography.

Media

Newspapers and Magazines

The main Italian papers (*Corriere della Sera, La Repubblica*) publish southern editions, but the local dailies are more popular. *Il Giornale di Sicilia* (http://gds.it/), Palermo's morning paper, includes practical listings (timetables, etc). *La Sicilia* (www.lasicilia.it), Catania's main paper, also has provincial supplements for Siracusa, Ragusa and Enna.

The following are Sicilian publications that may interest visitors:
Best of Sicily Magazine (www.bestofsicily.com) – English-language monthly online magazine.
Times of Sicily (www.timesofsicily.com) is a blog in English covering Sicilian news and topics spanning culture, food, art, history and politics.

Radio

Numerous private radio stations operate, as well as the three main national public stations (RAI Radio 1, 2, and 3). Most are broadcast on stereo FM. There are hourly traffic and weather bulletins on the RAI channels, in cooperation with ACI (Italian Automobile Association). In the summer bulletins are broadcast in English, German and French.
Television
In addition to the three main national radio and television broadcasting channels run by RAI (Italian Radio and Television), there are numerous others. Cable television and Euro-channels are also available, as well as satellite TV.

Money

The currency in Italy is the euro, written as €. A euro is divided into 100 cents, with 1, 2, 5, 20 and 50 cent coins. The euro notes are 5, 10, 20, 50, 100, 200 and 500.

Credit cards: Except in the smaller villages, major credit cards are accepted by shops, hotels and restaurants. They can also be used to pay *autostrada* tolls. ATMs, the automated cash dispensers (known here as *Bancomat*) are widespread.

Tipping: In restaurants, a service charge is included in the bill unless the menu indicates otherwise. It is customary to leave a few euros (€3–5), rather than a percentage of the total bill, if the service has been good. Taxi drivers will expect a passenger to round up the fare. For small services, including to guides, around €5 per person is fine. In many small villages, a custodian nearby may open closed churches and should be tipped around €5 per person with many *grazie*.

O

Opening Hours

Shops are generally open 9am–1pm and 4–7.30pm. Except for those in tourist resorts, shops are closed on Sundays. Food shops and fuel stations may also close on Wednesday afternoons. In cities, other shops are closed on

Monday mornings. **Bars and restaurants** close one day a week: a notice indicates which day.

Banks are open Mon–Fri 8.30am–1.20pm. Some also open from 2.45pm–4pm. Changing money can be a slow operation. ATMs are widespread, but often only in towns.

Post offices open Mon–Fri 8.30am–1.15pm, Sat and last day of the month 8.30–11.20am. The following open in the afternoon: **Palermo**: Corso Pisani 246; Piazza Verdi 7; Via Mariano Stabile 283; Via Roma 320 (Palazzo Poste). **Catania**: Corso Italia 33/35.

P

Postal Services

Post offices in the big towns and cities are generally open all day, with offices in smaller towns closing around 1pm. In Palermo, the main post office in Via Roma 320 (near Piazza Domenico) is open Mon–Sat 8.20am–7pm.

Stamps *(francobolli)* are also available from tobacconists *(tabacchi)* and bars that also sell cigarettes. Letters and postcards within the EU cost €1; outside the EU it is €2.20 (for less than 20g). The postal service is not renowned for its speed. If you need to send an urgent letter, send it by *Posta Prioritaria* (ask for the special stamps at the tobacconists, and the mail should be posted in the blue pillar boxes, not the red ones).

Public Holidays

Banks and most shops are closed on the following holidays:
1 January: New Year's Day *(Capodanno)*
6 January: Epiphany *(Befana)*
Easter Monday *(Lunedì di Pasqua)*: variable
25 April: Liberation Day *(Anniversario della Liberazione)*
1 May: May Day *(Festa del Lavoro)*
2 June: Republic Day *(Giorno della Repubblica)*
15 August: August holiday *(Ferragosto)*
1 November: All Saints' Day *(Ognissanti)*
8 December: Feast of the Immaculate Conception *(Immacolata Concezione)*

25 December: Christmas Day *(Natale)*
26 December: Boxing Day *(Santo Stefano)*

R

Religious Services

Italy is a Catholic country. The hours of Mass and services vary from city to country village, but Masses are usually held on Saturday afternoon and Sunday.

Each church has its own Mass timetable pinned inside its main door. Other denominations may practise their faith without hindrance and have their own services in Palermo and Catania.

S

Shopping

Sicily is not always as sophisticated as mainland Italy, but that is part of the island's charm, and the markets feel like a force of nature, especially in Palermo and Catania. Even so, designer shopping is readily available in the resorts. Sicilia Outlet Village, in Agira, just east of Enna, is Sicily's first luxury designer shopping mall, with all the big names (www.siciliaoutletvillage.com). It's a big deal in Sicily, and there's a free shuttle from Agrigento, Catania, Messina, Palermo, Siracusa and Trápani. Pottery, puppets and coral jewellery represent the best of traditional Sicilian handicrafts, while art books or special foodstuffs make excellent souvenirs.

T

Telephones

Telephone boxes have been phased out, as Italians have the highest use of mobile phones in Europe. In big cities, however, there are often combined call and internet centres.

For calls within Italy, telephone numbers must be preceded by the area code, even if the call is made within the same district. Mobile phones work well in Sicily.

Enquiries: 4176 for international directory enquiries; 170 for operator assisted calls.
International dialling codes:
To make international calls, dial 00, then the country code
Australia: 61
Canada and US: 1
Ireland: 353
UK: 44
Telephone offices
In Palermo, phone from: Piazza Giulio Cesare (24 hours); Via P. Belmonte 92 (8am–8pm); at the airport (8am–10pm).
In Catania, phone from: Via A. Longo (24 hours); Piazza Giovanni XXIII (8am–8pm); the airport (8am–8pm).

Time Zones

Italy and Sicily follow Central European Time (GMT + 1) but, from the last Sunday in March to the last Sunday in October, the clocks advance one addition hour to become GMT + 2. This means in summer when it is noon in Sicily it will be 11am in London, 6am in New York and 8pm in Sydney.

Toilets

Bars, cafés, restaurants and *autostrada* service stations have facilities. In a bar it is best to consume something first before heading for a toilet. Major sites now have reasonable facilities.

Tourist Information

The Sicilian tourism scene is still rather confusing, and information is hard to come by. On the other hand, Sicilian websites are improving, and many are very good, though often still only in Italian.

Tourism is now run by the Provinces, with varying degrees of success, and written material in short supply in many cases. Although the tourist office listings below are currently valid, addresses (and telephone numbers) change on a regular basis. Your first stop for information on the island is the National Tourist Board (Agenzia Nazionale del Turismo – ENIT; www.enit.it) which provides general background and practical information. Then try the specific provincial website.

In the absence of one tourist organisation for the entire island, a number of **tourism consortia**, either backed by local hoteliers, local interest groups or by the Chamber of Commerce, are beginning to take the place of some tourist offices.

Travel agencies or local tour operators can also be good sources of advice. In the more entrepreneurial resorts, especially in Taormina, Cefalù, Catania and Enna, some tour operators offer excellent, often adventurous day trips to anywhere from Mount Etna (explored in a 4x4) or a day trip to the Egadi or Aeolian islands. In Taormina, the Corso (the main street) is full of agencies offering such services.

Sicilian Tourist Offices

Official tourist offices are generally known as **IAT (Informazione Assistenza Turistica)**. Most big tourist offices will have staff who speak foreign languages, but this is far less true of smaller offices. When looking for the office, ask for *l'ufficio informazioni turistiche*. Tourist offices that can be singled out for their helpfulness include Palermo, Piazza Armerina and Taormina (which doubles as a tourist office for the Etna national park and Alcántara Gorge). The main offices are listed below; note that opening times tend to be unpredictable in many cases.

Acireale Via Oreste Scionti 15, tel: 095 891 999

Agrigento Via Empédocle 73, tel: 0922 20391

Caltanisetta Corso Vittorio Emanuele 109, tel: 0934 583 692

Catania: Via Beato Bernardo 5, tel: 095 747 7415

Catania airport tel: 095 093 7023

Cefalù Corso Ruggero 77, tel: 0921 421 458

Enna Piazza Napoleone Colajanni 6, tel: 0935 500 875

Messina Via dei Mille 87a, tel: 090 293 5292

Milazzo Piazza C. Duilio 20, tel: 090 922 2865

Palermo Via Notarbartolo 9, tel: 091 707 8035

Palermo airport tel: 091 591698

Palermo train station tel: 091 616 5914

Piazza Armerina Via Gen.le Muscarà, tel: 0935 680 201

Ragusa Via Ducezio 2, tel: 0932 675 837

Sciacca Corso Vittorio Emanuele 84, tel: 0925 22744

Siracusa Via Maestranza 33, tel: 0931 464 255

Taormina Piazza Santa Caterina (Palazzo Corvaja), tel: 0942 23243

Trápani Piazza Umberto I 15, tel: 0923 872 652

Tourist Information Abroad

Canada: Italian Government Tourist Board, 365 Bay Street, Suite 503, Toronto M5C 1T4.
Tel: 416 925 4882

UK and Ireland: Italian Government Tourist Board, 1 Princes Street, London W1B 2AY.
Tel: 020 7408 1254

US: Italian Government Tourist Board, 686 Avenue, New York, NY 10065. Tel: 212 245 5618
The official website is www.enit.it

Tour Operators and Travel Agents

Travel agents offer numerous holidays in Sicily.
Specialists include:
Just Sicily
14 Silver Business Park, Airfield Way, Christchurch, Dorset, BH23 3TA, tel: 01202-489040; www.justsicily.co.uk
Sicilian Places
Atlantic House, 3600 Parkway, Solent Business Park, Fareham, Hampshire, PO15 7AN, tel: 01489-866994; www.sicilianplaces.co.uk
The Sicilian Experience
6 Palace Street, London SW1E 5HY, tel: 020-7828 9171; http://thesicilianexperience.co.uk

Visas and Passports

Visas are not required by visitors from EU countries. A current passport or valid Identification Card is sufficient documentation for entry. Post-Brexit, UK nationals will need to check new regulations. For visitors from the US, Canada, Australia or New Zealand a visa is not required, but a valid passport is essential for entry to be granted for a stay of up to three months.

Nationals of most other countries require a visa. This must be obtained in advance from an Italian Embassy or Consulate.

Animal Quarantine: If you want to take a pet you need to have a Pet Passport, or the pet must be microchipped and have a vaccination

certificate for rabies and an official document stating that the pet is healthy.

W

Websites

Sicilian tourism
www.visitsicily.info (official site of Sicily)
Assessore al Turismo della Regione Sicilia:
www.regione.sicilia.it/turismo
www.bestofsicily.com
www.iat.it (tourist offices)
Sicilian heritage sites
Dipartimento dei Beni Culturali
www.regione.sicilia.it/beniculturali/dirbenicult
Palermo tourism
www.palermotourism.com
Parks and nature reserves
www.parks.it
Riserva Naturale dello Zíngaro
www.riservazingaro.it
Oasi di Vendícari
www.riserva-vendicari.it
Parco Regionale dei Nebrodi
www.parcodeinebrodi.it
Sicilian Transport
Airports
Trápani-Birgi airport: www.airgest.it
Palermo (Falcone-Borsellino) airport: www.gesap.it
Catania (Fontanarossa) Airport: www.aeroporto.catania.it
Comiso Airport: www.aeroportodicomiso.eu
Pantelleria airport: www.aeroportodipantelleria.it
Trains
Services: www.trenitalia.com
Train timetables: www.fsitaliane.it
Shipping lines
Ferry comparison: www.traghettiweb.it and www.directferries.co.uk
Grimaldi Lines: www.grimaldi-lines.com
Siremar: www.siremar.it
Snav: www.snav.it
Tirrenia: www.tirrenia.it
Liberty Lines: www.libertylines.it

Weights and Measures

All weights and measurements are in the metric system. As a rough but approximate guide:
A kilometre (1km) is five-eighths of a mile. So 80km equals 50 miles.
2.5cm = 1 inch
1 metre = approximately 1 yard
100 grams = 4oz
1 kilo = 2lb 2oz

LANGUAGE

The language of Sicily is Italian, supplemented by Sicilian dialects. Dialects may differ enormously within a few villages, and are an essential part of Sicilian culture.

In large cities and tourist centres you will find many people who speak English, French or German. In fact, given the number of returning immigrants – descendants of the families that were part of the massive emigration over the past 100 years – you may meet fluent speakers of these languages, often with a New York, Melbourne, Brussels or Bavarian accent.

One dialect with a difference is that of Piana degli Albanesi in Palermo Province: here Albanian is spoken. The population is descended from Albanians who arrived in the 15th century.

PRONUNCIATION

A few important rules for English speakers: c before e or i is pronounced ch, e.g. *ciao* ("chow"), *mi dispiace* ("mee dispyache"). Then ch before i or e is pronounced as k, e.g. *la chiesa* ("la kyesa"). Z is pronounced as ts, e.g. *la coincidenza* ("la coinchidentsa"), and *gli* is pronounced ly, e.g. *biglietto* ("bilyetto").

The stress is usually on the penultimate syllable of a word. In this book, where the stress falls elsewhere, we have indicated this with an accent (e.g. Trápani, Cefalù), although Italians often do not bother to use one (and, if they do, they may disagree about their direction).

Nouns are either masculine (*il*, plural *i*) or feminine (*la*, plural *le*). Plurals of nouns are most often formed by changing an o to an i and an a to an e, e.g. *il panino – i panini*; *la chiesa – le chiese*.

Like many languages, Italian has formal and informal words for "you".

In the singular, *Tu* is informal while *Lei* is more polite. For visitors, it is simplest and most respectful to use the formal form unless invited to do otherwise. To supplement the phrases below, we recommend the handy *Berlitz Italian Phrasebook & Dictionary*.

NUMBERS

1 Uno
2 Due
3 Tre
4 Quattro
5 Cinque
6 Sei
7 Sette
8 Otto
9 Nove
10 Dieci
11 Undici
12 Dodici
13 Tredici
15 Quindici
14 Quattordici
16 Sedici
17 Diciassette
18 Diciotto
19 Diciannove
20 Venti
30 Trenta
40 Quaranta
50 Cinquanta
60 Sessanta
70 Settanta
80 Ottanta
90 Novanta
100 Cento
200 Duecento
1,000 Mille

BASIC PHRASES

Hello (Good day) Buon giorno
Good evening Buona sera
Good night Buona notte
Goodbye Arrivederci
Hi/Goodbye (familiar) Ciao

Yes Sì
No No
Thank you Grazie
You're welcome Prego
All right (OK) Va bene
Please Per favore/per piacere
Excuse me (to get attention) Scusi (singular)/Scusate (plural)
Excuse me (in a crowd) Permesso
Can you show me...? Puo indicarmi..?
Can you help me, please? Puo aiutarmi, per piacere?
I'm lost Mi sono perso
Sorry Mi dispiace
I don't understand Non capisco
I am English/American Sono inglese/americano
Do you speak English? Parla inglese?
Do you like Sicily? (you will often be asked) Le piace la Sicilia?
I love it Mi piace moltissimo (correct answer)

QUESTIONS AND ANSWERS

I would like... Vorrei...
I would like that one, please Vorrei quello li, per favore
Is there ...? C'è (un) ...?
Do you have ...? Avete ...?
Yes, of course Si, certo/Ma certo
No, we don't No, non c'è (also used to mean: S/he is not here)
Where is the lavatory? Dov'è il bagno?
Gentlemen Signori or Uomini
Ladies Signore or Donne

TRANSPORT

airport l'aeroporto
aeroplane l'aereo
arrivals arrivi
boat la barca
bus il autobus/il pullman
bus station autostazione
connection la coincidenza

departures le partenze
ferry il traghetto
ferry terminal stazione marittima
flight il volo
hydrofoil l'aliscafo
left luggage il deposito bagaglio
no smoking vietato fumare
platform il binario
port il porto
railway station la stazione ferroviaria
return ticket un biglietto di **andata** e ritorno
single ticket un biglietto di andata sola
station la stazione
stop la fermata
train il treno
What time does the train leave? Quando parte il treno?
What time does the train arrive? Quando arriva il treno?
What time does the bus leave for Monreale? Quando parte l'autobus per Monreale?
How long will it take to get there? Quanto tempo ci vuole per arrivare?
Can you tell me when to get off? Mi può dire di scendere alla fermata giusta?
The train is late Il treno è in ritardo

DIRECTIONS

right a destra
left a sinistra
straight on sempre diritto
far away lontano
nearby vicino
opposite di fronte
next to accanto a
traffic lights il semaforo
junction l'incrocio, il bivio
Turn left Gira a sinistra
Where is ...? Dov'è ...?
Where are ...? Dove sono...?
Where is the nearest bank/petrol station/bus stop/hotel/garage? Dov'è la banca/il benzinaio/la

fermata di autobus/l'albergo/l'officina più vicino?
Can you show me where I am on the map? Potrebbe indicarmi sulla cartina dove mi trovo?
How do I get there? Come si può andare?
You're on the wrong road E sulla strada sbagliata

ROAD SIGNS

Alt Stop
Attenzione Caution
Caduta massi Danger of falling rocks
Deviazione Diversion
Divieto di campeggio No camping allowed
Divieto di passaggio No entry
Divieto di sosta, Sosta vietata No parking
Galleria Tunnel
Incrocio Crossroads
Limite di velocità Speed limit
Passaggio a livello Railway crossing
Parcheggio Parking
Pericolo Danger
Pericolo di incendio Danger of fire
Rallentare Slow down
Rimozione forzata Parked cars will be towed away (Tow Zone)
Semaforo Traffic lights
Senso unico One way street
Sentiero Footpath
Strada interrotta Road blocked
Strada senza uscita Dead end
Vietato il sorpasso No overtaking

SHOPPING

How much does it cost? Quanto costa?
(half) a kilo un (mezzo) kilo
100 grams un etto
200 grams due etti
a little un pochino
That's enough Basta così
That's too expensive E troppo caro

It's too small E troppo piccolo
It's too big E troppo grande
I like it Mi piace
I don't like it Non mi piace
I'll take it Lo prendo

IN THE HOTEL

I would like Vorrei
a single/double room (with a double bed) una camera singola/doppia (con letto matrimoniale)
with bath/shower con bagno/doccia
for one night per una notte
How much is it? Quanto costa?
Is breakfast included? E compresa la colazione?
half/full board mezza pensione/pensione completa
key la chiave
towel un asciugamano
toilet paper la carta igienica
Do you have a room with a balcony/view of the sea? C'è una camera con balcone/una vista del mare?
Can I see the room? Posso vedere la camera?
Is it a quiet room? E una stanza tranquilla?
We have one with a double bed Ne abbiamo una matrimoniale
Can I have the bill, please? Posso avere il conto, per favore?

FINDING THE SIGHTS

Custode Custodian
Suonare il campanello Ring the bell
Abbazia Abbey
Aperto Open
Chiuso Closed
Chiesa Church
Entrata Entrance
Museo Museum
Ruderi Ruins
Scavi Excavations/archaeological site
Spiaggia Beach
Tempio Temple

HISTORY AND CULTURE

The Leopard, Giuseppe Tomasi di Lampedusa (Vintage). This is both the classic Sicilian novel and Italy's greatest novel. A timeless masterpiece.

The Last Leopard: A Life of Giuseppe Tomasi di Lampedusa, David Gilmour (Quartet). This is a sensitive literary biography and companion to *The Leopard* itself, based on interviews with the author's adopted son and full access to the family archives.

The Normans in Sicily, John Julius Norwich (Penguin/Barnes & Noble). This remains the best introduction to the "other" Norman Conquest, including of Southern Italy and Sicily – led by the great Euro-adventurers.

CRIME AND SOCIETY

The Shape of Water, The Terracotta Dog, The Voice of the Violin and **The Snack Thief**, Andrea Camilleri. These detective stories/thrillers are worldwide best-sellers, helped by the Montalbano films. All are available in English paperback editions (Picador).

Boss of Bosses, Clare Longrigg (John Murray). This account covers the role and importance of Bernardo Provenzano, the Mafia boss *(capo di tutti capi)* who was finally arrested in 2006 near his home in Corleone.

The Day of the Owl, Leonardo Sciascia (Granta/Jonathan Cape). This novel about the Mafia was written by a rigorous writer and politician (1921–83) often known as 'the conscience of Sicily'.

Midnight in Sicily, Peter Robb (Panther). Personal insights and trenchant observations on Sicilian society, customs, relationships, art, food, history and the Mafia, especially centred on Palermo and western Sicily.

No Questions Asked, Clare Longrigg (Miramax Books). Subtitled "The Secret Life of Women in the Mob", this account covers the varied role of women in the Cosa Nostra, whom the author persuaded to talk.

TRAVEL AND GENERAL

Bagheria, Dacia Maraini (Rizzoli). The author, the daughter of a Sicilian princess, revisits the family's ancestral villa in Bagheria, in an attempt to come to terms with her past and with the desecration of this once glorious town close to Palermo.

Bitter Almonds, Mary Taylor Simeti and Maria Grammatico (Bantam).

⊘ Send us your thoughts

We do our best to ensure the information in our books is as accurate and up-to-date as possible. The books are updated on a regular basis using local contacts, who painstakingly add, amend and correct as required. However, some details (such as telephone numbers and opening times) are liable to change, and we are ultimately reliant on our readers to put us in the picture.

We welcome your feedback, especially your experience of using the book "on the road". Maybe you came across a great bar or new attraction we missed.

We will acknowledge all contributions, and we'll offer an Insight Guide to the best letters received.

Please write to us at:
Insight Guides
PO Box 7910
London SE1 1WE

Or email us at:
hello@insightguides.com

This foodie memoir is inspired by a disappearing Sicily, linked to the convents producing pastries, notably the almond pastries in Erice.

Clay Ghosts in Sicily, Angie Voluti (Bank House Books). Set in post-war Palermo, this quirky new novel features a lovelorn young Sicilian sculptress haunted by memories conjured up by visits to the capital, with its secret tunnels and dilapidated palaces.

Good Girls Don't Wear Trousers, Lara Cardella (Arcade Publishing). Living in a stifling Sicilian town in the early 1960s, teenage Annetta, the narrator, dreams that wearing trousers will give her freedom, but is told that "only two kinds of people in Sicily wear trousers: men and *puttane* (sluts)."

A House in Sicily, Daphne Phelps (Virago Press). An affectionate travel memoir centred on Casa Cuseni, a Taormina *pensione* that welcomed artists and writers such as Tennessee Williams, Bertrand Russell and Roald Dahl.

Made in Sicily, Giorgio Locatelli (Fourth Estate). This new gastronomic tour of Sicily presents the celebrity chef's simplest yet most authentic island recipes. As Locatelli says, "In a Sicilian village, you don't go out with a list, you just go out and see what there is."

The Silent Duchess, Dacia Maraini (Flamingo, also on Kindle). Set in the mid-18th century, this novel tells of a noble family, seen through the eyes of the deaf-mute duchess who strives for fulfilment in a society in which women's lives were circumscribed.

CREDITS

PHOTO CREDITS

COVER CREDITS

INSIGHT GUIDE CREDITS

Distribution
UK, Ireland and Europe
Apa Publications (UK) Ltd;
sales@insightguides.com
United States and Canada
Ingram Publisher Services;
ips@ingramcontent.com
Australia and New Zealand
Woodslane; info@woodslane.com.au
Southeast Asia
Apa Publications (SN) Pte;
singaporeoffice@insightguides.com
Worldwide
Apa Publications (UK) Ltd;
sales@insightguides.com
**Special Sales, Content Licensing and
CoPublishing**
Insight Guides can be purchased in
bulk quantities at discounted prices.
We can create special editions,
personalised jackets and corporate
imprints tailored to your needs.
sales@insightguides.com
www.insightguides.biz

Printed in China by CTPS

First Edition 1993
Seventh Edition 2019

Every effort has been made to provide
accurate information in this
publication, but changes are
inevitable. The publisher cannot be
responsible for any resulting loss,
inconvenience or injury. We would
appreciate it if readers would call our
attention to any errors or outdated
information. We also welcome your
suggestions; please contact us at:
hello@insightguides.com

www.insightguides.com

Editor: Carine Tracanelli
Author: Lisa Gerard-Sharp
Head of DTP and Pre-Press:
Rebeka Davies
Update Production: Apa Digital
Picture Editor: Tom Smyth
Cartography: original cartography
Berndtson & Berndtson, updated by
Carte

CONTRIBUTORS

This edition of *Insight Guide Sicily* was
commissioned and edited by Managing
Editor **Carine Tracanelli**.
    The book was largely written by **Lisa
Gerard-Sharp**, a writer with a special
interest in Italy. An award-winning
journalist, Lisa contributes to national
newspapers, travel documentaries and
magazines, and spends a large chunck
of the year travelling around Italy.
    Lisa is delighted to report that a
sunnier Sicily is emerging, from

"Mafia-free" holidays and the return
of "stolen" art treasures to the revival
of Ragusa, Siracusa and southeastern
Sicily, the resurgence of Palermo, and
the revitalisation of Sicilian wines.
    Added to the mix are chic boutique
hotels, Slow Food cookery courses,
new walking trails through nature
reserves, cruises around the Aeolian
islands, and helicopter rides over
Mount Etna. Sicily has never been
so beguiling.

ABOUT INSIGHT GUIDES

Insight Guides have more than 45
years' experience of publishing high-
quality, visual travel guides. We
produce 400 full-colour titles, in both
print and digital form, covering more
than 200 destinations across the
globe, in a variety of formats to meet
your different needs.
    Insight Guides are written by local
authors, whose expertise is evident in
the extensive historical and cultural

background features. Each destination
is carefully researched by regional
experts to ensure our guides provide
the very latest information. All the
reviews in **Insight Guides** are
independent; we strive to maintain an
impartial view. Our reviews are
carefully selected to guide you to the
best places to eat, go out and shop, so
you can be confident that when we say
a place is special, we really mean it.

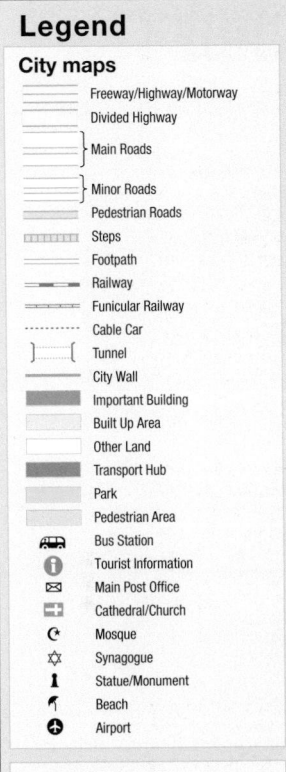

Legend

City maps

	Freeway/Highway/Motorway
	Divided Highway
	Main Roads
	Minor Roads
	Pedestrian Roads
	Steps
	Footpath
	Railway
	Funicular Railway
	Cable Car
	Tunnel
	City Wall
	Important Building
	Built Up Area
	Other Land
	Transport Hub
	Park
	Pedestrian Area
	Bus Station
	Tourist Information
	Main Post Office
	Cathedral/Church
	Mosque
	Synagogue
	Statue/Monument
	Beach
	Airport

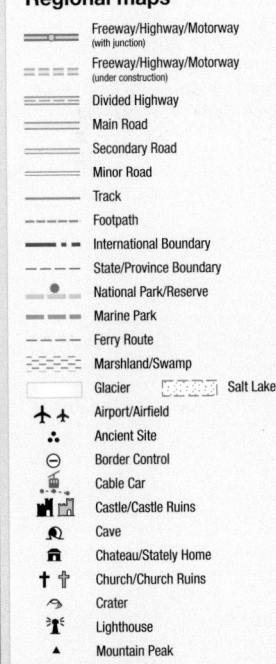

Regional maps

	Freeway/Highway/Motorway (with junction)
	Freeway/Highway/Motorway (under construction)
	Divided Highway
	Main Road
	Secondary Road
	Minor Road
	Track
	Footpath
	International Boundary
	State/Province Boundary
	National Park/Reserve
	Marine Park
	Ferry Route
	Marshland/Swamp
	Glacier / Salt Lake
	Airport/Airfield
	Ancient Site
	Border Control
	Cable Car
	Castle/Castle Ruins
	Cave
	Chateau/Stately Home
	Church/Church Ruins
	Crater
	Lighthouse
	Mountain Peak
	Place of Interest
	Viewpoint

INDEX

MAIN REFERENCES ARE IN BOLD TYPE

INSIGHT ● GUIDES

OFF THE SHELF

Since 1970, **INSIGHT GUIDES** has provided a unique perspective on the world's best travel destinations by using specially commissioned photography and illuminating text written by local authors.

Whether you're planning a city break, a walking tour or the journey of a lifetime, our superb range of guidebooks and phrasebooks will inspire you to discover more about your chosen destination.

INSIGHT GUIDES

offer a unique combination of stunning photos, absorbing narrative and detailed maps, providing all the inspiration and information you need.

PHRASEBOOKS & DICTIONARIES

help users to feel at home, when away. Pocket-sized with a free app to download, they go where you do.

CITY GUIDES

pack hundreds of great photos into a smaller format with detailed practical information, so you can navigate the world's top cities with confidence.

EXPLORE GUIDES

feature easy-to-follow walks and itineraries in the world's most exciting destinations, with our choice of the best places to eat and drink along the way.

POCKET GUIDES

combine concise information on where to go and what to do in a handy compact format, ideal on the ground. Includes a full-colour, fold-out map.

EXPERIENCE GUIDES

feature offbeat perspectives and secret gems for experienced travellers, with a collection of over 100 ideas for a memorable stay in a city.

www.insightguides.com

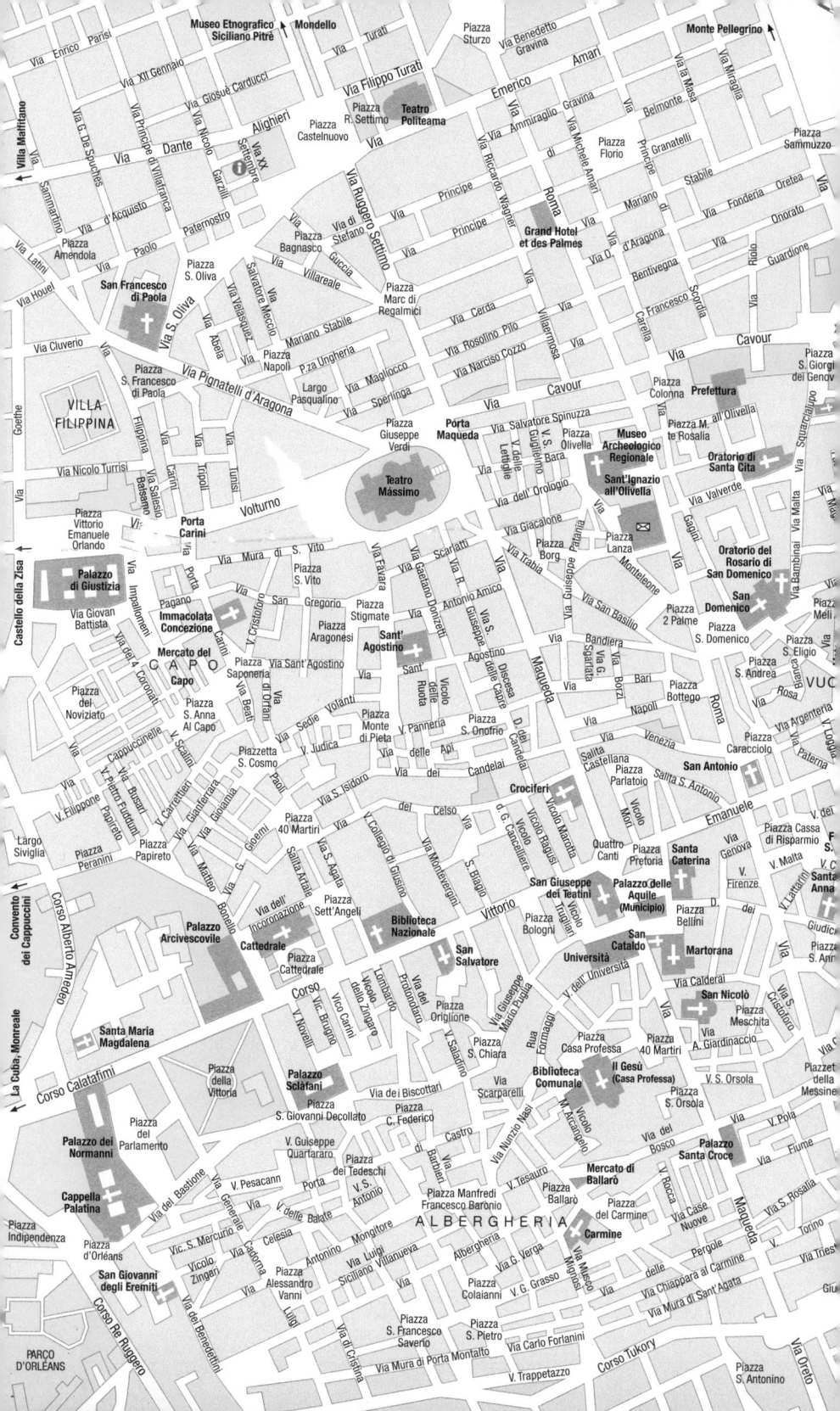